STATE TAX SYSTEMS

State governments are responsible for most of the direct domestic spending that affects the well-being of their citizens. Fiscal stability, important for state governments to serve the public, is influenced by both state tax systems and spending programs. This important new book explores how states' tax systems have changed, particularly in the aftermath of the Great Recession, why changes were made, and how these policies contributed to state fiscal stability. Author Yuhua Qiao examines tax systems, including state personal income tax, corporate income tax, sales and use tax, fuel tax, healthcare provider tax, and sin taxes. As fiscal stability largely depends on a tax system with a broad base and diverse sources, this book pays special attention to how changes affect the tax base, as well as the challenges and opportunities states face in broadening it.

Case studies within the book provide a rich discussion about the context under which a tax reform is adopted as well as its repercussions. The first book dedicated to a comprehensive examination of tax policy changes at the state level since the Great Recession, *State Tax Systems: Policy Making for Fiscal Stability* will help state government officials, public finance scholars, and students gain a better understanding of a given tax policy's impact on state fiscal health over the long term.

Yuhua Qiao is Professor in the Department of Political Science and Philosophy at Missouri State University, USA.

STATE TAX SYSTEMS

Policy Making for Fiscal Stability

Yuhua Qiao

NEW YORK AND LONDON

Designed cover image: Getty Images, MicroStockHub

First published 2025
by Routledge
605 Third Avenue, New York, NY 10158

and by Routledge
4 Park Square, Milton Park, Abingdon, Oxon, OX14 4RN

Routledge is an imprint of the Taylor & Francis Group, an informa business

© 2025 Yuhua Qiao

The right of Yuhua Qiao to be identified as author of this work has been asserted by her in accordance with sections 77 and 78 of the Copyright, Designs and Patents Act 1988.

All rights reserved. No part of this book may be reprinted or reproduced or utilised in any form or by any electronic, mechanical, or other means, now known or hereafter invented, including photocopying and recording, or in any information storage or retrieval system, without permission in writing from the publishers.

Trademark notice: Product or corporate names may be trademarks or registered trademarks, and are used only for identification and explanation without intent to infringe.

Library of Congress Cataloging-in-Publication Data
Names: Qiao, Yuhua, author.
Title: State tax systems : policy making for fiscal stability / Yuhua Qiao.
Description: New York, NY : Routledge, 2025. |
Includes bibliographical references and index.
Identifiers: LCCN 2024046785 | ISBN 9781032798868 (hardback) |
ISBN 9781032798851 (paperback) | ISBN 9781003494324 (ebook)
Subjects: LCSH: Taxation–United States–States. |
Fiscal policy–United States–States.
Classification: LCC HJ2385 .Q25 2025 |
DDC 336.2006973–dc23/eng/20241011
LC record available at https://lccn.loc.gov/2024046785

ISBN: 978-1-032-79886-8 (hbk)
ISBN: 978-1-032-79885-1 (pbk)
ISBN: 978-1-003-49432-4 (ebk)

DOI: 10.4324/9781003494324

Typeset in Times New Roman
by Newgen Publishing UK

This book is dedicated to
My Grandmothers, Shuzhen Yu (余淑贞) and Jinlian Guo (郭金莲), who taught me to be hardworking;
My parents, Zhenying Qiao (乔振英) and Congxian Chang (常从贤), to whom I owe everything;
My husband, Xinyuan Zhu, who always supports me;
My nephew, Boyan Qiao (乔伯岩), who is so kind and sharing and whom we all love.

CONTENTS

List of Illustrations   xi
Preface   xv
Acknowledgments   xvii

1 State Government Finance and the Fiscal Stability   1
   State Structural Deficits and Fiscal Stability   *1*
   Fiscal Stability and Taxation Goals   *4*
   Policy Making for State Fiscal Stability   *6*
   The Great Recession and Lessons for Fiscal Stability   *7*
   The Purpose of This Research   *8*
   Data Sources and the Attribution of This Book   *9*

2 State Expenditure Responsibilities: Trend and Cost Drivers   12
   Introduction   *12*
   State Expenditure on Elementary and Secondary Education   *14*
   State Expenditures on Medicaid   *18*
   State Spending on Higher Education   *23*
   State Transportation Expenditure   *28*
   State Expenditure on Corrections   *33*
   State Expenditure on Public Assistance   *35*

State "All Other Expenditures" 39
State Capital Expenditures 41
The Restricted State Expenditures 43
Conclusion 46

3 The Great Recession and State Tax Policies: An Overview   50
  Introduction 50
  The Great Recession and Its Impact on State Government Finance 50
  State Tax Actions Changes during and after the Great Recession 58

4 The Great Recession and Tax Increases: Stories in Three States   66
  Introduction 66
  The Story of California: Fiscal Crisis, Tax Increases, and Voter Initiatives 66
  The Story of New York: Wall Street, Millionaire Tax, Tax Progressivity 74
  The Story of Connecticut: Tax Increases, Legacy Costs, and Fiscal Instability 83
  Conclusion 91

5 The Great Recession and Tax Cuts: Stories in Two States   96
  Introduction 96
  Kansas Experiment: Big Income Tax Cuts and the Big Fiscal Hole 96
  Missouri's Story: Constant Income Tax Cuts and the Revenue Trigger 104
  Lessons Learned 111

6 State Income Taxes: How to Keep This Revenue Pilar Stable?   115
  Introduction 115
  State Personal Income Tax Changes during 2008–2020 118
  What Explains the Income Tax Changes? 125
  State Personal Income Tax and State Fiscal Stability 126
  Conclusion 132

7 State Corporate Income Taxes: How to Reform Them for
   State Fiscal Stability? 136
   Introduction 136
   State Corporate Income Tax Changes during 2008–2020 138
   Erosion of State Corporate Income Tax Bases 144
   Corporate Income Tax in Financing State Governments 149
   *State Fiscal Stability and Measures to Broaden the
      Tax Base 150*
   Conclusion 155

8 State Sales Taxes: How to Modernize Them for State
   Fiscal Stability? 159
   Introduction 159
   State Sales Tax Changes during 2008–2020 161
   Erosion of the State Sales Tax Bases 165
   *State Fiscal Stability and a Comprehensive Approach to
      Broaden the Sales Tax Base 179*

9 State Sin Taxes: Are They Stable Enough for State Fiscal
   Stability? 184
   Introduction 184
   Tobacco Taxes 185
   Alcohol Taxes 192
   Gambling Taxes 195
   Conclusion 203

10 Marijuana Tax: Is This New Revenue Source Reliable? 207
   Background of Legalizing Recreational Marijuana 207
   Tax Designs 208
   Marijuana Tax Revenue Trends and Prospect 213
   The Use of Marijuana Tax Revenue 217
   Conclusion 219

11 User Fees and Charges, Gasoline Taxes, and Healthcare
   Provider Taxes 221
   Introduction 221
   User Fees and User Charges 221
   State Motor Fuel Taxes 234
   Healthcare Provider Taxes 239
   Other Minor Taxes 248

12 State Tax Policies during the COVID-19 Pandemic 254
　Introduction 254
　States' Unprecedentedly Strong Fiscal Conditions 254
　State Tax Policies during the Pandemic—A Wave of Big
　　Tax Relief 256
　Impact on State Fiscal Stability 264

13 Conclusion: Have State Tax Policies Improved Their
　Fiscal Stability? 269
　Introduction 269
　State Tax Policy Reforms and State Fiscal Stability 269
　Rainy-day Fund and State Fiscal Stability 273
　Politics, Information, and Tax Policies 277
　Limitations of This Study 279

Appendices 282
Index 322

ILLUSTRATIONS

Figures

2.1	Percentage Change in Medicaid Spending and Enrollment, 1998–2023: Annual Percentage Changes	20
3.1	Nominal Annual Percentage Change in General Fund Spending	53
9.1	Steady Decline in Cigarette Consumption since the 1980s Per Capita Sales of Taxed Cigarette Packs	189

Tables

2.1	Total State Expenditure: Functional Categories as a Percentage of Total and Fund Sources	13
2.2	State Elementary and Secondary Education Expenditure: Sources of Funding (in $million) and Shares of State General Fund and Total	15
2.3	State Medicaid Expenditure: Sources of Funding (in $million) and Shares of State General Fund and Total	19
2.4	State Higher Education Expenditure: Sources of Funding and Share of State General Fund and Total (in $million)	24
2.5	State Higher Education Funding for Financial Aid, General Operation, and Net Tuition Revenue (2001–2022)	25
2.6	State Transportation Expenditures (in $million): Sources of Funding and Share of State General Fund and Total	30
2.7	State Corrections Expenditure (in $million): Sources of Funding and Share of State General Fund and Total	32

2.8	State Public Assistance Expenditure (in $million): Sources of Funding and Share of Total State Spending	36
2.9	State "All Other" Programs (in $million): Sources of Funding and Share of State General Fund and Total	40
2.10	State Capital Spending (in $million) and Sources of Funding	42
2.11	State Capital Spending: Different Programs (in $million) and Percentage of Total in Selected Years	43
3.1	State Revenue Shortages (in $billion) in FY 2009–FY 2013	52
3.2	The Number of States and Approaches and Strategies to Close Budget Gaps: 2009–2013	54
3.3	States Enacting Personal Income and Sales Tax Increases in FY 2009 or FY 2010	56
3.4	Budget Reserve Levels and Federal Recovery Grants (in $billion): FY 2008–FY 2013	56
3.5	Net State Tax Changes by Type of Tax (in $millions)	59
3.6	Number of States with Significant Tax Changes FY 2008–FY 2018 (as a Percentage of Previous Year's Tax Collection)	60
4.1	Budget Shortfalls for California, New York, and Connecticut: FY 2009–FY 2013	67
4.2	Personal Income Tax under Proposition 30	69
4.3	General Fund End Balances for FY 2013–FY 2018 (in $billion)	72
4.4	The Number of Tax Expenditures with CA Major Taxes in Selected Years	72
4.5	New York's Permanent and Temporary Tax Rates for Married Joint Filers	76
4.6	Number of Tax Expenditures with New York Major Taxes: 2009–2018	81
4.7	Connecticut OFA's Biennial Budget Deficit Projection General Fund (in $billion)	84
4.8	Connecticut Tax Expenditure in Select Years	88
4.9	Connecticut Total Liability as of June 16, 2016 (in $billion)	89
4.10	Pensions Are Getting the Biggest Slice of CT's Fiscal Pie	90
5.1	Budget Shortfalls for Kansas and Missouri: FY 2009–FY 2013	97
5.2	Kansas Tax Changes during 2008–2018 (in $millions)	97
5.3	Kansas Personal Income Tax Rates	98
5.4	Kansas General Fund Revenues, General Fund Expenditure, and Ending Balance (in current $million)	100
5.5	Kansas General Fund Nominal Percentage Expenditure Changes: FY 2012–FY 2018	101
5.6	Kansas General Fund Expenditures during FY 2014–FY 2017 (in $million)	102
5.7	Missouri Tax Changes during FY 2008–FY 2018 (in $millions)	105

List of Illustrations xiii

5.8	Missouri General Revenue (GR) FY 2012–FY 2017 (in $million) and Percentage Change over the Previous Year	109
5.9	Missouri Budget in Selected Years FY 2012–FY 2018 (in $million) and Percentage Change over the Previous Year	110
6.1	Individual Income Tax as a Share of State Tax Revenue (in $thousand)	116
6.2	State Income Tax Changes during 2008–2020	119
6.3	Tax Trigger Targets in Several States	124
7.1	Corporate Income Tax as Share of State Total Tax Revenue	137
7.2	State Corporate Income Tax Changes: 2008–2020	139
7.3	Corporate Income Tax Rate Changes during 2008–2022	140
7.4	North Carolina's Corporate Income Tax Rates	141
7.5	State Corporate Income Tax Base Changes: Selected Years	143
8.1	State General Sales and Gross Receipts Tax as a Percentage of State Total Tax Revenue: 2007–2021	160
8.2	State Sales Tax Changes: 2008–2020	162
8.3	State General Sales Tax Rates: 2008–2022	164
8.4	Sales Tax Breadth, Reliance, and Rates: 1970–2022	165
8.5	State Remote Sales Tax Revenue Collection: 2018–2021 (in $million)	174
9.1	State Excise Tax Rates on Cigarettes (January 1, 2023)	187
9.2	Tobacco Taxes Revenue: 2008–2022	188
9.3	State Alcohol Excise Tax Rates as of January 1, 2023	193
9.4	Alcohol Tax Revenues: 2008–2022	195
9.5	State and Local Lottery Revenue: 2008–2021	198
9.6	Casino and Racino Revenues (Inflation-adjusted) Per Adult Resident Declined Despite Overall Growth: FY 2008–FY 2017	200
9.7	Inflation-Adjusted Sin Taxes Revenue as Share of State Tax Revenue	204
10.1	State Legalizing Recreational Marijuana: Year and Way of Approval	208
10.2	Types of Cannabis Taxes by State as of November 2023	210
10.3	Marijuana Tax Revenue for State Governments (in $million)	214
10.4	Annual Marijuana Tax Growth Rates for Selected States	216
11.1	Current Charges and Miscellaneous General Revenue and as a Percentage of State General Revenue from Own Sources (in Constant $million)	225
11.2	States Fee Changes: FY 2008–FY 2020	227
11.3	Number of States with Medicaid Provider Taxes, 2004–2019	241
11.4	Number of States That Changed Medicaid Provider Tax Rates: 2007–2014	242
11.5	States' Provider Tax Changes: 2008–2020	243

11.6	Provider Tax and State General Revenue Funds as a Percentage of Nonfederal Share of Medicaid Payments: 2008 and 2018 ($billion)	245
11.7	Minor Tax Collections as a Percentage of Total State Tax Revenue in Selected Years	248
12.1	State Fiscal Conditions: FY 2020–FY 2023	255
12.2	State Tax Relief Measures: FY 2021–FY 2023	258
12.3	States with Flat Income Tax	260
13.1	State Expenditure and Tax Revenue: Annual Growth Rates	274
13.2	States' Rainy-day Fund Balance and Total Fund Balance: 2007–2024	275
13.3	Number of States with Rainy-Day Fund and Total Balance as a Percentage of State General Fund Expenditure: Selected Years	276

Boxes

4.1	Tax Base Broadening and Narrowing	80
6.1	Phasing in Tax Cuts	123
8.1	Three Cloud Computing Delivery Models	177
11.1	GFOA Best Practices on Establishing Government Charges and Fees	233

PREFACE

State governments are responsible for most of the direct domestic spendings that affect the well-being of their citizens. Yet, they constantly face challenges in meeting their obligations. This is apparent during economic recessions when state revenue collection declines but demand for service rises. Although economic recovery could correct these cyclical budget shortfalls, states face another more difficult challenge—long-term fiscal imbalance. Their revenue systems cannot generate adequate and stable revenue to meet their spending obligations in the long term.

Fiscal stability, important for state governments to serve the public, is influenced by both state tax systems and spending programs. During and in the aftermath of the Great Recession, when states faced such severe revenue shortages, the expectation was that states would undertake major tax and program reforms. That ignited my desire to study state fiscal stability, and I started my journey for this research endeavor—studying state tax policy making in the aftermath of the Great Recession.

The purpose of this book is to study how states' tax actions have changed their tax systems, particularly in the aftermath of the Great Recession, why they made these changes, and how these policies contributed to state fiscal stability. The tax systems that the book examines are state personal income tax, corporate income tax, sales and use tax, sin taxes (cigarette and tobacco–related tax, alcohol tax, gambling tax, and marijuana tax), fuel tax, healthcare provider tax, and user fees and charges. As fiscal stability largely depends on a tax system with a broad base and diverse sources, this research pays special attention to how the changes affect the tax base, what issues each tax has, what challenges states face in broadening the tax base, and how they could broaden it.

Tax policies are often political. They are shaped heavily by political and ideological beliefs, interest group politics, public preferences, and interstate competition. The long list of tax breaks granted to different groups contribute to a great deal of tax base erosion. Fiscal crises during and in the aftermath of the Great Recession did push states to raise tax rates and broaden tax bases. However, these efforts could not sustain once the fiscal crises subsided. At the same time, states have witnessed how the new service-oriented and digital economy affects their tax systems and raised additional issues and challenges.

Taxation is a sensitive, difficult, and complicated topic. Yet the government needs a stable and sustainable revenue system to perform its responsibilities. Therefore, it is important for us to understand the issues with each tax system, the policy options that are available, and the impact the policy choices have in both the short and long run. It is also important for elected officials and the public to seek information, engage in candid dialogue and thoughtful discussions about what we want, how we will pay for it, and what trade-offs we are willing to make.

ACKNOWLEDGMENTS

This writing is the result of years of hard work and support from various people. I want to thank the publisher for giving me this opportunity to share my research with readers. My sincere thanks go to Dr. Khi V. Thai, my major professor at Florida Atlantic University, for inspiring my interest in state government finance; to Dr. Mark Rushefsky, my professor, my colleague, and my trusted friend, for helping me in so many ways over the years; to Dr. Kant Patel for his valuable input and guidance in writing this book; to Dr. George Connor, for reading my manuscript and providing feedback; and to my graduate assistants, Ryan Ramaker, Emily Snodderly, and Matthew Carter, for all their assistance with this project.

I want to give my special thanks to my mother, Congxian Chang, and my late father, Zhenying Qiao, who provided unwavering support and unconditional love to me and my family, and who are models of dedication and commitment; to my husband, Xinyuan Zhu, who always supports me and helps take care of our family; to my children, Hui Zhou, Douan Alissa Zhu, Melinda Chenxi Qiao, and Alexander Yibin Zhu, for giving me joy and hope; to my brothers, Lijun Qiao and Lingjun Qiao, and sisters, Chuannv Qiao, Yuehua Qiao and Linghua Qiao, who always have confidence in me and encourage me; to the congregants of Springfield Chinese Church, who support me spiritually as I have handled numerous responsibilities in the midst of this writing.

1
STATE GOVERNMENT FINANCE AND THE FISCAL STABILITY

"State and local governments are the workhorses of the American public sector" (Gordon, Auxier, and Iselin 2016, p. 1). They are responsible for delivering most of the direct spending on domestic programs (e.g., non-national defense programs) and states play a particularly significant role in this. Nearly 50% of funding for public schools (U.S. Census 2019), 40%–50% for higher education (Pew Charitable Trust 2019), and 50% for transportation (CBO) come directly from state coffers. States undertake 80%–83% of social services. They incarcerate about 65% of the nation's inmates (Carson and Golinelli 2013). As an important partner, states work with the federal government to maintain a social safety net for millions of Americans who need financial assistance through their own public welfare programs and participation in joint programs (Gordon, Auxier, and Iselin 2016). Furthermore, state governments also administer economic development programs and give fiscal support to their local governments.

While state governments provide their citizens with a wide range of essential services, they constantly face fiscal challenges in fulfilling these expenditure responsibilities. The challenge is apparent during economic recessionary periods when state revenue collections decline, but service demands rise. Although economic recovery can correct cyclical revenue shortages, states encounter another more difficult fiscal challenge—long-term structural budget deficits.

State Structural Deficits and Fiscal Stability

It is a classic dilemma that all governments have restricted revenues but face unlimited demands for public services. In 1940, V. O. Key Jr. raised the central budgeting question: "On what basis shall it be decided to allocate x dollars to activity A instead of activity B?" (Key 1940, p. 24). He pinpointed the fact that public budgets were concerned with choices and invited scholars to study the question (Key 1940). These choices are inevitable since budgeting deals with "the allocation of scarce resources among competing demands" (Lewis 1952, p. 29).

This fiscal dilemma is magnified in the contemporary era. On the one hand, the state revenue system is not only restrained by the economic cycle but also by the change in economic structure, public anti-taxation attitudes, and continual efforts by lawmakers to reduce tax rates (Lav, McNichol, and Zahradnik 2005). However, state governments must provide ever-increasing public services in several categories because of voter demands, court orders, or elected officials' promises (Lav, McNichol, and Zahradnik 2005).

Literature on public budgeting by the mid-1990s had recognized structural deficits: revenue-expenditure gaps caused by revenue and spending policies, not economic downturns. Gold (1995) pointed to factors such as Medicaid, school enrollment, federal mandates, excessive spending patterns, and dysfunctional tax systems in some states. Wallace (1995) examined the impact of economic and demographic changes on state/local government revenue and predicted states might face long-term fiscal problems. The National Education Association (1998) found that 39 states faced structural gaps in their budgets. At that time, however, scholars did not recognize the chronic nature of these structural deficits.

Only since the late 2000s have policy makers and academia painfully realized that the fiscal challenges state/local governments are confronting will last not a few years but decades. They started to frame the discussion from "the broader and long-range perspective of fiscal sustainability" (Ward and Dadayan 2009, p. 460). The National Tax Association and its partners sponsored a special conference on the subject in 2008 in Washington, DC. State and local officials participated in the event and discussed how they could improve practical decision-making in light of fiscal sustainability. The Government Accountability Office (GAO) undertook a project studying long-term state/local fiscal outlook. Using historical revenue and expenditure data, GAO researchers built a simulation model and updated it regularly. The findings clearly showed that state and local governments will not be fiscally sustainable without policy changes. State expenditure as a percentage of Gross Domestic Product (GDP) increased faster than state revenue, and the mismatch between revenues and expenditures will steadily grow over the following years. By 2055, the budget deficit could be as much as over 5% of the national GDP (GAO 2008; 2009; 2010; 2016).

As indicated above, the problems underlying fiscal sustainability exist on the revenue and expenditure sides. Several spending pressures have been widely discussed, including Medicaid, public education, public infrastructure, and public pensions (Chapman 2008; Ward and Dadayan 2009). For instance, GAO (2018) found Medicaid expenditures would continue to rise at an average of 1% higher than GDP each year. On the revenue side, state and local governments have seen their revenue capability eroded by the numerous tax credits, the obsolete sales tax structure (Tannenwald 2001), and revenue caps and restrictions imposed by voters (Egan 2002; Lav, McNichol, and Zahradnik 2005; Gordon 2009; Qiao 2015). These studies reveal a growing misalignment between tax policy choices and spending needs" (Lav, McNichol, and Zahradnik 2005).

Murray, Clark-Johnson, Moro, and Vey (2011) traced the sources of structural deficits to three major categories: prevailing fiscal structures, economic and demographic trends, and critically, political decision-making. First, state constitutions and statutes define the tax structure (e.g., what to tax, tax base, and tax rates) and expenditure responsibilities (e.g., certain spending being considered mandatory and others discretionary). Economic changes affect tax collection. For instance, the general sales tax is designed for traditional and tangible goods transactions, not for a digital and service-based economy. Population shifts also affect state fiscal outlooks. The aging population tends to contribute less tax revenue but increases expenditures on health and social services. A growing number of middle-class and high-income taxpayers will bring in more tax revenue than government services consumed. Political decision-making made by elected officials and voters greatly affects the revenue policies and expenditure responsibilities and the long-term fiscal balance of state government. Murray et al. (2011) stated that "These three forces each have an independent influence on the budget and also can interact in such a way as to produce or magnify a fiscal crisis" (p. 4).

Revenue stability is always essential for state and local governments, as they lack borrowing flexibility but are legally required to balance their operation budgets. Taxation literature contains numerous studies that delve into the revenue volatility of specific taxes during specified periods and over time (Boyd 2022). However, this literature makes no connection to structural budget deficits. Due to states' severe fiscal problems during the Great Recession and its aftermath, fiscal stability became an important topic for state policy discussion. For instance, the state of Connecticut established the *Commission on Fiscal Stability and Economic Growth* with the mission "to develop and recommend policies to achieve state government fiscal stability and promote economic growth and competitiveness within the state" (Connecticut Commission on Fiscal Stability and Economic Growth 2018, p. 6). The Commission delivered its reports, stating that "Connecticut's fiscal stability has deteriorated to crisis levels, eroding the general public and business confidence. Fiscal stability is a condition precedent to competitiveness" (p. 15). The U.S. News Report ranks the fiscal stability of the 50 states, emphasizing that "the fiscal stability of a state's government is vital to ensuring the success of government-sponsored programs and projects, trickling down to affect the quality of life of state residents" (U.S. News No Date).

Interestingly, these discussions have never defined the term of fiscal stability. Though the meaning seems obvious, additional articulation is warranted. According to The Content Authority (No Date), "stability refers to the ability of a system to remain consistent and predictable over time. In other words, a stable system is able to maintain a certain level of performance or output without experiencing significant fluctuations or disruptions (p.1)." Based on this definition, fiscal stability refers to a fiscal system that can support public services without experiencing significant disruption.

Fiscal stability can have short- and long-term orientations. From a short-term perspective, fiscal stability requires governments to have adequate resources to cover their current expenditures and fulfill their immediate financial obligations. For these reasons, Connecticut's *Commission on Fiscal Stability and Economic Growth* (2018) stated that Connecticut's ongoing budget deficits of $2–3 billion in FY 2020 and beyond constituted a primary explanation for the state's fiscal instability. Typically, a cyclical economy imposes severe challenges to fiscal stability. It can be corrected when the economy recovers, but the fiscal instability will persist if the fiscal system is distressed with a growing fiscal imbalance.

Furthermore, fiscal stability also looks at the outputs of a fiscal system in the long term, referring to states' ability to fund long-term obligations where the revenue system can support the expenditure needs while also "securing stable economic future, incorporating a state's credit rating and its ability to cover pension obligations" (U.S. News No Date, p. 1). In this sense, fiscal stability resembles fiscal sustainability as both emphasize the governmental ability to maintain public services over long run.

Structural deficits inevitably threaten long-term fiscal stability. At the same time, they also "further complicate the resolution of cyclical fiscal problems. Together they can produce devastating consequences for state economies and their residents" (Murray et al. 2011, p. 4). While fiscal stability in both short- and long-term perspectives is vital for state governments to provide essential public services, achieving the latter requires greater efforts.

This book uses "fiscal stability" in its title to imply the broad perspective this research takes. That is, it presents a general discussion about state fiscal policies and their short- and long-term impacts.

Fiscal Stability and Taxation Goals

Tax policies embody different values which are not always consistent with fiscal stability. Equity and revenue adequacy are two of the important goals for a tax system to incorporate. Equity requires a progressive system of taxing high-income families with a higher effective rate. Revenue adequacy, a crucial test for state fiscal health, requires a tax system to have a broad base and reasonable rates. There is a consensus in public finance literature that a broad base is desirable for tax policies. Tax base refers to the total value of all the items and economic activities that a tax is applied to. What is a reasonable rate is highly debatable. Higher rates do not necessarily lead to more tax revenue collection because people may change their market behaviors. However, rates considered too low will result in unnecessary revenue losses for state governments. Tax rate changes at any point in time affect not only current revenue generation but also revenue availability for future uses (Mikesell 2018).

Revenue adequacy is more consistent with fiscal stability, but equity is not. Income taxes with graduate tax brackets are considered progressive but are more volatile over economic cycles. The sales tax is deemed a stable revenue source but is regressive, imposing a higher tax burden on low-income families. As the share of income tax increases, the system will become more progressive but less stable. When making policies, state lawmakers may choose to prioritize values other than stability (Chernick, Reimers, and Tennant 2014). For instance, many states levy capital gains tax even though studies show that including capital gains increases income tax volatility.

Revenue adequacy also includes a dynamic component, requiring the tax to be responsive or have a high elasticity. That means the tax revenue can increase faster than the economy so that governments can have adequate revenue to meet the service demands in the long run. This responsiveness complements long-term fiscal stability but may conflict with cyclical fiscal stability. In Boyd's words, "There is a tradeoff between growth (e.g., responsiveness) and volatility (lack of stability)" (p. 6). For instance, some taxes that are stable during economic cycles are not responsive, meaning that they fall behind economic growth over time. The fuel tax, applied to the quantity of fuel consumption rather than the value, is considered stable, but as one of the least responsive taxes, it cannot generate the needed revenue for the transportation system. Research findings show that income taxes typically are the most responsive revenue source due to their graduate rates and sensitive tax base. The general sales tax occupies a median rank in terms of revenue volatility. That is, it is less volatile than income tax but more volatile than fuel tax. There is also another issue with responsiveness. It can be a double-edged sword. During economic slowdowns, the more responsive the tax, the more sharply its revenue tends to fall, causing more severe fiscal instability. For instance, income taxes, the most responsive taxes, can have their revenue falling more sharply than other tax revenues.

Literature offers some generalizations about the volatility of specific taxes. However, Boyd (2022) stated that "there is no such thing as 'volatility' of a tax or a state tax system" (p. 4). The fiscal stability of a specific tax depends on how the tax system is designed, its tax base components, its rate structure, and economic conditions. Additionally, Boyd (2022) recommends analyzing all tax sources as a package or tax portfolio instead of focusing on a specific tax. He asserts, "Some taxes tend to grow rapidly but are highly variable. Some taxes grow slowly but are stable" (p. 6). Some taxes serve equity purposes well, while others do not. Understanding how an entire tax portfolio affects fiscal stability is more important.

Policy Making for State Fiscal Stability

When Murray et al. (2011) discussed three major categorical sources of structural deficits (e.g., prevailing fiscal structures, economic and demographic trends, and political decision-making), they noted the critical role of political decision-making in state fiscal health. Political decisions affect budgetary dynamics as changes to a state's fiscal system at one point in time often significantly impact long-term fiscal stability. During periods of economic prosperity, lawmakers resort to cutting taxes and increasing program spending. While the boom is temporary, these changes to the fiscal apparatus are permanent. Similarly, voters often use ballot measures to restrict government revenues but demand new and expanded services. These policy decisions are inconsistent, contributing to a permanent gap between tax and expenditure policies.

To improve fiscal stability, states need to improve their fiscal policy making. To be specific, "states need to improve the quality of their fiscal policymaking by steadily working to broaden, balance, and diversify their revenue bases while looking to the long-haul balance of taxing and spending" (Murry et al. 2011, p. 13). This process contains several basic and widely recognized practices: "balanced approaches, broad tax bases, diverse revenue sources, and a close fit of revenue adequacy to necessary expenditures" (Murray et al. 2011, p. 13).

- Balanced Approach: As state fiscal imbalances are driven by both restrained revenue capacities and expanded spending responsibilities, it is imperative and prudent to address both revenue and expenditure policies. A balanced approach also means diversifying the revenue system.
- Revenue Diversification: This tenet can ensure a greater adaptation to economic and demographic changes. Although absolute protection "against the vagaries of the business cycle" does not exist (Murray et al. 2011, p. 14), a balanced revenue system with a variety of tax revenue sources will allow the tax system to be less vulnerable to the economic cycle and changes in economic structure.
- Broadening the Base: A broad tax base is crucial for revenue adequacy and responsiveness. The broader the base, the easier it is to generate tax revenue and the less distortion the tax will have on the economy, which will further help preserve the tax base. Over the past decades, tax bases have been eroded with a long list of tax breaks and economic and technological advances. Murray et al. (2011) point out, "Tax policies that increase the base and elasticity of state tax systems would help mitigate structural deficits and reduce the need

for discretionary rate increases" (p. 14). Including digital goods and services in the sales tax broadens the tax base and generates additional revenue without rate increases. Collectively, a wide range of revenue sources, together with a broad base, will enable the fiscal system to respond better to economic occurrences and the emerged budgetary needs.

The work by Murray et al. provides an insightful framework for studying state fiscal stability. This research will apply the three elements—a balanced approach, revenue diversification, and broadening the tax base, with special attention to broadening the tax base—to examine state tax policy changes over the years and their impacts on state fiscal stability. As tax rates are an important variable for revenue adequacy, this research will also examine tax rate changes over the years and their impact on state fiscal stability.

Other measures are also necessary to improve state fiscal decision-making. Murray et al. (2011) discussed the importance of maintaining adequate rainy-day funds and improving budget process and information sharing through which fiscal problems are identified, analyzed, and addressed. These topics will briefly be discussed in the conclusion chapter, given the focus of this research is on state tax policies.

The Great Recession and Lessons for Fiscal Stability

The Great Recession of 2007–2009, the worst fiscal time since the Great Depression, constituted a perfect storm for state public finance (National Association of State Budget Office 2009). The severe budget shortfalls that accompanied this period not only demonstrated cyclical fiscal instability but also exposed the dire fiscal imbalance for many state governments and the urgency of finding practical solutions. Therefore, the Great Recession and its aftermath provided fertile terrain for studying state fiscal stability.

During the Great Recession, states employed pro-cyclical measures such as cutting expenditures and raising revenue and fees, as they had done in the previous recessions. However, the Great Recession and the ensuing budget crisis pressured state government officials to reexamine their tax systems and service priorities, as well as address long-term structural imbalances. Many states have made changes to program areas, such as employee retirement systems and corrections (NASBO 2013). On the revenue side, in recent years, some states have expanded the tax base to capture advancements in the new digital and service-based economy by taxing digital goods and services and collecting online sales. States such as Oregon started re-evaluating current tax expenditures and other forms of spending through tax policy assessments. Some states even eliminated certain tax expenditure programs (NASBO 2013). A number of states have also raised the rates for major taxes (e.g., personal income tax and sales tax) and other taxes. Among the various proposed and enacted tax changes, some are minor and temporary, but some called for significant, substantial, and structural changes (NASBO 2013).

At the same time, we should also note that during the Great Recession, states pursued easy and short-term measures such as temporary tax raises, cross-board cutting, and reducing local aid. In addition, with economic recovery in recent years, elected officials in many states have turned back to tax cuts and delayed addressing fiscal issues. Did the Great Recession change the dynamics of state fiscal policy making? What happened in the post-Great Recession era in terms of state tax policies and expenditure programs? How do these policies affect state fiscal stability and long-term fiscal health? These are important inquiries that require further exploration and discussion.

The Purpose of This Research

This book examines state tax policy making from the perspective of fiscal stability. The objective is to assess whether state tax policy making has improved fiscal stability in the last decades, particularly the period following the Great Recession. The focus rests on tax policy making, but state spending responsibilities are also examined in one of the chapters. To be specific, the author examines the following topics.

Regarding state revenue systems,

- What policy changes have states undertaken with each of the following tax systems—personal income tax, corporate income tax, sales tax, sin taxes, fuel tax, healthcare provider taxes, and fees and charges? And what led to the changes?
- Have state tax actions (i.e., changes to the tax base, rates, and diversification) made state revenue systems fiscally stable?

Regarding state spending responsibilities,

- What are the spending trends of major state spending responsibilities (e.g., public education, higher education, Medicaid, public welfare, public infrastructure, corrections, and all others)?
- What are cost factors and issues contributing to spending increases?

It is important to understand how tax policy changes in the past decades affect state fiscal stability. Although government officials may pursue other tax goals, such as equity, they need to know how to maintain fiscal stability when practical and necessary (Boyd 2022). Fiscal stability is important for public service delivery in both the short and long terms.

Data Sources and the Attribution of This Book

The analysis in this study pursues a qualitative approach. It utilizes four major data sources: (a) *the State Tax Action* database collected and maintained by the National Conference of State Legislatures (NCSL) from 2008 to 2024; (b) *State Expenditure Reports* published by the National Association of State Budget Officers from 2000 to 2022; (c) *State & Local Government Finance Historical Datasets and Tables* maintained by U.S. Census Bureau, and (d) various states' government budget documents. Additionally, the discussion draws information from reports by various think tanks related to state tax and fiscal policies, including the Tax Foundation, Urban Institute, Brookings Institution, and the Pew Charitable Trusts. Finally, the author reviews a wide range of literature on state taxes and expenditures.

While the literature has seen much discussion regarding state fiscal structural deficits and fiscal stability, no one has analyzed how state tax policy changes in recent decades affect states' long-term fiscal health. This research will provide the most updated and comprehensive review and discussion on this topic. In addition to examining each tax policy change in general, five states—New York, California, Connecticut, Kansas, and Missouri—will serve as case studies to explain how and why each state has changed its tax policies and the impact on state fiscal stability.

References

Boyd, Don. 2022. "State Tax Revenue Volatility and Its Impact on State Governments." *The Pew Charitable Trusts.* (June 30).

Carson, E. Ann and Daniela Golinelli. 2013. *Prisoners in 2012: Trends in Admissions and Releases, 1991–2012.* Washington, DC: Bureau of Justice Statistics. (December).

Chapman, Jeffrey I. 2008. "State and Local Fiscal Sustainability: The Challenges." *Public Administration Review.* (Special issue). pp. 115–131. www3.interscience.wiley.com/cgi-bin/fulltext/121473545/PDFSTART

Chernick, Howard, Cordelia Reimers, and Jennifer Tennant. 2014. "Tax Structure and Revenue Instability: The Great Recession and the States." *IZA Journal of Labor Policy*, 3, pp. 1–22.

Connecticut Commission on Fiscal Stability and Economic Growth. 2018. "Final Report." (March).

Egan, Timothy. 2002. "They Give, but They Also Take: Voters Muddle States' Finances." *New York Times.* (March 2).

Gold, Steven D. (ed.). 1995. *Fiscal Crisis of the States: Lessons for the Future.* Washington, DC: Georgetown University Press.

Gordon, Tracy M. 2009. "Bargaining in the Shadow of the Ballot Box: Causes and Consequences of Local Voter Initiatives." *Public Choice*, 141, pp. 31–48.

Gordon, Tracy, Richard Auxier, and John Iselin. 2016. Assessing Fiscal Capacities of States: A Representative Revenue System – Representative Expenditure System Approach, Fiscal Year 2012. *Urban Institute.*

Key, V. O. Jr. 1940. "The Lack of Budgetary Theory." In Hyde, Albert. 2002. *Government Budgeting: Theory, Process, Politics*. 3rd ed. Toronto, Canada: Thomson Learning, Inc. pp. 24–28.

Lav, Iris J., Elizabeth McNichol, and Robert Zahradnik. 2005. "Faulty Foundations: State Structural Budget Problems and How to Fix Them." *Center on Budget and Policy Priorities*. (May).

Lewis, Verne B. 1952. "Toward a Theory of Budgeting." In Hyde, Albert (2002). *Government Budgeting: Theory, Process, and Politics*. Toronto, Canada: Wadsworth/Thomas Learning. pp. 27–38.

Mikesell, John. 2018. *Fiscal Administration*. Bostin, MA: Cengage Learning.

Murray, Matthew, Sue Clark-Johnson, Mark Murro, and Jennifer Vey. 2011. "Structurally Unbalanced: Cyclical and Structural Deficits in California and the Intermountain West". *Brookings Mountain West, Morrison Institute for Public Policy*.

National Association of State Budget Officers (NASBO). 2013. *State Budgeting and Lessons Learned from the Economic Downturn: Analysis and Commentary from State Budget Officers*.

National Education Association. 1998. *The Outlook for State and Local Finances: The Dangers of Structural Deficits for the Future of Public Education*.

National Governor Association and National Association of State Budget Office. 2009. *The Fiscal Survey of States*. (December).

Pew Charitable Trust. 2019. Two Decades of Change in Federal and State Higher Education Funding: Recent Trends across the Levels of Government. The Pew Charitable Trusts.

Qiao, Yuhua. 2015. "Voter Initiatives and Their Impact on State Budget Balance." *Journal of Budgeting, Accounting & Financial Management*, 27 (1), pp. 1–36.

Tannenwald, Robert. 2001. "Are State and Local Revenue Systems Becoming Obsolete?" *New England Economic Review*, 4, pp. 27–43.

The Content Authority. No Date. Stability vs. Sustainability: Meaning and Differences.

U.S. Census Bureau. 2019. *2019 Public Elementary Secondary Education Finance Data*. www.census.gov/data/tables/2019/econ/school-finances/secondary-education-finance.html

U.S. Congressional Budget Office (CBO). 2022. *Federal Financial Support for Public Transportation*. www.cbo.gov/publication/57940#:~:text=Because%20state%20and%20local%20governments%20together%20account%20for,an%20important%20impact%20on%20finances%20for%20public%20transportation.

U.S. Government Accounting Office (GAO). 2008. *State and Local Governments: Growing Fiscal Challenges Will Emerge During the Next Ten Years*.

U.S. Government Accounting Office (GAO). 2009. *Update of State and Local Government Fiscal Pressures*.

U.S. Government Accounting Office (GAO). 2010. *State and Local Governments' Fiscal Outlook*.

U.S. Government Accounting Office (GAO). 2016. *State and Local Governments' Fiscal Outlook: 2016 Update*.

U.S. Government Accountability Office (GAO). 2018. *State and Local Governments' Fiscal Outlook*. (December). www.gao.gov/assets/gao-19-208sp.pdf

U.S. News. No Date. "Fiscal Stability." www.usnews.com/news/best-states/rankings/fiscal-stability

Wallace, Sally. 1995. *The Effects of Economic and Demographic Changes on State and Local Budgets*. Washington, DC: The Finance Project.

Ward, Robert B. and Lucy Dadayan. 2009. "State and Local Finance: Increasing Focus on Fiscal Sustainability." *Publius*, 39 (3), pp. 455–475.

2
STATE EXPENDITURE RESPONSIBILITIES

Trend and Cost Drivers

Introduction

This chapter examines the major state spending responsibilities, the cost factors that drive up spending, and the issues that states face in fulfilling expenditure needs. Such an overview will help readers understand where state tax revenues are spent and why a large share of state spending is outside the annual budgetary control.

State governments spent $2.1 trillion in 2019 to provide a wide range of services. The National Association of State Budget Officers (NASBO) classifies state expenditures into seven main functional categories: elementary and secondary education, Medicaid, higher education, transportation, corrections, public assistance, and "all others." States have three major fund categories to fund these programs: state general revenue, federal funds, and "state other funds." The federal funds include various federal grants, nearly all of which are designated for certain programs. The Medicaid grant is used to fund Medicaid programs. The Highway Trust Fund (HTF) supports interstate highway construction projects. Few federal grant programs allow states to supplement general revenue sources. "Other states funds" account for nearly one-third of state revenue coming from a wide range of revenue streams, including sin taxes, fuel tax, vehicle-related fees, severance tax, and even part of the general sales tax. These taxes are usually earmarked for certain expenditure programs. The gasoline tax is earmarked for highway transportation. Lottery revenue is often designated for public education. General fund revenue allows state lawmakers the most discretion on how to spend it. It is usually supported by personal income tax, general sales tax, and corporate income tax.

Table 2.1 shows total state spending by functional categories and by fund sources. It reveals four key observations. First, overall state expenditures during 2000–2022 increased in both current and constant dollars. Second, the three largest spending categories were always elementary and secondary education, Medicaid, and all other expenditures. Third, Medicaid spending, which used to constitute the second largest expenditure, surpassed elementary and secondary education in the early 2000s, mainly due to the expansion of Medicaid grants. Fourth, general fund revenue as a share of total state revenue has declined over the years while the share of state other funds has increased, although, in dollar amounts, state other funds are still smaller. This means that state governments have expanded earmarking revenue for designated programs. Meanwhile, federal funds have increased significantly after 2008. The large increase in total state spending after 2019 was led by a significant increase in federal COVID-19-related legislation and strong state revenue performance in the last three years.

The following sections provide a more in-depth examination of state expenditures. For each spending category, the discussion will examine funding sources, spending trends, and cost factors that contribute to spending increases.

TABLE 2.1 Total State Expenditure: Functional Categories as a Percentage of Total and Fund Sources

		Fiscal Year	*2000*	*2008*	*2019*	*2022*
Total Spending		Current $	945,271	1,425,028	2,101,503	2,775,897
		Constant $	1,403,634	1,692,427	2,101,503	2,424,997
Functional Categories		K-12	22.5%	21.6	19.5%	18.6%
		Medicaid	19.5%	20.7%	28.9%	29.6%
		High Ed	10.9%	10.2%	10.1%	8.7%
		Transportation	8.8%	7.9%	8.1%	7.2%
		Corrections	3.8%	3.5%	3.0%	2.5%
		Public Assistance	2.4%	1.7%	1.2%	1.1%
		All others	32.1%	34.6%	29.1%	32.2%
		Total	100%	100%	100%	100%
Funding Sources		State General Fund source	48.1%	45.7%	40.8%	38%
		State Other Funds	24.0%	25.7%	26.6%	25.1%
		Federal Funding	26.0%	26.3%	30.7%	35.3%
		Bonds	1.9%	2.4%	1.9%	1.5%
		Total Funding Sources	100%	100%	100%	100%

Sources: NASBO (2000; 2008; 2019; 2022).

To show these trends, data are expressed in both current and constant inflation-adjusted dollars (in 2019 dollars). Spending is also presented as a share of total state spending and as a share of state general revenue. Bonds usually issued to generate funding for capital projects will be discussed in the capital expenditure section.

State Expenditure on Elementary and Secondary Education

Public schools provide K-12 education services for approximately 51 million school-age children, roughly nine out of ten school-age children in the United States. Funding is needed for school operation, maintenance, and facility construction (Urban Institute No Date a). While all levels of government contribute funding, state government is typically the largest provider, accounting for 47.1% of the total spending in 2019, followed by local governments, mainly with property tax revenue, at 44.9 %. The federal government contributes the remaining 8.0% of funding (NASBO 2022).

States do not provide public education services directly. Rather, they distribute funding to schools through general funds on a per-pupil basis and through "categorical grants to support specific programs or needs" (NASBO 2019, p. 18). The federal government provides pass-through grants to state governments, who then transfer them to local school districts (Urban Institute No Date a).

In 2019, total state spending on elementary and secondary education was $413,367 million. About 74%, or $305,519 million, was derived from state general revenue. This $305,519 million accounts for 35.6% of state general revenue. Indeed, elementary and secondary education is the largest spending category for the state general revenue fund, consuming 34%–36% of state general revenue, and the state general fund typically contributed over 70% of state public education spending until the COVID-19 pandemic arrived (see Table 2.2).

While most states support their public education with general revenue funds, some states (e.g., Michigan, New Hampshire, Vermont, and Wyoming) have set up separate and large "education funds." In addition, states have used sizable revenue from "other state funds" to support public education. Other state funds contain various designated revenue streams, including lotteries and other earmarked tax revenues (NASBO 2008; 2016; 2019; 2022). Table 2.2 shows that other state funds exhibit larger annual growth rates than general revenue funds before 2019 (see Table 2.2), indicating states expanded other funds for public education at a larger rate.

During COVID-19, state shares (e.g., state general fund and other state fund) dropped slightly because of the large influx of federal spending for public schools. Before the pandemic, federal grants from the Elementary and Secondary

TABLE 2.2 State Elementary and Secondary Education Expenditure: Sources of Funding (in $million) and Shares of State General Fund and Total

	2000	2008	2019	2022	Annual Growth Rate (%) 2000–2008	Annual Growth Rate (%) 2008–2019	Annual Growth Rate (%) 2019–2022
Funding Sources in Current Dollar Percentage of Total							
State Gen Fund	162,588 76.4%	236,963 73.2%	305,519 74.4%	362,601 66.5%	5.53	2.34	5.88
Federal Fund	25,857 12.2%	45,224 14.0%	55,789 13.6%	118,914 22.4%	8.31	1.93	28.69
Other State Funds	20,713 9.7%	38,192 11.8%	49,362 11.4%	53,993 10.2%	9.13	2.36	3.03
Bonds	3,543 1.7%	3,545 1.1%	2,697 0.6%	4,842 1.0%	0.01	-2.45	21.54
Total State K-12 Spending	212,701 100%	323,924 100%	413,367 100%	540,350 100%	6.19	2.24	9.34
Funding Sources in Constant Dollar							
State Gen Fund	241,427	281,428	305,519	316,765	2.21	0.75	1.21
Federal Fund	38,395	53,710	55,789	103,882	4.91	0.35	23.03
Other State Fund	30,757	45,359	49,362	47,168	5.71	0.77	(1.50)
Bonds	5,261	4,210	2,697	4,230	(3.13)	(3.97)	16.19
Total K-12 State Spending	315,840	384,707	413,367	472,045	2.86	0.66	4.52
K-12 Spending as Share of							
State Total Expenditure	22.5%	21.6%	19.5%	18.8%			
State Gen Fund Expenditure	35.0%	34.5%	35.6%	34.2%			

Sources: NASBO (2000, 2008, 2019, 2022).

Education Act mainly provided supplemental funding for economically disadvantaged school districts and special education needs (NASBO 2023, p. 21). During COVID-19, the federal government expanded the scale and scope of its grant distribution, allowing the funds to be used for "a wide variety of public health safety measures, technology needs, and efforts to address learning loss and other impacts of school closures" (NASBO 2023, p. 21).

Cost Drivers for Elementary and Secondary Spending

Table 2.2 shows that between 2000 and 2019, state elementary and secondary education spending grew in both current and constant dollars in all sources except bonds. The annual growth rates for the state general fund were 5.53% during 2000–2008, 2.34% during 2008–2019, and 5.88% after 2019. The annual growth rates for other state funds were larger. In real terms, the annual growth rates were smaller but still positive, except for other funds during the pandemic.

Data from the National Center for Education Statistics (No Date), the primary federal agency for collecting and analyzing education data in the United States, clearly show significant growth of state spending per student over the past half-century. In constant dollars, state spending per pupil was $2,457 in 1970, then increased to $5,022 in 1990, and $7,335 in 2019. That is an increase of about $1,000 per decade. State contributions as a share of the total national public education funding was 39.9% in 1970, increasing to 47.1% in 1990, and have remained at and above that level in nearly all the years after.

Court Actions

What are the forces behind these steady and significant increases? The major factor is court decisions that demand state governments provide equitable and adequate funding for public education. Since the landmark decision, *Serrano v. Priest*, in 1970, most states have been subject to lawsuits seeking to reform their education funding systems. For those who have not, the prospect of litigation also prompted revisions of their funding systems (Candelaria, McNeill, and Shores 2022a). In *Serrano v. Priest (1971)*, the California Supreme Court agreed with the plaintiff that the traditional use of local property taxes to fund public schools created inequity across school districts, violating equal protection under the state constitution. Such "equalization" cases insist that children are entitled to the same amount of money spent on their education. By 1999, at least 19 states' school funding systems had been struck down.

Many later litigations, starting from 1990, took an "adequacy" approach. While the equity approaches demand fiscal equity within the resources the state can provide, "adequacy" cases successfully argue that "spending on education must be adequate to provide all students with an education of the quality guaranteed by their constitution" (West and Peterson 2016, p. 5). These cases are much more open and robust and set ambiguous standards, requiring much more significant fiscal commitment from state governments.

In response to litigations and court decisions, state legislatures revised and implemented new funding formulas and increased their share of educational spending. During the 1990s and early 2000s, the growth of public education spending often outpaced the growth in total state expenditures. In some states, many fiscal years saw double-digit percentage growth rates. Governors often made public education policy, including funding policies, their top priorities (NASBO 1995; 1997; 1999; 2000). State governments pursued many specific measures, including raising basic student funding levels, increasing state aid to poor districts, requiring a minimum local tax effort to participate in the state aid program, and expanding adjustments for at-risk persons, special needs students, and high-cost district conditions. Another state-sponsored measure included equalizing school facility funds to ensure adequate school construction and repair (NASBO 1995; 1997; 2003).

The Public Demands and Other Factors

Public attitudes and their actions are another force behind the observed spending increases. In several cases, voters passed ballot measures and amended state constitutions, resulting in states increasing funding for public education. One example is Oregon's Measure 5, a constitutional amendment in FY 1991 that limited local property tax rates and required the state to increase state education funding to replace lost property tax revenue. Another notable example is Colorado's Amendment 23, which voters passed in 2000, requiring the state government to increase funding for public education (Candelaria, McNeill, and Shores 2022a).

Demographic variables also elevated state public education spending. The growth of school enrollment over the years and the responsibility to teach students with special needs demanded more resources (NASBO 1995; 1999). In recent years, many states have made efforts to provide pre-K education services. Teacher shortages in recent years prompted many state governments to raise funding for public school teachers to promote retention and recruitment.

Candelaria, McNeill, and Shores (2022b) state that public education funding systems reflect an array of policy goals and processes. Many factors, such as "the economic conditions, relationship with teacher unions, and political party dynamics, are all likely important contextual factors that give rise to legislation" (p. 6). For instance, public school teacher unions are extremely active and strong. The widespread teacher walkouts in 2018 and 2019 pressured many state governments to raise funding for public education.

18 State Tax Systems

Over the years, there has been a large push toward linking funding to outcomes per national education standards and goals. State governments have supported school innovation, choice, and accountability, and funding has accompanied the efforts to attain these goals.

State spending on elementary and secondary education will likely keep growing in the years to come. The historical trend in the past century shows a continuous increase in constant dollars, except during economic recessions (e.g., 2003, 2009, and 2012) years. The forces behind the growth discussed above are well present today. Public education also enjoys overwhelming public support as it reinforces the basic right for every child to have quality education and experience equal opportunity.

State Expenditures on Medicaid

While elementary and secondary education remains the largest general fund spending, Medicaid is the largest component in total state spending. Medicaid is a jointly funded and means-tested entitlement program providing comprehensive and long-term medical services to low-income individuals (NASBO 1999). In 2019, 75 million relied on Medicaid services; in 2022, 80 million (NASBO 2019; 2022), or one out of five Americans use this program. The federal government provides broad guidelines, and states administer the program with considerable discretions about the specifics of the services. State funds are matched with federal grants based on a federal Medicaid Assistance Percentage (FMAP) that varies depending on state per capita personal income (Smith and Ellis 2001).

Table 2.3 shows funding sources for Medicaid in the selected years. Federal spending is typically larger than state funding (see Table 2.3). Among state funding are the general fund ($170.1 billion in 2019) and other state funds ($64.1 billion), with the latter largely supported by healthcare provider taxes, to be discussed in Chapter 11. Total Medicaid spending accounts for 28.9% of total state spending in fiscal 2019 and 19.7% of state general fund spending.

Between 2019 and 2022, total Medicaid spending increased by 10% every year to $801.2 billion in 2022. This dramatic increase was due to Congress' action to increase FMAP by 6.2 percentage points to provide state fiscal relief and address increasing Medicaid spending (NASBO 2022).

Cost Factors Driving Up Medicaid Expenditures

Table 2.3 shows increasing expenditures for the Medicaid program from 2000 to 2022 in all funding sources in both current and constant dollars. The annual growth rates between 2000 and 2019 were all much higher than those for elementary and secondary education, ranging from 3.84% to 8.18% in current

TABLE 2.3 State Medicaid Expenditure: Sources of Funding (in $million) and Shares of State General Fund and Total

Fiscal Year	2000	2008	2019	2022	Annual Growth Rate (%) 2000–2008	2008–2019	2019–2022
	Funding Sources in Current Dollar Percentage of Total						
State Gen Fund	65,491 / 35.5%	111,711 / 35.9%	169,018 / 27.8%	172,044 / 22.9%	6.90	3.84	0.59
State Other Funds	14,332 / 7.8%	26,884 / 8.6%	62,541 / 10.5%	72,303 / 8.6%	8.18	7.98	4.95
Federal Funding	104,555 / 56.7%	172,290 / 55.4%	372,516 / 61.8%	552,969 / 68.5%	6.44	7.26	14.35
Total Medicaid Spending	184,378 / 100%	310,885 / 100%	604,075 / 100%	801,276 / 100%	6.75	6.22	9.87
	Funding Sources in Constant Dollar						
State Gen Fund	97,248	132,673	169,018	150,296	3.96	2.23	(3.84)
State Other Funds	21,282	31,929	62,541	63,163	5.20	6.30	0.33
Federal Funding	155,254	204,619	372,516	486,528	3.51	5.60	9.31
Total Medicaid Spending	273,783	369,221	604,075	699,987	3.81	4.58	5.03
	Medicaid Spending as a Share of						
Total State Expenditure	19.5%	20.7%	28.9%	28.6%			
Total Gen Fund Expenditure	n.a.	16.3%	19.7%	17.3%			

Sources: NASBO (2000; 2008; 2019; 2022).

dollars and 2.30% to 6.30% in real dollars. Total spending annual growth ranged from 3.81% to 5.03% between 2000 and 2022.

Medicaid costs have been increasing ever since the program's inception. Total Medicaid expenditures were $0.9 billion in 1966 when implemented, $5.1 billion in 1970, and $25.2 billion in 1980. In the early 1990s, the program experienced double-digit growth (NASBO 2000). For many years, Medicaid has increased faster than the general economy. For instance, the Centers for Medicare and Medicaid Services Office of the Actuary 2012 Actuarial Report shows that while the average annual growth rate of gross domestic product was projected to be 5.5% from 2012 to 2021, the rate of Medicaid expenditures would be around 6.4% (NASBO 2012). As a result, Medicaid expenditure increased from 10.8% of total state spending in 1988 to 19.6% in 1999. By 2004, the share of Medicaid spending (22.3%) surpassed that for elementary and secondary education (21.4%) and became the largest state spending item (NASBO 2004).

Although much of Medicaid's spending increase came from federal funding, the program also remains a large spending pressure for state governments. State spending experienced an annual percentage increase every year except during recession years. In some years, especially amid economic downturns, Medicaid expenditures exceeded budgeted amounts.

Increasing Enrollment

Several factors contributed to Medicaid expenditure increases, the major one being continuous enrollment increases. Medicaid is a countercyclical program. During economic downturns, enrollment and spending increase, but state revenue decreases. Figure 2.1 shows sharp enrollment growth during 2002 (9.3%), 2009 (7.8%), and 2021 (11.2%) (Williams 2022).

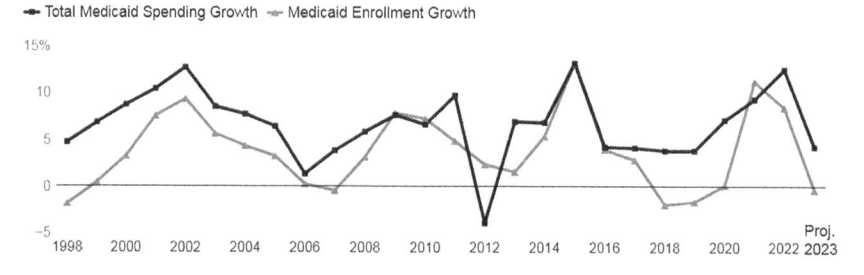

FIGURE 2.1 Percentage Change in Medicaid Spending and Enrollment, 1998–2023: Annual Percentage Changes.

Source: Williams, Elizabeth. 2022. "Medicaid Enrollment & Spending Growth: FY 2022 & 2023." Kaiser Family Foundation, p. 6. Permission granted.

To address the rise in Medicaid spending and provide state fiscal relief, Congress authorized temporary enhanced FMAP three times in the past three major recessions (in 2003, 2009, and 2021) by 2.95%, 6.2%, and 6.2%, respectively. For instance, the American Recovery and Reinvestment Act (ARRA) of 2019 brought states an additional approximately $103.1 billion between October 2008 and June 2011. To receive a higher FMAP, states are required to meet certain "maintenance of eligibility" (MOE), including not making eligibility harder. The Families First Coronavirus Response Act (FFCRA) of 2020 also requires states to ensure "continuous coverage for current enrollees" (Williams 2022, p. 1). MOE requirements keep enrollment numbers up.

Enrollment has also increased because of changes to Medicaid policy. In the early 2000s, the large enrollment growth of children in Medicaid resulted from the extensive outreach effort by the State Children's Health Insurance Program (S-CHIP). The Affordable Care Act (ACA) is another example that showcases the policy changes led to significant enrollment growth. ACA encourages states to expand Medicaid eligibility to non-pregnant and non-elderly individuals whose income is under 138% of the federal poverty line. The federal government would cover all the expanded costs for 2014, 2015, and 2016. From 2017, states were required to share 5% of the expanded cost, gradually increasing to 10% in January 2020 (NASBO 2017). The large increase in enrollment during 2014–2017 was due to the implementation of the ACA. The ACA added approximately 18.3 million individuals to the lists by 2021. High rates of enrollment growth during the Great Recession and the implementation of the ACA were the major drivers of total Medicaid spending growth over the last decade.

The only years that witnessed enrollment declines were FY 2018 (–2.1%) and FY 2019 (–1.7%), reflecting the tapering of ACA-related enrollment after the peak. Improving economic conditions was also a significant factor. Lower unemployment rates relieved pressure on Medicaid enrollment growth (Rudowitz and Hinton 2018).

Prescription Drug Costs

The increase in Medicaid expenditure is also due to the growth of overall healthcare costs and prescription drug costs. Healthcare, in general, became more expensive largely because of the aging population and the advancement of medical technology (Lav, McNichol, and Zahradnik 2005). The rising cost of prescription drugs reflects higher prescription drug prices and a larger volume of drugs consumed. Prices of prescriptions grew at a double-digit rate of approximately 18% every year in the late 1990s and early 2000s, partially attributed to newly developed drugs. The volume increases were the result of the aging population, direct consumer advertisement from pharmaceutical companies, and the movement into managed care plans (NASBO 1999; 2000).

The rapid growth of prescription drug cost concerned state officials in the late 1990s and early 2000s. Then since 2014, rising drug prices, together with the expansion of Medicaid services under the ACA, renewed state focus on controlling rising prescription drug costs. Many states "identify high cost and specialty drugs [such as hepatitis C antivirals] as a significant cost driver for state Medicaid program" (Smith, Gifford, Ellis, Rudowitz, Snyder, and Hilton 2015, p. 3). As a result, they have refocused on pharmacy cost containment efforts, including refining and enhancing their pharmacy programs, particularly those related to new and emerging specialty and high-cost drug therapies (Smith et al. 2015; Smith, Gifford, Ellis, Edwards, Rudowitz, and Hilton 2016; Rudowitz and Hinton 2018).

Seniors, Disabled, and Long-term Care Services

Several program and demographic factors also explain the growth of the Medicaid program. About 25% of Medicaid beneficiaries are seniors and disabled, but they are responsible for 70% of the program cost (NASBO 2004). The implementation of the ACA also saw an increase in disabled persons receiving long-term care services under Medicaid. As the population ages, the number of seniors who need long-term care will also increase dramatically.

As more seniors and disabled persons use long-term institutional care (e.g., nursing home) or other home and community-based care settings (HCBS), the overall costs will continue to increase. In a 2018 survey, state officials reported that per enrollee cost for the aged and persons with disabilities increased at a higher rate than for other groups. In addition, Medicaid is also responsible for the rapid growth of HCBS alternatives designed for this population group (NASBO 2000). State officials also report other factors accelerating Medicaid expenditures. This includes medical inflation (usually higher than general CPI), the policy decision to raise provider rates, the shortage of labor in the healthcare industry, and wage pressures in the healthcare industry (Rudowitz and Hinton 2018; 2020).

Medicaid plays a key role in the U.S. healthcare system, providing healthcare services to 20% of Americans and accounting for 17% of health expenditures. Medicaid also has a significant impact on the state budget. It is the largest spending category for state total spending and is the second largest category for state general fund expenditures. As its expenditures increase at a rate faster than other programs and the general economy, Medicaid places major spending pressure on state finances. How to make it sustainable is one of the greatest challenges and concerns for state and federal governments. States have experimented with different management models and cost-controlling methods, but some of the drivers behind program costs, such as long-term care costs and recession-inserted enrollments, cannot be removed and will remain.

State Spending on Higher Education

States are responsible for funding higher education institutions (e.g., public universities, community colleges, and career and technical education institutions) through general operation support and student financial aid programs. General operation support assumes a lion's share of total state funding. Student financial aid never exceeds 10%. Higher education is the third largest category of total state spending and also the third largest component of general fund spending. Total spending on higher education was $213.7 billion in fiscal year 2019 and $247 billion in 2022 (see Table 2.4).

Funding for higher education comes primarily from state general funds and other state funds (e.g., tuition and fees). Higher education expenditures, as a share of state general spending, have been shrinking in recent decades because spending in other program areas, particularly Medicaid, has expanded (NASBO 2022). For instance, higher education spending was 14% of state general fund spending in 1990, declined to 12.2% in 2000, and even further to 9.6% in 2019 (NASBO 2019; Okunade 2004). Also see Table 2.4.

With the share of state general funds declining, the share of state other funds increased (see the annual growth rate between 2000 and 2019). This is particularly true in the years immediately after the Great Recession, continuing the trend that started after the 2001 recession (see Table 2.4). During 2009–2012, states significantly reduced their general fund support for higher education by $13.9 billion or 17.5%. Although federal stimulus funds offset most funding, states increased their reliance on "state other funds" to support higher education. As a result, the inflation-adjusted tuition and fees increased by 44% at public four-year institutions between 2009 and 2019 after taking into account grant aid and federal education tax breaks (NASBO 2019).

As the economy started to improve, states increased their funding for higher education to support the operations and provided more student financial aid, as well as scholarship programs, to make higher education affordable and accessible. Many states implemented promise programs and last-dollar scholarship programs to guarantee free tuition for state residents. Laws were also passed to restrict tuition increases and freeze tuition rates. There is also a movement toward public investment for community and technical colleges via more student financial aid and targeting more resources to career and technical education programs. The purpose is "to better align their education systems with workforce changes" (NASBO 2019, p. 29). As a result, the net tuition (tuition minus financial aid and tax benefits) for two-year community colleges declined from 2009 to 2019 (NASBO 2019). Also see the declining annual growth rates of "other state funds" between 2019 and 2022 in Table 2.5. States also adopted strategies to hold institutions accountable for results through outcome-based funding models (NASBO 2013; 2019).

TABLE 2.4 State Higher Education Expenditure: Sources of Funding and Share of State General Fund and Total (in $million)

Fiscal Year	2000	2008	2019	2022	Annual Growth Rate (%) 2000–2008	2008–2019	2019–2022
	Funding Sources in Current Dollar						
	Percentage of Total						
State Gen Fund	$55,412	$77,521	82,434	$94,587	4.29	0.56	4.69
	53.8%	50.7%	38.8%	39.1%			
State Other Funds	$31,524	$54,871	103,230	105,584	7.17	5.91	0.75
	30.6%	35.9%	48.7%	43.4%			
Federal Funding	$12,657	$14,938	22,287	36,507	2.09	3.70	17.88
	12.3%	9.8%	10.1%	15.2%			
Bonds	3,450	$5,494	$5,100	5,043	5.99	(0.67)	(4.30)
	3.3%	3.6%	2.4%	2.3%			
Total Higher Edu. Exp.	103,043	152,824	213,051	241,721	5.05	3.07	4.30
	100%	100%	100%	100%			
	Funding Sources in Constant Dollar						
State Gen Fund Source	82,281	92,067	82,434	82,630	1.41	(1.00)	0.08
State Other Funds	46,810	65,167	103,230	92,237	4.22	4.27	(3.68)
Federal Funding	18,794	17,741	22,287	31,892	(0.72)	2.10	12.69
Bonds	5,123	6,525	5,100	4,406	3.07	(2.21)	(4.76)
Total Higher Edu. Spending	153,009	181,501	213,051	211,165	2.16	1.47	(0.30)
	Higher Education Spending as a Share of						
Total State Expenditure	10.9%	10.2%	10.1%	8.7%			
Total Gen Fund Expenditure	12.2%	11.3%	9.6%	9.2%			

Sources: NASBO (2000; 2008; 2019; 2022).

TABLE 2.5 State Higher Education Funding for Financial Aid, General Operation, and Net Tuition Revenue (2001–2022)[a]

	2001	2012	2021	2022	Percentage Changes		
					2022–2021	2022–2012	2022–2001
Current Dollars (in Millions)							
State Appropriation	$56,118	$69,203	$98,210	$105,515	7.4%	52.5%	88.0%
Financial Aid	$2,834	$6,584	$9,767	$10,205	4.5%	55.0%	260.1%
General Operations	$53,298	$62,502	$84,818	$92,824	9.4%	48.5%	74.2%
Net Tuition Revenue	$22,816	$59,234	$73,644	$74,665	1.4%	26.1%	227.2%
Total Edu. Revenue	$78832	$127,737	$170,911	$179,265	4.9%	40.3%	127.4%
Constant Inflation-Adjusted Dollars (in Millions)							
State Appropriation	$95,264	$87,682	$103,219	$105,515	2.2%	20.3%	10.8%
Financial Aid	$4,811	$8,342	$10,265	$10,205	-0.6%	22.3%	112.1%
General Operations	$90,477	$79,191	$89,144	$92,824	4.1%	17.2%	2.6%
Net Tuition Revenue	$38,732	$75,050	$77,400	$74,665	-3.5%	-0.5%	92.8%
Total Edu. Revenue	$133,807	$161,846	$179,628	$179,265	-0.2%	10.8%	34.0%
Constant Inflation-Adjusted Dollars (FTE)							
FTE Enrollment	8,709,255	11,521,192	10,573,262	10,306,924	-2.5%	-10.5%	18.3%
State Appropriation	$10,938	$7,610	$9,762	$10,237	4.9%	34.5%	-6.4%
Financial Aid	$552	$724	$971	$990	2.0%	36.8%	79.3%
General Operations	$10,389	$6,874	$8,431	$9,006	6.8%	31.0%	-13.3%
Net Tuition Revenue	$4,447	$6,514	$7,320	$7,244	-1.0%	11.2%	62.9%
Total Revenue	$15,364	$14,048	$16,989	$17,393	2.4%	23.8%	13.20%

Source: Revised based on State Higher Education Executive Officers Association (2023), p. 23.

[a] State spending on Higher Education may slightly differ from those in Table 2.4, even for the same year, due to different data sources.

Federal funding has remained relatively stable, contributing roughly 10% of total funding for higher education before COVID-19. The large increase in federal funding during 2020–2022 is attributed to COVID-19 fiscal relief funds. States reported at least $23.6 billion in additional federal aid distributed to higher education during 2020–2022 through the Higher Education Emergency Relief Fund programs and other COVID-19 relief legislations. Some federal relief funds went to higher education institutions directly and are not reflected in state expenditure data (NASBO 2022). These federal funding levels are not permanent, and the share is expected to return to normal levels.

State Higher Education Funding Per FTE Trend

Data in Table 2.5 illustrate the story of higher education financing by showing state funding for student financial aid, general operations, and net tuition revenue over the years. The top panel is in current dollars, showing state funding in 2022 increasing by 7.4% over 2021. State general operating support increased by 9.4%, student aid by 4.5%, and the net tuition increase (tuition minus financial aid) was 1.4%. Comparing 2022 with 2012, state financial aid increased at a larger scale (i.e., 55%) than general operations (i.e., 48%). The picture is more striking if we look further back to 2001. Student aid increased by 260% as compared with 74% for general operations. Tuition increased by 227% in the same period. After being adjusted with inflation, the increases in all areas are smaller. State financial aid in 2022 declined by 0.6% from 2021 (State Higher Education Executive Officers Association 2023).

When examining the inflation-adjusted per full-time equivalent (FTE) funding, the data in the bottom panel show that state education appropriation in 2022 was 6.4% lower than in 2001. All declines occurred in state general operation funds—a 13% decline. State general operating spending per FTE has continually declined since 2001. Only until 2022, per FTE funding rose, attributing to the following three factors: the large federal fiscal relief as mentioned, the state's robust economic recovery with unprecedented revenue collection, and the declining student enrollments. Student financial aid per FTE was relatively more stable and increased by 79% between 2001 and 2022.

Cost Drivers and Issues with Higher Education Spending

Unlike elementary and secondary education and Medicaid, whose expenditures are mostly mandated by laws or courts, higher education is one of the few remaining areas in the state budget that is at the complete discretion of state lawmakers. When facing revenue shortages, state officials disproportionately cut funding for higher education institutions. Therefore, state funding for higher education is "closely tied to economic cycles and fluctuates widely as tax revenue rises or falls with changing economic conditions" (NASBO 2000, p. 24). This is particularly true with general operating support funding, as discussed above. According to Cummings, Laderman, Lee, Tandberg, and Weeden (2021), during the last four recessions, state higher education appropriations per FTE in constant dollars not only dropped but dropped further down each time, and recoveries took longer. State funding in FY 2012 reached an all-time low in recent history and did not get back to the pre-Great Recession level even by 2019. State funding also fluctuates because of the notion that public universities and colleges can obtain revenues by raising tuition and fees while other spending areas cannot.

As discretionary spending, funding for higher education does not impose legal obligations to state finance. However, states do face pressures to make more investments in higher education. First, state governments always play an important role in supporting higher education. Higher education generates both private and public benefits. McMahon (2009) and Cummings et al. (2021) believe the public benefit exceeds the private outcomes. The public benefits include increased citizen engagement, lower crime rates, lower poverty rates, lower healthcare costs, and higher tax revenue. Additionally, higher education has assumed increasing and varying missions, such as producing an educated workforce, improving local economies, advancing research endeavors, and ensuring all citizens the access to education regardless of their circumstances. These missions generate substantive and long-term positive spillovers, and state funding is critical to accomplish these missions.

Second, with the changing economy, the nation faces a shortage of skilled workers and high-quality credentials for the technical market. There is also an increasing income gap between those with a college degree and those without. Higher education is expected to play a special role in developing specific attainment goals to address these gaps. College success and access are important policy issues for higher education funding. State governments must not only increase student college enrollment but also provide financial support for those who cannot afford it and ensure their successful completion. In addition, states need strategies to reduce the attainment and completion gaps among different racial, ethical, and socio-economic groups. Empirical studies show state funding contributes to student success in higher education. State investment in higher education leads to increasing enrollment, persistence, and completion (Zhao 2018; Chakrabarti et al. 2020). Studies also show that financial aid influences student behaviors and increases student persistence, credential attainment, as well as income tax revenue (Bettinger Gurantz, Kawano, Sacerdote, and Stevens 2019; Nguyen, Kramer, and Evans 2019).

Third, although higher education funding reached pre-Great Recession levels in the last three years, that was mostly due to the large federal fiscal relief fund that effectively reduced state budget strains and allowed states to have room to show their commitment to higher education. It is important to realize that "these one-time funds are not a replacement for long-term state investments" (SHEEO 2023, p. 76). When the federal funds run out, states will face pressure as to how to continue supporting higher education.

Fourth, the net tuition FTE declined in the last few years, partially due to low tuition growth rates as a result of the restrictions imposed by state laws. The State Higher Education Executive Officers Associations (SHEEO) (2023) also shows that in 2021 and 2022, for the first time since 2016, student's share to support higher education was below 50% of the total in more than half of states. This is good news for students and their families. However, more pressure is placed on states to expand their funding shares. Student affordability and student loan debts are considered important public concerns. States should proceed with caution to avoid raising and exacerbating student burdens that later may complicate college affordability and attendance rates.

States need to increase student financial aid, and they also need to keep up state general operation funding support as both are important for student success. Over the decades, states have increased student financial aid programs, but funding for general operation per FTE has fallen behind. Cummings et al. (2021) insist that the growth of financial aid should not come at the expense of state general operating support. State operating appropriation, according to Cummings et al., "serves to support the entire mission of schools, contribute to the overall quality of education experience, and directly impact student access and success" (p. 13). General operation funding is an essential and undervalued tool for higher education institutions to achieve student completion, state attainment rates, and other positive interests (Cummings et al. 2021).

Similar to any other policy area, state higher education funding policies face some basic but important questions. How should states and students share the financial burden of higher education? How should states allocate their funding between general operations and student aid programs? What is the most efficient use of state funding to achieve desired outcomes? Debates around these questions started in the 1980s. The questions are still relevant to current state funding policy. The answers to these questions vary at different times and to different groups. As a discretionary spending item, higher education is always vulnerable to state fiscal conditions. However, it is important for state lawmakers to balance competing needs and recognize the critical need for direct investment in higher education general operations.

State Transportation Expenditure

The nation's "roads, bridges, and transit are funded through a partnership among the levels of government in which financial contributions are substantial and deeply intertwined" (Oliff, 2015, p. 1). State governments are an important player in this partnership, primarily responsible for funding, operating, and constructing the highways, tollways, and bridges (Urban Institute No Date b). The federal grants also provide a significant amount of resources for these projects. Local governments are mainly responsible for local streets and roads.

Transportation spending is unique in that roughly 60% of funding is directed to capital spending. In comparison, all other spending categories typically have less than 10% used for capital construction. In 2020, 57% of state and local highway and road spending went toward capital spending, such as highway construction. The other 43% of funding went toward operational costs, including maintenance, repair, snow and ice removal, highway and traffic design, operation, and safety (Urban Institute No Date b).

Total state transportation funding was $164 billion in 2019 and $189 billion in 2022 (see Table 2.6). Although only about 5% derives from the state general fund, states have larger "other funds" and issue a sizable amount of bonds to support transportation. The "other state funds" contain numerous earmarked revenues designated for transportation. At least 47 states retained separate transportation funds, with 40% of funding deriving from all or some fuel taxes. Forty-three states also include vehicle registration and license fees (19.4% of the fund), and 24 states deposit vehicle sales and user taxes (7.6%) into the transportation fund. States also include toll revenue (1.5% of the fund) and many other funding sources (31.7%) (NASBO 2019). The "other state funds" exhibit higher annual growth rates than state general funds between 2000 and 2019, indicating the expansive use of alternative transportation funding.

The federal government contributes 26%–29% of total funding, mainly via the HTF, which is primarily financed by dedicated revenue streams from gasoline and diesel taxes. The HTF, with 90% distributed to states based on a formula, is used for highway planning and construction, not for operation and maintenance. The fund is not provided upfront but reimbursed to states after the project has started, costs are incurred, and a voucher is submitted to the Federal Highway Administration. About 90% of the fund is dedicated to interstate system projects, accounting for 25% of all U.S. public roads (Kirk and Mallett 2021).

Over the years, each funding source as a share of total expenditures has remained relatively stable, but there has been a noticeable increase in the state share (the combination of state general fund, other funds, and bonds) from 67.1% in fiscal year 2010 to 73.1% in fiscal year 2019 (NASBO 2019). This is due to state efforts to update their transportation funding by including charges and fees for hybrid cars, electric cars, road use fees, and other innovative financing.

Cost Drivers for State Transportation Expenditures

Transportation plays a crucial role in facilitating commerce and providing personal mobility. According to the Urban Institute (No Date b), the increase

TABLE 2.6 State Transportation Expenditures (in $million): Sources of Funding and Share of State General Fund and Total

Fiscal Year	2000	2008	2019	2022	Annual Growth Rate (%) 2000–2008	2008–2019	2019–2022
	Funding Sources in Current Dollar Percentage of Total						
State Gen. Fund	4,013 / 4.8%	$5,390 / 4.5%	6,044 / 4.8%	$7,708 / 6.0%	3.76	1.05	8.44
State Other Funds	51,717 / 62.2%	$67,985 / 57.3%	100,618 / 61.1%	$112,251 / 57.4%	3.48	3.63	3.71
Federal Funding	22,724 / 27.4%	$33,457 / 28.2%	43,742 / 26.9%	$49,105 / 26.7%	4.95	2.47	3.93
Bonds	4,683 / 5.6%	$11,754 / 9.9%	14,035 / 7.3%	$20,280 / 9.9%	12.18	1.63	13.05
Total State Transportation Spending	83,137 / 100%	$118,586 / 100%	164,439 / 100%	189,344 / 100%	4.54	3.02	4.81
	Funding Sources in Constant Dollar						
State Gen. Fund Source	5,959	$6,401	6,044	$6,734	0.90	(0.52)	3.67
State Other Funds	76,795	$80,742	100,618	98,061	0.63	2.02	(0.85)
Federal Funding	33,743	$39,735	43,742	$42,898	2.06	0.88	(0.65)
Bonds	6,954	$14,838	14,035	$17,716	9.10	0.05	8.07
Total State Transportation Spending	123,450	$141,413	164,439	165,409	1.66	1.42	0.20
	Transportation Spending as a Share of						
Total State Expenditure	8.8%	7.9%	8.0%	8.1%	7.3%		

Sources: NASBO (2000; 2008; 2019; 2022).

in state and local transportation expenditure was one of the slowest growing areas from 1977 to 2020. Table 2.7 also shows that over the years, total transportation spending as a share of total state spending decreased slightly from 8.8% in 2000 to 8.1% in 2019 and to 7.3% in 2022. While the annual growth rate from other sources grew at 3.48%–3.71% over the years, the consensus is that U.S. transportation systems have been severely underfunded and cannot meet the nation's 21st-century needs by many measures. The system is facing "the dual challenges of better managing demand and increasing investments in capacity" (Burwell and Puentes 2021, p. 1).

First, the demand for road use far outpaces the addition of capacity. From 1980 to 2010, vehicle miles traveled increased by 95%, whereas road capacity only added 4%, resulting in serious congestion in densely populated regions and great inefficiency. In 2005 alone, "congestions nationwide cost 2.9 billion gallons of waste fuel, and the economy $200 billion in lost productivity" (Burwell and Puentes 2021, p. 4).

The second challenge for the transportation system is the inadequate amount of investment "needed to add new capacity and to preserve, operate, and maintain and upgrade the existing system" (Burwell and Puentes, 2021, p. 5). The American Society of Civil Engineers (ASCE 2021) stated that "the U.S. has underfunded its roadway system for years, resulting in a $786 billion backlog of road and bridge capital needs" (p. 3). The lack of investment is mainly due to the out-of-date revenue structure of transportation funds, which rely on fuel tax as the primary source. The issues with fuel tax will be discussed in Chapter 11.

The federal HTF has also become insolvent due to its reliance on gasoline and diesel tax revenues. Since 2001, the outlay from HTF has consistently exceeded its revenue. In 2008, Congress began to bridge the gap by transferring funds from the U.S. Treasury general fund. Under the Fixing America's Surface Transportation Act, $157 billion from the U.S. Treasury general fund was transferred to the HTF from 2008 to 2020. The Infrastructure Investment and Jobs Act (IIJA) of 2021 transferred another $118 billion to the general fund. However, the underlying gap between HTF revenue and outlay persists and will worsen as fuel efficiency increases and more hybrid cars and electric vehicles are used. The Congressional Budget Office projects that the HTF will be depleted in 2028, and the accumulative shortfall in funding for the HTF will grow rapidly over the next 10 years to reach $250 billion in 2033 (Peter G. Peterson Foundation).

Due to inadequate investment, the U.S. transportation infrastructure has severely deteriorated. According to an ASCE (2021) report, 43% of roads are in poor or mediocre conditions, and 7.5% of bridges were considered structurally deficit.

With climate change becoming a top public policy concern, the government needs to invest in transportation systems to address the challenges. As

TABLE 2.7 State Corrections Expenditure (in $million): Sources of Funding and Share of State General Fund and Total

Fiscal Year	2000	2008	2019	2022	Annual Growth Rate (%)		
					2000–2008	2008–2019	2019–2022
	Funding Sources in Current Dollar Percentage of Total						
State Gen. Fund	$31,714 87.8%	$47,730 91.8%	$56,726 89.4%	$54,999 81.3%	5.24	1.58	(1.03)
State Other Funds	$1,961 5.4%	$2,494 4.8%	$5,425 8.5%	$6,683 10.0%	3.05	7.32	7.20
Federal Funding	$1,041 3.1%	$856 1.6%	$607 1.0%	$5,524 7.9%	(2.42)	(3.08)	108.78
Bonds	$1,323 3.7%	$916 1.8%	$694 1.1%	$705 0.9%	(4.49)	(2.49)	0.53
Total State Corrections Spending	$36,102 100%	$51,996 100%	$63,452 100%	$67,911 100%	4.69	1.83	2.29
	Funding Sources in Constant Dollar						
State Gen. Fund	$47,291	$56,686	$56,726	$48,047	2.34	0.01	(5.38)
State Other Funds	$2,924	$2,974	$5,425	$5,838	0.21	5.66	2.48
Federal Funding	$1,546	$1,017	$607	$4,826	(5.10)	(4.58)	99.58
Bonds	$1,965	$1,088	$694	$616	(7.12)	(4.00)	(3.90)
Total State Corrections Spending	$53,835	$61753	$63,452	$59,326	1.81	0.25	(2.22)
	Corrections Spending as Share of						
Total State Expenditure	3.8%	3.5%	3.0%	2.5%			
Total Gen Fund Expenditure	7.0%	7.0%	6.6%	5.5%			

Sources: NASBO (2000; 2008; 2019; 2022).

transportation emissions are responsible for greenhouse gases, investment in transportation systems should find methods to reduce total emissions. This may involve enhancing land use planning to make it possible for people to make fewer trips or to walk and bicycle on trips. Building additional public transit systems is also a viable solution. At the same time, investment commitments need to make transportation systems more resilient to the impact of climate change and advance climate and environmental justice (U.S. Department of Transportation 2023).

An effective, efficient, and resilient transportation system is critically important for our economy and the well-being of the people. It requires all levels of government to work together, finding innovative strategies to fund, build, and update the system. Creating long-term sustainable funding for the construction of the nation's surface transportation will remain a significant issue for state lawmakers and Congress.

State Expenditure on Corrections

State corrections expenditures reflect states' obligations to "build and operate state prison systems and may also include the spending on juvenile justice system and alternative to incarceration such as probation and parole" (NASBO 2019, p. 60). States spent $63,452 million on corrections in 2019 and $67,911 million in 2022 (see Table 2.7). During the pre-COVID-19 years, state spending as a share of state total spending and as a share of state general fund spending was relatively stable, around 3% and 7%, respectively. State general funds are the primary funding source for correction expenditures, contributing 87%–91% of all the funding. As a matter of fact, no other state spending category has such a heavy reliance on state general funding.

Federal funding increased substantially at an annual rate of 108% during 2019–2022 by at least $14.6 billion (NASBO 2022). States could technically use the Coronavirus Aid, Relief, and Economic Security Act (CARES Act) funds to cover COVID-19-related expenses, including correction officer payroll costs and equipment. States could also direct part of the American Rescue Plan Act (ARPA) to respond to a public health emergency (NASBO 2022). However, this funding will soon expire, and federal funding will return to its normal level.

Cost Drivers for the Correction Expenditures

While state correction expenditure has remained relatively constant as a share of state general fund spending and the annual growth rate became smaller after 2008 (see Table 2.7), it has experienced extraordinarily high growth rates in some periods. For instance, 1990 saw state corrections expenditure growing by 19% over the previous year and 1995 by 15%. The annual average growth rate was 7.5% in the 1990s. Between 1986 and 2013, inflation-adjusted correction spending more than doubled, growing from $20 billion to $47 billion. Growth in corrections spending outpaced spending in public education and higher education. Inflation-adjusted state spending on higher education grew by less than 6% during 1986–2013. Meanwhile, state spending on K-12 education grew by 69%, and spending on corrections grew by 141% (Mitchell and Leachman 2014).

The substantial growth of state correction spending caused serious concerns because it diverted scarce public resources from other major functions, such as public education and higher education. Investment in education for children and young adults, particularly in those in high-poverty communities, is believed to bring better long-term economic growth.

The Prison Population

Several factors pushed up correction costs. Before mid-2010, the state prison population was the primary driver of the expenditure spike. State prison populations experienced extraordinary growth during the 1980s and 1990s due to tough-on-crime legislation passed by state lawmakers. These laws imposed "longer sentences, mandatory sentences for repeat offenders, and less generous parole and higher sentencing rates for the most serious crimes" (NASBO 1997, p. 77). For instance, the "three strikes" laws sentenced repeat offenders to life imprisonment (NASBO 2001). As a result, the state prison population grew from 270,000 in 1978 to over 1.3 million in 2013. Once incarcerated, costs were incurred as inmates needed to be appropriately fed, housed, and medically cared for.

Facing overcrowded prisons and rapid cost increases, states began to reform their criminal justice system in the early 2000s. The strategy was to focus resources on the most violent criminals and return other inmates to communities with the support and tools they need. The measures include alternatives to incarceration, earning sentence credits for good behaviors, other sentencing changes, parole reforms, and increased treatment to address mental health and substance abuse disorders. As a result, the prison population started to decline by mid-2010. States held 325,500 fewer inmates in 2020 than in 2009. A drop of 181,250 during 2019–2020, or 14%, took place due to COVID-19-related reasons. Some states expedited inmate releases to minimize the possible COVID-19 spreading. The courts altered their operation in 2020, slowing down inmate admissions (NASBO 2022).

Healthcare Expenditure

Even with the prison population declining, state correction expenditures continued to increase. First, the decline in the prison population does not automatically translate to state correction savings. The decline needs to be large enough to result in closing a prison unit and reducing staff (NASBO 2020). Second, other factors still push up the cost. Similar to the general population, healthcare services for inmates are costly. In addition, the mix of inmate populations affects healthcare costs. Certain groups are more costly because they require more medical care. The high number (22,518) of HIV-positive inmates increased healthcare costs in the 1990s (NASBO 1999). Older inmates tend to have more health issues and require more accommodations at the facilities. According to the Census Bureau, the number of inmates aged 55 and older has increased from 7.9% of the sentenced prisoners in 2011 to 13.1% in 2019 (NASBO 2020).

Personnel Cost and Other Factors

In the last decade, with the tightening of the labor market, states have increased salaries and benefits to retrain current correctional officers and improve recruitment and retention for some critical positions (NASBO 2016; 2019). Other factors pushing up state correction costs include contract costs for community-based programs, maintaining aged and large physical plants, and continuing criminal justice reforms to reduce prison populations and improve outcomes (NASBO 2020).

State Expenditure on Public Assistance

States are responsible for cash assistance provided through the Temporary Assistance for Needy Families (TANF) program and other public assistance programs—those optional state programs for Supplemental Security Income and General Assistance. The optional programs are not guaranteed in all states. For those states that offer the program, each designs its own program structure. Some have state-wide eligibility rules, while others just require county residency (NASBO 2008).

Table 2.8 shows states' public assistance expenditure in selected years. The total spending level remains relatively stable. The primary state funding sources come from the general funds, which have declined over the years, even in nominal dollar amounts. In constant dollars, state funding for this spending category has consistently declined every year from 2000 to 2022 (see Table 2.8).

Federal funding increased both in nominal terms and as a share of total funding. While TANF is the major funding source, the federal government also provides additional funding at emergency times. For instance, during 2020–2022, states received at least $14.5 billion more funding from COVID-19 relief aid for public assistance programs.

TABLE 2.8 State Public Assistance Expenditure (in $million): Sources of Funding and Share of Total State Spending

Fiscal Year	2000	2008	2019	2022	Annual Growth Rate (%) 2000–2008	2008–2019	2019–2022
	Funding Sources in Current Dollar Percentage of Total						
State Gen Fund	11,345 49.2%	12,568 50.3%	7,752 29.8%	7,917 27.8%	1.29	(4.30)	0.70
State Other Funds	1,847 8.0%	377 1.5%	2,534 9.8%	3,025 8.5%	(18.02)	18.91	6.08
Federal Funding	9,866 42.8%	12,064 48.2%	14,715 60.4%	16,879 63.7%	2.55	1.82	4.68
Total State Public Assistance Spending	23,058 100%	25,009 100%	25,001 100%	27,821 100%	1.02	0.00	3.63
	Funding Sources in Constant Dollar						
State Gen Fund	16,846	14,926	7,752	6,916	(1.50)	(5.78)	(3.73)
State Other Funds	2,754	448	2,534	2,643	(20.27)	(5.78)	(3.73)
Federal Funding	14,650	14,386	14,715	14,745	(0.28)	0.24	0.07
Total State Public	34,323	29,702	25,001	24,304	(1.76)	(1.55)	(0.84)
Total State Public Assistance Spending	34,323	29,702	25,001	24,304	(1.76)	(1.55)	(0.84)
	State Public Assistance Spending as Share of						
Total State Expenditure	2.4%	1.7%	1.2%	2.5%			

Sources: NASBO (2000; 2008; 2019; 2022).

TANF and the Decline of Public Assistance Caseload

In 1996, Congress passed the Personal Responsibility and Work Opportunity Reconciliation Act (PRWORA) and overhauled the public welfare system by replacing its 60-year-old Aid to Families with Dependent Children (AFDC) with the TANF program. While AFDC was a dedicated and open-ended funding source for family cash assistance, TANF, a block grant, provides states with a fixed amount of $16.5 billion per year. As a result, states are given more flexibility and responsibilities to design and run their system. States are required to maintain at least 75%–80% of their own 1994 AFDC-related spending level—$10.3 billion—as maintenance of effort (MOE) requirement. For any year, if states have any TANF funding left, they can save it to build up "rainy day" funds. There is also a contingency fund within TANF that can provide additional funding to states during economic downturns (Blank 2001).

One of the statutory goals of TANF is "to end the dependence of needy parents on government benefits by promoting job preparation, work, and marriage" (CRS 2023, p. 5). The program requires families to work in exchange for time-limited cash assistance. Those who received the benefit over five cumulative years are not eligible for federally funded assistance, though states have discretion to determine how the rule is applied for each individual case (NASBO 2016). "The program defines work, work verification requirements, and the penalty if a state fails to meet the requirement" (NASBO 2022, p. 40). Most states must significantly increase work participation rates to meet the requirement.

Under the broad federal guidelines, state governments have considerable discretion regarding how to spend TANF and MOE funds. As a result, states tend to spend only a small portion of total TANF funds (41% in 2006, 25% in 2016, and 21% in 2019) on cash assistance payments. The majority of funds are directed to supportive services for recipients to achieve self-sufficiency. States have experimented with a variety of methods to assist recipients in overcoming work barriers and remaining in the workforce. These services include child-care services and pre-kindergarten, transportation, job training and education, job retention training, transitional rental assistance, and programs to address substance abuse and domestic violence.

Since the reforms in 1996, the number of people who received cash assistance has declined significantly. The average monthly recipients fell from its historical peak of 18.0 million in 1994, prior to the reforms, to 4 million in December 2009, 2.0 million in March 2019, and 1.8 million in 2022 (NASBO 2019; 2022). Indeed, the constant decline of cash assistance caseloads is a distinctive characteristic of welfare reform with PRWORA, often seen as an indicator of the reform's success.

However, this is not the entire story. The number of people eligible for benefits is always much higher. For instance, in 2010, the number of people eligible for TANF reached approximately 23 million, almost as many as pre-TANF era, but only about 30% of them received the benefit. In 2018, about 14.3 million were eligible for the benefit, but only 26%, or 3.8 million, received it. This means those who need help are not able to receive it, not even on a temporary basis, leaving them, including children, in poverty and deep poverty (below 50% of the poverty threshold). According to the Congressional Research Service (CRS), the number of children who are in poverty increased by 4.3 million between 2000 and 2012, but only 20% of them received TANF assistance compared to 30.7% in 2000. This raises an important issue for discussion. Although the intention of welfare reform is to end dependence on government benefits, it also has another goal of providing assistance so that "needy children can live in the homes of their parents or other relatives" (CRS 2017, p. 13). The low rate of receiving assistance contradicts the second goal.

Several reasons explain why so many people who are eligible for benefits do not receive them. One reason offered by economists is that the gains from applying for the benefit (e.g., the cash payment) may be smaller than the cost (i.e., time spent in the application process and transportation cost to get to the office). There is also a social stigma attached to people receiving welfare assistance. Third, the TANF policy design incentivizes states to reduce their receiving rates. As the grant is capped at $16.5 billion annually, not even adjusted for inflation, states can save more if the cash assistance caseload is lowered and funds are directed for other services and benefits. In addition, TANF requires states to keep certain "work participation standards," and states can meet these expectations by partially or entirely reducing their caseload rather than engaging recipients in work or other activities (CRS 2017). Furthermore, TANF also gives states the authority to reduce their caseloads. If the parents fail to conform to work requirements, states can terminate the benefits to entire families (CRS 2017).

Given that TANF funds and the required MOE are set at a fixed level, state spending on public assistance will remain small, and the inflation-adjusted amount will continue to shrink. Public assistance programs have evolved over time. Under TANF, fewer families in need received cash assistance. Although there are other income-security programs, such as earned income tax credits and child tax credits, they do not provide cash assistance on a monthly basis. Policy makers might pay attention to the diminishing impact of TANF on deep poverty and find the right balance between ending dependence on the government and providing a safety net for those who are in need.

State "All Other Expenditures"

The category "all other state expenditures" contains the bulk of state government agencies and a list of programs that do not belong to previous categories. Among the list are

> State the Children's Health Insurance Program (S-CHIP), care for the mentally ill and developmentally disabled, public health programs, child welfare and family services, constitutional offices, legislative and judicial branches, some employer contributions to pensions and health benefits, economic development, state police, environmental protection, parks and recreation, other natural resources program, unemployment insurance, housing, general aid to local governments, and debt services.
>
> *(NASBO 2019, p. 78)*

Altogether, these items consume a substantial amount of state funding. The amount started at $303,071 million in 2000, increased to $518,269 million in 2008, and to $618,289 million in 2019 (see Table 2.9). The primary funding source originates from state funds, particularly state general funds. Over the years, the share of "other state funds" increased from 34.6% in 2000 to 38.2% in 2019, but dropped to 32.5% in 2022.

The significant increase in all other spending during 2019–2022 was attributed to federal COVID-19 relief funds and state revenue collection increases. States spent at least $431 billion of federal COVID-19 relief funds for "all other" categories in these three years (NASBO 2023a). For instance, most of the CARES Act funds can be used for unemployment insurance, public health programs, housing assistance, emergency management, economic relief, aid to local governments, broadband, and other technology upgrades. The Coronavirus State and Local Fiscal Recovery Fund in the ARPA of 2021 can be used to support a wide range of activities in "all other state expenditure" (2023). Collectively, these expenditures tend to be temporary as some have recently expired, and others will soon in the coming years. States' robust revenue collection in recent years also allows them to increase spending for various programs in this category.

All other expenditures have displayed relatively high annual growth rates, 6.96% during 2000–2008, 1.60% during 2008–2019, and 10% after 2019. Inside this omnibus spending category are numerous programs whose spending is committed by existing laws or previous state actions (see the discussion in the next section). Among them are S-CHIP, debt services, public employee pension funding, unemployment compensation, care for the mentally ill and developmentally disabled, child welfare, and family services. Debt services are used to retire the principal and interest on bonds that states have issued. States must pay to avoid default. In fiscal year 2023, debt service spending sat at $55.2

40 State Tax Systems

TABLE 2.9 State "All Other" Programs (in $million): Sources of Funding and Share of State General Fund and Total

Fiscal Year	2000	2008	2019	2022	Annual Growth Rate (%)		
					2000–2008	2008–2019	2019–2022
	Funding Sources in Current Dollar Percentage of Total						
State Gen Funds	124,256 41.0%	194,686 37.5%	232,076 37.3%	310,280 34.2%	5.77	1.61	10.16
State Other Funds	104,960 34.6%	119,861 37.5%	235,172 38.2%	299,956 32.5%	1.67	6.32	8.45
Federal Funds	68,807 22.7%	116,005 22.3%	133,002 21.3%	279,531 31.4%	6.75	1.25	28.09
Bonds	5,048 1.7%	13,716 2.6%	18,039 3.2%	17,712 1.9%	13.31	2.52	(0.51)
Total "All Other"	303,071 100%	519,268 100%	618,289 100%	907,479 100%	6.96	1.60	13.64
	Funding Sources in Constant Dollar						
State Gen Fund Source	185,508	232,208	232,076	271,058	2.86	0.03	5.31
State Other Funds	155,866	142,352	235,172	262,039	(1.13)	4.67	3.67
Federal Funding	102,172	137,773	133,002	244,196	3.81	(0.32)	22.45
Bonds	7,496	16,290	18,039	15,473	10.19	0.93	(4.99)
Total "All Other" Spending	450,031	616,706	618,289	792,975	4.02	0.02	8.64
	"All Other" Spending as Share of						
Total State Expenditure	32.1%	34.6%	29.1%	34.0%			

Sources: NASBO (2000; 2008; 2019; 2022).

billion. The state general fund covered 55% of it, and "state other funds" paid the other 44.4% (NASBO 2023a). States earmarked certain tax revenues for debt services. Many programs in "All Other" are means-tested. If individuals meet eligibility requirements, their benefits cannot be denied. One example is the S-CHIP. Jointly funded by the federal and state governments, S-CHIP targets children in families with income levels too high for Medicaid but too low to purchase individual health insurance. About two million children were enrolled in 2000, and the number increased to 9.6 million in 2018. The spending levels for S-CHIP increased from $127 million in 1998, only 0.1% of total health spending, to $18.6 billion in 2022 (NASBO 2022).

State Capital Expenditures

State governments fund capital expenditures for "new construction, infrastructure, major repairs and improvements, land purchases and the acquisition of major equipment and existing structures" (NASBO 2016, p. 80). Minor repairs and routine maintenance are included in the operating budgets. Traditionally, funding for capital spending comes from non-general funds, primarily "state other sources" (no less than 35% of the total) and bonds (25%–31%), closely followed by federal funds (see Table 2.10). State reliance on debt financing, bonds, experienced a downward trend from 2008 to 2019 but increased shortly thereafter. The "state other funds" category included funds set aside for capital projects, such as transportation funds and other designated funds, as well as higher education tuition and fees. The federal funds for capital purposes are primarily used to finance transportation projects.

Capital spending has fluctuated from year to year, reflecting the demands for capital projects, long construction timetables, and unforeseen or delayed project costs. The average annual growth rate since 1991 is 4.6%. Total state capital expenditures reached $114,810 million in 2019. The large increases after that—$139,631 million in 2022—stemmed largely from federal funds through the ARPA of 2021 and the IIJA of 2021 and from one-time state spending on infrastructure resulting from state large revenue surpluses in fiscal years 2021 and 2022.

Among the different program areas, capital spending on transportation comprises the largest share (54%–65%) of all capital spending (see Table 2.11). Since 2010, the average annual growth for transportation capital spending was 4.9%, "reflecting states' efforts at addressing both the maintenance and expansion of its transportation systems with tax and revenue actions to raise funds" (NASBO 2019, p. 86). The second largest program area is "all others," consuming 13%–21% of the total state capital spending. This may include items such as zoo improvements, healthcare infrastructure, or sports facilities, behavioral health and hospital facilities, parks and tourism, large information

42 State Tax Systems

TABLE 2.10 State Capital Spending (in $million) and Sources of Funding

Fiscal Year	2000	2008	2019	2022	Annual Growth Rate (%)		
					2000–2008	2008–2019	2019–2022
	Funding Sources in Current Dollar Percentage of Total						
State Gen Fund Source	$4,122	7,697	7,119	16,456	8.12	(0.71)	32.22
	6.8%	9.4%	8.2%	9.3%			
Other State Funds	$26,557	28,745	45,217	47,801	0.99	4.20	1.87
	43.9%	35.3%	37.8%	35.0%			
Federal Funding	$14,269	19,286	29,889	32,546	3.84	4.06	2.88
	23.6%	23.7%	26.8%	25.2%			
Bonds	$15,575	25,759	32,586	$42,828	6.49	2.16	9.54
	25.7%	31.6%	27.1%	30.6%			
Total Capital Spending	$61,281	81,488	114,810	139,631	3.63	3.17	6.74
	100%	100%	100%	100%			
	Funding Sources in Constant Dollar						
State Gen Fund	$6,121	$9,141	$7,119	$14,376	5.14	(2.25)	26.40
Other State Funds	$39,436	34,139	45,217	41,759	(1.79)	2.59	(2.62)
Federal Funding	$21,188	22,905	29,889	28,432	0.98	2.45	(1.65)
Bonds	$23,127	30,593	32,586	$37,414	3.56	0.58	4.71
Total Capital Spending	$90,996	96,779	114,810	121,980	0.77	1.57	2.04

Sources: NASBO (2000; 2008; 2019; 2022).

TABLE 2.11 State Capital Spending: Different Programs (in $million) and Percentage of Total in Selected Years

	1998	2004	2008	2010	2014	2018	2020	2022
Total Capital spending	57,488	69,386	80,356	85,904	94,186	108,197	119,702	139,631
K-12	n/a	n/a	n/a	n/a	n/a	2%	3%	4%
Higher Edu	9%	12%	13%	15%	12%	11%	0%	9%
Corrections	4%	2%	2%	2%	1%	1%	1%	2%
Transportation	60%	62%	55%	57%	63%	65%	66%	61%
Housing	1%	1%	2%	2%	1%	1%	1%	2%
Environmental	7%	8%	7%	6%	5%	6%	5%	5%
All others	20%	15%	21%	19%	18%	13%	13%	17%
	100%	100%	100%	100%	100%	100%	100%	100%

Source: Author's calculation based on data provided in NASBO (2023), p. 92.

technology systems, other state facilities, and other criminal justice facilities. The primary funding source for this category is bonds.

Higher education is the third largest expenditure category in the area. It reached its peak of 15.2% in fiscal 2009 and then started to decline. On average, capital spending for higher education is 11% of state total spending. Capital spending on environmental affairs includes projects for environmental cleanup and drinking water, accounting for 6%–8% of total capital spending. Corrections capital spending supports major institutional construction and renovation projects. It reached its peak around 1998–2000 when states had to construct more prisons due to overcrowding (NASBO 2023a). Housing capital expenditures comprise only 2% of total fiscal 2023 capital spending at $3.2 billion. States vary in how they provide capital funding for public schools. The data are not collected in earlier years. For the most recent years, it is relatively small.

The Restricted State Expenditures

While the discussion above examines state spending on each functional category, this section integrates them and explains state expenditures from a different angle. That is, how much spending is within the discretion of state lawmakers, and how much is beyond annual budgetary control? Previous discussions indicate that federal funding and other state sources are largely designated for certain programs. At the same time, numerous cost drivers examined above are beyond the control of state lawmakers such as economic conditions, demographics, legal restrictions, and court decisions. Literature on state budgets often identified several pressures that impose spending demands on states, including public education, infrastructure, Medicaid, public pensions, and other post-employment benefits (OPEBs) (Chapman 2008; Lav, McNichol, and Zahradnik 2005).

The federal government classified its spending into mandatory spending and discretionary spending. Although state governments do not employ the same terminology in their budgets, they are facing similar structural restrictions with their spending. For the federal government, 70% of its spending is classified as mandatory spending—those items that are not subject to the annual appropriation process because the spending level is committed by existing laws. For state governments, a substantial share of spending is also committed even before the annual budget process starts. Gordan, Randall, Steuerle, and Boddupalli (2019) name it "restricted spending" (p. v) or the "spending that requires policymakers to clear identifiable hurdles, beyond the normal appropriations process, to reduce obligations or pare their growth" (Gordan et al. 2019, p. v). Several types of restricted spending will be explained below, some of which have appeared in previous discussions (Gordon et al. 2019).

- **Long-Term Obligations:** This includes debt service, pension obligations, as well as OPEBs. For instance, in 2017, Connecticut accumulated $87 billion in long-term obligation debt, including pension liabilities of $33.9 billion, unfunded OPEBs of $21 billion, general obligation debt of $18.4 billion, and non-GO debt of $11.3 billion. As a comparison, that same year, general fund revenue sat at $18 billion (Connecticut Commission of Fiscal Stability and Economic Growth 2018).
- **Programmatic:** There are provisions in laws requiring state governments to spend certain amounts on specific programs or areas of services (e.g., public education) or designating all or part of certain revenue sources for specific services (e.g., earmarking lotteries for public education, gasoline tax for transportation fund). States normally spend funds to comply with certain federal grant requirements, such as MOE for TANF and the non-federal matching share of Medicaid.
- **Federal:** Federal grants are typically earmarked for certain programs and services and attached with strings, as indicated earlier.
- **Judicial:** Court decisions dictate states' spending obligations. For instance, state courts ruled that states must provide equitable and adequate funding for public education.
- **Institutional:** Many states have adopted Tax and Expenditure Limitations that indirectly affect the overall revenue or expenditure levels, and thus reduce lawmakers' flexibility. States may also have certain legal requirements to deposit a certain amount of revenue into a Budget Stabilization Fund.
- **Local aid:** Some states have revenue-sharing programs that obligate states to provide fiscal assistance to their local governments.

- **Other restricted spending:** They can also stem from inflexible caseloads and costs that grow with program enrollment or inflation. Corrections are considered restricted spending because inmates must be appropriately fed, housed, and medically attended to. Changing sentence laws would reduce the overall prison population but that takes time and takes certain scales of reduction.

Gordon et al. (2019) studied the five most populous states based on data from 2000 to 2015 and the interviews with state budgetary personnel. They estimated that at the high end (i.e., including all types of restrictions), 70%–90% of total state spending was potentially restricted in 2015. At the low end (i.e., only including Medicaid and debt services), restricted spending comprised a quarter to half of state spending. Furthermore, Gordon et al. also found that at the low end, state-restricted spending as a share of total state spending increased over the years, largely attributive to Medicaid obligations.

Although Gordon et al.'s study covers only five states with 2015 data, the larger messages are clear and applicable to states in general. For example, based on the Missouri 2024 Operating Budget of $51 billion total expenditure, only 28% (or $14.28 billion) are general fund spending. Federal funds and other state funds supported the other 72%, most of them are designated. Among $14.28 billion general fund spending, 75% was to support other restricted spending, leaving only 25% (or $3.57 billion) of the general revenue as discretionary spending (Division of Budget and Planning 2024). That means Missouri state lawmakers have discretion over roughly 7% of the total state spending. Connecticut called restricted spending a "fixed cost" in contrast to a "discretionary cost." Based on the *Fiscal Accountability Report* issued by the Connecticut Office of Fiscal Analysis (2023), the fixed cost—a combination of Medicaid, debt payments, pension and retiree health benefits, adjudicated claims, and supplemental payments to hospitals—accounts for roughly 53% of state general budget expenditures in 2023 and is predicted to rise to 54% in 2028. In 2006, the fixed cost constituted only 37% of total general revenue.

Although states utilize different terms and classifications, officials are concerned that a substantial share of state spending is "on autopilot" (Gordon et al. 2019, p. v) or committed before governors can propose a budget and lawmakers adopt a budget. State lawmakers have limited flexibility in directing expenditures and deciding spending levels. In theory, state lawmakers could loosen almost all the restrictions. However, they face big hurdles and political risk. For instance, state lawmakers could override the minimum spending requirement for public education, but this will only invite legal challenges and public discontent.

State lawmakers must "weave their way through a multifaceted and complex mase of restriction" (Gordon et al. 2019, p. ix). Advocacy groups, for fear of inadequate funding from this small slice of discretionary revenue, will push for revenue to be earmarked for their program, further reducing spending flexibility (Gordon et al. 2019).

This has significant implications for state fiscal stability. To maintain fiscal stability, the ideal practice is to maintain spending on a relatively stable growth path and develop a revenue system that is broad enough to generate sufficient revenue. When spending is "on autopilot" (Gordon et al. 2019, p. v), state lawmakers have little room or flexibility to control its usage, increasing fiscal instability, and inserting more pressure on the revenue system.

Conclusion

This chapter first explains the major state spending responsibilities by analyzing the spending trends of each spending category, as well as the cost drivers and the issues states face in meeting these responsibilities. Total state spending rose from $1.4 trillion in 2000 to $2.4 trillion in 2022 in real terms. All spending categories, except public assistance, experienced positive annual growth rates in constant dollars in most fiscal years. Medicaid is the largest spending category for all state spending. Meanwhile, elementary and secondary education continues to remain the largest spending category for state general funds. Medicaid exhibits the highest annual growth rates of over 6%, followed by higher education, transportation, "all others," and corrections, whose annual growth rate in current dollars is around 3.02%–3.9%. Although the cost drivers for each category may not be the same, many of them are outside the control of state lawmakers, including the economic cycle, the aging population, federal actions, rising healthcare costs, court actions, and citizens' actions. The discussion in the last section of this chapter focuses on state-restricted spending. A significant portion of state spending is pre-committed, leaving state lawmakers limited discretion over future spending decisions.

References

American Society of Civil Engineers (ASCE). 2021. A Comprehensive Assessment of America's Infrastructure: 2021 *Reporting Card for American Infrastructure*. 2021-IRC-Executive-Summary-1.pdf

Bettinger, Eric, Oded Gurantz, Laura Kawano, Bruce Sacerdote, and Michael Stevens. 2019. "The Long-run Impacts of Financial Aid: Evidence from California's Cal Grant." *American Economic Journal: Economic Policy*, 10 (1), pp. 64–94.

Blank, Rebecca M. 2001. "Welfare and the Economy." *Brookings* (September 2).

Burwell, David and Robert Puentes. 2021. "Innovative State Transportation Funding and Financing: Policy Options for States." *National Governor Association Center for Best Practices*.

Candelaria, Christopher A., Shelby M. McNeill,., and Kenneth A. Shores, 2022a. "What Is a School Finance Reform? Uncovering the Ubiquity and Diversity of School Finance Reforms Using a Bayesian Changepoint Estimator." *EdWorking Paper* No. 22-587 (June). https://edworkingpapers.com/sites/default/files/ai22-587.pdf

Candelaria, Christopher, Shelby McNeill, and Kenneth Shores A. 2022b. "Commentary What Drives Increases in State Funding for Education?" *Brookings* (August 11).

Chakrabarti, Rajashri, Nicole Gorton, and Michael Lovenheim. 2020. "State Investment in Higher Education: Effects on Human Capital Formation, Student Debt, and Long-term Financial Outcome of Students." *Federal Reserve Bank of New York Staff Report*, 941.

Chapman, Jeffrey. 2008. "State and Local Fiscal Sustainability: The Challenges." *Public Administration Review*, 68 (1), pp. S115–S131. (December).

Congressional Research Service (CRS). 2017. "Temporary Assistance for Needy Families (TANF): Size of the Population Eligible for and Receiving Cash Assistance." (January 3).

Congressional Research Service (CRS). 2023. "Temporary Assistance for Needy Families: The Decline in Assistance Receipts among Eligible Individuals." (April 10).Connecticut Commission on Fiscal Stability and Economic Growth. 2018. *Connecticut Commission on Fiscal Stability and Economic Growth: Final Report.* (March). https://files.schoolstatefinance.org/hubfs/Resources/Commission%20on%20Fiscal%20Stability%20Report.pdf.

Cummings, Kristen, Sohpia Laderman, Jason Lee, David Tandberg, and Dustin Weeden. 2021. "Investigating the Impacts of State Higher Education Appropriations and Financial Aid." *State Higher Education Executive Officers Association* . (May).

Division of Budget and Planning, Office of Administration of Missouri. 2024. *The Fiscal Year 2024 Executive Budget* . https://oa.mo.gov/sites/default/files/FY_2024_Budget_Summary_Docs.pdf

Gordon, Tracy, Megan Randall, Eugene Steuerle, and Aravind Boddupolli. 2019. "Fiscal Democracy in the States: How Much Spending is on Autopilot?" *Urban Institute*. (July).

Kirk, Robert S. and William J. Mallett. 2021. "Highway and Public Transit Funding Issues." *Congressional Research Services*. IF10495 (congress.gov)

Lav, Iris J., Elizabeth McNichol, and Robert Zahradnik. 2005. "Faulty Foundations: State Structural Budget Problems and How to Fix Them." *Center on Budget and Policy Priorities*. (May).

McMahon, Walter W. 2009. *Higher Learning, Greater Good: The Private and Social Benefits of Higher Education*. Baltimore: Johns Hopkins University Press.

Mitchell, Michael and Michael Leachman. 2014. "Changing Priorities: State Criminal Justice Reforms and Investments in Education." *Center on Budget and Policy Priorities.* (October 28).

National Association of State Budget Officers (NASBO). 1995. *State Expenditure Report*.
National Association of State Budget Officers (NASBO). 1997. *State Expenditure Report*.
National Association of State Budget Officers (NASBO). 1999. *State Expenditure Report*.
National Association of State Budget Officers (NASBO). 2000. *State Expenditure Report*.
National Association of State Budget Officers (NASBO). 2001. *State Expenditure Report*.
National Association of State Budget Officers (NASBO). 2003. *State Expenditure Report*.
National Association of State Budget Officers (NASBO). 2004. *State Expenditure Report*.

National Association of State Budget Officers (NASBO). 2008. *State Expenditure Report*.
National Association of State Budget Officers (NASBO). 2012. *State Expenditure Report*.
National Association of State Budget Officers (NASBO). 2013. *State Expenditure Report*.
National Association of State Budget Officers (NASBO). 2016. *State Expenditure Report*.
National Association of State Budget Officers (NASBO). 2017. *State Expenditure Report*.
National Association of State Budget Officers (NASBO). 2019. *State Expenditure Report*.
National Association of State Budget Officers (NASBO). 2020. *State Expenditure Report*.
National Association of State Budget Officers (NASBO). 2022. *State Expenditure Report*.
National Association of State Budget Officers (NASBO). 2023a. *State Expenditure Report*:
National Association of State Budget Officers (NASBO). 2023b. *The Fiscal Survey of the States*. (Spring).
Nguyen, Tuan D., Jenna W. Kramer, and Brent J. Evans. 2019. "The Effects of Grant Aid on Student Persistence and Degree Attainments: A Systematic Review and Meta-Analysis of the Causal Evidence." *Review of Educational Research*, 89 (6), 831–874.
Okunade, Albert A. 2004. "What Factors Influence State Appropriations for Public Higher Education in the United States?" *Journal of Education Finance*, 2 (2) (Fall): 123–138.
Oliff, Philip. 2015. "Funding Challenges in Highway and Transit: A Federal-State-Local Analysis." *The Pew Charitable Trust*. (February 24).
Peter G. Peterson Foundation. No Date. "The Highway Trust Fund Explained." www.pgpf.org/budget-basics/budget-explainer-highway-trust-fund
Rudowitz, Robin, Elizabeth Hinton, and Larisa Antonisse. 2018. "Medicaid Enrollment & Spending Growth: FY 2018 & 2019." *Kaiser Commission on Medicaid and the Uninsured*. (October 25).
Rudowitz, Robin, Elizabeth Hinton, Madeline Guth, and Lina Stolyar. 2020. "Medicaid Enrollment & Spending Growth: FY 2020 & 2021." *Kaiser Commission on Medicaid and the Uninsured*. (October 14).
Smith, Vernon K. and Eileen Ellis. 2001. "Medicaid Budgets under Stress: Survey Findings for State Fiscal Year 2000, 2001, and 2002." *Kaiser Commission on Medicaid and the Uninsured*. (October).
Smith, Vernon K., Kathleen Gifford, Eileen Ellis, Barbara Edwards, Robin Rudowitz, Elizabeth Hinton, Larisa Antonisse, and Allison Valentine. 2016. "Implementing Coverage and Payment Initiatives: Results from a 5—State Medicaid Budget Survey for State Fiscal Years 2016 and 2017." *Kaiser Commission on Medicaid and the Uninsured*. (October 13).
Smith, Vernon K., Kathleen Gifford, Eileen Ellis, Robin Rudowitz, Lauran Snyder, and Elizabeth Hinton. 2015. "Medicaid Reforms to Expand Coverage, Control Costs and Improve Care: Results from a 50-state Medicaid Budget Survey for State Fiscal Years 2015 and 2016." *National Association of Medicaid Directors*. (October).
State Higher Education Executive Officers Association (SHEEO). 2023. *State Higher Education Finance*: FY 2022.
U.S. Department of Education, National Center for Education Statistics. No Date. *Digest of Education Statistics*. https://nces.ed.gov/programs/digest/d20/tables/dt20_235.10.asp
U.S. Department of Transportation (USDOT). 2023. *Climate Action*. www.transportation.gov/priorities/climate-and-sustainability/climate-action (January 13).
Urban Institute. No Date a. "Elementary and Secondary Education Expenditures – State and Local Backgrounders."

Urban Institute. No Date b. "Highway and Road Expenditures – State and Local Backgrounders."

West, Martin R. and Paul E. Peterson. 2016. *The Adequacy Lawsuit: A Critical Appraisal*.

Williams, Elizabeth. 2022. "Medicaid Enrollment & Spending Growth: FY 2022 & 2023." *Kaiser Family Foundation* . (October 25).

Zhao, Bo. 2018. "Disinvesting in the Future? A Comprehensive Examination of the Effects of State Appropriations for Public Higher Education." *Federal Research Bank of Boston, New England Public Policy Center*.

3
THE GREAT RECESSION AND STATE TAX POLICIES

An Overview

Introduction

As mentioned in Chapter 1, the Great Recession delivered a heavy blow to state budgets. The severe revenue shortages not only reflected state financial vulnerabilities to the economic cycle but also exposed their long-term fiscal imbalances. This chapter and the following ones analyze state tax policy changes during and after the Great Recession. The questions asked are: What changes did state governments make regarding their tax policies? Did the changes translate into a tax system that supports fiscal stability?

This chapter contains two sections. The first section highlights the fiscal impact of the Great Recession on state budgetary systems. The second section provides an overview of state tax actions during and after the Great Recession and discuss the impact on the state's long-term fiscal health.

As every state has its own political dynamics and mechanisms for policy making, it will be insightful to examine tax policy reforms in certain states and the impact on their fiscal stability. For this purpose, five states are selected and will be examined in the two succeeding chapters. These states are California, New York, Connecticut, Kansas, and Missouri. After that, each chapter is devoted to examining the policy changes in one of the state taxes (i.e., PIT, CIT, SUT, sin taxes, fuel taxes, and healthcare provider taxes).

The Great Recession and Its Impact on State Government Finance

The Great Recession started in December 2007 and was technically over by June 2009. As the worst recession since the 1930s, its impact on state budgets was larger, wider, and lasted longer than any other recession. State governments started to see weak revenue collection in the fourth quarter of 2008, first with the sales tax and then "income tax ultimately fell harder and faster" (Gordon 2012, p. 3). By the second quarter of 2009, state tax revenue had fallen by 17% compared with a year earlier, and personal income taxes (PITs) by 27%. State and local source revenues fell by "$100 billion in real terms" from the fourth quarter of 2007 to the second quarter of 2009 (Gordon 2012, p. 3).

At the same time, with high unemployment rates, demands for public welfare, particularly Medicaid and unemployment insurance, escalated. The combination of revenue declines and demands for more services brought the largest revenue shortfalls in decades. Shortfalls are gaps between state revenue and the cost of providing services (Oliff, Mai, and Palacios, 2012).

Table 3.1 shows revenue shortages from FY 2009 to FY 2013. The worst year was FY 2010, with the gaps accounting for 29% of state general funds, or over 40% in at least five states (see Table 3.1), affecting all states except Montana and North Dakota. In the subsequent years, serious revenue shortages persisted partially due to a slow economic recovery. Even though state governments took active measures to close the shortfalls during budget adoptions, many still confronted gaps in the mid-fiscal year, necessitating further actions (see Table 3.1). State governments had to address $540 billion shortfalls during FY 2009–FY 2013 (Oliff, Mai, and Palacios 2012) and $430 billion for FY 2009–FY 2011.

The performance of state general funds also exemplified the fiscal brutality of the Great Recession. The general fund is important for state budgets because it gives state officials the most budgetary flexibility. The general fund revenue declined in two consecutive years by a 11.1% total, from $676 billion in FY 2008 to $606 billion in FY 2010 causing general fund expenditures to experience negative nominal growth rates of –3.8% in FY 2009 and –5.7% in FY 2010 (see Figure 3.1). To place this into context, the general fund expenditure had a health growth pattern between 1979 and 2008 with an average of 1.6% real annual growth or 5.6% nominal growth. The only other year that has a negative nominal growth was FY 1983 which observed a negative growth of –0.7% (NASBO 2014). The consecutive significant negative growth in FY 2009–FY 2010 situated state governments in a fiscal crisis they had rarely experienced.

How Did States Close the Revenue Gaps?

All states, except Vermont, are legally required to balance their operating budgets. To balance their budgets, state governments used a combination of spending cuts, reserve withdrawals, revenue increases, one-time federal stimulus dollars, and other strategies. Table 3.2 shows some strategies under each approach and the number of states that used specific strategies to reduce the budgetary gaps.

TABLE 3.1 State Revenue Shortages (in $billion) in FY 2009–FY 2013

Fiscal Year	Rev gap closed upon budget adoption	Additional mi-year gaps	Total Revenue Shortages	Total Shortage as a Percentage of State Gen Fund Revenue	# of States with Revenue Shortages	Top 5 States with the Largest Percentage of Shortfalls
2009	46.8	63.1	109.9	15.2%	46	AZ 36.8% CA 36.7% RI 26.6% FL 22% NA 19.9%
2010	158.5	32.3	190.8	29.0%	49	AZ 65% CA 52.8% NV 46.8 IL 43.7% NJ 40%
2011	122.6	7.4	130.0	19.9%	47	NV 54.5% IL 40.2% AZ 39% NJ 38.2% ME 34.7%
2012	102.9	4.4	107.3	15.5%	43	NJ 37.5% NV 37% CA 27.8% LA 25.1% OR 24%
2013	27.0	28.0	55.0	9.5%	30	NV 36.2% OR 24.3% TX, 24.2% NH 19.9% WA 19.6%

Source: Oliff, Mai, and Palacios (2012).

Budget Reductions

Budget cuts tend to be the initial government responses to budget shortages since other measures, particularly tax measures, take time to deliberate and formulate. When the recession began in December 2007, states were in the middle of their FY 2008 and had already passed their FY 2009 budgets. As tax revenue deteriorated rapidly, state governments were forced to implement serious midterm budget cuts for FY 2008 and FY 2009 through either executive orders or legislative actions. FY 2009 witnessed a total of $31.3 billion in mid-year budget cuts by 41 states for a wide range of service areas, representing the largest mid-year cuts in recent history (NASBO 2013).

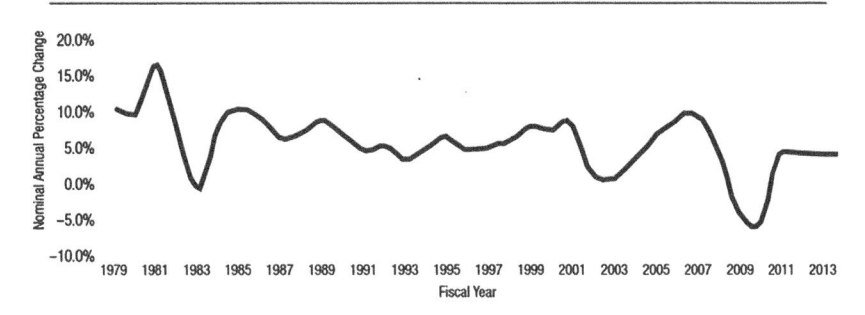

FIGURE 3.1 Nominal Annual Percentage Change in General Fund Spending.
Source: NASBO 2014. State Fiscal Survey (Spring), p. 3.

The FY 2010 budget contained decreased spending authorizations. States' general fund expenditures in FY 2010 were $623 billion, approximately $64 billion lower than $687 billion in FY 2008. Even these reduced budgets turned out to be too optimistic, resulting in 39 states enacting mid-year budget cuts totaling $18.3 billion.

After FY 2010, the budget cuts were considerably smaller due to several reasons. The economy began to stabilize. State legislatures were able to enact tax increases in 2009 and 2011. The American Recovery and Reinvestment Act (ARRA) made federal stimulus funding available to state governments. Without these measures, states would have continued to make large spending cuts (NASBO 2013). General fund expenditures started to pick up in FY 2011 but did not reach pre-recession levels until 2013.

Cuts to state general funds affected all functional areas, including public education and healthcare. For instance, in FY 2010, states cut nearly all functional areas, some by large margins, 5.2% for public education, 6.7% for corrections, and 9.6% for Medicaid (Leachman, Albares, Masterson, and Wallace 2016). These cuts were clearly caused by severe revenue shortages, but state officials also knew that federal recovery funding would replenish these expenditure cuts. Medicaid services and K-12 education are considered the most expensive programs for state governments.

In making the numerous rounds of budget cuts during FY 2009–FY 2013, states employed both targeted cuts and across-the-board cuts (see Table 3.2). Although across-the-board cuts are typically easy to implement, targeted cuts allow policy makers to assess the importance of each program, effectively utilizing limited revenue. It is also important to note that states made targeted cuts at least 151 times, indicating states were making structural changes in their fiscal systems. Some states started with across-the-board cuts, followed by targeted cuts. Other states did the opposite. Over the years, state legislators

TABLE 3.2 The Number of States and Approaches and Strategies to Close Budget Gaps: 2009–2013

Approaches and Strategies	2009	2010	2011	2012	2013	Total
Revenue and Tax Measures						
Enacted Tax Increases	24	11	9	3	6	49
Lottery Expansion	1	1	4	3	3	12
Gaming/Gambling Expansion	0	2	4	1	1	8
User Fees	6	11	14	9	4	44
Higher Education-Related Fees	6	7	7	8	4	32
Court Related Fees	6	6	9	6	2	29
Transportation/Motor Vehicle Fees	6	12	8	8	4	38
Business Related Fees	3	9	6	5	3	26
Budget Cuts Measures						
Layoffs	16	17	20	15	5	73
Furloughs	17	15	19	3	2	56
Early Retirement	6	4	6	3	1	20
Salary Reductions	7	10	9	6	2	34
Cuts to State Employee Benefits	7	16	13	12	6	54
Across-the-Board Cuts	23	16	20	15	10	84
Targeted Cuts	36	30	34	30	21	151
Reduce Local Aid	18	20	16	17	5	76
Using Rainy-day Fund						
Rainy-day Fund	23	15	9	5	5	57
Others Including Using Federal Recovery Grants						
Reorganize Agencies	6	16	12	16	7	57
Privatization	3	2	5	4	4	18
Others*	18	24	15	16	12	85
Total Strategies Used by States by Year	**208**	**233**	**230**	**182**	**101**	

Sources: Author's calculation based on NASBO: *Fiscal Survey of States (2009–2013)*.

* These represent various activities, including Federal Medical Assistance Percentage (FMAP) and Stabilization Stimulus Funds, fund transfers, tax collection enhancements, redirecting funds previously allotted to other entities, suspending mandates, and tax amnesty payments.

have lost their budgetary discretion over a large portion of state programs due to federal mandates and state laws, as discussed in Chapter 2. This meant that across-the-board cuts were only applicable to a certain extent, and heavier cuts were imposed on those programs such as higher education, local government assistance, and public welfare assistance (NASBO 2013). States also used other methods to reduce expenditures, including agency consolidation, employee layoffs, furloughs, reduced local aid, decreased state employee benefits, and scaled-down services (NASBO 2013).

According to NASBO's (2013) interview of state budget officers, inefficient programs existed, but eliminating them was difficult. Each program developed a client group base dedicated to preserving its respective program. In most situations, spending for these programs and services was trimmed rather than eliminated. However, some structural changes were implemented by state governments, such as agency consolidation and decreased state employee benefits, as shown in Table 3.2.

Revenue Measures

Raising revenue coupled with budget cuts represents a balanced approach to reducing large budgetary gaps (Lav and Grundman 2011). This has been an established practice for state governments in recent recessions. The severity of fiscal problems experienced during the Great Recession necessitated revenue increases. These actions provided short-term benefits and did not impose an adverse impact on long-term economic performance (Johnson, Collins, and Singham 2010). During FY 2009–FY 2013, many states adopted revenue measures. The $23.9 billion tax and fee generated in FY 2010 were not only the largest in the Great Recession but also the largest in recent decades. However, tax increases were smaller as a share of general fund revenues (NASBO 2013).

Tax increases assumed different forms: eliminating tax exemptions and deductions, broadening tax bases, and raising tax rates and fees (NASBO 2013). Numerous states raised their income and sales taxes (see Table 3.3). New York and California both raised their income tax on higher-income brackets. More states raised their PITs during the Great Recession than in the 2001 recession (NASBO 2013). However, some raises were temporary for only two years (Gordon 2011). The temporary increases made it easy to get political support, but the fiscal problems might not have been over when they expired, adding more uncertainty. Further discussion over tax increases during the Great Recession and subsequent periods will be provided in the second part of this chapter.

Using the Reserves and the Federal Stimulus Grants

The primary purpose of reserves, both the year-end revenue and rainy-day fund, is to help states circumvent service disruptions experienced during economic downturns (NASBO 2013). States began to utilize end balances immediately upon facing severe revenue shortfalls. As Table 3.4 shows, the ending balance dropped significantly from $34.5 billion in FY 2008 to $4.5 billion in FY 2009, another illustration of the severity of these fiscal problems.

The decision about whether and when to use rainy-day funds differs from state to state. The legal requirements, the way to replenish the fund, and certainty about the future all influence these decisions (NASBO 2013). Some states used

TABLE 3.3 States Enacting Personal Income and Sales Tax Increases in FY 2009 or FY 2010

Personal Income Tax Increase	Sales Tax Increases
One state raised income tax rates for all taxpayers: California (temporary). Nine states created a new high-income bracket or increased the top existing rate: Connecticut (permanent), Delaware (temporary), Hawaii (temporary), Maryland (temporary and permanent), New Jersey (temporary), New York (temporary), North Carolina (temporary), Oregon (temporary and permanent), and Wisconsin (permanent). Nine states restricted deductions or broadened their tax bases: • Limited Capital Gains Exclusion: Colorado, Rhode Island, Vermont, and Wisconsin. • Included Lottery Winnings: Delaware and New Jersey. • Limited Itemized Deductions, Exemptions, or Credits: California, New Jersey, New York, Oregon, and Vermont.	Eight states increased sales tax rates: • Temporary Increase: California (1%), Nevada (0.35%), and North Carolina (1%). • Permanent Increase: Utah (0.05%), Indiana (1%), and Massachusetts (1.25%). • Increase on Specific Goods/Services: Illinois and Maine. Nine states expanded the sales tax base to include the following: • Tobacco: Colorado. • Alcohol: Kentucky, Massachusetts, and Vermont. • Digital Downloads (e.g., music and movies): North Carolina, Vermont, and Wisconsin. • Other Computer Software: Tennessee and Wisconsin. • Internet Transactions: New York, North Carolina, and Rhode Island.

Sources: Johnson, Collins, and Singham (2010, p 6–7) and NASBO (2013, p. 22).

TABLE 3.4 Budget Reserve Levels and Federal Recovery Grants (in $billion): FY 2008–FY 2013

Fiscal Year	Rainy-day Fund	End Balance	Federal Recovery Grant
FY 2008	$32.9	$34.5	–
FY 2009	29.0	4.5	$31.6
FY 2010	21.0	8.0	61.1
FY 2011	25.0	22.1	50.1
FY 2012	34.0	24.5	5.8
FY 2013	41.3	38.9	0.9
Total	n/a	n/a	149.5

Sources: NASBO (2009; 2010; 2011; 2012, 2013a; 2014) and NASBO (2013b).

Data on the Federal Recovery Grant (FRG) are from NASBO (2013b, p. 15). All other data are from NASBO (2009, 2010; 2011; 2012; 2013a; 2014).

the rainy-day funds before budget cuts were enacted. In a few extreme cases, such as in Vermont, the rainy-day fund was not used at all throughout the entire economic downturn because its rainy-day fund was legally required to avoid a deficit near the end of the fiscal year, not to close the budget gap prior to fiscal year end. Overall, the use of the rainy-day fund was more gradual than the use of the year-end reserve. Some state officials were concerned about future fiscal uncertainties, and access to rainy-day funds was also cumbersome. At its peak in FY 2006, the total state rainy-day fund amounted to $69 billion or 11.5% of the general fund expenditure. By 2009, it was 4.8% of expenditures or only 2.7% if Texas and Alaska were excluded. States could have depleted these funds entirely if not for trying to save for years beyond 2009 (NASBO 2009).

To help state governments weather these harsh financial situations, the federal government provided $149 billion of fiscal assistance to state and local governments as a part of the ARRA in FY 2009 (see Table 4.4). Approximately $90 billion was used to temporarily increase federal funding share to the Medicaid program or the Federal Medical Assistance Percentage. The remaining funds went to the State Fiscal Stabilization Fund with two block grants: $39.5 billion for education and $8.8 billion for other services (Lav, Johnson, and McNichol 2010). The large amount of federal fiscal assistance provided timely and temporary support for various state programs and services. Without it, cuts to state programs would have been much deeper. Yet, when they expired, state government officials still had to make the tough budgetary choices.

Lessons Learned

While the revenue collapse states experienced during FY 2008–FY 2010 was a direct result of the cyclical downturn, they also exposed the structural weaknesses of state tax systems. Over the years, state tax structures have become less stable in the face of changing economic conditions and more sensitive to market fluctuations. These trends have increased the vulnerability of state budgets and rendered them more vulnerable to business cycle fluctuations. For example, sales tax, an important source of state tax revenue, has its base eroded with numerous exemptions, significant increases in service consumption and online sales, costing states billions of revenue dollars every year. For income taxes, another important state revenue, the types of income (capital gains, dividends, salaries and wages, etc.), and corresponding rates determine if the revenue collection is stable. The tax cuts enacted in many states during the previous decades and heavier reliance on capital gains and investment income, as well as on earnings from high-wage earners in the finance sector, have resulted in a more volatile revenue collection system (Deitz, Haughwout and Steindel 2010; NASBO 2013). When the recession came, the impact was severe, and few people could comprehend the full impact. Not only did the revenue fall significantly, but the revenue forecasting was also off a lot. For instance, in FY 2009 and FY 2010, 41 and 36 states, respectively, overestimated their projected revenue collections. Even the most conservative revenue forecasters overestimated revenue projections.

During and after the Great Recession, states employed pro-cyclical measures such as cutting expenditures and raising revenues and fees, similar to the measures used in previous recessions. They also adopted many short-term budgetary tactics such as hiring freezes, layoffs, sales leasebacks of state properties, and bond refinancing. These short-term solutions could work properly under normal fiscal conditions. However, slow economic growth and prolonged fiscal hardships revealed an embedded structural fiscal imbalance and forced state governments to examine the current tax system and search for long-term revenue system changes. The changes included diversifying revenue sources and expanding the tax base. Some states expanded the sales tax base to capture technological advancements in the new digital and service-based economy, thereby taxing digital goods and services and collecting online sales taxes. States such as Oregon began to re-evaluate and scrutinize their tax expenditures and other spending items. Other states eliminated certain exemptions (NASBO 2013). The Great Recession served as a catalyst for state policy changes, and states took action in this direction. However, there were obstacles, as in other times. The question remains whether the efforts to search for long-term solutions could be sustained during economic rebounds.

Going through the recession with its severe revenue collapse, state government officials generally saw the need to expand rainy-day funds and to loosen the repayment requirement. Additionally, some states understood the necessity and importance of employing long-term planning to better prepare for the worst. Massachusetts and Washington started to require a long-term budget outlook to forecast future fiscal and economic circumstances. As NASBO highlights, "projecting revenues and expenditures beyond the budget cycle can preemptively inform decision-makers of pending issues that need to be addressed, increasing the likelihood that necessary changes will be made before fiscal problems worsen" (NASBO 2013, p. 25). Long-term budget forecasts can also help states assess the need for greater reform.

State Tax Actions Changes during and after the Great Recession

As outlined above, state governments took several approaches to responding to the fiscal crisis during and immediately after the Great Recession. This section focuses on state tax policy changes and the impact these changes could have on their fiscal stability.

Table 3.5 presents a summary of state tax changes during FY 2008–FY 2019 for PIT, corporate income tax (CIT), sales and use tax (SUT), healthcare tax,

TABLE 3.5 Net State Tax Changes by Type of Tax (in $millions)

Fiscal Years (1)	PIT (2)	CIT (3)	SUT (4)	Healthcare Tax (5)	Tobacco Tax (6)	Alcohol Tax (7)	Motor Fuel Tax (8)	Total (9)
2008	−254.3	2,347.0	688.9	237.2	464.0	141.1	35	3,803.4
2009	11,406.1	2,014.5	7,236.5	2,535.4	1,898.2	192.6	1,871.2	28,588.2
2010	−656.4[a]	494.3	1,736.5	1,298.1	602.7	34.2	48.2	3,959.4
2011	2,994.9	−804.9	−5244.7[a]	1955.9	51.9	24.1	12.0	−1,960.4[a]
2012	2,837.2	822.0	428.1	−393.9[a]	372.4	0.0	−57.1	4,082.3
2013	−1,956.1	82.1	770.4	474.6	384.4	5.1	−531.9	−978.0
2014	−2,985.0	−1,150.3	−420.4	520.5	−8.7	0	89	−3121.7
2015	−1,999.8	−514.6	151.5	311.9	547.6	7.7	1,120.2	−324.0
2016	−884.3	−736.7	788.6	1,348.8	1,008.2	18.2	923.3	2,340.8
2017	4,333.0	335.4	−1915.2[a]	530.0	47.7	6.9	2,762.0	6,931.8
2018	−44.2	29.6	847.1	−3.8[a]	298.6	0.0	143	1,295.6
2019	−864.4	−23.1	1,456.8	663.3	149.1	8.0	2,492.3	4,960.8

[a] Indicating the negative amount resulting from the expirations of an earlier tax increase.

Source: Based on the author's review of the National Conference of State Legislatures *State Tax Actions Database* by Waisanen and Haggerty 2010; Rafool and Haggerty 2011; Rafool 2013; 2014; 2015; NSCL 2009; 2012; NCSL 2016-2019.

60 State Tax Systems

tobacco tax, alcohol tax, motor fuel tax, and total revenue changes. The total revenue changes include all these tax revenues plus the miscellaneous revenue, which is not listed here. These changes can be attributed to rate changes, base changes, or both.

Annual Tax Changes

Among the 12 years, eight years witnessed net tax increases and four net tax decreases (see Column 9 in Table 3.5). The period of FY 2008–FY 2012 saw net tax increases in four of the five years. Although FY 2008 had a net total tax increase, state governments were reducing income taxes at the midpoint of the recession (see Column 2). This may be puzzling to readers, but there are two explanations. First, it usually takes time for the legislature to deliberate on tax increases. Second, tax reductions are traditionally used to reduce taxpayer burdens during recessions.

FY 2009 saw the largest tax increase since 1991, with a $28.5 billion, or 3.7% increase over the previous year. Twenty-four states increased their taxes that year by more than 1% (see Table 3.6), reflecting states' desperation for additional

TABLE 3.6 Number of States with Significant Tax Changes FY 2008–FY 2018 (as a Percentage of Previous Year's Tax Collection)

Fiscal Year	Increase Tax = or >5% (Names of States)	1%–4.9%	No Significant Changes	Decrease Tax = or >1% (Names of States)
2008	1 (IN)	6	39	4 (GA, NM, ID, OR)
2009	7 (CT, DE, WI, CA, NV, OR, NY)	17	25	1 (ND)
2010	3 (KS, AZ, WA)	9	37	1 (N.J.)[a]
2011	2 (CT, IL)	7	32	8 (ME, NY, MI, OH, IA, ND, NC, CA, WV)
2012	0	3	44	3 (ID, KS, NY)
2013	1 (MN)	6	36	7 (AK, AZ, IA, ME, OH, ND, WI)
2014	0	5	41	4 (IL, IN, MN, OH)
2015	3 (CT, LA, NV)	12	29	6 (FL, IN, ND, OH, RI, TX, NY)
2016	2 (LA, SD)	4	39	5 (GA, IN, MS, NM, WI)
2017	3 (DE, IL, KS)	7	38	2 (NJ, TN)
2018	2 (KS, OK)	6	36	6 (ID, IA, MO, NE, NH, WI)

[a] NY: This indicates the expiration of a previous temporary tax increase, not a deliberate cut.

Sources: Based on the author's review of the National Conference of State Legislatures State Tax Actions Database by Waisanen and Haggerty 2010; Rafool and Haggerty 2011; Rafool 2013; 2014; 2015; NSCL 2009; 2012; NCSL 2016-2020.

revenue to provide needed services. State legislatures continued to pursue efforts to raise taxes in FY 2010 to resupply their budgetary reserves.

FY 2011 observed the first-time overall tax reduction of nearly $2 billion. This is the result of the expiration of several temporary tax increases passed by state legislation in 2009. For instance, the California state legislature voted to allow the 2009 temporary income and sales tax increases to expire as planned, and the result was a $8.3 billion tax revenue decline. Excluding California, a different picture emerged. State governments, primarily Connecticut and Illinois, enacted a $9 billion tax increase (Rafool 2013). In 2012, the net tax increase of over $4 billion reflected various state tax actions in all tax categories, including California's Proposition 30 with its $5.5 billion income and sales tax increases that were approved by voters.

However, the subsequent years from FY 2013 to FY 2019 witnessed net tax revenue reductions or small tax increases except in 2017 and 2019. The relatively large tax increases for FY 2017 were from the combined state tax actions, including large income tax increases in Kansas and Illinois and significant CIT increases occurring in Delaware. Both Kansas and Illinois faced severe revenue shortages at the time, and Delaware was positioned to reform its corporate franchise tax (Quinn and Gilmore 2018). The large tax increases of FY 2019 derived from sales tax increases resulting from the Supreme Court *South Dakota v. Wayfair, Inc.* ruling. This landmark case gives states the authority to require remote sellers to collect sales tax for states.

Individual Tax Changes

When looking at individual taxes, readers will see the following patterns: states almost always increased healthcare tax, tobacco tax, alcoholic beverage tax, and motor fuel tax (see Columns 5–8 in Table 3.5). Only in two years (FY 2012 and FY 2018) did the net amount of revenue collected from the healthcare tax decline. However, these reductions were the result of a single state action. In 2012, California allowed the temporary 2.35% tax on MediCal managed care plans to expire (Rafool 2013). In 2018, Washington lawmakers authorized an exemption for Accountable Communities of Health funds (NCSL 2019). The motor fuel tax declined in FY 2012 because North Carolina enacted a gas tax cap. The decline in FY 2013 was due to Virginia's effort to replace its motor fuel excise tax with an increase of its general sales tax to fund state infrastructure (Rafool 2014).

The story is different for the major taxes (e.g., PIT, CIT, and SUT) (see Columns 2–4 in Table 3.5). States tend to increase these taxes only during a recession or years immediately after. For example, from FY 2009 to FY 2012, there was a net increase in PIT every year except 2010. The decline in FY 2010 resulted from the expiration of temporary tax increases in New Jersey and Idaho's continuing implementation of previous tax cut legislation (Rafool and Haggerty 2011). On the contrary, FY 2013–FY 2019 saw a multi-year trend of lowering both PIT and CIT. The desire and the tendency to cut income taxes were always strong. Tax actions in 2017 interrupted this trend partially due to extensive tax increase packages in a few states, including Illinois and Kansas, as mentioned above.

Compared with the income tax, state governments tend to increase sales/use taxes because the tax burden can be exported to nonresidents. In all the twelve years examined, nine years witnessed an increase in SUT revenue, and cutbacks were observed in three years. Among those three years, FY 2012 and FY 2017 reductions resulted from the expiration of California's temporary sales tax increases enacted in previous years (Rafool 2013; Quinn and Gilmore 2018). The trend of increasing sales tax continued in FY 2018 and FY 2019 when many states expanded their collection to remote sales after the U.S. Supreme Court *South Dakota v. Wayfair* decision.

Tax Changes among States

Table 3.6 shows the number of states with tax changes in each year during FY 2008–FY 2018. During the period, some states raised their taxes, while others reduced them. The magnitude of these reforms differed greatly. State tax policies are always influenced by fiscal stresses, tax structures, state political party leadership, and the legal-imposed restraints each state faces.

FY 2009 observed the largest number of states raising their taxes and raising significant amounts of their tax (i.e., with a 5%, or greater, of their previous year's tax collection). In later years, fewer states undertook significant tax increases, and more states reduced their taxes. It is important to note that in all the years besides 2009 and 2015, more than 30 states did not pursue any significant actions.

Tables 3.6 also show that significant tax actions took place in several states. Large PIT increases occurred in California, Connecticut, Illinois, Kansas, and New York. Significant PIT cuts took place in Ohio, North Carolina, Indiana, and Missouri. Most state governments pursued a mixture of these fiscal policies.

The Impact of Tax Actions on State Tax System

The discussion above supports several generalizations regarding the impacts of state tax actions on state tax systems and their fiscal stability. First, in the post-Great Recession period, state lawmakers in several states have pursued a multitude of tax actions, displaying an effort to reform their tax systems. However, significant tax changes come from a select number of states, as shown in Table 3.6. The tax actions enacted in many states were not significant. Some years saw a greater number of tax-related actions than others. For the income tax, most of the tax actions occurred in FY 2009, when 24 states increased their income taxes, and in 2011 and 2015. Other years were quiet, during which states could implement tax changes that were adopted.

Second, state governments increase taxes only when facing a dire fiscal situation. In 2009, many states started raising their taxes, which was the largest increase in recent decades. However, without fiscal pressures, the effort to raise taxes could not be sustained. This is shown by the declining number of states that raise their taxes in the later years.

Third, in the post-Great Recession years, tax cuts were still popular. Compared to the post-2001 fiscal period, there were more tax cuts in the post-Great Recession period. For income taxes, most recent fiscal years witnessed more tax reductions. After FY 2009, there were six fiscal years of PIT cuts and four fiscal years of CIT reductions. These findings are surprising as many assumed that state officials would learn lessons from the Great Recession and reform their major revenue taxes to improve fiscal stability.

Fourth, the non-major taxes (e.g., healthcare tax, tobacco tax, alcohol tax, and motor fuel tax) are easy targets for state governments to increase their revenues. However, these items are often earmarked for certain programs and do not improve the fiscal health of general fund reserves.

Fifth, the overall changes made for income and sales taxes, the major revenue sources for state general funds, do not provide strong evidence of improvement in state fiscal stability. More than half of states made no major changes to their tax system. As stated earlier, significant increases occurred only in a handful of states. Many tax increases were temporary and would not correct the fiscal imbalances. Additionally, state tax action databases show states made effort to expand their tax bases, but some tax expenditures that were eliminated were restored, and new tax expenditures were added. Literature for public finance is consistent in that a good tax policy is one with a broad base. A stable tax system depends on a broad tax base and reasonable tax rates. In the post-Great Recession years, state tax changes have made limited progress in raising the tax rates or expanding the tax base.

Several factors explain the tax changes that state governments pursued during and after the Great Recession. The principal force for tax increase was the presence of fiscal crisis. Without it, tax increases would not take place. The anti-tax movement has grown since the late 1970s, and pro-business culture tends to push for tax cuts. The political parties that control the state legislature also shape the tax policies. Although it is politically difficult to expand the tax base and keep the tax rate reasonable in the absence of a fiscal crisis, a broad base with a reasonable rate is important for states to improve their fiscal stability in both the short term and the long term.

References

Deitz, Richard, Andrew F. Haughwout, and Charles Steindel. 2010. "The Recession's Impact on the State Budgets of New York and New Jersey." *Current Issues in Economics and Finance*, 16 (6), 1–9.

Gordon, Tracy. 2011. "State Budgets in Recession and Recovery." *Brookings Institute*. (October 27).

Gordon, Tracy. 2012. "State and Local Budgets and the Great Recession." *The Rusell Sage Foundation and the Stanford Center on Poverty and Inequality.* (July).

Johnson, Nicholas, Catherine Collins, and Ashali Singham. 2010. "State Tax Changes in Response to the Recession." *Center on Budget and Policy Priorities*. (March 9).

Lav, Iris J. and Dylan Grundman. 2011. "A Balanced Approach to Closing State Deficits." *Center on Budget and Policy Priorities.* (February 25).

Lav, Iris J., Nicholas Johnson, and Elizabeth McNichol. 2010. "Additional Federal Fiscal Relief Needed to Help States Address Recession's Impact." *Center on Budget and Policy Priorities*.

Leachman, Michael, Nick Albares, Kathleen Masterson, and Wallace Marlana. 2016. "Most States Have Cut School Funding, and Some Continue Cutting." *Center on Budget and Policy Priorities.* (January 25).

National Association of State Budget Officers (NASBO). 2008. *The Fiscal Survey of States*. (Fall).

National Association of State Budget Officers (NASBO). 2009. *The Fiscal Survey of States*. (Fall).

National Association of State Budget Officers (NASBO). 2010. *The Fiscal Survey of States*. (Fall).

National Association of State Budget Officers (NASBO). 2011. *The Fiscal Survey of States*. (Fall).

National Association of State Budget Officers (NASBO). 2012. *The Fiscal Survey of States*. (Fall).

National Association of State Budget Officers (NASBO). 2013a. State Budgeting and Lessons Learned from the Economic Downturn: Analysis and Commentary from State Budget Officers. (Summer).

National Association of State Budget Officers (NASBO). 2013b. *The Fiscal Survey of States*. (Fall).

National Association of State Budget Officers (NASBO). 2014. *The Fiscal Survey of States*. (Fall).

National Conference of State Legislature (NCSL). 2012. *State Tax Actions 2011: Special Fiscal Report.* Denver, Colorado: National Conference of State Legislature.

National Conference of State Legislature (NCSL). 2015-2019. *State Tax Actions. State Tax Actions Database*

Oliff, Phil, Chris Mai, and Vincent Palacios. 2012. "State Continue to Feel Recession's Impact." *Center on Budget and Policy Priorities.* (June 27).

Rafool, Mandy and Todd Haggerty. 2011. *State Tax Actions 2010: Special Fiscal Report.* Denver, Colorado: National Conference of State Legislature.

Rafool, Mandy. 2013. *State Tax Actions 2012: Special Fiscal Report.* Denver, Colorado: National Conference of State Legislature.

Rafool, Mandy. 2014. *State Tax Actions 2013: Special Fiscal Report* Denver, Colorado: National Conference of State Legislature.
Rafool, Mandy. 2015. *State Tax Actions 2014: Special Fiscal Report.* Denver, Colorado: National Conference of State Legislature.
Waisanen, Bert and Todd Haggerty. 2010. *State Tax Actions 2009: Special Fiscal Report.* Denver, Colorado: National Conference of State Legislature.

4

THE GREAT RECESSION AND TAX INCREASES

Stories in Three States

Introduction

Chapter 3 provides an overall picture of the tax policy changes in the post-Great Recession years. This chapter investigates three states (i.e., California, New York, and Connecticut), examining how and why they raised their major taxes (i.e., personal income tax (PIT), corporate income tax (CIT), and sales tax). The discussion will first reveal the political and fiscal context under which the taxes were increased, then explain the impact these measures will have on their long-term fiscal health and highlight issues that impede state fiscal stability. While tax policy in every state deserves research attention, California, New York, and Connecticut are chosen because they were among the states with the largest revenue shortfalls during FY 2009 - FY 2013 (see Table 4.1). They are also the states that made significant tax reforms during the post-Great Recession years.

The Story of California: Fiscal Crisis, Tax Increases, and Voter Initiatives

California is considered the origin of the modern tax revolt movement. Since its voters passed Proposition 13 in 1978, which cut property tax, among others, California has been "on the leading edge of the tax cut movement that has spread across the nation" (Nagourney 2011, p. 1). Voters also used ballot measures to impose other revenue restraints and to expand services. As a result, it is extremely difficult to raise taxes, particularly income and sales taxes, and California lawmakers always have difficulties balancing their budgets. Then, in 2009 and

DOI: 10.4324/9781003494324-4

TABLE 4.1 Budget Shortfalls for California, New York, and Connecticut: FY 2009–FY 2013

FY	Total Shortfall (in $billion)			Total Shortfall as % of General Fund Spending			National Average
	CA	NY	CT	CA	NY	CT	
2009	37.1	7.4	2.7	36.7%	13.2%	15.5%	15.2%
2010	45.5	21.0	4.7	52.8%	38.8%	27.0%	29.0%
2011	17.9	8.5	1.8	20.7%	15.9%	25.1%	19.9%
2012	23.9	10.4	3.2	27.8%	18.2%	17.1%	11.3%
2013	15.0	2.0	3.0	11.3%	3.4%	16.0%	9.5%

Source: Oliff, Mai, and Palacios (2012).

2012, California enacted two big tax increases. What made it possible for these to happen? Will these tax increases improve California's fiscal stability?

Fiscal and Political Context for Tax Policy Changes

As indicated, California's budget has been marred by severe fiscal crises, and lawmakers constantly "relied on borrowing and short-term solutions (Taylor 2018b, p. 5). When the Great Recession hit, California was in even bigger fiscal trouble. Taylor (2018b) from the California Legislative Analyst's Office (LAO) states:

> On December 31, 2008, Governor Schwarzenegger's proposed budget projected a $42 billion deficit. This shortfall was stunning, but it turned out to be optimistic. A few months later, the Governor's deficit projection was $15 billion larger. In the subsequent weeks, the Governor released two more revised budgets, each one addressing a larger shortfall. In the months that followed, California was called "ungovernable," "a wreck," and a "failed state."
>
> *(Taylor 2018b, p. 1)*

California's fiscal crisis was also exemplified by its cash crisis, which started in the fall of 2008. The cash flow was dangerously low and then reached the minimum cash level in January 2009. The governor had to approach the U.S. Treasurer, alerting him to the possibility of asking for short-term financing assistance. The state also launched a campaign to encourage Californians to buy state short-term bonds to help the state out. To ease the cash crisis, the state issued $2.6 billion IOU, a form of debt in July and August 2009 (Taylor 2018b).

California had effectively no reserves at that time. Even with the help from federal stimulus grants, state lawmakers still had to cut a wide range of programs and services, including healthcare services, public education, and even releasing inmates early to eliminate costs. There were other short-term methods, such as fund transfers, cost deferrals, and various cash management measures to mitigate the state's fiscal crisis.

Facing such a severe fiscal crisis, state lawmakers knew that tax and revenue measures had to be part of the solution. During FY 2009–FY 2018, state lawmakers were able to enact several tax increases, resulting in billions of dollars in revenue (Appendix A). In addition to increasing the health-related tax, cigarette tax, and motor fuel tax that are usually designated for certain programs, California lawmakers were also able to raise income tax and sales tax to shore up the general fund spending.

2009 Tax Increase in the Midst Fiscal Crisis

California pursued two major tax actions with its income tax and sales tax. The first increase was enacted in the February *2009 Budget Act* by lawmakers during the fiscal wrecking moment when state lawmakers had to settle $42 billion of deficits before the new FY 2009 started. Due to the magnitude and urgency of the state fiscal crisis, state lawmakers passed the *2009 Budget Act* five months ahead of the constitutional deadline with both spending cuts and revenue increases to balance the budget for FY 2008–FY 2009 and FY 2009–FY 2010. Among the tax measures, the law increased all PIT rates by 0.25% and raised sales tax by 1% from 7.25% to 8.25% for two years. The measure also suspended businesses' ability to deduct net operating losses (NOL). As described by the California Department of Finance, the act was sweeping in scope and immediate in effect. The tax measures generated much-needed revenue of over $8 billion, representing one of the largest tax increases among all states in 2009 (California Department of Finance). When other tax increases are included, the total additional revenue amounted to over $11 billion. This temporary tax increase lasted only two years, and California lawmakers let it expire in 2011 as planned.

Governor Brown and Proposition 30

Despite the 2009 tax increases, the California budget continued to face deterioration due to several underlying factors. Many measures used to address budget gaps were temporary fixes. For instance, the heavy reliance on borrowing added more uncertainties. The economy was recovering slowly. More importantly, California's budget was fundamentally misaligned as long-term expenditure exceeded revenues that the tax system could generate. In other words, even if the lawmakers could pass a balanced budget in one year, they

TABLE 4.2 Personal Income Tax under Proposition 30

Rate	Single Filer	Joint Filer
10.3%	$250,001–$300,000	$500,000–600,000
11.3%	$300,001–$500,000	$600,000–$1 million
12.3%	Over $500,000	Over $1 million

Source: Chen (2016).

would still face a large "operating budget" deficit in future fiscal years (Taylor 2018b).

When Jerry Brown became the governor in 2011, the state was facing another $15.7 billion revenue gap for FY 2012. Tax increases became the legislative focus that year as spending cuts on essential programs were much deeper and wider than in other states. Proponents of tax increases had to use the initiative process this time because they did not have the supermajority votes (i.e., two-thirds votes) in the legislature to approve it, which is required by California law. The Republican lawmakers had made it clear that they would not give Democrats the needed votes (Nagourney 2011). Governor Brown, a Democrat, during his gubernatorial campaign, also promised that he would not raise taxes without directly asking voters.

Governor Brown made Proposition 30 the hallmark of his administration, telling the public that increasing income tax for the high income was the only way to save the public school (Dayen, 2013). The official name for Proposition 30 was the Temporary Taxes to Fund Education. Under the leadership of Governor Brown and with a broad support coalition, California voters approved Proposition 30 with 54% of the vote. This constitutional amendment added three new PIT rates for individuals earning over $250,000 a year (see Table 4.2) for seven years and increased the sales tax by ¼ cents for four years. Furthermore, the law requires multi-national corporations to adopt a single sales factor, replacing the traditional four-factor apportionment formula based on sales, payroll, and property (see Appendix A).

This is the first time that California voters approved a major tax increase since 2004 (Onishi 2012). Two years later, in 2016, Governor Brown and a coalition of his political allies led by teacher unions went back to voters for reauthorization. Voters approved Proposition 55, allowing an additional 12 years for the income tax portion. The sales tax portion expired as planned.

Why Did Voters Approve Proposition 30?

It was remarkable that California's electorate supported Proposition 30, helping chart a path for the state to experience a budgetary rebound. An important and interesting question asked here is: What convinced California voters to approve this significant tax increase? The fiscal crisis and the urgent need are important factors, and several other factors also contributed to its passage.

Urgent Need and Catastrophic Consequence if not Passed

During the campaign, Governor Brown continuously reminded the public that his administration had cut many public services. He told voters if they wanted the wealthy to keep all they had and not give to the public school, "we suffer the consequences" (Jerry Brown quoted in DeCastro 2012). The consequences would be $6 billion of further cuts into public education, additional tuition raises, large classes, and many school districts being forced into bankruptcy.

Leadership, Framing the Issue, and Campaign Strategies

Governor Brown was instrumental in passing Proposition 30. He was the major architect behind the measure, sponsoring the bill and campaigning tirelessly to push its passage. In the last weeks preceding the election, Governor Brown visited campuses, mobilizing college students to vote for Proposition 30. On the last day before the election, he campaigned in five cities.

Brown's effective leadership was also reflected in how he delivered his campaign messages: tax the rich to save public schools. According to Bradley (2012), Governor Brown was able to capitalize on popular support for funding public schools and universities and against cutting them further. He successfully explained to voters that the initiative was essential for California to expand innovation opportunities for the future. At the same time, Governor Brown was also able to convince voters taxing the wealthy would not hurt the businesses.

Design of the Measure

Proposition 30 specified how the increased tax revenue would be used. It would be deposited into a newly created "Education Protection Account" (EPA) within the state's general fund. A large share, 89% of EPA funds, would go directly to K-12 school districts, county education offices, and charter schools. The remaining 11% would be directed to community college districts. "No school districts would receive less than $200 in EPA funds per student, and no community college district would receive less than $100 in EPA funds per student" (California Budget Project 2012, p. 2). Such a stipulation guarantees the benefit spread to every student and every school. Under Proposition 30, schools and colleges decide how the funds could be used but are "required to hold public meetings when making spending decisions" (California Budget Project 2012, p. 2).

In terms of tax burden distribution, 78% of the new revenue derives from the top 1% of Californians with an annual income of $533,000 and above and 81.2% from the top 5% with an annual income of at least $206,000. The remaining 18.8% comes from the sales tax increase. Although the sales tax increase affects everyone, it is a small share (California Budget Project 2012). Overall, a small number of Californians bear a larger share of the tax burdens associated with Proposition 30, but the benefits spread to all schools, students, and their parents.

The measure also protects the revenue from politics. The legislature cannot touch the funds, and audits are mandated each year to ensure the money is spent on public education and safety. When the measure expires, any renewal will need to be approved by voters (California Budget Project 2012).

Broad Grassroots Coalitions and Community-based Voter Mobilization

Proposition 30 was supported by a broad coalition consisting of teacher unions, progressive groups, faith-based organizations, community leaders, and grassroots organizations. In the largest community-led voter mobilization effort in the state's recent history, Reclaim California's Future—an organization committed to restore critical funding for schools—had more than 5,000 community members in 23 counties across California reaching out to hundreds of thousands of voters in the final 24 hours before the Election Day. The campaign led by Governor Brown with a broad coalition and grassroots mobilization brought about a massive increase in political participation, resulting in a key victory.

The Impact of Tax Changes on the State Fiscal Stability

Together, the 2009 tax measure and Proposition 30 provided much-needed revenue to California at a time when the state faced daunting fiscal challenges. According to Chen (2016), the PIT and sales tax rate changes approved in Proposition 30 generated $7–8 billion annually, not only allowing the state to avert further substantial cuts in public programs but also increasing state investment in preschool and K-14 education. The state also increased spending for other public services and even boosted rainy-day fund deposits and debt repayment. LAO *Fiscal Outlook* reports revealed an increasing trend of year-end reserves and rainy-day funds after the passage of Proposition 30 (see Table 4.3). Raising the tax rates for the top earners also makes the system more progressive.

However, these tax actions have not improved California's long-term fiscal stability. First, the two major tax increases are temporary, and they already expired or will expire. The state will largely retain a similar tax structure as before. Second, lawmakers did not address a fundamental problem with the tax system—the erosion of the tax base. Like all other states, the California tax base has eroded over the years with a plethora of tax expenditures. In the post-Great

TABLE 4.3 General Fund End Balances for FY 2013–FY 2018 (in $billion)

	FY 2013	FY 2014	FY 2015	FY 2016	FY 2017	FY 2018
Ending Fund Balance	3.6	2.157	3.7	1.7	10.1	10.3
Budget Stabilization Account	n/a	1.6	3.4	6.7	11.0	13.8

Sources: Taylor (2015, p. 5; 2016, p. 8; 2018a, p. 16).

TABLE 4.4 The Number of Tax Expenditures* with CA Major Taxes in Selected Years

	FY 2007–FY 2008	FY 2019–FY 2020
PIT	41	44
CIT	13	18
SUT	19	30

* The Department of Finance is legally required to provide a tax-expenditure report to the legislature, covering major tax expenditures whose revenue losses exceed $5 million.

Source: The author's compilation is based on California Department of Finance, *Tax Expenditure Report* (various years).

Recession era, California lawmakers attempted to reduce tax expenditures in the first few years. For instance, the state reduced the dependent credit in PIT and required more businesses to suspend their ability to deduct NOL. However, from 2013, the state legislature began to provide more CIT credits. In its 2013 tax-expenditure program reforms, the state eliminated the enterprise zone program but authorized other new tax incentives. Among them are a new hiring credit equal to 35% of qualifying wages for certain new employees hired by businesses in specific areas, a new negotiated tax credit package to targeted businesses, and a partially exempted purchase of manufacturing equipment from the sales tax. The annual film incentive program was expanded, and the state also authorized and expanded earned income tax credits in recent years.

As a result, the number of major tax expenditures has increased, not decreased (see Table 4.4). The large number of tax breaks not only complicates the tax system but also causes substantial tax revenue loss and undermines fiscal sustainability. The tax breaks for PIT and CIT combined cost California $63 billion in tax revenue every year. That equals 40% of the 2019–2020 general fund budget (Kitson 2020). The revenue loss from sales tax exclusion and exemptions represented another $9 billion (California Commission on the 21st Century Economy 2009). Without a broad tax base, high tax rates alone will not improve government revenue capability.

Third, the tax actions did not represent comprehensive reforms and were not designed to restore balance among the major tax systems. According to California's Commission on the 21st Century Economy, the state's tax system has become less diverse in its sources and more volatile in its performance. When established in the 1930s, the sales tax accounted for 60% of state tax revenue. Over the years, its base has been shrinking, covering few intangible goods and only 21 services and containing a whole range of deductions and exemptions. Its share had dropped to 31% of state tax revenue by 2009. Proposition 30, while increasing the sales tax rate, did not extend the sales tax to additional services or intangible goods and did not eliminate any exemptions. As a result, the share of sales tax, a relatively stable revenue source, continued to fall to 21.7% in 2015, pushing California to rely on PIT, a more fluctuating revenue. During FY 2009–FY 2010, the PIT accounted for 54% of the state's general fund revenue, up from 11% in the 1950s. By 2022, the total share increased to 58%.

In addition, over the years, California's PIT has shifted from wages/salaries to include more variable forms of pay, such as capital gains realizations, bonuses, and stock options. These changes seem to expand the income tax base, but they effectively induce PIT to rely on "a narrow band of taxpayers who have the volatile sources of income" (California Commission on the 21st Century Economy 2009, p. 6). In the short term, relying on the variable income leaves state tax revenue at the mercy of the economic cycle. In the long term, critics say that higher rates on the top bracket will lead to an exodus of wealth and investment out of the state, further undermining the tax base, although this claim is debatable.

California needs a comprehensive tax reform to stabilize its tax system. Betty T. Yee, California State Controller, stated that the "fiscal imbalance will persist until we dig deep into structural changes" (California State Controller Betty T. Yee and the Controller's Council of Economic Advisor on Tax Reform 2016, p. ii). However, a comprehensive reform is impossible to attain. Every year, the state legislature considers an average number of 245 tax proposals, but these measures are mostly incremental, addressing a single tax at a particular bracket or or adjusting tax rates (California State Controller Betty T. Yee and the Controller's Council of Economic Advisor on Tax Reform 2016). Although considered major, the tax actions that occurred after the Great Recession are not comprehensive.

Voter Initiatives and California Fiscal Stability

Furthermore, the California budget process is complicated by voters' initiatives. As stated earlier, these procedures impose restraints on tax revenues and are not always consistent. For instance, Proposition 13 stipulates that tax increases be approved by either two-thirds of the legislature or by voters. However, tax cuts and adding tax credits only require a simple majority of legislature votes. While voters approved measures to restrain tax increases, they also approved program spending measures. For instance, in 1988, voters passed Proposition 98, establishing a minimum constitutional funding guarantee for K-14 education.

In the post-Great Recession years, voters have continued to add restrictions to the budget process. In 2010, when state lawmakers were desperately looking for additional revenue, voters passed Proposition 26 mandating two-thirds votes, not the original simple majority, from the legislature to enact "fees, charges, levies, and tax allocations" (California State Controller Betty T. Yee and the Controller's Council of Economic Advisors on Tax Reform 2016, p. 51). The impact of such a change is estimated to be $1 billion annually.

In 2014, voters passed Proposition 2, requiring the state to set aside minimum amounts of funding each year for reserves and debt payments. One provision, specifically, mandates the state to deposit a share of capital gains revenues that exceeds a specific threshold into a separate fund. The extraordinary revenue gains that usually happen during booming stock market years can only be used under specific circumstances and cannot be used to build on an unsustainable spending base. The intention is to help the state build up reserves and "moderate spending swings associated with capital gains revenue" (California State Controller Betty T. Yee and the Controller's Council of Economic Advisors on Tax Reform 2016, p. 7). This requirement should reduce the revenue volatility and improve fiscal stability.

Proponents believe ballot measures give people a voice in public policy decisions. Critics say that "ballot box budgeting hemmed in public officials and prevented sound tax and spending policies" (Gordon, Randall, Steuerle, and Boddupalli 2019, p. 37). Regardless of how they are perceived, ballot politics will continue to complicate California's budget process, shape tax reforms, and add further challenges for lawmakers to achieve fiscal stability. Therefore, it is imperative for elected officials to communicate with the public about the revenue needs, the impact of the ballot actions, and what is needed to achieve fiscal stability.

The Story of New York: Wall Street, Millionaire Tax, Tax Progressivity

For decades, the Empire State struggled to balance its budgets. Spring borrowing became a routine, not an exception. Critics refer to New York State as a high-tax capital with free-spending habits. When the Great Recession brought unprecedented revenue shortfalls, state lawmakers had to make even more difficult fiscal decisions. They must find ways to meet the state's budgetary needs but not hurt economic recovery. What tax actions did state lawmakers take to address these historic challenges? Were these actions able to improve the state's overall fiscal stability?

Fiscal and Political Context for Tax Policy Changes

New York State relies heavily on PIT, accounting for nearly two-thirds of all its tax revenue (New York State Tax Reform and Fairness Commission 2013). Among income tax revenue, a majority derives from the financial service sector, generating 20% of state tax revenue. Since Wall Street is the international financial center and the pillar of New York's economy, the Great Recession was devastating to the state economy and state government finance, resulting in severe revenue shortfalls during FY 2009–FY 2013, ranging from 13.2% to 38.8% of the state general fund (see Table 4.1).

Heavy Spending Cuts and the 2009 Temporary Tax Increase

Governor David Paterson took office in March 2008 amid the Great Recession. He immediately implemented two rounds of spending reduction measures by over 10% and then called for a special legislative economic session to enact another $1 billion in savings for the next two years. These aggressive spending cuts, aiming to rein in government spending, fell virtually in every area of state government services, including public education and healthcare.

Still, FY 2008 ended with a $2.2 billion deficit, and FY 2009 was projected to have a budget gap of $17.9 billion. The combined revenue shortfall of $20.1 billion was the largest in state history. Due to the urgency of the problem, Governor Paterson delivered his executive budget more than one month prior to the constitutional deadline and urged the legislature to act quickly. His FY 2009–FY 2010 executive budget proposal projected a five-year cumulative budget gap of $70.7 billion (Paterson 2008).

New York had $1.3 billion in rainy-day reserves, but state lawmakers did not touch it for the first two years. It was small compared with the revenue gap. Therefore, state officials relied on heavy cuts and federal fiscal relief to close the revenue shortfalls. Governor Paterson also proposed a series of reforms to address long-term costs, including agency consolidations, Empire Zone reform, public employee pension reform, and a workforce reduction of 8,690 positions (Paterson 2008).

For months, Governor Paterson had been insisting that new income taxes would be the last resort in balancing the budget. Then, in early 2009, with the rapid revenue decline, it was clear the state needed that last resort. Closing the $20.1 billion gap without a tax measure would mean an $18 billion general fund spending cut. A reduction of this magnitude would be detrimental to public health, public safety, and economic recovery and would impose a grave burden on local property tax (Paterson 2009). The Democratic-controlled state legislature, supported by unions and liberal groups, negotiated with the governor and included an income tax increase as part of the FY 2009–FY 2010 budget. After Governor Paterson won significant spending cuts in areas such as healthcare and education, he accepted the package and signed it into law on April 7, 2009.

The tax deal reflected the new political power balance among the powerbrokers in Albany. First, as mentioned before, the Democrats controlled both the legislature and the executive office after the 2008 election. Second, the major architect of the tax increase legislation, Mr. Sheldon Silver, was a powerful Assembly speaker. He exercised tremendous leverage during the negotiation process over Governor Paterson, who had a low approval rate, and Mr. Malcolm A. Smith, the Senate leader, who had a 32–30 narrow margin of Democrat majority in the chamber.

While the governor preferred a simple tax system, Mr. Malcolm A. Smith and his Senate Democrats proposed a more radical income tax reform by creating nine brackets for five years and raised as much as $5 billion a year, including some to be used for property tax relief. Mr. Silver did not believe the Senate's plan would succeed and did not like the idea of using income tax increases to offset property taxes, which would largely benefit residents in the suburbs and upstate. The final version of the tax legislation, largely hammered out by Mr. Silver, entailed three-year tax increases with two rates over the top bracket income individuals (Confessore 2009).

Dubbed as "millionaire tax," its two new top brackets, 7.85% and 8.97%, were applied to joint filers whose taxable incomes were over $300,000 (see Table 4.5). The new top rates would generate $3.95 billion in revenue in FY 2010 and $4.77 billion in FY 2011 (Waisanen and Haggerty 2010). The law also eliminated various tax credits and exemptions and increased taxes on beer, cigarettes, and cigars (see Appendix B). It was the largest state income tax increase in recent state history, significantly larger than the previous recession surcharges imposed from 2003 to 2005 (Waisanen and Haggerty 2010).

TABLE 4.5 New York's Permanent and Temporary Tax Rates for Married Joint Filers

Taxable Income	Permanent Law (Before 2009)	Temporary 2009–2011 Rate	2012–2014 Rate
$40,000–$150,000	6.85%	6.85%	6.45%–>5.5%
$150,000–$300,000	6.85%	6.85%	6.65%–>6.0%
$300,000–$500,000	6.85%	7.85%	6.85%
$500,000–$2 million	6.85%	8.97%	6.85%
Over $2 million	6.85%	8.97%	8.82%

Source: New York State Tax Reform and Fairness Commission (2013, p. E-4); McMahon (2012a, p. 705). Permission granted.

Governor Cuomo and His Middle-class Tax Cuts

The lawmakers allowed the 2009 temporary tax increases to expire in 2011 as planned. However, the state was still facing large and persistent revenue shortfalls, ranging from $10 billion to $21 billion each year.

- $10 billion in FY 2011–FY 2012
- $15.3 billion in FY 2012–FY 2013
- $17.9 billion in FY 2013–FY 2014
- $21.4 billion in FY 2014–FY 2015

The new governor, Andrew Cuomo, told the public correctly that the budget gaps

> reflected the short-term impact of the recession on state tax receipts and economically sensitive programs, the long-term impact of current statutory provisions that have allowed spending to grow beyond the State's ability to pay for it, and the phase-out of the Federal government's increased share of Medicaid costs.
>
> *(Cuomo 2011, p. 3)*

According to Cuomo, the solution was not raising taxes but slowing down or eliminating the state's unsustainable spending growth, entirely redesigning government operations, and promoting economic development. Although a Democrat, "at times, Mr. Cuomo found himself more closely aligned with Republicans than Democrats" (Kaplan 2011, p. 3).

During his election campaign, Governor Cuomo promised voters numerous times he would not raise taxes. True to his promise, in his first budget, he eliminated the $10 billion budget deficits for FY 2011 without raising taxes. He also reduced $55 billion projected budget gaps (out of $64 billion total) for the upcoming four fiscal years by cutting programs. In addition, the state would implement a 10% year-to-year reduction of its operation spending to entirely redesign government agencies' operations to meet contemporary needs (Cuomo 2011). The governor also appointed an advisory commission to examine the current program operation and to make recommendations to reduce the state's long-term spending burdens. By limiting tax and spending growth, the governor wanted to "remind the world that New York is open for business" ("Director's Message" in Cuomo 2011, p 1).

However, by November 2011, the state budget was projected to end with a $350 million deficit for the current fiscal year and a $3.5 billion revenue gap for FY 2012–FY 2013. Further cuts would be difficult, given the several rounds of deep cuts and adamant opposition from the unions and other advocacy groups who were calling to extend the temporary tax increases (McMahon 2012a).

Furthermore, Governor Cuomo had promised to increase spending on public education and Medicaid by 4% after additional spending cuts in his first year. This would effectively lock 40% of the state budget, reducing options available for the governor. At the same time, the Democrats, emboldened by the Occupy Wall Street movement, pushed the governor to pursue a more progressive tax system (Kaplan 2011).

Tax measures were inevitable, but any move to raise taxes could be risky for the governor. It was a dilemma, but the governor found a way out. When Governor Cuomo decided to tackle tax change, he presented it not as a measure to generate more revenue but as a measure to bring fairness into the system, arguing that New York income tax took away the same percentage of income from the middle class as from the wealthy since the permanent law imposes 6.85% on all income brackets (see Table 4.5). According to Kaplan, by "appropriately changing the terms of debate," Governor Cuomo made it possible to raise revenues without "inflammatory rhetoric and driving businesses and wealth out of the state" (Kaplan 2011, p. 4).

In the December 2011 special session, Governor Cuomo and the legislature passed the second tax legislation to restructure the New York income tax system for tax years 2012 through 2014. The law lowered the rates on lower income brackets and added a new top rate of 8.82% on taxable incomes of $1 million for individuals and $2 million for married couples. The lawmakers defined the measure as a middle-class tax cut, but critics called it a millionaire tax (McMahon 2012b). The new top rate is lower than the rate in the FY 2009–FY 2010 law but higher than the permanent law. According to McMahon (2012b), the tax increase for the targeted high-income earners collected $2.6 billion in new revenue. Compared to the 2009 temporary tax measure, this package cost the state $1.2 billion in revenue.

The 2011 law also linked tax rate brackets and standard deductions to the consumer price index, the first attempt in New York history. The law was reauthorized in 2013, 2017, and 2019. The top rate is currently scheduled to expire in 2024. In FY 2016, the tax rate for the middle class was permanently reduced from 6.85% to 5.5% or 6%, depending on income level.

2014 CIT Reform

New York State also undertook a major CIT reform in 2014, the most significant CIT reform since the 1940s. By 2013, the New York corporate franchise tax system had not only been unduly complex and vulnerable to tax avoidance but also seriously outdated (New York State Tax Reform and Fairness Commission 2013). For instance, different tax rules were applied to banks and other financial institutions, even if the services they provided were essentially the same. The 2014 reform merged the bank tax and corporate franchise tax, attempting to modernize and streamline the tax code. The reform "also includes tax cuts that bring the corporate tax rate to the lowest level since 1960" (New York State Department of Taxation and Finance No Date, p. 1). Governor Cuomo also simplified the CIT by eliminating the corporate Alternative Minimum Tax, one of the four tax bases used to calculate the tax, and aligning the NOL rule with most states. Walczak from the Tax Foundation stated that these reforms improved New York's competitiveness among other states (Walczak 2020).

The Impact of Tax Changes on State Fiscal Stability

New York's tax actions did little to improve the tax system in terms of long-term fiscal stability. First, similar to the tax changes in California, New York's tax actions are considered temporary fixes. These measures were adopted in response to the fiscal crisis and political pressures. Although renewed three times, these tax actions will expire eventually, and the additional revenue will be gone as well. Back in December 2011, Governor Cuomo described the tax reform as "the first major restructuring of the tax code in decades" (McMahon 2012a, p. 708). McMahon from the Manhattan Institute stated that "the bill did not represent true tax reform but an expedient short-term response to a combination of fiscal and political pressures" (McMahon 2012a, p. 708).

Furthermore, the tax actions did not stop the fundamental problem of tax base erosion, just like in California. The major tax systems in New York saw a dramatic increase in tax expenditures before the Great Recession, and this trend continued after the Great Recession. For instance, the number of business tax credits increased from 9 in 1995 to 38 in 2009, with costs rising from $200 million in 1995 to $821 million in 2009 (New York State Tax Reform and Fairness Commission 2013).The years immediately after the Great Recession witnessed some efforts to reduce a number of tax expenditures (see Box 4.1). However, after 2011, state lawmakers started to establish more tax breaks and extend existing ones. According to the NCSL *State Tax Actions Database* (Waisanen and Haggerty 2010; Rafool and Haggerty 2011; Rafool 2013, 2014, 2015; NSCL 2009, 2012, 2016–2019), New York State lawmakers established or expanded 24 PIT expenditure programs while only reducing or eliminating 12 PIT credits. For CIT, 43 tax actions narrowed the base, while only 14 effectively broadened the base. Several new tax credits were expensive. One was the property tax freeze in the form of a PIT credit for homeowners in 2014, which cost the state $400 million for FY 2015 and $976 million for FY 2016. The other one was the conversion of the School Tax Relief (STAR) program rate reduction into a state PIT credit in 2017, costing the state $340 million for the next fiscal year.

Based on the data from the *Annual Report on New York Tax Expenditures* (New York State Department of Taxation and Finance, Division of the Budget,

BOX 4.1   TAX BASE BROADENING AND NARROWING

The efforts to expand the major tax bases in the years immediately after the Great Recession:

- Applying the PIT to gains from the sales of certain partnerships and non-residents' past compensation
- Limiting itemized deductions for high-income earners
- Reverting the federal tax deductions to state taxable income
- Reducing PIT deduction for charitable donations for taxpayers who earn more than $10 million a year
- Adopting a measure to treat gains from S-corporations and installment income as taxable for non-residents
- Applying the sales tax to several services, and removing the exemption on clothing of less than $55 (it was reinserted in the next year, 2011)
- Defining "vendor" to include internet companies with local affiliates
- Closing several CIT loopholes

New expensive tax credits

- Freezing the property tax in the form of PIT credit for homeowners (2014)
- Conversion of the STAR program rate reduction into a state PIT tax credit (2017)

Changes to state CIT tax bases authorized in 2014 are

- Applying the STAR tax credits to manufacturers equal to 20% of taxes paid
- Approving an income tax credit equal to 15% of wages for hiring the developmentally disabled
- Approving an income tax credit equal to 25% of qualified costs for musical and theatrical productions
- Increasing the income tax credit for low-income housing, enhancing the youth works tax credit
- Extending alternative duel tax exemptions

Source: Rafool (2015).

TABLE 4.6 Number of Tax Expenditures with New York Major Taxes: 2009–2018

	FY 2009	FY 2018
PIT	55	69
CT	38	50 (2013)*
SUT	143	160

* Due to the 2014 corporate tax reform, the classification of business tax expenditure is slightly different from those in 2009. Therefore, the 2013 number is used.

Sources: Author's compilation based on data from New York State Department of Taxation and Finance, Division of the Budget (2008–2018).

2008;2018), the number of tax expenditures for all the major taxes in the post-Great Recession years has increased (see Table 4.6).

Each of the tax expenditures has laudable purposes. For instance, business tax incentives are designed to encourage economic development and promote job growth in distressed areas. PIT breaks are intended to achieve social goals, such as using earned income tax credits to assist low-income families. Many sales tax exemptions are used to alleviate the tax regressivity. However, there is no conclusive evidence that these policy goals can be best achieved through employing tax credits. In some cases, direct spending may represent a better option for achieving policy goals.

These tax incentives violate the principles of good tax policy and the tenets of effective budgeting. Aside from distorting economic decisions and complicating the tax system, tax expenditures erode the tax base, causing the government to lose significant revenue and undermining fiscal stability. The New York State Tax Reform and Fairness Commission (2013) concluded that in 2013, the 50 business tax credits would cost New York State $1.7 billion. As Rubin and Boyd (2013) stated,

> If all New York State business tax credits were eliminated, the potential revenue gain would be used to reduce the top personal income tax rate, cut both personal and corporate income tax rates, lower the sales tax rate or reduce other tax rates.
>
> *(p. 2)*

Tax Progressivity, Capital Gain Tax, and State Fiscal Stability

Similar to the tax actions pursued in California, New York's two major income tax changes increased the system's progressivity. The 2012 tax action introduced two new higher marginal rates for high-income families and lowered the tax rates for middle- and lower-income households.

New York is one of the several states that imposed top tax rates on the wealthy. Other states with the so-called millionaire tax include California (13.3% top rate on $1 million income earners), New Jersey (10.75% on $5 million plus earners), Connecticut (6.99% over $1 million), Washington, DC (8.95% top rate on $1 million-plus earners). Although the top rate for New York is lower than that of California, the combined rate of state and New York City taxes of 13.9% is the highest in the nation.

Applying top marginal rates to top earners improves the fairness of the tax system and generates additional tax revenue for states. However, critics argue that higher tax rates will hurt state economic competitiveness and lead to high-income household outmigration. According to Walczak (2020), New York lost nearly one million people in the 2010–2017 period. This translated into $51 billion in annual adjusted gross income in current dollars or 4%–5% of the state operating budget. He did recognize that tax is only one of many factors influencing individual and business decisions to relocate. The impact on the state economy is still subject to further study.

Another concern with the millionaire tax is that it will increase tax collection volatility. Two related issues are behind this concern: the progressive structure of the millionaire tax system and the sources of income that the tax captures (e.g., capital gains). The questions become: Does a progressive tax structure lead to tax collection volatility? Does capital gains tax lead to tax collection volatility?

Top income earners tend to have capital gains, bonuses, and other investment-related income in their income profile. Studies have shown that, in some cases, taxes on these incomes lead to more revenue volatility because they are prone to fluctuations in the stock market. The top rates within progressive tax usually apply to the top income brackets, which include capital gains and bonuses, thus making the system vulnerable to economic cycles and tying tax revenue closely to a small group of taxpayers. Yet, other studies found weak or no relation between state capital gains tax and revenue volatility. To reconcile the different findings, Boyd (2022) suggests the impact of capital gains tax on a state's revenue vitality "depends on their magnitude and how they are taxed" (p. 4). If the top tax rates are high and the capital gains tax accounts for a large share of tax revenue, the impact on revenue volatility will be high, like in California.

Another study conducted by Chernick, Reimers, and Tennant (2014) found that income concentration and capital gains incomes are the major contributors to fiscal instability, and the progressivity of a tax system only has a secondary effect. While further discussion on this topic will be provided in Chapter 6, this brief discussion indicates that New York's progressive tax structure is not necessarily the major contributor to its fiscal instability. What matters more is how the state taxes capital gains, bonuses, and other investment-related income, how high the income concentration is, and how large the share of these revenues is in the state revenue. The fact that Wall Street is the pillar of the New York State economy and the state's finance relies heavily on the financial service sector will continue to expose the state's government budget to economic volatility.

The Story of Connecticut: Tax Increases, Legacy Costs, and Fiscal Instability

Connecticut is considered one of the wealthiest states in terms of per capita income. Her rolling and picturesque landscape is the home of a disproportionate number of high-income residents. However, when the Great Recession hit, the state faced significant financial troubles like many other states (see Table 4.1). What is striking is its fiscal trouble—large annual budget deficit—persists year after year for an entire decade. Connecticut was one of the few states that adopted a series of significant tax increases between 2009 and 2017, not only raising the tax rates of the major taxes but also expanding the tax bases. What are these tax measures? How did they take place? Did they improve the state fiscal stability?

Fiscal and Political Context for Tax Policy Changes

2009: From No Tax Increase to the First Big Increase

The Great Recession imposed a dramatic fiscal crisis for Connecticut. As Connecticut's economy relied heavily on the financial services section, Governor Jodi Rell recognized the severe fiscal consequences of the revenue system. During the first six months of FY 2009, Governor Rell issued three rounds of rescissions, hiring freezes, and implementing other cost-saving initiatives (Rell 2009). However, the state ended FY 2009 with a $976 million deficit on June 30, 2009 (Connecticut State Comptroller 2009).

Budget forecasts for the biennial FY 2010 and FY 2011 were more ominous. The governor's office in February 2009 projected a $6.1 billion revenue shortage or roughly 20% of total state spending. Large as it was, it was much smaller than the nonpartisan Office of Fiscal Analysis (OFA) estimate of $8.7 billion (Connecticut Office of Fiscal Analysis October 2009) (see Table 4.7). Governor Rell, a Republican, relying on her office budget forecast, attempted to close the $6.1 billion revenue gap by cutting spending, transferring funds from "off-budget" accounts, increasing fees, using rainy-day funds, and delaying pension payments, but not implementing tax increases. She stated, "Taxing our way out of this downturn was simply not a viable option" (Rell 2009, p. 32).

The Democratic-controlled state legislature, trusting OFA's projection, insisted that tax actions were needed to avert further fiscal chaos. The difference between the two sides was so big that the FY 2010 started without a budget. Only after the Connecticut Office of Policy and Management (OPM) and OFA agreed to a consensus revenue projection on July 24, 2009, the governor and

TABLE 4.7 Connecticut OFA's Biennial Budget Deficit Projection General Fund (in $billion)

Projection date	February 2009			February 2011		November 2012		November 2014		February 2017	
For FY	2009	2010	2011	2012	2013	2014	2015	2016	2017	2018	2019
Deficits	1.35	3.97	4.71	3.2	3.0	1.1	1.0	1.3	1.43	1.7	1.9
Percentage of State General Fund	15.5%	27.0%	28.8%	17.1%	n/a	n/a	n/a	n/a	n/a	n/a	n/a

Sources: Office of Fiscal Analysis, Connecticut General Assembly. *Connecticut State Budget FY 2018–FY 2019; Connecticut State Budget FY 2016–FY 2017; Connecticut State Budget FY 2018–FY 2019; Connecticut State Budget FY 2014–FY 2015; Connecticut State Budget FY 2012–FY 2013; Connecticut State Budget FY 2009–FY 2011.*

the legislature reassumed budget actions. Although the governor negotiated the tax increase, she declined to sign the budget. Instead, she used a legal technique and let the budget become law without her signature on September 8, 2009 (Connecticut Office of Fiscal Analysis 2009).

The budget contains various tax increases, including raising PIT rates from 5% to 6.5% for high-income earners and imposing a tax surcharge of 10% on corporations with over $100 million annual gross revenue. This is the first time that Connecticut has raised its income tax since the adoption of this tax in 1991.

More Tax Increases in 2011, 2015, and 2017

Even if the 2009 tax increases brought in $797 million additional tax revenues or nearly $1 billion of revenue if fees and other sources were included, Connecticut continued to experience a fiscal crisis. As Table 4.7 shows, OFA projected deep budget gaps, one of the worst in the nation, for each of the future fiscal years. The actual revenue shortages were even greater because the state consistently ended several fiscal years in the red. Economic recovery was slower in Connecticut than in the nation and the region, and the high unemployment rates persisted.

In 2010, Daniel Malloy was elected as governor. This is the first time Connecticut had a Democratic governor in 20 years, and the state legislature had a supermajority of Democrats. In his proposed FY 2012–FY 2013 Biennial Budget, Governor Malloy outlined a balanced approach to address the state's fiscal challenges by reducing half of the budgetary gap through program cuts and the other by tax changes (Malloy 2012). He also pointed to the large amount of unpaid state's long-term liabilities, including the state pension obligations for state employees and teachers. "The state's long-term liabilities have also grown to crushing levels through short-sighted neglect" (Malloy 2012, p. 9). For instance, the state employee pension was less than 43% funded, and unfunded liabilities were $11.7 billion as of June 2010. Governor Malloy warned other lawmakers that Connecticut could no longer ignore this daunting fiscal challenge. "If left unchanged, the state's contributions to the retirement fund would reach unsustainable levels—levels that the governor believes no administration will be able to honor" (Malloy 2012, p. 9).

Working with his fellow Democratic lawmakers, Governor Malloy was able to push through a $1.8 billion tax increase, the largest tax increase in Connecticut State history. This included a $1.4 billion increase from the state's three major taxes and $408 million from the healthcare provider tax. Among the changes, the law increased the number of marginal rates and tax brackets from three (3%, 5%, and 6.5%) to six (3%, 5%, 5.5%, 6%, 6.5%, and 6.7%), raised the sales tax from 6.0% to 6.25%, and extended sales tax to a long list of items and services. Additional changes included the elimination of several sales tax exemptions, raising the CIT surcharge from 10% to 20%, and extending the surcharge for two years (see Appendix C for specific information.).

During his re-election campaign in 2014, Governor Malloy pledged that the period of repeated deficits and tax increases was over. He was right to pursue a balanced approach to address the large budget deficits and made a great effort to tackle the state's unpaid long-term debt. However, the fiscal situation did not improve. Two weeks after his reelection, his Budget Director, Ben Barnes, declared that Connecticut had entered a "permanent state of fiscal crisis" (Phaneuf 2017b, p. 1). The projected budget deficits continue to be high. The state remains one of the most indebted states in the nation.

The year 2015 was a turbulent year. It started with a projected budget deficit of $2.7 billion for the upcoming fiscal years—FY 2016 and FY 2017. Governor Malloy proposed to reduce spending and increase revenue. The revenue measures included extending current levels of corporate surcharges and postponing certain scheduled tax cuts and sunset dates (Malloy 2015). Since these measures would not result in tax increases relative to existing taxes, Governor Malloy did not label them as tax increases. The final budget that the state legislature approved in June 2015 included $806 million in additional revenue, the second largest tax increase after that of 2011. The legislation did increase the top PIT rate from 6.7% to 6.9% and created a new top rate of 6.99%.

Yet, tax revenue collections were low. "In November 2015, OFA projected a fiscal deficiency of $552 million for FY 2017", growing to $963.2 million in a few months (Connecticut Office of Fiscal Analysis 2017, p. 1). Business communities also complained about the tax burden from these changes. A special legislative session was called to address both the deficits and tax burden on businesses. As a result, the legislature provided tax relief measures to reduce businesses' tax-related burdens (Bigger, Casella, Lieberman, and Schatz 2015).

The budgetary process in 2017 was even more difficult and messier, clearly showcasing the magnitude of Connecticut's fiscal troubles. Malloy told the lawmakers that "The state [was] fac[ing] a daunting scenario of slow-growing revenues to support fast-growing fixed costs, particularly pension and health care costs" (Malloy 2017, p. 8). Given the large projected budget shortages, revenue increase seemed inevitable, but lawmakers tried hard to avoid that. There was an increasing concern that the tax hikes would hurt economic growth and lead to the out-migration of the wealthy (Bennett, 2018). Republicans had used tax hikes as a campaign strategy to gain more seats in the state House and Senate. At the same time, lawmakers also tried to avoid further cuts of aid to cities and towns.

In that Spring, Democrats, with their slim majority in the state House and Senate, could not reach a consensus on a new budget. When they reached out to the Republicans for a bipartisan proposal, the Republicans agreed but had one condition: excluding Governor Malloy—a lame-duck Democrat who had an uneasy relation with legislators in his second term—from the budget talk (Phaneuf 2024).

With the budget gap remaining wide and tax measures off the table, legislators could not balance the budget when the regular legislation session ended in early June, nor even after autumn came (Phaneuf 2024). Finally, in the middle of November 2017, four and half months after the start of FY 2018, a budget was enacted (Connecticut Office of Fiscal Analysis 2018b).

The adopted budget eliminated the large deficits without raising income or sales tax rates but reduced numerous income tax credits, enacted healthcare provider tax hikes, increased fees and tobacco taxes, and other revenue sources, which was worth roughly $500 million per year for the biennium. Lawmakers also drew $87.5 million per year from three energy conservation programs and offered a seventh amnesty program to tax delinquents since 1990. Again, the budget tightened social service safety net programs (Phaneuf, Thomas, and Pazniokas 2017).

Toward the end of the budget battle, the lawmakers, who were desperate to find ways to reduce the state's fiscal instability, enacted several caps—critics called them "fiscal restraints' while supporters dubbed them "fiscal guardrails." These measures include "volatility adjustments" and "revenue caps." The former attempts to capture tax receipts from two traditional volatile sources. One source is quarterly income tax payments, mainly from capital gains, dividends, and other investment incomes that are closely tied to the performance of the stock market. The other source is quarterly filings by certain partnerships, limited liability corporations, and other business entities that do not have to pay the state's corporation tax. Under the arrangement, once the total revenue from the two sources reaches $3.1 billion, any excess must be deposited into the state's rainy-day fund, and when the rainy-day fund reaches its legal limit at 15% of annual operating expenses, the funds are used to pay for pension debt. The threshold of $3.1 billion was chosen simply because it was the amount in 2017. The "revenue cap" stipulates that annual appropriations cannot exceed 98.75% of projected revenues. There must be a 1.25% cushion to offset cost overruns (Phaneuf 2024).

The Impact of the Tax Actions on State Fiscal Stability

Connecticut lawmakers made a series of major tax reforms during 2009–2017, overhauling both the major tax systems and other taxes as well. Appendix C lists most of the specific tax actions. Among the three states under examination, the tax reforms in Connecticut were relatively comprehensive and far-reaching, not only raising major tax rates but also expanding their bases. This is especially true for the 2011 and 2015 tax reforms that covered the major taxes, tobacco tax, and health provider taxes. Lawmakers not only raised rates for the PIT, CIT, and sales and use tax (SUT) but also expanded the SUT base by extending existing rates to new products, services, and entities; and eliminating, reducing, or limiting tax credits and deductions.

These tax increase packages generated sizable revenue (see Appendix C). The $1.8 billion tax increase in 2011 was considered the largest in Connecticut's state history. The $806 million tax increase in 2015 was the largest among all the states in that year (NCSL 2012; 2016–2019). Without these tax measures, Connecticut would not have been able to balance its budget, or the cuts to essential services such as public education and safety net programs would have been even deeper.

It is also true that even with tax increases, the state was still in fiscal crisis. Critics say tax increases created a less competitive business environment and, therefore, could not generate the amount of tax revenue they promised. This assertion is debatable. As will be discussed shortly, significant legacy costs played a major role in perpetuating state fiscal crisis and influencing the state's economic climate.

Connecticut also retained many tax breaks and enacted new ones in its major tax systems. Table 4.8 shows that during FY 2009–FY 2018, the number of tax expenditures for SUT and CIT were reduced. The dollar amount for CIT breaks has also declined, although the values for sales tax have increased. Overall, the reforms during 2009 and 2017, by adjusting major tax rates and expanding the tax bases, helped stabilize the state tax system in the years to come.

The fiscal situation in Connecticut started to improve after FY 2018. According to an analysis by the Pew Charitable Trusts, by mid-2018, Connecticut was among the leaders in the nation in terms of tax revenue growth, with 16.3% higher than its pre-recession peak after adjustments to inflation (Phaneuf 2019b). This was impressive growth, even though some of this was due to a one-time

TABLE 4.8 Connecticut Tax Expenditure in Select Years

Tax Type	FY 2009		FY 2018	
	Quantity	*Dollar Amount ($million)*	*Quantity*	*Dollar Amount ($million)*
PIT	11	517.0	15	373.1
CIT	64	556.2	23	338.5
SUT	89	2568.4	68	3,928.7

Source: Connecticut Office of Fiscal Analysis (2008, 2018a).

factor—the change in federal tax law. In recent years, Connecticut has seen budget surpluses of $1.8 billion a year on average. Various factors explain this budgetary improvement, including the booming stock market, COVID-19 fiscal relief funds, and the fiscal restraints imposed on the state government in 2017 that forced the state to cap spending and reserve volatile revenue. However, the tax reforms in the 2010s that broadened the tax base and raised rates did the heavy lifting and allowed Connecticut to transition toward a fiscally stable environment (Phaneuf 2024).

Legacy Cost and Other Challenges to Connecticut Fiscal Stability

Connecticut still faces important challenges that threaten its long-term fiscal stability. The challenges derive from several sources. Some are related to the tax system. For instance, the tax system is still filled with exemptions and credits. There are also the concerns that high tax rates might reduce state competitiveness and tie tax revenue closely to a small group of taxpayers (i.e., high-income earners). The heavy reliance on income tax (51% of state revenue) also makes the system vulnerable to economic cycles. These are the same issues as those discussed under the millionaire tax earlier.

In addition to these tax-structure-related issues, Connecticut is facing other challenges to its fiscal stability. The most noticeable is its legacy costs that continue to impose daunting costs on the state. Additionally, the fragmented local government structure also imposes a heavy burden on the state to provide financial assistance.

High Legacy Costs

Connecticut has long-term spending issues. They illustrate well how structural issues on the spending side can threaten its fiscal stability and sustainability. As stated by Greenblatt, "Long blessed with a disproportionate number of high-income residents, the state has entertained lavish spending habits for decades"

TABLE 4.9 Connecticut Total Liability as of June 16, 2016 (in $billion)

G.O. Debt	$17.4
Non-G.O. Debt	$10.6
Unfunded Other Post-employment Benefits (OPEB)	$21.9
Unfunded Pension	$33.8
State Employees	$20.4
Teachers	$13.1
Judicial	$0.2
Others	$1.9
Total	$85.58

Source: Connecticut Commission on Fiscal Stability and Economic Growth (2018).

(Greenblatt 2017, p. 1), yet it omitted adequate payment for pension plans, other post-employment benefits, and infrastructure maintenance. Connecticut is considered one of the most indebted states in the nation. The unpaid liabilities always existed, but the amount exploded during the Great Recession and has overshadowed the state's finance ever since. Connecticut Commission on Fiscal Stability and Economic Growth (2018) estimated that the total debt and unfunded liabilities were approximately $85.5 billion as of June 2016 (see Table 4.9).

Connecticut's bond-debt burden, measured as a share of personal income, was the third highest among all states, according to a 2016 report by the Pew Charitable Trust. The ratio of debt service to state revenue was 13%, the highest in the nation (Connecticut Commission on Fiscal Stability and Economic Growth 2018).

For the retirees' healthcare benefits, the state did not save anything before 2009. Malloy inherited $19 billion in retiree healthcare obligations from the previous administrations. Because of medical inflation and the increasing number of state employees, the costs grew exponentially. According to a study conducted back in 2010, the state would pay more than $1.15 billion annually in the late 2010s, and by 2032, the bill would be quadrupled to $4.4 billion (Phaneuf 2017b).

Although lawmakers promised good pensions for state employees and public-school teachers, Connecticut saved very little between 1939 and the mid-1980s. Partially as a response to this situation, Connecticut adopted a PIT in 1991. However, when Connecticut had tax revenue, it failed to make adequate contributions as recommended. It also missed out on the good investment returns from the dot-com stock-market boom in the 1990s (Phaneuf 2024). As a result, Connecticut has become one of the worst underfunded pension plan state in the nation, only topped by Alaska and Illinois. The state's unfunded liabilities per capita were $14,746, while the national average was $4,383 in 2014 (Phaneuf 2017a).

A study by the Center for Retirement Research at Boston College in 2015 shows that, without any policy changes, the annual pension contribution to the State Employees Retirement System would increase to $6 billion in the early 2030s, and contributions for the public-school teacher retirement system would be another $6 billion (Phaneuf 2017b). Either of the payment plans would crush the state's fiscal stability. For this reason, Governor Malloy repeatedly stated that his budgets had to compensate for current program costs and the costs accrued from previous administrations. About 80% of the state retirement pension payments are to make up for the contributions that were not made or the investment returns that they missed in the past.

During Malloy's administration, through several rounds of negotiations, state employee unions made a series of concessions. The government also refinanced the state's pension obligations three times, shifting billions of dollars of debt to future taxpayers. As a result, the payment for the state employee pension became stabilized, meaning that funding spike in 2030 could be avoided. However, the state cannot restructure the teacher pension contribution because, in 2008, when it issued $2.3 billion of pension-obligation bonds to elevate the pension fund, it signed away any ability to defer contribution.

Table 4.10 shows that 10%–13% of the state general fund went to pension contributions between 2014 and 2020. In recent years, the share increased to 15%–28% when some of the state used some of its budget surplus to pay for the pension debt as required by the volatility adjustment. Even with such a large amount of constant annual contributions, Connecticut still has to continue the pension debt payment well into the 2040s and even the 2050s.

Overall, the Connecticut budget has been burdened with significant legacy costs, including pensions, retirees' healthcare obligations, and bonded debt. Their share in the annual budget increased from 12% in the mid-1990s to nearly 30% in 2017. The total estimated legacy cost was $88 billion in 2023, still

TABLE 4.10 Pensions Are Getting the Biggest Slice of CT's Fiscal Pie

Fiscal Year	Total Contributions (in $billion)	Percentage of General Fund Revenue	Fiscal Year	Total Contributions (in $billion)	Percentage of General Fund Revenue
2014	1.86	10.6%	2020	2.47	12.5%
2015	1.96	11.3%	2021	4.19	19.2%
2016	2.07	11.7%	2022	7.02	28.0%
2017	2.14	12.1%	2023	5.03	20.8%
2018	2.32	11.8%	2024 (est.)	3.48	15.1%
2019	2.46	11.9%			

Source: Phaneuf (2024, p. 12). Permission granted.

rendering Connecticut one of the most indebted states per capita in the nation (Phaneuf 2022b).

Burden from the Local Governments

Connecticut has no counties, and many functions that counties perform in other states, such as road and courthouse services, are performed by the state. Local governments in Connecticut only levy the property tax, so the state must provide them a large amount of aid (Greenblatt 2017). Municipal aid that includes funding for public education is the second largest state expenditure. Additionally, within the fragmented local government system, each of the 165 towns and cities guards its political independence, resulting in significant duplications of basic services and causing inefficiencies. All of these add to the state's fiscal burden.

In sum, the tax reforms Connecticut undertook during 2009–2017 expanded the tax base and raised the rates, placing the state on the right track for fiscal stability. However, the overhang of unfunded liabilities and debt threatens the state's fiscal stability and future economic growth. Despite increased pension funding over the years, the substantial debt costs are still pressing. Even if recent years have seen the state budgets end with record-setting surpluses, the same issues remain (Phaneuf 2023). The legacy costs will continue to consume 30% or more of general fund revenue. The population has increased in recent years, but many people work outside the state for high-paying jobs. The booming stock market can cover the underlying problems but does not remove the cause. Although the budget has witnessed large surpluses in the past few years, spending on social services, healthcare, and education programs, which were cut heavily in the previous years, remains low because the spending cap and volatility cap lead to mandatory savings (Phaneuf 2022a).

Conclusion

This chapter has examined tax policy changes in three states. Each case reveals how and why each state increased its major taxes. Each has its unique development, but they share commonalities in many other ways. First, the stories show that the dominant force contributing to the tax increases was the fiscal crisis. All the tax increases were enacted at a time when the states were facing severe revenue shortfalls. Second, other contextual factors also explain how these tax increases took place, including partisan control of the state legislature, leadership commitments, the framing of the debates, and the influence of stakeholders in the negotiation. In terms of the impact on fiscal stability, these states have made major tax reforms that generated needed revenues for states going through fiscal crises and even helped state finances turn around. Compared with California and New York, Connecticut's tax efforts were more comprehensive. Yet, these tax changes did not correct the structural issue, including tax base erosion and lack of source diversification. They were largely short-term fixes, and no systematic efforts have been made to expand the tax bases and diversify tax revenues. Furthermore, these states rely heavily on income tax and the financial/technological sector, making their tax systems still vulnerable to the economic cycle. While California and Connecticut implemented a system to capture volatile revenues (e.g., capital gains and bonuses) into a special fund, New York did not pursue any related actions.

Each story ends by discussing one specific issue that complicates the state's fiscal stability: voter initiatives in California, the millionaire tax in New York, and legacy costs in Connecticut. Although each issue is presented within the context of one specific state, its implications go to many states or states in general. The impact of voter initiatives discussed in California's case applies to half of the states where direct democracy is instituted and voters are allowed to decide tax policies through the ballot box. The legacy costs are not only present in Connecticut but in nearly all states. The discussion about restricted spending in Chapter 2 echoes this fiscal challenge. The issues regarding the millionaire tax, capital gain tax, and heavy reliance on income tax do not only trouble New York public finance but also California, Connecticut, and many other states that raised the top income tax. Just as the three states are still facing structural imbalance, states, in general, are also facing the structural imbalance. While it is difficult to restructure their revenue system, the key is to broaden the tax bases and diversify the revenue sources.

References

Bennett, Jared. 2018. "Connecticut is in Crisis – And Its Troubles Are Hardly Unique." *HuffPost*. (July 25).

Bigger, David O., Ray Cassella, Alan E. Lieberman, and Louis B. Schatz. 2015. "Connecticut Tax Developments 2015 – Legislative Session: Tax Increases and Mea Culpas." *Connecticut State & Local Tax Alert, Shipman & Goodwin LLP.* (December 29).

Boyd, Don. 2022. "State Tax Revenue Volatility and Its Impact on State Governments." *The Pew Charitable Trusts.* (June 30).

Bradley, William. 2012. "How Jerry Brown Pulled Off the Big Prop Win" *Huffington Post*. www.huffingtonpost.com/william-bradley/jerry-brown-prop-30_b_2094749.html

California Budget Project. 2012. "What Would Proposition 30 Mean for California?" *Budget Brief.* (September).

California Commission on the 21st Century Economy. 2009. *Report on the Commission on the 21st Century Economy*. (September).

California Department of Finance (DF). *California Tax Expenditure Reports* (series) www.dof.ca.gov/Forecasting/Economics/Tax_Expenditure_Reports/index.html

California Department of Finance. No Date. *2009 Budget Act.*
California State Controller Betty T. Yee and the Controller's Council of Economic Advisors on Tax Reform. 2016. *Comprehensive Tax Reform in California: A Contextual Framework.* (June).
Chen, William. 2016. "What has Proposition 30 Meant for California?" *California Budget Project.* https://calbudgetcenter.org/resources/what-has-proposition-30-meant-for-california/ (September).
Chernick, Howard, Cordelia Reimers, and Jennifer Tennant. 2014. "Tax Structure and Revenue Instability: The Great Recession and the States." *IZA Journal of Labor Policy,* 3: 1–22.
Confessore, Nicholas. 2009. "Albany Agrees on a Plan to Raise Taxes on Top Earners." *New York Times.* (March 28).Connecticut Commission on Fiscal Stability and Economic Growth. 2018. *Connecticut Commission on Fiscal Stability and Economic Growth: Final Report.* (March). *https://files.schoolstatefinance.org/hubfs/Resources/ Commission%20on%20Fiscal%20Stability%20Report.pdf.*
Connecticut Office of Fiscal Analysis. 2008. *Connecticut Tax Expenditure Report.*
Connecticut Office of Fiscal Analysis. 2009. *Connecticut State Budget: 2009–2011: A Summary of Revenue Appropriations and Bonds Authorized by the General Assembly.* (October).
Connecticut Office of Fiscal Analysis. 2016. *Connecticut State Budget: FY 16 & FY 17 Budget.*
Connecticut Office of Fiscal Analysis. 2017. *Connecticut State Budget: FY 17 Revision.*
Connecticut Office of Fiscal Analysis. 2018a. *Connecticut Tax Expenditure 2018.* (February).
Connecticut Office of Fiscal Analysis. 2018b. *Connecticut State Budget: FY 18 & FY 19 Budget.*
Connecticut Office of Fiscal Analysis. 2022. *Connecticut Tax Expenditure 2022.* (February).
Connecticut State Comptroller. 2009. "Wyman Says State Ends Fiscal Year with $925.9 million Deficit." (September 1). https://osc.ct.gov/public/pressrl/2009/september01.htm
Cuomo, Andrew M. 2011. *State of New York: 2011-12 Executive Budget Briefing Book.*
Dayen, David. 2013. *Back from the Brink: Progressives have Achieved the Impossible: They Balanced California's Books.* www.newrepublic.com/article/112257/california-balances-its-budget-how-progressives-balanced-books
DeCastro, Bob. 2012. "Voters Pass Proposition 30; Proposition 38 defeated." *Los Angeles Local News.* www.myfoxla.com/story/20028238/california-voters-pass-Propositionositionosition-30-tax-increase-for-education
Division of the Budget of State of New York. 2009. "Division of the Budget Releases Enacted Budget Financial Plan." (August 28).
Division of the Budget of State of New York. 2010. "Division of the Budget Releases Enacted Budget Financial Plan." (August 20).
Gordon, Tracy, Megan Randall, Eugene Steuerle, and Aravind Boddupalli. 2019. "Fiscal Democracy in the States: How Much Spending Is on Autopilot?" *Urban Institute.* (July).
Greenblatt, Alan. 2017. "How Did America's Richest State Become Such a Fiscal Mess?" *Governing Magazine.* (August 29).

Kaplan, Thomas. 2011. "Cuomo Pushes New Tax Rates for Big Earners." *New York Times.* (December 4).

Kitson, Kayla. 2020. "Tax Breaks: California's $60 Billion Loss: High-Income Households and Corporations Benefit the Most from California's Tax Breaks." *California Budget & Policy Center.* (January).

Malloy, Dannel P. 2011. *Fiscal Year 2012–2013 Biennial Budget Address.* (February 16).

Malloy, Dannel P. 2012. *2012-2013 Biennial Budget.* https://portal.ct.gov/OPM/Bud-Budgets/20122013_BiennialBudget/2012_2013_Biennial_Budget_Home

Malloy, Dannel P. 2015. *Budget Address for the FY 2016 and FY 2017 Biennium.* (February 18).

Malloy, Dannel P. 2017. "Budget Address for the FY 2018 and 2019 Biennium" (February 8).

McMahon, E. J. 2012a. "The Tax Reform That Wasn't." *Manhattan Institute and Its Empire Center for New York State Policy.*

McMahon, E. J. 2012b. "Cuomo's Pivot." *City Journal,* www.city-journal.org/html/cuomo%E2%80%99s-pivot-13457.html

"Millionaires Tax Supporters Launch Grassroots Campaign to Pass Proposition 30." *Reclaim California Future.*

Nagourney, Adam. 2011. "In California, Asking Voters to Raise Taxes." *New York Times.* (November 30).

National Conference of State Legislature (NCSL). 2009. *State Tax Actions 2008: Special Fiscal Report.* Denver, Colorado: National Conference of State Legislature.

National Conference of State Legislature (NCSL). 2012. *State Tax Actions 2011: Special Fiscal Report.* Denver, Colorado: National Conference of State Legislature.

National Conference of State Legislature (NCSL) (2016–2019). *State Tax Actions Database.* https://www.ncsl.org/fiscal/state-tax-actions-database State Tax Actions Database.

New York State Department of Taxation and Finance. No Date. "Corporate Tax Reform." Corporate Tax Reform (ny.gov).

New York State Department of Taxation and Finance, Division of the Budget. 2008 *Annual Report on New York State Tax Expenditures.* www.tax.ny.gov/research/stats/statistics/annual-tax-expenditures.htm

New York State Department of Taxation and Finance, Division of the Budget, 2018 www.tax.ny.gov/research/stats/statistics/annual-tax-expenditures.htm

New York State Tax Reform and Fairness Commission. 2013. *New York State Tax Reform and Fairness Commission Final Report.*

Oliff, Phil, Chris Mai, and Vincent Palacios. 2012. "State Continue to Feel Recession's Impact." *Center on Budget and Policy Priorities.* (June 27).

Onishi, Norimitsu. 2012. "Californians Back Taxes to Avoid Education Cuts." *New York Times.* (November).

Paterson, David A. 2008. *2009-10 New York State Executive Budget.* (December 16).

Paterson, David A. 2009. *New York State: 2009-10 Enacted Budget Financial Plan.* (April 28).

Phaneuf, Keith M. 2017a. "A Legacy of Debt: Whether Taxing or Cutting, CT Faces Painful, Contentious Fiscal Future." *CT Mirror.* (February 1).

Phaneuf, Keith M. 2017b. "A Legacy of Debt: Connecticut Standing on Its Own Fiscal Cliff." *CT Mirror.* (January 30).

Phaneuf, Keith M. 2019a. "Has CT Broken Its Cycle of Budget Deficits?" *CT Mirror*. https://ctmirror.org/2019/08/07/has-ct-broken-its-cycle-of-budget-deficits/ (August 7).
Phaneuf, Keith M. 2019b "CT's Budget Reserve on the Brink of Hitting Unprecedented High." *CT Mirror*. https://ctmirror.org/2019/08/01/cts-budget-reserve-on-the-brink-of-hitting-unprecedented-high/ (August 1).
Phaneuf, Keith M. 2022a. "CT's Government Was Once Broke. Is It Now Holding Too Much Cash?" *CT Mirror*. (March 20). https://ctmirror.org/2022/03/20/is-ct-holding-too-much-cash-in-its-rainy-day-fund/
Phaneuf, Keith M. 2022b. "Best, or Worst, of Times? The Battle to Frame CT's Finances Is Underway: Long-term Debt Expands Even as CT's Budget Surpluses Reach Historical Levels." *CT Mirror*. (March 13).
Phaneuf, Keith M. 2023. "Is CT's Budget Boom Over? Report Likely to Show Eroding Revenue." *CT Mirror*. (November 9).
Phaneuf, Keith M. 2024. "A Question of Volatility: Are Connecticut's Fiscal Guardrails in the Right Place?" *CT Mirror*. (January 28).
Phaneuf, Keith M., Jacqueline R. Thomas, & Mark Pazniokas. 2017. "After 117-day Marathon, Senate Passes Bipartisan Budget." *CT Mirror*. (October 26).
Rafool, Mandy and Todd Haggerty. 2011. *State Tax Actions 2010: Special Fiscal Report*. Denver, Colorado: National Conference of State Legislature.
Rafool, Mandy. 2013. *State Tax Actions 2012: Special Fiscal Report*. Denver, Colorado: National Conference of State Legislature.
Rafool, Mandy. 2014. *State Tax Actions 2013: Special Fiscal Report* Denver, Colorado: National Conference of State Legislature.
Rafool, Mandy. 2015. *State Tax Actions 2014: Special Fiscal Report*. Denver, Colorado: National Conference of State Legislature.
Rell, Jodi. 2009. "FY 2010-FY 2011 Biennium Budget."
Rubin, Marilyn M. and Donald J. Boyd. 2013. *New York State Business Tax Credits: Analysis and Evaluation: A Report Prepared for the New York State Tax Reform and Fairness Commission*. (November).
Taylor, Mac. 2015. *The 2016-17 Budget: California's Fiscal Outlook*. California Legislative Analyst's Office. (November).
Taylor, Mac. 2016. *The 2017-18 Budget: California's Fiscal Outlook*. California Legislative Analyst's Office. (November).
Taylor, Mac. 2018a. *The 2019-20 Budget: California's Fiscal Outlook*. California Legislative Analyst's Office. (November).
Taylor, Mac. 2018b. "The Great Recession and California Recovery." *California Legislative Analyst*. (December)
Waisanen, Bert and Todd Haggerty. (2010). *State Tax Actions 2009: Special Fiscal Report*. National Conference of State Legislatures. (February).
Walczak, Jared. 2020. "Taxes and New York's Fiscal Crisis: Evaluating Revenue Proposals to Close the State Budget Gap." *Tax Foundation*. (December 8).

5
THE GREAT RECESSION AND TAX CUTS

Stories in Two States

Introduction

This chapter discusses Kansas and Missouri's tax-cut efforts and their fiscal impacts. During the Great Recession and its aftermath, Kansas and Missouri encountered large revenue shortfalls, although not as bad as New York, California, or Connecticut. In terms of the percentage of state general revenue, their revenue gaps were bigger than the national averages in some years (see Table 5.1).

In the post-Great Recession era, the national economy was on a slow recovery, and the states were still facing the same structural imbalance and fiscal uncertainty that jeopardized their finance. Those who advocate for tax cuts argue that a tax cut would help stimulate the economy and would pay for itself. There may never be a way to verify the argument, but what happened in Kansas and Missouri shows the argument was not true. While tax cuts are always politically popular, the lesson these cases offer is that decisions to cut taxes should be cautious and should consider the long-term fiscal impact.

Kansas Experiment: Big Income Tax Cuts and the Big Fiscal Hole

During the Great Recession, Kansas relied heavily on spending cuts to address the severe revenue shortfalls when it could have utilized a more balanced approach by including new revenue sources. When the recession hit, Governor Kathleen Sebelius decided to resolve the budget gap "in a realistic way without raising taxes" (Sebelius 2008, p. 1). For the first three years and the next few years,

DOI: 10.4324/9781003494324-5

TABLE 5.1 Budget Shortfalls for Kansas and Missouri: FY 2009–FY 2013

FY	Total Shortfall (in $million) KS	MO	Total Shortfall as a Percentage of General Fund Spending KS	MO	National Average
2009	186	542	2.9%	6.0%	15.2%
2010	1,800	1700	33.9%	22.7%	29.0%
2011	570	730	10.1%	9.4%	19.9%
2012	492	704	8.1%	8.8%	11.3%
2013	n/a	800	n/a%	10.0%	9.5%

Source: Oliff, Mai, and Palacios (2012).

TABLE 5.2 Kansas Tax Changes during 2008–2018 (in $millions)

Year	Personal Income Tax	Corporate Income Tax	Sales and Use Tax	health care Related	Tobacco	Alcohol	Motor/ Fuel
2008	−2.0	−47.4	−2.6	0.0	0.0	0.0	0.0
2009	3.0	10.2	13.7	0.0	0.0	0.0	0.0
2010	−15.0	4.5	339.1	0.0	0.0	0.0	0.0
2011	−1.5	−4.5	8.9	0.0	0.0	0.0	0.0
2012	−249.2	0.0	0.0	0.0	0.0	0.0	0.0
2013	59.4	0.0	−64.4	0.0	0.0	0.0	0.0
2014	−5.0	0.0	−2.0	0.0	0.0	0.0	0.0
2015	149.8	0.0	164.2	0.0	0.0	0.0	0.0
2016	0.0	0.0	0.0	0.0	40.0	0.0	0.0
2017	582.0	0.0	0.0	0.0	0.0	0.0	0.0
2018	633.0	0.0	−3.3	0.0	−1.6	0.0	0.0

Source: Rafool (2013, 2014, 2015); NCSL (2012, 2017, 2018).

Kansas relied heavily on budget cuts and fund transfers. The state's financial situation became dire in FY 2010 when the revenue shortage amounted to 33.9% of Kansas' general revenue, and the year ended with only $875.05 cash balance in its general fund. To address the fiscal crisis, the lawmakers decided to raise the sales tax by one cent in 2010 (see Table 5.2 and Appendix D).

During his gubernatorial election campaign in 2010, Sam Brownback called for fiscal responsibility and economic prosperity as ways to solve the state's long-term budget problems (Brownback 2012). Central to his policy agenda was cutting the income tax, and he successfully pushed it through in the 2012 and 2013 legislative sessions. As a matter of fact, his tax cut was considered the biggest ever enacted by any state in percentage terms, and many tax-cut proponents deemed it a fiscal model for other states to follow. Before examining his tax reform, readers may also notice from Table 5.2 the personal income tax increases in 2015, 2017, and 2018. The increase in 2015 reflected the slowing down of Brownback's tax-cut implementation. The tax increases in 2017 and 2018 were at least a partial reversal of Brownback's tax cut by state legislators when the state was fiscally collapsing.

Governor Brownback's Tax Reform Package

Governor Brownback's tax reform package contained several elements. First, it eliminated the top tax bracket of 6.45% for the individual income tax. Thus, those who make $1 million would be taxed at the same rate as those making $30,001 annually (see Table 5.3). Eliminating the top tax bracket equaled almost a 30% rate cut for the high-income earners. Second, the plan would also gradually reduce tax rates for the remaining two brackets and raise standard deductions. As the income tax generated approximately 50% of state general revenue at the time, the rate cuts to the income tax contributed to 70% of the revenue loss (Kansas Center for Economic Growth, No Date b).

Third, Governor Brownback's tax plan contained a "March to Zero" provision with the intention to eliminate the income tax. Under this provision, state government spending after 2018 was capped at a 2.5% annual nominal growth rate regardless of the demand for public services. Any higher growth rate with general fund revenue would be used to buy down income tax rates for the next year until all individual income taxes were eliminated. At that point in time, the formula would be applied to corporate income tax rates until they were erased (Leachman and Mai 2014). There are several issues with this provision. Government spending is influenced by many uncontrollable forces, such as population growth and healthcare cost increases. Yet, this mechanism did not take these into consideration and did not allow adjustment for inflation, which often surpasses the 2.5% threshold. Furthermore, no exception is given to the economic recovery time when the government needs to pick up its spending.

TABLE 5.3 Kansas Personal Income Tax Rates

Taxable Income	Tax Rate in 2012	Brownback's Tax Policy	Rate Set in 2017
$0–30,000	3.5%	2.6%	3.1%
$30,001–60,000	6.25%	4.6%	5.25%
Over 60,000	6.45%	4.6%	5.7%

Source: Kansas Center for Economic Growth (No Date a). Permission granted.

Fourth, the signature feature of Governor Brownback's tax-cut plan involved the exemption of all income taxes for pass-through businesses (e.g., limited liability companies or LLCs, and other pass-through business owners). He argued that this would bring in additional business activities and, therefore, facilitate job growth in the state. This pass-through income tax cut was an innovation by Governor Brownback, and no other states had utilized it. To compensate for his tax cuts, Governor Brownback eliminated certain tax breaks that could have helped the average citizens. This included child and dependent care credits, medical deductions, mortgage interests, and property tax deductions (Leachman and Mai 2014).

As the largest income tax cut a state had ever enacted by then, Governor Brownback called it a "red state model" that would act "like a shot of adrenaline into the heart of the Kansas economy" (Leachman 2017a, p. 1). The tax cuts were enacted in FY 2012, and implementation started in January 2013.

Fiscal Impacts of Tax Cuts

The fiscal impact on Kansas was immediate and devastating. The estimated revenue losses provided by Kansas' non-partisan legislative Research Department were $231 million in FY 2013 and $802 million in FY 2014. By 2019, the cumulative revenue loss would exceed $5 billion (Leachman and Mai 2014). The loss was substantial for the state's $6 billion annual general fund budget.

Table 5.4 shows the state's major tax collections during FY 2011–FY 2017. Kansas' personal income tax revenue in current dollars declined by 24% in FY 2014 and again by 1.3% in FY 2016. The corporate income tax witnessed slow growth rates in FY 2014–FY 2015 and then experienced a double-digit decline in FY 2016–FY 2017. Total state tax revenue growth was either very minimal or negative. For instance, total tax revenues declined by 11.1% in FY 2014 and again in FY 2017 by 0.2%.

In the years that followed the tax cuts, the state of Kansas was constantly in the national news because of its financial crisis: severe revenue shortages, deep program cuts, twice bond downgrading, and still billions of dollars of budget gaps (Leachman 2017a). The immediate and tremendous personal income tax revenue decline after the tax cut led to a revenue shortage of $688 million in FY 2014, $293 million more than initial predictions. The state government was able to cut spending by $152 million. The remainder of the fiscal gaps were filled by using reserves and reducing itemized deductions. A planned state sales tax cut was also delayed.

For FY 2015, deficits were even greater, with estimated revenue shortfalls of $1 billion for the biennial budget of FY 2015 and FY 2016 (Copper 2014). The state government had to tap into its fund balance to "fix" the problem. As

TABLE 5.4 Kansas General Fund Revenues, General Fund Expenditure, and Ending Balance (in current $million)

Tax Source	Fiscal Year						
	2011	2012	2013	2014	2015	2016	2017[a]
PIT	2,709	2,908	2,931	2,218	2,277	2,248	2,305
% Change over the Previous Year	12.1%	7.3%	0.8%	(24.3%)	2.7%	(1.3%)	2.5%
CIT	224	284	371	399	417	354	270
% Change	0.0%	26.5%	30.5%	7.6%	4.5%	(15.0%)	(23.9%)
Sales Tax	1,965	2,136	2,184	2,102	2,132	2,273	2,272
Use Tax	287	325	340	344	351	384	380
% Change	21.3%	9.3%	2.6%	(3.1%)	1.6%	7%	(0.02%)
Total Tax Revenue	5,693	6,160	6,333	5,632	5,717	5,758	5,745
% Change	14.2%	8.2%	2.8	(11.1%)	1.5%	0.7%	(0.2%)
Total Receipts	5,882.1	6,412.8	6,341.1	5,653.2	5,928.8	6,171.3	6,326.0
Expenditures	5,666.6	6,098.1	6,134.8	5,982.8	6,237.0	6,202.6	6,270.4
Ending Balance	188.3	503.0	709.3	379.7	71.5	40.2	95.8
% Gen. Fund Expenditure	3.3%	8.2%	11.6%	6.3%	1.1%	0.6%	1.5%
Rainy-day Fund[b]	0	0	0	0	0	0	0

Source: Comparison Report: The Governor's Budget Report with Legislative Authority (FY 2014, FY 2015, FY 2017).

[a] All values are actual valuations except FY 2017. FY 2017 was the estimated value.
[b] The state of Kansas did not establish a budget stabilization fund at that time.

shown in Table 5.4, the end balance after FY 2013 declined significantly. In 2016, Kansas was one of four states with little end balance, and it had almost depleted all its reserves. Although Kansas is legally required to maintain at least 7.5% of total expenditures as its year-end fund balance, the only years it could do this were FY 2012 and FY 2013 before the implementation of the tax cuts.

In FY 2016, revenue shortages grew even bigger, and cutbacks on programs were difficult. Kansas raised its sales tax rate from 6.15% to 6.5% (see Appendix D), making the state the eighth highest sales tax rate in the nation. The cigarette tax rate was increased from 79 cents per pack to $1.29 per pack, and a new tax was imposed on e-cigarettes. The state also eliminated several deductions in the individual income tax and implemented the one-time tax amnesty program.

In FY 2017, Governor Brownback proposed adding another dollar to the cigarette tax. There was also a proposal "to securitize funds from the tobacco

Master Settlement Agreement, which would dry up a future revenue stream to solve this year's budget problem" (Drenkard and Henchman 2017a).

As the state continued to be in a financial crisis and as its reserves were depleting, two major bond agencies, Standard and Poor's and Moody's, downgraded Kansas' bond twice, in 2014 and again in 2016. The downgrading made it more costly for the state to invest in infrastructure projects (Copper 2014; Leachman 2017a).

The tax cuts were not only fiscally unsustainable but also harmful to the state's long-term economic vitality and irresponsible for future generations. For all the years since the beginning of the Great Recession, Kansas relied heavily on cuts to balance its budget. Schools and pension programs were drastically underfunded, infrastructure repairs were delayed, and state aid to local governments and was cut. For instance, cuts for public schools amounted to $358 million between 2009 and 2014 and $154.5 million between 2015 and 2017. As a result, the Kansas Supreme Court in 2018 ruled that the funding for public schools was inadequate and ordered the state government to increase its funding (Kansas Center for Economic Growth 2015). By the late 2010s, Kansas' general fund spending per capita was lower than its FY 2008–FY 2009 level, and its annual general fund expenditure growth was lower than the national average for all years except FY 2012 and FY 2015 (see Table 5.5).

Table 5.6 shows the growth rates for state general fund expenditures. Over the years, funding for each major function has either reduced, stagnated, or only increased slightly. There was a serious need to expand Medicaid funding and increase contributions to the Kansas Public Employees Retirement System. Funding is also needed for corrections, higher education, the judicial branch, state employee salaries, and other state services.

The tax cuts also rendered the Kansas tax system significantly regressive. The wealth gap between the top and low incomes widened as the tax cuts substantially benefitted the high-income families while the increase in sales and cigarette taxes imposed greater burdens on lower-income families. For instance, in 2015, the lowest 20% of the income bracket (e.g., those with less than $20,000) bore an

TABLE 5.5 Kansas General Fund Nominal Percentage Expenditure Changes: FY 2012–FY 2018

Fiscal Year	2012	2013	2014	2015	2016	2017	2018
Kansas	8.1	1.1	(2.2)	5.0	(2.0)	2.3	0.1
National Average	3.4	4.3	4.9	3.1	3.2	4.8%	1.0

Source: (Rafool 2013; 2014; 2015; NCSL 2012; 2017; 2018).

TABLE 5.6 Kansas General Fund Expenditures during FY 2014–FY 2017 (in $million)

Expenditure	FY 2014	FY 2015	FY 2016	FY 2017	% Change FY 2014–FY 2017
Aid to K-12 Schools/KPERS	2,951.8	3,105.4	3,071.6	3,152.4	6.8%
Higher Edu.	761.9	779.9	752.6	753.1	(1%)
Human Services Caseloads	1,006.1	1,129.0	1,075.1	1,026.5	2%
KPERS State Employer Contribution	41.0	46.8	51.6	49.7	21.2%
Judiciary	96.5	97.4	96.0	99.3	2.9%
General Government	252.7	107.3	152.0	196.1	(29%)
Public Safety	383.9	388.5	370.2	382.7	(1%)
Agriculture and Natural Resources	16.4	16.9	14.1	14.5	(14%)
All Other Exp.	472.5	565.8	619.4	596.1	20.8%
Total Exp.	5,982.8	6,237.0	6,202.6	6,270.4	4.8%

Source: Brownback (2016). The last column is the author's calculation.

effective tax rate of 11.1%. Meanwhile, the top 1% of the income bracket (those with income over $439,000) only faced a 3.6% rate. Kansas was ranked as the ninth most unfair state and local tax system in the country (Kansas Center for Economic Growth, No Date b).

Rollback the Tax Cuts

The public and the legislators came to realize Kansas' experiment did not work, and tax cuts had to be rolled back. The tax cuts not only led to the financial crisis but also failed to create jobs, as Governor Brownback promised. Job growth over the years of 3.3% was one of the lowest in the nation while the national average at that time was 8.4% (Leachman 2017b). Politically, the flaw of the pass-through income cut was obvious. Average workers who earn wages started to question why they paid income tax when their bosses who owned the pass-through businesses did not.

In the 2017 legislative session, lawmakers passed Senate Bill 30 to terminate the tax cuts. Governor Brownback vetoed the bill, but the Republican-controlled legislature combined with Democrats had enough votes to override the veto.

Even Republican legislators realized that they had to roll back the tax cut to end the state budget crisis and invest in the future.

The new law contained the following major provisions: 1) restoring a top income tax bracket and adjusting the tax rates (see Table 5.3), 2) closing the LLC loopholes, 3) ending the "March to Zero" provision, and 4) restoring the child and dependent care credits and other important deductions to help the average citizens (Kansas Center for Economic Growth No Date a). The tax increases were projected to bring in an estimated revenue of $600 million annually for FY 2018 and FY 2019.

Lessons Learned

Kansas' story is a classic case where political ideology dictates the tenets of state tax policy. Governor Sam Brownback blamed income taxes for the state's population losses and the economic declines. He was determined to transform the state into "a fiscal conservative paradise" and promised to cut income taxes to bring in "astronomical jobs" everywhere in the state (Cillizza 2017, p. 1). His conservative views barred him from considering the situation from a more balanced and comprehensive perspective.

Kansas' failed experiment provides a good lesson for Kansas, other states, and the federal government. The experiences of Kansas show us once again that deep cuts to the income tax create large revenue losses. The large revenue losses undermined funding for public programs, including public education, universities, infrastructure, and community services. The main lesson is to be cautious with tax cuts and not count on the trickle-down effect. The tax cuts in Kansas did not lead to exceptional economic growth as promised, and there is no evidence that the cuts will improve the state's economic climate in the future (Leachman and Mai 2014; Mazerov 2018). The experiment also showed cutting income tax made the tax system more regressive.

Kansas' experiment has its special features that deserve extra attention. Specifically, the so-called pass-through exemption embedded in the income tax cut offers some important takeaways. In their testimony to the Kansas House Committee on Taxation, Scott Drenkard, the Director of State Projects for the Tax Foundation, and Joseph Henchman, the Executive Vice President of the National Taxpayers Union Foundation, stated that "the pass-through exemption encourages tax avoidance without generating desired growth" (Drenkard and Henchman 2017b, p.2). Since incomes for pass-through businesses are exempted, a person who used to make wages and pay income taxes can ask employers to turn them into an independent contractor or pass-through business. In 2012, when the tax cut was passed, 191,000 entities were estimated to qualify for the exemption. By 2015, the real claimants jumped to 393,814, more than twice the original number. This alone created an annual revenue loss of

$200-$300 million. In other words, this provision reduced the tax base when the reforms should have broadened the base. The presumed trickle-down effects did not happen because the provision did not generate new economic activities (Drenkard and Henchman 2017b). Therefore, Drenkard and Henchman (2017b) warned lawmakers not to include a pass-through provision in any tax reform to avoid serious fiscal consequences.

From a broader policy perspective of restoring state fiscal balance, Kansas' experiment illustrates that significant tax cuts further erode the state's fiscal health and stability. The income tax comprises over 50% of all revenue collected for the Kansas general fund in 2012. In the first year after Governor Brownback's tax cut, the revenue losses were more than all the revenue losses during the Great Recession combined. Eliminating the income tax through the "March to Zero" would greatly destabilize the state's finances. Instead of restoring viable revenue streams and replenishing program funding, tax cuts further undermined Kansas' capability to maintain basic public services.

While pushing for cut tax rates, Governor Brownback and other lawmakers did not make much effort to expand the tax bases. According to the data from the *Tax Expenditure Report* prepared by the Kansas Department of Revenue, the number of tax credits for the three major taxes remained the same or increased. In dollar amount, the total tax expenditure programs increased from $6,655 million in 2009 to $9,526 million in 2017 (Wagnon 2009; Burghart 2018). In addition, the exemption of all income taxes for pass-through businesses significantly undermines the income tax base, as stated earlier. Tax rate cuts coupled with a narrower tax base led to state fiscal instability.

Missouri's Story: Constant Income Tax Cuts and the Revenue Trigger

During the Great Recession and the years immediately after, Missouri faced constant and severe revenue shortages (see Table 5.1). To balance the budgets, the state legislature and Governor Nixon relied heavily on spending cuts, including cuts on core services (Ehresman 2009; Kruckemeyer and Blouin 2010; MBP 2010; Ehresman and Blouin 2011).

According to the Missouri Budget Project (MBP), part of Missouri's funding crisis was a revenue issue. Lawmakers enacted several tax reductions in the 1990s and 2000s along with increases in tax credits, resulting in the lowest revenue collections as a percentage of the state economy in 2011 over the past 25 years (Kruckemeyer and Gleason 2011). In the years following the Great Recession, and even during it, the Republican-controlled state legislature continued to push for another series of decade-long efforts to cut both personal income and corporate income taxes. Although it did not garner as much national attention as Kansas, Missouri's tax-cutting efforts in the aftermath of the Great Recession,

TABLE 5.7 Missouri Tax Changes during FY 2008–FY 2018 (in $millions)

Fiscal Year	Personal Income Tax	Corporate Income Tax	Sales and Use Tax	Health Related Tax	Tobacco Tax	Alcohol Tax	Motor/Fuel Tax
2008	0.0	0.0	–0.8	0.0	0.0	0.0	0.0
2009	0.0	–42.0	0.0	0.0	0.0	0.0	0.0
2010	0.0	0.0	0.0	0.0	0.0	0.0	0.0
2011	0.0	0.0	0.0	0.0	0.0	0.0	0.0
2012	0.0	0.0	0.0	0.0	0.0	0.0	0.0
2013	0.0	0.0	0.0	0.0	0.0	0.0	0.0
2014	0.0	–16.5	0.0	0.0	0.0	0.0	0.0
2015	0.0	–16.5	0.0	0.0	0.0	0.0	0.0
2016	–88.3	0.0	0.0	0.0	0.0	0.0	0.0
2017	–90.3	0.0	0.0	0.0	0.0	0.0	0.0
2018	–238.3	0.0	0.0	0.0	0.0	0.0	0.0

Source: Rafool (2013, 2014, 2015); NCSL (2012, 2017, 2018).

to a certain extent, resembled those pursued in Kansas. Missouri lawmakers reduced the top income tax rates and provided various tax credits. Table 5.7 shows the overall dollar impacts of these tax actions. Appendix E provides a detailed overview of these actions.

From 2008 to 2018, the only tax increase was a new tax imposed on medical marijuana with 4% on retail sales. Lawmakers made assertive and constant efforts to reduce personal and corporate income taxes. These efforts included phasing out the franchise tax by 2016, cutting corporate tax and personal income tax rates, creating pass-through business tax reductions, and adding more tax credits and deductions. The actions in 2014 and 2018 are particularly significant, with the 2018 tax reform deemed as the largest tax reduction in Missouri history.

Major Income Tax Cut Measures: SB 509 and Revenue Trigger

In 2013, the state legislature approved a broad tax-cut measure in their regular session, but Governor Nixon, a Democrat, vetoed it. In the 2014 session, the Republicans who controlled the General Assembly by a large margin pushed for a big income tax cut. Governor Nixon vetoed the measure again. However, this time, the legislature had enough votes to override his veto. The result was the passage of Senate Bill 509 (SB 509), which contains one of the biggest tax cuts in Missouri's history.

While continuing the state's tax-cut effort, SB 509 incorporates a revenue trigger that sets tax cuts in the future. The law states that when the net state general revenue collected in the previous year grows by more than $150 million over any of the three years prior to that, the individual income tax rate will be reduced from 6% to 5.5% in a period of five years at a 0.1% increment each time (Missouri Budget Project 2017a). The trigger threshold is not adjusted for inflation or population growth.

The law also provides a 25% income deduction for pass-through business owners using the same revenue trigger. The phase-in started in 2017. If the revenue threshold is met, these business owners can deduct 5% of their income from individual income tax. The increase to the deduction amount will be 5% each time when the trigger kicks until the 25% deduction is reached. It is important to emphasize that this pass-through tax cut mirrors the design used in Kansas. The new exemptions would incentivize businesses to transform their corporate structure to avoid paying state taxes. There could be more registered LLCs but no increase in economic activities (Missouri Budget Project 2017a).

The state official fiscal notes indicated that business tax deductions alone would cost $95.8 million annually, and the entire tax-cut package would cost $620 million annually after being fully implemented. Later, based on the updated data on reported business income, the MBP estimated higher costs would be exhibited (MBP 2017a; MBP 2017b).

2018 Tax cuts

In the 2018 legislative session, the Republican-controlled legislature started to pursue another round of tax cuts. In January 2018, three versions of tax-cut measures were introduced.

> The most sweeping and the one that got most attention would not only cut most top income tax rates, and eliminate the bottom four brackets, but also would slowly phase out the income tax altogether over the next few decades.
> *(Hancock 2017, p. 1)*

The final version of the tax-cut legislation was HB 2540, dealing with personal income tax, and SB 884, dealing with corporate income tax.

Under SB 509 enacted in 2014, the state's personal income taxes are already set to gradually decrease to 5.5% from 6%, provided the revenue trigger kicks in. The new law (i.e., HB 2540) exacerbates the cut to 5.4% in 2019 and gradually to 5.1% over several years if the net state general revenue collected meets the revenue target. Additionally, the law phases out the federal income tax deduction. Before January 2019, a single tax filer could deduct $5,000 federal tax liability from their Missouri tax return. A married couple could deduct $10,000. Under the new law, this deduction was phased out for individuals based on Missouri's adjusted gross income levels. The deduction percentage is determined as follows (Deloitte 2018):

Missouri Adjusted Gross Income	Deduction Percentage
$25,000 or less	35%
$25,001 to $50,000	25%
$50,001 to $100,000	15%
$100,001 to $125,000	5%
$125,000 or more	0%

SB 884 implements significant changes to business taxes starting with the 2020 tax year. This measure reduces the corporate income tax from 6.25% to 4%, making Missouri's rate one of the lowest in the nation at that time. The law also changes how business income is calculated. It removed the earlier practice where businesses could choose among the options: the default of traditional-equally-weighted three factors (i.e., their property, payroll, and sales in the state) or an elective single-sales factor. The new law mandates the use of the single-receipts factor method, requiring all corporate income taxes to be based on Missouri sales. Generally speaking, tangible personal property sales will be considered Missouri sales if the final sales destination is in the state. Under this new law, services and intangible property will be sourced to Missouri if the market for the sales activity occurs in the state. By these changes, Missouri joins most states that already use that method for calculating corporate income taxes (Beckwith 2018).

The corporate income tax rate cuts benefit businesses, but the fiscal impact of changing the income calculation is not certain. Upon its passage of SB 884, legislative research staff projected the first-year impact ranged from a $4.4 million revenue loss to a $4.9 million tax increase (Lieb 2019). After the first year of application, these estimates ranged even wider "from an $8.8 million net tax cut to a $9.7 million tax increase in FY 2021" (Lieb 2019, p. 2). The nonprofit MBP estimated that the measure could lead to a net $28 million tax cut (Lieb 2019).

At the signing ceremony of the tax-cut legislation, Governor Mike Parson stated, "This is the first step in an ongoing process. We need to continue to make the Missouri tax code simple and fair" (Office of Governor Mike Parson 2018, p. 1) He pledged to continue to work with the state legislature to offer broad-based tax relief measures that mutually benefit taxpayers and businesses

Why Tax Cuts in Missouri?

Usually, during economic booming years, when the government collects excess tax revenue, lawmakers will push for tax cuts. That is not the case with Missouri's efforts. In the post-Great Recession years, Missouri's tax cuts were purely driven by political and ideological convictions, with little consideration given to the state's fiscal reality and the consequences it would cause. In the past two decades, Missouri has had such a favorable political environment for tax cuts when Republicans controlled the Missouri legislature, normally by supermajority margins. For Republican lawmakers, tax cuts have long been their legislative goal. From 2009 to 2016, Governor Jay Nixon, a Democrat, opposed the tax cuts, but the supermajority of Republicans in both chambers could easily override his veto. In 2014, the tax-cut laws were enacted after the Republican-controlled legislature overrode Governor Nixon's veto. After the 2016 election, Republicans continued to dominate the state legislature and won over the Governor's Office. For a while, it looked like Republicans could pass any legislation they wanted. The new and ambitious governor, Eric Greitens, was haunted by extramarital affair scandals and had a contentious relationship with the legislature. Even so, they were able to work together and accomplish their tax-reduction goals. After Greitens resigned, his successor, Mike Parson, pursued tax reform as one of the major issues of his tenure.

Republicans argue that lower tax rates would allow taxpayers to keep more money in their own pockets, improve the state's competitiveness, and generate more economic activity. They also argue that tax cuts would make the government more efficient. The Democrats criticized the tax actions, comparing them to those Kansas passed under then-Governor Brownback, yet Democrats were outnumbered by their Republican counterparts.

Fiscal Impacts

When Missouri Republican lawmakers pursued these tax-cut measures, the state government was experiencing severe revenue shortfalls and intensive spending cuts. The sluggish revenue further worsened budget prospects for the state. In some years, the governor (both Governor Nixon and Governor Greitens) made huge cuts and withholdings to the enacted budget right before the fiscal year started. These were after initial sizable cuts throughout the budget negotiation season. For instance, on June 24, 2014, a week before FY 2015 started, Governor Nixon reduced $1.1 billion from the Missouri FY 2015 budget, including a $276 million line-item veto and $846 million withholding. These cuts were in response to a looming huge revenue shortfall, partially caused by various tax cuts passed in the final days of the 2014 legislative session.

On June 30, 2017, on the night right before the start of FY 2018, Governor Greitens cut $250 million from the state budget that affected higher education, K-12 education, the Medicaid program, and many other public services (Lieb and Ballentine 2017). Universities received a 9% budget cut and were instructed to identify areas that could be cut. Reductions took place in online teaching, staff positions, travel money, and community outreach efforts. Faculties were told to be economical, saving any money that was possible. Governor Greitens claimed that he inherited a fiscal mess and Missouri was spending money that it did not have. Indeed, when taxes were cut, the revenue would fall, and Missouri did not have that money. The constant tax cuts result in Missouri ranking 45th among all states in terms of state tax revenue per capita (MBP 2024).

Table 5.8 shows the revenue collections (not adjusted for inflation) during FY 2012–FY 2018. Both individual income and corporate income taxes grew either at a minimal or negative rate. Personal income tax collections declined in 2014 when SB 509 passed, and corporate income tax collections declined in three of the eight years under examination. The phase-out of the franchise tax passed in 2009 was officially completed in 2016. That year, the state had a 16% decline in corporate income/franchise tax collections. In 2016, the state legislature enacted additional tax reductions, causing a roughly $55–$64 million revenue loss for each fiscal year (MBP 2017b).

What is shown in Table 5.8 does not include the revenue loss that would be caused by the SB 509 revenue trigger If threshold was met, the top income tax would be reduced from 6% to 5.5% in five years, and pass-through businesses would be given 25% of deductions. If, like in Kansas, registration of pass-through businesses dramatically increased, the fiscal hole for Missouri was expected to grow bigger.

TABLE 5.8 Missouri General Revenue (GR) FY 2012–FY 2017 (in $million) and Percentage Change over the Previous Year

Fiscal Year	2012 (actual)	2013 (actual)	2014 (actual)	2015 (actual)	2016 (actual)	2017 (actual)	2018 (actual)
Taxes							
PIT	5,840	6,370	6,350	6,890	7,158.2	7,320	7,728
% Change	3.8%	9.0%	(0.2%)	8.5%	3.9%	2.3%	5.6%
CIT	502	525	540.7	558.6	468.3	435.1	461.7
% Change	(6.4%)	4.5%	2.9%	3.3%	(16.2%)	(7.1%)	6.1%
SUT	1,870	1,906	1,970	2,010	2,102	2,150	2,196
% Change	3.5%	1.3%	3.8%	2.3%	4.4%	2.1%	2.1%
All Others	398.4	470.9	419.3	468	462	529	533
% Change	(14.6%)	18.2%	(10.9%)	11.6%	(1.2%)	14.4%	0.08%
Gross GR	n/a	n/a	n/a	n/a	10,191.8	10,535.7	10,920
% Change					2.6%	3.37%	3.6%
GR Refunds	1,280	1,180	1,280	1,220	1,405	1,420	1,499
% Change	(4.4%)	7.8%	8.4%	(4.4%)	14.9%	0.8%	2.2%
Net GR	7,340	8,086	8,000	8,710	8,787	9,029	9,468
% Change	3.2%	0.1%	(1.1%)	8.8%	0.9%	2.6%	4.9%

Sources: Missouri Office of Administration, Division of Budget and Planning (2012-2018); Parson (2019).

As a result of low revenue collections, Missouri experienced slow or negative growth in a wide range of public services. Table 5.9 presents the total expenditures, general fund expenditures, and major expenditure categories. Over the years, the average annual growth rate for all these measures was relatively moderate at 2%–3% except for transportation services (see the last column of Table 5.9). These rates are reported in nominal terms, not adjusted for inflation. In some years, the growth rate was negative (e.g., human services in 2013 and 2018 and corrections and public safety in 2013, 2016, and 2018). Notably, negative growth occurred for almost every category in FY 2018. The general fund expenditure declined by 3%, higher education by 9%, transportation by 69%, corrections and public safety by 6%, and human services by 3%. Even though funding for public education expenditure increased by 3%, the funding level was still lower than what the foundation formula requires. At this rate, it would take ten years to fund public education fully (Altman 2017).

TABLE 5.9 Missouri Budget in Selected Years FY 2012–FY 2018 (in $million) and Percentage Change over the Previous Year

Fiscal Year	2012 (actual)	2013 (actual)	2014 (actual)	2015 (actual)	2016 (actual)	2017 (appr.)[a]	2018 (appr.)	Avg. Annual Growth Rate 2012–2018
Total Exp.	22,933	22,738 (1%)	23,093 2%	23,925 4%	24,628 3%	27,695 12%	27,882 1%	3.4%
General Fund Exp.	7,848	7,950 1%	8,327 5%	8,669 4%	9,017 4%	9,692 7%	9,449 (3%)	3.2%
Elementary and Secondary Education	2,769	2,913 5%	2,922 0.3%	3,140 7%	3,236 3%	3,318 3%	3,369 3%	3.4%
Higher Education	789	827 5%	837 1%	900 8%	905 1%	996 10%	909 (9%)	2.6%
Human Services	2,403	2,359 (2%)	2,554 8%	2,573 1%	2,781 8%	2,980 7%	2,902 (3%)	3%
Corrections and Public Safety	646	541 (16%)	659 22%	714 8%	703 (2%)	759 8%	710 (6%)	2.3%
Transportation	9.0	9.3 3%	13.5 45%	13.9 3%	17.9 29%	37.6 110%	11 (69%)	20%

[a] The annual growth rate for FY 2017 over FY 2016 needs to be interpreted with caution. The data for 2016 are the actual expenditure data, while the 2017 data were from the appropriated expenditure. Before FY 2017 finished, Governor Nixon cut roughly $400 million.

Sources: Missouri Office of Administration, Division of Budget and Planning (2011; 2012; 2013); Nixon (2014; 2015; 2016); Greitens (2017).

From the fiscal stability perspective, these tax cuts created more instability and uncertainty for the state to provide basic services. Over the years, the Republican-controlled state legislature cut income tax rates, but their efforts to broaden the tax base were limited. The number of tax expenditure programs in the state budget increased by 408% between 1998 and 2010, when the general revenue only grew by 14%. Facing such a growth, Governor Nixon appointed the Tax Credit Review Commission in 2010 to review the state's tax credits and give recommendations. The Commission studied 61 tax credits that amounted to more than $500 million each year and made recommendations on how to reform them (Ehresman 2010). However, eliminating tax expenditures is difficult due to the influence of special interest groups. The state still keeps some credits that have become obsolete. For instance, the state still offers a timely filing discount, allowing retailers to retain a portion (2%) of the sales and use tax collected from customers if they remit those taxes to the state in a timely manner. This measure was established at a time when vendors had to manually calculate sales tax (MBP 2016). The "vendor discount" is not capped and remains the second most generous in the country, costing the state government $144 million in 2016.

In recent years, lawmakers have added tax breaks instead of reducing them.. According to Amy Blouin, Director of the Missouri Budget Project, the combined costs of the numerous tax breaks offered to businesses amounted to $1 billion annually (Altman 2017). The combination of tax rate cuts and the base not being broadened translates into state fiscal instability.

Lessons Learned

Again, tax cuts lead to revenue loss. Revenue loss leads to service reduction, which in turn undermines investment in education and in the future. In 2014, Tom Kruckemeyer, Director of Fiscal Policy and Chief Economist of Missouri Budget Project, warned that "Missouri has no 'surplus revenues' and is not in a position to cut taxes and further erode its revenue base. Missouri should be aware of the consequences of declining revenue collections coupled with future tax cuts." (Kruckemeyer 2014a, p. 2). Many critics of the tax-cut efforts compared the actions to those pursued in Kansas. The critics also correctly point out that Missouri's circumstances are even more troublesome to the state's fiscal health because Kansas lawmakers can undo their tax actions themselves through legislative remediations, whereas Missouri lawmakers cannot. Since reversing a tax cut equals a tax increase, such a measure must be approved by voters as required by the Missouri state constitution.

According to Missouri State Auditor Nicole Galloway, Missouri ranked 49th in the nation in funding its public schools (Fortino 2021). Its public education funding contributions were always below its legal level, and the General Assembly, in recent years, revised the foundation formula to make it easier to reach the funding targets. In terms of per capita spending, including federal funds, Missouri ranked 43rd in the nation (MBP 2024). As a conservative state, Missouri voters and their elected officials can choose the fiscal policies based on their preferences, but investment in education, workforce, and infrastructure and the improvement of public service and healthcare are critical for the state's economic development and long-term fiscal health.

References

Altman, Maria. 2017. "Corporate Income Tax Revenue Drop in Missouri, But Not Because of the Economy." *St. Louis Public Radio*. (April).

Beckwith, Heather. 2018. "Missouri Cuts Corporate and Individual Tax Rates – and More." *Tax Strategies*.

Blouin, Amy. 2014. "Fiscal Year 2015 Budget Contains Critical Increases for Public Services; However, Weak State Revenue and a Plethora of Tax Breaks Make Funding Uncertain." *Missouri Budget Project*. (May 20).

Brownback, Sam. 2012. "Fiscal Year 2013 Budget Report (Vol 1)." (January). https://budget.kansas.gov/wp-content/uploads/fy2013-gov-bdg-rpt-vol-1-2012-03-08.pdf

Brownback, Sam. 2016. *State of Kansas FY 2017 Comparison Report: The Fiscal Year 2017 Governor's Budget Report with Legislative Authorizations.*.

Burghart, Mark. 2018. *Tax Expenditure Report: Calendar Year 2018*. Kansas Department of Revenue.

Cillizza, Chris. 2017. "How the Grand Conservative Experiment Failed in Kansas." *CNN*. (June 10).

Copper, Brad. 2014. "Kansas Revenues Will Fall $1 Billion Short of 2015 and 2016 Expenses, Fiscal Experts Say." *Kansas City Star*. (November 10).

Deloitte. 2018. "Enacted Missouri Legislature Includes Personal Income Tax Changes." (July 31).

Drenkard, Scott and Joseph Henchman. 2017a. "Kansas Sends Tax Overhaul to Governor Brownback." *Tax Foundation* . (February).

Drenkard, Scott and Joseph Henchman. 2017b. "Testimony: Reexamining Kansas' Pass-Through Carve-Out." *Tax Foundation* . (January).

Ehresman, Ruth. 2009. "Still Trying to Balance the Budget: Governor Approves New Round of Cuts." *The Missouri Budget Project*. (August).

Ehresman, Ruth. 2010. "Tax Credit Review Commission Offers Recommendations to Curb Growth in Tax Credits." *The Missouri Budget Project*. (December 16).

Ehresman, Ruth and Amy Blouin. 2011. "FY 2012 Budget Approved with Additional Spending Reductions." *The Missouri Budget Project*.

Fortino, Jodi. 2021. "Missouri Ranks Next-To-Last Nationally in Funding K-12 Schools, State Auditor Finds." *KCUR*. (May 28).

Greitens, Eric R. 2017. *The Missouri Budget Fiscal Year 2018*. (February) https://oa.mo.gov/sites/default/files/2018_Summary_Information.pdf

Hancock, Jason. 2017. "Missouri Republicans Hope to Pass a Massive Tax Cut. Can They Avoid Kansas' Trouble?" *The Kansas Star*. (December 26).

Hardenbrook, Jay. 2014. "Governor's Vetoes and Restrictions Span Entire Budget" *Missouri Budget Project*. (June 24). Gov_Budget_June2014.pd f

Kansas Center for Economic Growth. 2015. "Tax Cuts Taking Toll on Kansas Communities." (April).

Kansas Center for Economic Growth. No Date a. "Senate Bill 30: The Legislature Sets Kansas on the Road to Recovery."

Kansas Center for Economic Growth. No Date b. "Who Pays: The Cost of Kansas' Tax Cuts for Local Communities."

Kruckemeyer, Tom. 2014a. "State General Revenue Declines Sharply in April: Could Lead to Budget Reductions." *The Missouri Budget Project*. (May 15).

Kruckemeyer, Tom. 2014b. "There is No Surplus: Missouri Still Falling Short of Pre-Recession Funding." *The Missouri Budget Project.* (February 7).

Kruckemeyer, Tom and Amy Blouin. 2010. "Following a Decade of Deficits: Missouri's Revenue Crisis Continues." *The Missouri Budget Project*.

Kruckemeyer, Tom and Traci Gleason. 2011. "Missouri General Revenue Collections Still in a Deep Hole." *The Missouri Budget Project*. (January).

Leachman, Michael. 2017a. "Timeline: 5 Years of Kansas' Tax-Cut Disaster." *Center on Budget and Policy Priorities*. (May 24).

Leachman, Michael. 2017b. "A Kansas Wake-Up Call for Other States Considering Big Income Tax Cuts." *Center on Budget and Policy Priorities*. (February 23).

Leachman, Michael and Chris Mai. 2014. "Lessons for Other States from Kansas' Massive Tax Cuts." *Center on Budget and Policy Priorities*. (March 27).

Lieb, David A. 2019. "New Law Makes Missouri Corporate Tax One of the Lowest in U.S.: Thousands of Missouri Businesses Will Receive Tax Cuts with the New Year." *Associated Press.* (December 30).

Lieb, David A. and Summer Ballentine. 2017. "Missouri Governor Signs Budget, Cuts $250 M in Spending." *Associate Press.* (June 30).

Mazerov, Michael. 2018. "Kansas Provides Compelling Evidence of Failure of 'Supply-Side' Tax Cuts." *Center on Budget and Policy Priorities.* (January 22).

Missouri Budget Project. 2010. "Fiscal Year 2011 Belt-tightening Has Broad and Deep Impact: Almost $900 Million in Cuts to Service that Affect all Missourians." (June 28).

Missouri Budget Project. 2016. "Timely Filing Discount Costs Missourians Millions." (October).

Missouri Budget Project. 2017a. "Creating Winners and Losers: Lessons for Missouri on the Implication of the Business Income Deduction." (April 5).

Missouri Budget Project. 2017b. "Missouri Faces Additional Cuts to Services in Both Current Year, Fiscal Year 2018." (January).

Missouri Budget Project. 2024. "How Missouri Taxes & Revenue Compare to Other States." (January).

Missouri Office of Administration, Division of Budget and Planning. 2011. *The Missouri Budget Fiscal Year 2012.*

Missouri Office of Administration, Division of Budget and Planning. 2012. *The Missouri Budget Fiscal Year 2013.*

Missouri Office of Administration, Division of Budget and Planning. 2013. *The Missouri Budget Fiscal Year 2014.*

MO Office of Administration, Division of Budget and Planning. 2012-2018. *General Revenue Report* (for FY 2012–2018). https://oa.mo.gov/budget-planning/revenue-information

National Association of the Budget Officers. *Fiscal Survey of States* (series 2012–2017).

National Conference of State Legislature (NCSL). 2012. *State Tax Actions 2011: Special Fiscal Report*. Denver, Colorado: National Conference of State Legislature.

National Conference of State Legislature (NCSL). 2017. *State Tax Actions 2016: Special Fiscal Report*. Denver, Colorado: National Conference of State Legislature.

National Conference of State Legislature (NCSL). 2018. *State Tax Actions 2017: Special Fiscal Report*. Denver, Colorado: National Conference of State Legislature.

Nixon, Jeremaih W. 2014. *The Missouri Budget Fiscal Year 2015*. (January). https://oa.mo.gov/sites/default/files/FY%202015%20Executive%20Budget%20comp.pdf

Nixon, Jeremaih W. 2015. *The Missouri Budget Fiscal Year 2016*. (January).

Nixon, Jeremaih W. 2016. *The Missouri Budget Fiscal Year 2017*. (January). https://oa.mo.gov/sites/default/files/FY_2017_Executive_Budget_download.pdf

Office of Governor Mike Parson. 2018. "Governor Mike Parson Signs Income Tax Cut for Missourians." Governor Mike Parson Signs Income Tax Cut for Missourians | Governor Michael L. Parson

Oliff, Phil, Chris Mai, and Vincent Palacios. 2012. "State Continue to Feel Recession's Impact." *Center on Budget and Policy Priorities*. (June 27).

Parson, Michael L. 2019. *The Missouri Budget Fiscal Year 2020*.

Rafool, Mandy. 2013. *State Tax Actions 2012: Special Fiscal Report*. Denver, Colorado: National Conference of State Legislature.

Rafool, Mandy. 2014. *State Tax Actions 2013: Special Fiscal Report* Denver, Colorado: National Conference of State Legislature.

Rafool, Mandy. 2015. *State Tax Actions 2014: Special Fiscal Report*. Denver, Colorado: National Conference of State Legislature.

Rafool, Mandy. 2016. *State Tax Actions 2015: Special Fiscal Report*. Denver, Colorado: National Conference of State Legislature.

Sebelius, Katherine. 2008. *Governor's Budget Report: Fiscal Year 2009 (Vol 1)*. Dear Kansan:

Wagnon, Joan. 2009. *Tax Expenditure Report: Calendar Year 2009*. Kansas Department of Revenue.

6
STATE INCOME TAXES
How to Keep This Revenue Pilar Stable?

Introduction

In the United States, 41 states and Washington, DC collect a broad-based personal income tax (PIT) by imposing a tax on salaries, wages, dividends, interest, and other sources of income. New Hampshire has a narrow-based one, taxing only dividends and interest, and will be repealed soon. Washington does not tax regular income, but only capital gains. Seven states do not have a PIT: Alaska, Florida, Nevada, South Dakota, Tennessee, Texas, and Wyoming. These states have other revenue sources (e.g., natural resources or tourists) to tax. Income tax is not an ideal local revenue source because residents can easily avoid the tax by moving away to non-income tax localities. Only a limited number of local governments in 13 states collect PIT (Urban Institute No Date).

Among the 41 states, 30 states and Washington, DC use graduate rates for their PIT. The other eleven states have flat rates, including five that converted their graduated rates to a flat rate in 2022. Among the graduated rate states, Hawaii has the largest number of income brackets, 12 of them. State income taxes, even for those with graduated rates, are generally flatter than the federal structure. For example, in Alabama, the top tax rates can start as low as $3,001 of taxable income. In recent years, many states have reduced their tax rates, particularly the top rates. Right now, states' income tax top rates range from 2.5% in Arizona to 13.3% in California. The top rate states, after California, are Hawaii (11%), New York (10.9%), and New Jersey (10.75%). On the other end, 18 states have top rates at 5% or lower (Urban Institute No Date). State income tax varies in other aspects, including personal exemptions, standard deductions, and whether the brackets and exemptions are indexed to inflation. Generally,

DOI: 10.4324/9781003494324-6

the tax is imposed by the state where the income is earned. Some states, usually neighboring ones, do have reciprocal agreements to allow income earned in one state to be taxed by the earner's resident state (Urban Institute No Date).

States usually tie their income tax systems to the federal system. For instance, 31 states use the federal adjusted gross income (AGI) as the starting point, and five use federal taxable income. A few others use their own definitions of income but still mirror the federal AGI (Urban Institute No Date). In addition, some states link their standard deductions and personal exemptions to the federal tax codes (Vermeer 2023). This means that federal tax code changes will affect state income tax collection. To avoid this, states can decouple their tax codes from federal tax provisions (Urban Institute No Date).

PIT has a longer history than the state's general sales tax. Ten states had already collected PIT before the 1920s. But similar to sales tax, the wide adoption of PIT was the state's response to the collapse of property tax revenue during the Great Depression. Seventeen states instituted income tax during the 1930s (Drenkard 2014). PIT revenue as a share of states' total tax revenue increased steadily over the 1950s–1990s from 9.3% in 1950 to 19% in 1970 and passed the 30% mark in 1990 (see Table 6.1). Its steady growth is attributable to two factors. First,

TABLE 6.1 Individual Income Tax as a Share of State Tax Revenue (in $thousand)

Year	Total State Tax Revenue	Total PIT	As % of Total Tax Revenue
2020	1,068,784,950	387,987,371	36.30
2019	1,093,452,066	411,234,520	37.61
2018	1,041,365,054	395,740,284	38.00
2017	957,498,317	353,137,071	36.88
2016	930,875,000	344,284,337	36.99
2015	918,539,656	338,426,933	36.84
2014	865,752,089	310,828,815	35.90
2013	847,096,988	309,736,583	36.56
2012	796,917,528	280,589,983	35.21
2011	761,836,690	259,849,070	34.11
2010	705,929,253	236,986,784	33.57
2009	713,474,529	245,880,786	34.46
2008	779,716,635	277,996,021	35.65
2000	539,655,337	194,573,057	36.05
1990	300,488,565	96,076,243	31.97
1987	246,509,508	76,216,412	30.92
1980	137,075,178	37,089,481	27.05
1970	47,961,994	9,182,862	19.15
1960	18,035,927	2,209,294	12.25
1950	115,918	14,314	9.3

Source: U.S. Census Bureau. Annual Survey of State Government Tax Collections Tables (Various Years) (census.gov).

more states came to adopt a PIT. Pennsylvania, Rhode Island, Ohio, and New Jersey adopted PIT in the 1970s, and Connecticut was the last to adopt it in 1991. Second, the booming economy and the robust stock market in the middle and late 1990s led to the ballooning of personal income. The booming economy was fueled by a high technology industry, the "proliferation of employee stock options," and the rapid growth of the real estate market (Brunori 2016, p. 27). Though personal income declined during economic downturns, such as in the early 2000s and the height of the Great Recession, the economy recovered, and the tax revenue rebounded. Interestingly, while economic and technological developments have eroded the sales tax and fuel tax bases and created increasing issues for corporate income tax, they have generated enormous income and expanded the state income tax base (Brunori 2016).

In total, individual income tax has been the largest tax revenue source for state governments for many years. Its share has remained around 34%–38% of state total tax revenue in the last two and a half decades (see Table 6.1). Some states rely more on PIT than others. For example, in 2017, Oregon, a state without sales tax, collected 70% of tax revenue from its PIT, followed by Virginia (58%), New York (56%), and California (54.1%). Massachusetts, Missouri, Georgia, Colorado, and Utah all collected over 40% of tax revenue from income tax. On the other end is North Dakota, which collects about 10% of its tax revenue from PIT (U.S. Census Bureau).

Paradoxically, while PIT is the most productive tax and the pillar for state finances, it is one of the most heavily attacked targets by many elected officials, particularly conservative governors and legislators. They oppose PIT because they see a tax on personal income as a tax on labor, deterring people from working hard. They also believe an income tax reduces the competitive edge of their state, which in turn will harm economic growth (Brunori 2016). Therefore, they constantly call for tax cuts, rate reductions, flattening the tax structure, and providing more tax breaks. On the other side of the political spectrum are those, usually liberals, who support PIT and insist the tax structure be more progressive. They cite the evidence that tax cuts do not necessarily lead to economic growth. Indeed, PIT policies reflect the clash of different political ideologies and beliefs.

PIT is also used to serve various purposes. In addition to generating revenue, it is often employed as a policy tool to implement a wide range of public policies involving economic development, income distribution, education policy, and even environmental policies, to name a few. The latter role is not compatible with revenue generation because it narrows the tax base and complicates the system.

Furthermore, PIT is also one of the most volatile revenue sources, just after the corporate income tax. Directly tied to the economic cycle, PIT revenue fall sharply during economic downturns, making it hard for states to balance their budgets. The Great Recession was extremely devastating. The severe and persistent revenue shortages during that time led to the expectation that states would have to restructure their tax systems, particularly PIT, to make them stable.

How have state governments reformed their income tax in the past decades? What explains the changes? Did the fiscal crisis during the Great Recession change PIT political dynamics and reverse the tax-cutting mentality? How did these changes help states improve their fiscal stability? These are the major questions that this chapter addresses.

State Personal Income Tax Changes during 2008–2020

Table 6.2 presents the state PIT policy changes by showing the overall net PIT revenue changes in each year over the period of 2008–2020 (the period of 2021–2023 is discussed in Chapter 12), the number of PIT rate changes each year, tax base changes, and conformation to the federal tax codes. Appendix F shows the specific changes in PIT rates for different states.

Table 6.2 and Appendix F reveal six observations regarding state PIT policy changes. First, the dire fiscal situation changed states' tax policy dynamics, making it possible to increase PIT. The length and severity of the Great Recession forced more states to turn to PIT (and other taxes as well) for needed revenue during the Great Recession and years immediately after that. FY 2009 saw the largest net revenue gains, for which nine states increased PIT rates. In 2010, states took another measure to raise PIT revenue by reducing or eliminating tax credits, resulting in tax base expansion. Here are a few examples:

- New Mexico and New York adopted similar measures to add back state income tax deducted from federal taxable income.
- New York limited PIT deduction for charitable donations made by high-income taxpayers.
- Arizona required nonresident taxpayers to pro-rate standard deductions.
- Minnesota and Oklahoma suspended several PIT credits.
- New Jersey reduced its Earned Income Tax Credit (EITC).

Although FY 2010 had a net negative dollar impact, the net cut was due to New Jersey's surtax expiration on the wealthy enacted in the previous year. This is also due to Idaho and Iowa continuing to phase in previously enacted tax cuts. FY 2011 and FY 2012 saw net PIT revenue increase. The significant tax increase in FY 2017 was the response to the financial crisis affecting states, particularly Illinois and Kansas. Illinois had not been able to enact a budget in the previous two years, and Kansas had pursued deep spending cuts in a wide range of public services. The financial troubles pushed the two states to enact large PIT increases. In both states, the legislatures had to override the governors' vetoes to pass the tax increase measures.

State Income Taxes 119

TABLE 6.2 State Income Tax Changes during 2008–2020

Year (1)	Overall # States with Net Raise (2)	Overall # States with Net Cut (3)	Net $ Impact (Million) (4)	Tax Rate # of State Tax Actions Raise (5)	Tax Rate # of State Tax Actions Cut (6)	Tax Base # of State Tax Actions Broaden (7)	Tax Base # of State Tax Actions Narrow (8)	Conform to IRS Codes # of State Tax Actions That Lead to Raise (9)	Conform to IRS Codes # of State Tax Actions That Lead to Cuts (10)	States with Big Tax Raise (Cut)[b] (11)
2008	6	16	−261	1	1	4	28	1	11	MD
2009	15	12	11,406	14	2	9	13	2	12	CA, CT, NJ, NY, NC, OR, WI
2010	7	12	−656	1	2[a]	18	15	2	5	NY, (NJ)
2011	6	22	2,995	3	8[a]	8	31	2	12	CT, IL, MI, (GA, NY, NC, OH)
2012	3	11	2,830	2	7[a]	4	16	0	1	CA, MD (KS, MI, NY)
2013	6	18	−1,956	6	9	22	45	7	12	MN, (NC, IA, ME, NC, ND, OH, WI)
2014	2	18	−2,985	0	5[a]	4	48	0	5	(IL, MA, MN, NY, OH, WI)
2015	9	20	−1,999	1	7	29	41	2	3	CT, KS (CA, IN, MA, NJ, NC, OH)
2016	6	17	−884	2	4	7	41	1	7	OK (IN, MA, NC)
2017	8	14	4,333	5	4	16	68	1	3	IL, KS (CA, MN)
2018	9	16	−100	2	6	5	40	5	2	GA, KS, NJ, OR (ID, IA, KY, MI, MO, NE)
2019	5	17	−859	2	7	10	37	17	6	CA (AZ, MN, OH, NC, WI)
2020	6	17	1,517	2	1	7	10	1	0	
Total	87	210	13,384.8	41 104	63	184 617	433	41 121	80	

[a] When a state lets its previous tax increase expire, it is counted as a tax cut. In 2011, four out of the eight states that let tax rate increases enacted in 2009 expire. Also, see the states stricken out in the last column.

[b] States with big cuts are those that cut their income tax by more than $100 million. States with major tax increase are those that raised their income tax by more than $100 million. The changes included both tax rate and tax base changes. Those in parenthesis are the states that cut more than $100 million of income tax revenue. Those that are stricken out are the states that let the previous tax increase expire.

Source: Based on the author's review of the National Conference of State Legislatures *State Tax Actions Database* by Waisanen and Haggerty 2010; Rafool and Haggerty 2011; Rafool 2013; 2014; 2015; NSCL 2009; 2012; NCSL 2016–2020.

Second, for tax increase measures, particularly rate hikes, states often created a new bracket or set of brackets for the top-income families. This surtax, also called the millionaire tax, tended to be temporary, not permanent. The millionaire tax was mentioned in Chapter 4, and more will be discussed shortly.

Third, when fiscal pressure subsides, the pressure to push for tax cuts prevails. Even in 2012, seven states cut their PIT rates. This includes the ambitious tax cuts in Kansas, which would phase out income tax, the cross-border rate cuts in Michigan and Nebraska, as well as top rates consolidation and reduction in Oregon. FY 2013, FY 2014, and FY 2015 had net revenue cuts, with more states passing new tax cut measures (cutting tax rates and increasing tax credits) or continuing to implement their previously enacted cuts. Column 11 in Table 6.2 shows that during 2011–2019, more states cut than raised their income tax revenue by $100 million. The pandemic years saw another big wave of cuts, which is discussed in Chapter 12. Tax politics did not seem to change even with the Great Recession. As usual, cutting taxes has been a dominant theme in state PIT policy.

Fourth, two emerging features are noticeable when reviewing these tax cut efforts. An increasing number of states began using phase-in and tax triggers to implement their tax cuts and establish future tax cuts. More detailed discussions follow in the next section.

Fifth, Table 6.2 also shows that compared with tax rate changes (104), state legislatures had made much more efforts affecting income tax bases (616). In addition, in all years, except 2010, the efforts to narrow the tax base outnumbered the effort to broaden it. The tax breaks cover a wide range of areas, including higher standard deduction, more personal tax exemptions, exemptions for retirement income, credits for small businesses, renters, education, energy efficiency, healthcare premiums, as well as earned income tax credits and child tax credits. Narrowing tax base narrowing reduces tax revenue and makes tax rate changes less productive. That is, a given tax rate increase will bring less revenue increase if the base is narrower than otherwise. This point is also discussed in Chapter 7.

Sixth, many states' PIT policy actions were the responses to federal income tax changes. The federal individual income tax policies influence states' income tax performance. Every year, state lawmakers passed legislation to conform to IRS codes or decouple from the federal income tax. Many of these actions resulted in state PIT revenue decreases, except 2018 to 2020 when the federal Tax Cuts and Job Act expanded the tax base.

State Personal Income Tax Rate Increases and Surtax (Millionaire Tax)

Over these years, states' tax increase efforts often targeted high-income households with a few exceptions (see Appendix F). From 2008 to 2020, states raised the top marginal rates or added new higher rates for high-income households 19 times. In 2009, seven states enacted surtaxes. As mentioned earlier, that was the year with the most tax rate hikes. Maryland and North Carolina added new top rates in 2008, Connecticut in 2015, New Mexico in 2019, and New Jersey in 2020. Appendix F shows that the millionaire tax is concentrated in several states, including California, Maryland, New Jersey, New York, and Hawaii. These states enacted the tax more than once.

There were four occasions when the raises were across the board. One was in California in 2009, when it increased all rates by 0.25%. The other was in Illinois in 2011, when the flat rate increased from 3% to 5%, and again in 2017, the rate increased from 3.75% to 4.95%. Another occasion is when Kansas lawmakers decided to reverse the previously enacted tax cuts, resulting in higher rates for all income brackets.

Two reasons explain why states turned to the millionaire tax to generate the needed tax revenue. First, as income tax is the major state revenue source, high income households is where the large amount of revenue lies. Second, over the decades, income distribution has grown increasingly uneven. The income concentration on the top makes high-income earners an attractive target when states are desperate for revenue. Those states that imposed surtaxes tended to be liberal states with severe revenue shortages, or the states that were under fiscal crisis.

These millionaire taxes all have sunset dates, ranging from a single year (New Jersey) to six years (Hawaii). They have expired on schedule or been renewed again when the challenging time strikes again. Only Delaware's surtax became permanent after several changes. After raising the top rate (over $60,000 taxable income for single filers) from 5.95% to 6.95% in 2007, Delaware reduced it to 6.75% in 2012 and again to 6.6% in 2014, and then made it permanent (Francis and Moore 2014).

As tax increases are always controversial and difficult, temporary increases make it easier for lawmakers to present their case and can serve as a useful tool to generate needed revenue. In addition to PIT, state lawmakers also tend to use the same strategy for other tax increases (e.g., sales/excise tax and business tax) (Francis and Moore 2014). The downside of a temporary tax raise is that it provides financial relief but is not a fundamental structure change. The uncertainty of funding in the future makes it difficult for governments to plan for long-term projects and address underlying fiscal issues.

State PIT Cuts, Phasing in, and Tax Triggers

The pressure to cut income tax taxes always remains strong. Even during the Great Recession, several states continued to implement tax cuts enacted in previous years. Starting in 2011, more states turned toward tax cuts. The effort increased in 2013, 2014, 2015 and also remained high in other years (see Appendix F). The following are examples of how states cut their PIT.

- Some states cut their top rates. For instance, North Dakota cut the highest rate from 4.8% to 3.99% in 2012. Missouri reduced the top rate in 2014 by 0.5% over a five-year period. In 2019, Ohio lowered its top rate from 4.997% to 4.79%.
- Some reduced all rates across the board, such as Idaho in 2018, Wisconsin in 2013, and Oregon in 2019.
- Some cut the rates for middle- and low-income families. Mississippi, in 2016, phased out PIT on the first $5,000 of taxable income from 3% to 0% over a five-year period. Arkansas, in 2017, lowered the middle- and low-income rates. Wisconsin, in 2014, dropped the bottom marginal rate from 4.4% to 4.0%. New York in 2012 cut the rates for middle- and low-income families but raised the top rate.
- Some consolidated the number of brackets, making the tax system flatter, like Maine in 2009. Kentucky, in 2018, lowered its rate, expanded the tax base by collapsing brackets, and imposed a flat rate of 5%. While nearly all tax increases are temporary, as we just discussed, tax cuts are all permanent, no matter how they are structured.

Some tax cuts are highly controversial, like the one in Kansas where Governor Sam Brownback pushed through a tax cut package not only with deep cuts but also attempting to eliminate income tax. It was eventually reversed because Kansas was in a dire fiscal situation (see Chapter 5 discussion). Tennessee, in 2016, enacted a reform package that would eliminate the PIT over six years by 2022. Tennessee's plan was feasible since the income tax revenue was a minor portion of its tax revenue.

Some of the tax rate changes are part of comprehensive tax reform packages in which states' lawmakers also altered PIT exemptions, deductions, and credits. North Carolina, in 2013, adopted a tax reform measure to reduce PITs by broadening the base and lowering the rate. The lawmakers changed the tax to a flat rate of 5.8% in 2014 and then dropped the rate to 5.75% in 2015 and thereafter. At the same time, the tax reform packages often contained changes to other taxes like sales tax, corporate income tax, and property tax.

Two features emerged in their tax cuts efforts: phasing in and tax triggers. Rather than letting the tax rate cut take effect all at once, these states phase in the implementation over several years. Ohio may be the first to practice this mechanism. It enacted a five-year income tax reduction plan in 2005 to cut income taxes by 21%. From 2011 to 2017, 11 states phased in their tax cuts (Figueroa, Leachman, and Mazwrov 2017). See Appendix F and Box 6.1 for

> **BOX 6.1 PHASING IN TAX CUTS**
>
> - Maine in 2011 reduced its PIT from 7.95% to 7.15% over the next four years.
> - North Carolina's tax reform packages that were adopted in 2013 and 2017 took several years to implement.
> - In 2013, Arkansas reduced its PIT rate and number of brackets over multiple years. In 2019, it used two years (till 2021) to consolidate its brackets and to reduce its top rate from 6.9% to 5.9%.
> - Indiana reduced the PIT rate from 3.4% in 2013 to 3.23% in 2017. Then, in 2022, it reduced it again from 3.23% to 3.15% by 2024. After that, a revenue trigger can be used to further cut PIT to 2.9% by 2029 (Loughead 2022).
> - In 2016, New York lawmakers enacted a tax reduction for middle-class taxpayers, cutting the rate from 6.85% to 5.5% (for $40,000–$150,000 income bracket) and to 6% (for $150,000–$300,000 bracket) over an eight-year period.
> - In 2016, Tennessee passed legislation to eliminate PIT over a six-year period. PIT was eliminated in 2022
>
> Sources: Figueroa, Leachman, and Mazwrov (2017); NCSL (Various Years). *State Tax Actions Database*; Loughead (2022).

most of them. During the pandemic years, more states came to phase in their tax cuts.

Tax triggers are mechanisms that will set off a series of automatic tax reductions if pre-established revenue (or similar) targets are met. In other words, the current lawmakers are setting up cuts for the future. At least ten states and Washington, DC had instituted tax triggers by 2020. They are applied to PIT or corporate income tax. The benchmarks vary from state to state. Some rely on year-to-year revenue changes. Others set a baseline. Some rely on revenue projections. Others use the prior year's revenue collection. Only two are adjusted to inflation. Table 6.3 is a summary of the trigger designs for seven states.

Chapter 5 has already discussed the revenue trigger used in Missouri and touched on that in Kansas. Two other states (i.e., Michigan and Oklahoma) are also worth mentioning. Michigan adopted revenue trigger to set tax cuts eight years down the road. It was included in a 2015 tax reform package to increase the fuel tax and increase property tax relief to middle- and low-income families, but the implementation was set to start in 2023. For any year that has

TABLE 6.3 Tax Trigger Targets in Several States

State	Year Adopted	Benchmarks	Final Target Rate
Massachusetts	2002	2.5% inflation-adjusted year-over-year revenue growth.	Reduce PIT from 5.3% to 5%
W. Virginia	2009 (CIT)	Rainy-day Fund at 10% of budgeted general fund revenue.	Cut CIT from 8.75% to 6.5%
Kansas	2013 (repealed in 2017)	2.5% year-over-year revenue growth. Scheduled to begin on or after FY 2020.	Fully repeal PIT and CIT
North Carolina	2013 (CIT)	Revenue exceeds statutory benchmarks.	Reduce CIT from 5% to 3%
Oklahoma	2013	Projection of adequate funding to reduce rates on a revenue-neutral basis.	Reduce PIT from 5.25% to 4.85%
Missouri	2014	General fund revenue exceeds the highest of the past 3 years by $150 million.	Reduce the PIT top rate from 6% to 5.5% top rate
Michigan	2015	Inflation-adjusted revenue growth.	Indefinite
Iowa	2018	General fund revenue must equal or exceed $8.3 billion. State revenue must grow by at least 4% from the previous fiscal year. Both triggers are met for changes to take effect on January 1, 2023.	

Sources: Mazerov and Wallace (2017) and Walczak (2016).

an inflation-adjusted general revenue fund/ growth over FY 2021 collection, a statutory formula will be used to calculate the amount of PIT reduction (Walczak 2016; Mazerov and Wallace 2017). Oklahoma's case is interesting because its trigger is based on revenue projection not on the actual revenue collection (Walczak 2016, p. 10).

During the pandemic, state governments launched another wave of big tax cuts, and the tax-cut proponents have pushed the use of tax triggers and phase-in mechanisms to a larger scale. According to ITEP (2023), at least 14 states have enacted revenue triggers and phasing-in mechanisms by 2023. More states are considering their adoption. The intention is to set future tax cuts and keep the tax low even though the future is full of uncertainties.

What are the advantages and issues with these mechanisms? Will they promote revenue stability, as proponents claim? These questions are addressed in a later section.

What Explains the Income Tax Changes?

Several empirical studies have found the following variables statistically significantly related to tax policy changes. Hansen (1983) found that tax increases happen most during fiscal stress. Berry and Berry (1992) examined factors affecting states adopting a new tax, including income tax. Their findings are consistent with Hasen (1983) in that the existence of a fiscal crisis is one of the three variables explaining why states adopt a new tax. The poorer a state's fiscal health, the more likely it is to adopt a new tax. Two other variables are the length of time before the next election and the presence of neighboring states that have previously (or recently) adopted the tax. All three variables created opportunities for elected officials to shield themselves from the political costs of supporting a tax increase.

Phillips and Jolla (2004), using 47 states' data from 1968 to 2000, examined whether market competition (e.g., the actions of neighboring states) or electoral competition (e.g., party control of state legislature) drives state tax policy. They found both do, but different forces influence different taxes.

> Taxes that fall on capital or specific consumer goods such as gasoline, tobacco, and alcohol appear to be more responsive to interstate competition, not state-level electoral outcomes. Conversely, tax on labor and the general sales tax respond to partisan politics, but not inter-jurisdictional competition.
>
> *(p. 1)*

Partisan politics is measured by whether a political party (either Republican or Democrat) controls the state legislature and whether the state legislature is split. They stated that

> in fact, personal incomes tax appears to be the tax that is most responsive to political factors internal to the state. It is the only tax for which annual change is statistically significantly related to both the partisan control of the state legislature and voter ideology.
>
> *(p. 16)*

The current review of state income tax policy changes reveals the same forces (e.g., fiscal condition and partisan control of state legislature) behind income tax policy changes. As shown earlier, the severe revenue shortages during the Great Recession pushed several states to raise PIT. Kansas and Illinois raised their PITs also because of the serious financial trouble they were facing. Those states that raised the millionaire taxes had Democratic majorities in the state legislature and Democratic governors and dire financial conditions. The tax cuts typically happened under conservative controlled state legislatures when the fiscal crisis was less pressing.

State Personal Income Tax and State Fiscal Stability

Since PIT is the largest tax revenue source for most states, its performance directly affects their fiscal health. To have a productive and stable PIT is critical for state governments to provide public services. This section examines how the changes in PIT policy affected state fiscal stability, first by examining the impact on the PIT base in general and then discussing several specific issues related to PIT revenue stability. These issues include how income concentration and tax progressivity are related to PIT stability and how revenue triggers affect fiscal stability.

Personal Income Tax Base and Its Revenue Stability

As stated previously, a productive and stable tax needs a broad base and reasonable rates. Have the tax reforms in the past decade yielded a PIT system with a broad base and reasonable tax rates? The changes in tax rates took two different directions. Fourteen states raised their top rates or imposed a surtax, but nearly all of them are temporary and cannot help states address big and long-term financial needs. The dominant trend is tax cuts. Are the cuts affordable? The answers are subjective. Proponents believe that the cuts will create jobs and grow the economy, which in turn will bring in more tax revenue. However, this was not the case in Kansas, where deep tax cuts hurt the state's ability to finance their essential services. In addition, tax cuts may not prove to be prudent because it is always difficult to reverse the cuts. Since reversing tax cuts equals a tax increase, they need to be approved by voters in many states.

In terms of the tax base, several parameters affect the state's PIT base: federal income tax policies, the overall economy, and state policies regarding exemptions, deductions, and tax credit programs. As shown in Table 6.2, the federal policy changes frequently narrow state income tax base. In theory, states can decouple their PIT from the federal income tax when these provisions erode the tax base.

Personal Income Tax Changes and State Economy

The overall economy should be the most crucial factor influencing PIT base. Since the tax is imposed on income, a strong economy with low unemployment and a booming stock market will expand the tax base and generate substantial tax revenue. While the overall economy is primarily outside the control of a state legislature, many, particularly conservatives, believe that tax policies contribute to economic development. They believe low taxes on labor and capital can help the economy grow, whereas high-income taxes hurt the economy. They also cite empirical studies to support their position. For example, Vermeer (2022) reviewed a series of empirical studies on the national level regarding the changes in marginal tax rates and their impacts. He outlined several findings.

- "Research invariably shows a negative relationship between income tax rates and gross domestic product (GDP)" (p. 1).
- "Cuts to marginal tax rates are highly correlated with decreases in the unemployment rate" (p. 1).

Those on the other side of the political spectrum—usually liberals—cite studies that show the opposite.

Tharpe (2019) from the Center for Budget and Policy Priorities states:

- "Real-world experiences suggest that raising top income tax rates is unlikely to harm state economies in the short run" (p. 1). Among the eight states that imposed a millionaire tax since 2000, most of them did equally well or better than their neighboring states in terms of per-capita income growth and state gross domestic product.
- Empirical studies from the past 40 years do not support the proposition that high taxes hurt the economy and low taxes help it (Tharpe 2019).

It is difficult to assess the impact of state income tax changes on the state economy because economic growth depends on a wide range of non-tax factors, including local workforce participation, state economic development policies, technology innovations, international competition, the nature of the business cycle, and even some unpredictable forces. As income tax policy is always politically charged, there may never be a consensus about the impact of PIT on the economy. Most mainstream academic research shows that state tax rates may have a role at the margins but are not likely to affect states' overall economic growth (Tharpe 2019, p. 2).

Personal Income Tax Changes and Population Migration

At the same time, tax cut proponents also argue high PIT leads to a high rate of outmigration (Brady, 2021), particularly among top earners, who are important contributors to the PIT base. This proposition has received extra support in recent years when remote working enhanced the mobility of workers. But again, it is debatable. According to Tharpe (2019), a landmark study conducted by U.S. Treasury and Stanford University reviewed the tax returns of those who earn more than $1 million over 13 years. The finding is that millionaires rarely moved away due to tax reasons. Their migration rate is 2.4%, while the rate among the general population is 2.9%. Millionaire tax flights are taking place, but "only at the margins of statistical and socioeconomic significance" (Young, Varner,

Lurie, and Prisinzano 2016, p. 1). Decisions to move from one place to another depend on many factors, including the quality of public service, climate, and closeness to family.

There may never be straightforward evidence about the impact of PIT changes on the economy and outmigration. Therefore, it may not be wise for states to use population migration as the rationale to cut income tax. Lawmakers should consider a broader group of factors and long-term impact. Otherwise, the tax cuts, which may not expand the tax base, can only add pressure to the race to the bottom, where states compete to reduce their tax rates, resulting in tax revenue losses for all.

State Tax Breaks and Tax Base

The part of a tax base that the state legislature has more control over is their PIT codes dealing with exemptions, deductions, and tax credits. The more exemptions, deductions, and other preferential treatments, the narrower the base, and the less stable the tax will be. The current examination has shown that while there are times (e.g., the year 2010) that some states did expand the tax base, in most years, most states, in general, increased the number of tax breaks. Based on the NCSL *State Tax Actions Database,* the expensive ones, those costing $10 million or more annually, occur in the areas of healthcare (e.g., income tax credits for health insurance premiums), education (tax credit for tuition and donation for scholarships), property tax credits, small business tax credits, capital gains tax relief, retirement income exemptions (pension and social security benefit), EITC (either establishing a new program or expanding the existing ones), and Child Tax Credit (CTC). The most frequently enacted credits are retirement benefits, EITC, and CTC. This trend continues during the pandemic years.

CTC and EITC target financial assistance to low-income families. These programs are useful tools to address the increasing income inequality. However, policy makers need to know how effective they are and whether they are the best way to use public funds. An increasing number of states have adopted Social Security benefit exemptions. As Social Security benefits are a sizable portion of ordinary income, these exemptions effectively affect the tax base and are found to be statistically significant in increasing the volatility of state tax revenue (Boyd 2022).

In theory, state legislatures have the authority to reverse these exemptions. The forces to implement more tax breaks are always strong. As shown, only when state fiscal conditions are dire, state lawmakers would have enough courage and support to repeal or reform tax credit programs. Due to interest group politics, it is inevitable to use income tax as a tool to achieve a wide range of policy outcomes. Like those for corporate income tax, state income tax credits are costly, and lawmakers need to review these programs on a regular basis and assess their effectiveness.

Income Concentration, Capital Gains Tax, Tax Progressivity, and State Fiscal Stability

The tax structure and income concentration also influence state fiscal stability. The discussion in Chapter 4 touches on this briefly. Experts have observed that recession-related revenue volatility has increased over time, as shown by the severe and persistent revenue shortages during the Great Recession. They attribute this to the growing income concentration and increasing share of capital gains tax. Capital gains are "the profits an investor realizes when selling an asset that has grown in value, such as shares of stock, mutual funds, real estate, or artwork" (McNichol 2021, p. 1). Income concentration and capital gains go hand in hand because 85% of capital gains are concentrated in the top 5% of income households, and 75% of capital gains in the top 1%. As capital gains are closely tied to the value of stocks, they are more volatile than ordinary income. During a recession, not only will the stock values decline, but capital gains realizations also do. For instance, the realization of capital gains declined 95% from 2007 to 2009, while total AGI only fell 12.2% (Chernick, Reimers, and Tennant 2014). Academic studies have dominantly confirmed the impact of capital gains on state revenue volatility (Sjoquist and Wallace 2003; Vasche and Williams 2005; Mattoon and McGranahan 2012).

The conventional view also holds that a tax's progressivity may lead to more revenue volatility. The reasoning is that during a recession, the tax base at the top end (i.e., the high-income earners) will experience a larger drop since this group tends to hold capital gains income, as just explained. When a higher rate is applied, the effect (revenue loss) will be amplified.

However, income concentration/capital gains and tax progressivity play different roles in affecting state revenue volatility. Chernick, Reimers, and Tennant (2014) conducted a study to test the extent to which revenue decline is influenced by income concentration compared with the progressivity of state tax structure. Their findings are

> while potential revenue exposure (a measurement of revenue volatility) is greater in more progressive states, the most important source of interstate variation in revenue exposure was not tax structure, but differences in the importance of income concentration and capital gains income, as well as the state-specific severity of the recession.
>
> *(p. 2)*

They explained that economic recession affects state revenue collection through two different channels. First, a recession affects the stock market. The sharp decline in stock values and high tax burden can cause big revenue loss. The state tax base is affected "in proportion to their pre-recession reliance on capital gains income" (p. 18). Second, economic recession also affects tax revenue by reducing employment and output. This Channel has more impact on those who are below the top 5% of income distribution than those who are in the top 5%. Chernick, Reimers, and Tennant (2014) found that progressive state tax systems "tended to mitigate rather than exacerbate recession-induced declines in tax revenues" (p. 2). The reason is that as ordinary income is more stable, the higher tax burden on the 80th to 95th percentiles provide a cushion to revenue declines. As explained in their evaluation, "Regressive taxation failed to insulate the state from revenue shocks" (p. 18).

These are insightful findings. They might not be final, but they do provide important policy implications. That is, since the income concentration affects state revenue stability much more than the progressivity of the tax system, states that have graduated rates or raised the top rates may not necessarily experience more revenue volatility during a recession than those that cut the top rates or those who shift to a flat rate. A more critical factor is the income concentration of the states and the share of capital gains tax in the state income system.

How to Handle Capital Gains Tax

If capital gains tax is a major contributor to revenue volatility, how should it be treated in a state income tax system? At present, among the 41 states with broad-based income tax, 33 tax capital gains income at ordinary income rates, and the other eight offer special tax breaks. The reliance on capital gain tax varies. On the heavy end are California, New York, Massachusetts, Connecticut, and Colorado. One view regarding capital gains is to cut tax rates on capital gain income to encourage investment and reduce their share in the tax base. The opposing view holds that a heavier tax should be imposed given the increasing income inequality, and it is not fair to tax ordinary income at a higher rate (McNichol 2021).

Capital gains generate substantial revenue. With the increasing income inequity, capital gains should at least be taxed as ordinary income. To address its volatility, state governments can set up an account to direct capital gain tax revenue, separating it from the general revenue fund. In fact, some states have already offered some useful examples. Massachusetts deposits all capital gains tax revenue above a specific threshold ($1 billion) into its rainy-day fund. A similar program is used in Connecticut and California, where tax revenue from investment income is deposited into state reserves after exceeding a certain level (McNichol 2021).

Another issue, similar to the capital gains tax, is state income tax on financial sector income. This stream of income can be large and grow rapidly during the booming time, but recessions can also hit it harder, exacerbating revenue shortfalls and volatility. New York, New Jersey, and Connecticut experienced this revenue shock during the Great Recession (Deitz, Haughwout, and Steindel 2010). A similar question also arises: Should states keep taxing financial sector income or reduce it for fiscal stability? State legislatures do have to make difficult policy choices, but because this is a high-income sector and a substantial amount of revenue can be generated, it should be taxed for revenue and equity purposes. States can treat it the same way as capital gain incomes and design a similar account to mitigate its sharp revenue fluctuations.

Tax Triggers and State Fiscal Stability

As discussed earlier, an increasing number of state governments utilize phasing in tax cuts and tax triggers to establish future tax cuts. Proponents hailed these mechanisms as fiscally responsible and promoting revenue stability because tax cuts occur only in a small and incremental fashion and only when the condition is met. They also see tax triggers as a valuable way to "balance the economic impetus for tax reform with a governmental need for revenue predictability" (Walczak 2016, p. 1).

However, opponents criticize these mechanisms as politically unaccountable. First, they lock in tax cuts before full and real impacts are known and deny future lawmakers the real-time decision-making power. Second, those who enact these mechanisms may never have to face the consequences of revenue loss because most states have strict term limit requirements. Third, lawmakers often do not consider the long-term affordability of their actions. In Kansas and Michigan, triggers remain until PITs are entirely phased out (Kansas' was repealed in 2017). This means states would either cut deep into basic services or raise tax revenue significantly from other sources. The former is not desirable, and the latter is not feasible. Revenue triggers "almost never consider every state's need to maintain adequate financial reserves for fiscal and other emergencies" (Mazerov and Wallace 2017, p. 2).

The proper use of phasing in can help stabilize revenue changes, but phasing in deep cuts will not. Revenue triggers may not be a good sound policy tool. While the impact on fiscal stability varies depending on the structure, those improperly designed caused issues. Here are a few examples. First, when trigger revenue thresholds are expressed in dollar amounts, such as the ones in Missouri and Oklahoma, they should be adjusted for inflation. Otherwise, as time goes by, inflation will erode the value of the dollar and make it much easier to meet the revenue goal, leading to unwarranted cuts. Among current triggers, only two are indexed for inflation. Second, the benchmark should not be based on revenue projections like Oklahoma's. It should be based on actual baseline revenue increases. Using projection is problematic, as it can often be inaccurate, especially during an economic downturn, resulting in unaffordable tax cuts. Third, several states use revenue growth year over year, and this is not a good design, either. In the years immediately after the recession, the revenue may still be lower than pre-recession levels, even with a positive annual growth rate. This trigger could lead to tax revenue cuts when states need more revenue. For instance, in Oklahoma, automatic tax cuts took place in 2012 and 2016 when states were still in harsh fiscal conditions and facing severe revenue shortages (Mazerov and Wallace 2017). Fourth, tax triggers aimed at eliminating PIT and corporate income tax will not help state fiscal stability at all because it is difficult to have another revenue source that can be as productive as income taxes. Revenue triggers should be limited to a specific period and should not be indefinite. Many budget experts say voting for tax cuts when states do have revenue surplus is more prudent than relying on these formulas (Povich 2015).

In sum, the discussion in this section indicates that PIT may face an even bigger challenge today in terms of fiscal stability. The rates in most states are lower, but it is debatable whether they will promote economic growth. The base that state legislatures have the most control over is narrower. Increasing income concentration also makes the system more volatile.

There is also the concern that more reliance on income tax, while bringing in more tax revenue, will put states' revenue systems more at the mercy of the economic cycle. It is true that income taxes are volatile, but this does not mean the share of income taxes should be reduced or eliminated. Instead, states need to examine their tax structure, broaden the base by keeping the ordinary income tax base broad and including non-wage income. States could put income revenue that is sensitive to the economic cycle into a special reserve fund, isolating it from the general fund as several states have already done. This also requires states to diversify their revenue system, modernize the sales tax system, create a more stable revenue source, and build strong rainy-day funds.

Conclusion

Used in 41 states, PIT is important for many states' finances. The fiscal crisis during the Great Recession did disrupt the tax cut mentality associated with PIT and forced numerous state governments to raise rates and expand the base. Yet, when fiscal pressure receded, the dominant policy theme was tax cuts. The empirical studies show ideological, political, and fiscal forces explain these tax actions. Although tax cut proponents often insist lowering taxes promotes economic growth, the evidence is not consistent with that claim.

For PIT to serve as a stable tax revenue source, it is important to keep its base broad and rate reasonable. State officials need to consider the impact of further cuts on the tax base. The government does need to use PIT to serve as a policy tool to achieve many policy goals, such as economic development and income redistribution. As these tax expenditure programs erode the tax base, policy makers should study the effectiveness of these programs and understand the trade-offs before taking any action.

State governments are responsible for many fundamental public services. Income tax policies involve important policy choices and considerations. Whenever proposing PIT changes, lawmakers should ask: How do these changes affect state revenue capacity in the short and long terms? If it is a tax cut, is it affordable? Where else can we generate revenue? Will that result in service cuts? If yes, what are the consequences of these cuts? These are basic, but important policy questions lawmakers should consider when they reform PIT.

References

Berry, Frances S. and William D. Berry. 1992. "Tax Innovation in the States: Capitalizing on Political Opportunity." *American Journal of Political Science*, 36 (3) (August), pp. 715–742.

Boyd, Don. 2022. "State Tax Revenue Volatility and Its Impact on State Governments. *Pew Trust*. state-tax-revenue-volatility-and-its-impact-on-state-governments.pdf (June 30)

Brady, Demian. 2021. "Taxpayers are Fleeing from High-Tax States, Shifting $43 Billion in Wealth." *National Taxpayers Union Foundation* (November 17).

Brunori, David. 2016. *State Tax Policy: A Primer* (4th ed.). New York: Rowman & Littlefield.

Chernick, Howard, Cordelia Reimers, and Jennifer Tennant. 2014. "Tax Structure and Revenue Instability: The Great Recession and the States" *IZA Journal of Labor Policy*, 3 (3).

Deitz, Richard, Andrew F. Haughwout, and Charles Steindel. 2010. "The Recession's Impact on the State Budgets of New York and New Jersey." *Current Issues in Economics and Finance*, 16 (6).

Drenkard, Scott. 2014. "When Did Your State Adopt its Income Tax?" *Tax Foundation*. (June 10).

Figueroa, Eric, Michael Leachman, and Michael Mazwrov. 2017. "Phasing in State Tax Cuts Doesn't Make Them Fiscally Responsible." *Center on Budget and Policy Priorities*. (February 6).

Francis, Norton and Brian David Moore. 2014. "Temporary Taxes: States' Response to the Great Recession." *Urban Institute*.

Hansen, Susan B. 1983. *The Politics of State Taxation: Revenue without Representation*. New York: Praeger.

Institute on Taxation and Economic Policies (ITEP). 2023. "Which States Have Tax Cut Triggers or Phase Ins?"

Loughead, Katherine. 2022. "Indiana Should Use Surplus to Expedite Rate Cuts, Index Exemptions for Inflation." *Tax Foundation.* (July 29).

Matton, Rick and Leslie McGranahan. 2012. "Revenue Bubbles and Structural Deficits: What's a State to Do?" Working Paper. Federal Reserve Bank of Chicago. Revenue Bubbles and Structural Deficits: What's a State to Do?

Mazerov, Michale and Marlana Wallace. 2017. "Revenue 'Triggers' for State Tax Cuts Provide Illusion of Fiscal Responsibility." *Center on Budget & Policy Priorities.* (February 6).

McNichol, Elizabeth. 2021. "State Taxes on Capital Gains." *Center on Budget and Policy Priorities.* (June 15).

National Conference of State Legislature (NCSL). 2009. *State Tax Actions 2008: Special Fiscal Report.* Denver, Colorado: National Conference of State Legislature.

National Conference of State Legislature (NCSL). 2012. *State Tax Actions 2011: Special Fiscal Report.* Denver, Colorado: National Conference of State Legislature.

National Conference of State Legislature (NCSL) (2016-2020). *State Tax Actions Database.* State Tax Actions Database.

Philips, Justin H. and La Jolla. 2004. "Does Market Competition or Electoral Competition Drive State Tax Policy?" Conference paper prepared for presentation at the annual meeting of the Midwest Political Science Association. (April).

Povich, Elaine S. 2015. "Triggers Cut State Taxes: But Are They Good Policy?" *Stateline.* (November 16).Rafool, Mandy and Todd Haggerty. 2011. *State Tax Actions 2010: Special Fiscal Report.* Denver, Colorado: National Conference of State Legislature.

Rafool, Mandy and Todd Haggerty. 2011. *State Tax Actions 2010: Special Fiscal Report.* Denver, Colorado: National Conference of State Legislature.

Rafool, Mandy. 2013. *State Tax Actions 2012: Special Fiscal Report.* Denver, Colorado: National Conference of State Legislature.

Rafool, Mandy. 2014. *State Tax Actions 2013: Special Fiscal Report* Denver, Colorado: National Conference of State Legislature.

Rafool, Mandy. 2015. *State Tax Actions 2014: Special Fiscal Report.* Denver, Colorado: National Conference of State Legislature.

Rafool, Mandy. 2016. *State Tax Actions 2015: Special Fiscal Report.* Denver, Colorado: National Conference of State Legislature.

Sjoquist, David L. and Sally Wallace. 2003. "Capital Gains: Its Recent, Varied, and Growing (?)Impact on State Revenues." *State Tax Notes*, p. 10. (November 3).

Tharpe, Wesley. 2019. "Raising State Income Tax Rates at the Top a Sensible Way to Fund Key Investments." *Center on Budget and Policy Priorities.* (February 7).

Urban Institute. No Date. "State and Local Backgrounders." *State and Local Backgrounders.*

U.S. Census Bureau. Annual Survey of State Government Tax Collections Tables (census.gov). (various years)

Vasche, J. and B. Williams. 2005. "Revenue Volatility in California." *State Tax Notes*, 35 (April).

Vermeer, Timothy. 2022. "The Impact of Individual Income Tax Changes on Economic Growth." *Tax Foundation – Fiscal Fact No. 793* (June).

Vermeer, Timothy. 2023. "State Individual Income Tax Rates and Brackets for 2023." *Tax Foundation*. (February 21).

Walczak, Jared. 2016. "Designing Tax Triggers: Lessons from the States." *Tax Foundation Fiscal Fact No. 526.* (September).

Waisanen, Bert and Todd Haggerty. 2010. *State Tax Actions 2009: Special Fiscal Report.* Denver, Colorado: National Conference of State Legislature.

Young, Cristobal, Charles Varner, Ithai Lurie, and Richard Prisinzano. 2016. "Millionaire Migration and Taxation of the Elite: Evidence from Administrative Data." *American Sociological Review*, 81 (3).

7
STATE CORPORATE INCOME TAXES
How to Reform Them for State Fiscal Stability?

Introduction

Corporate income tax (CIT) is widely used among state governments. Forty-four states and the Washington D.C collect CIT. Ohio, Nevada, Texas, and Washington levy a gross receipts tax that is applied to a company's gross income without deducting any operating expenses. South Dakota and Wyoming do not collect either tax. Seven states also allow their local governments to levy CIT.

CIT generated $60 billion in revenue for state governments in 2019, $53 billion in 2020, and $90 billion in 2021. As a share of total state revenue, CIT is small (see Table 7.1), and the share has continued to decline over the decades. It was 9.5% of state tax revenue in the 1970s (Brunori 2005) and fell to 6.9% in 2007 and further down to 4.9% in 2020. There were several rebounds, but they were minor, except for in 2021. The 2021 number raises an interesting question. Does it represent a reverse of the declining trend or just a one-time phenomenon? Three factors contributed to the increase: strong economic performance after the COVID-19 lockdowns, the postponement of state 2020 tax due date to 2021, and state implementation of pass-through entity taxes, which usually count personal income tax as CIT. Are there any other more durable factors? The answer will not be clear until we have future data.

Like all other state taxes, CITs vary among states regarding tax rates and importance to state finances. In 2022, the highest rate was 11.5% imposed in New Jersey, followed by Illinois (9.5%), Iowa (9.8%), Washington, DC (8.5%),

TABLE 7.1 Corporate Income Tax as Share of State Total Tax Revenue

Years	CIT % of State Total Tax Revenue	Years	CIT % of State Total Tax Revenue
2007	6.985	2015	5.341
2008	6.394	2016	4.956
2009	5.051	2017	4.718
2010	5.384	2018	4.707
2011	5.390	2019	5.518
2012	5.235	2020	4.949
2013	5.298	2021	7.092
2014	5.345		

Source: Author's calculation based on data from U.S. Census *Annual Survey of State Governments Tax Collection.* www.census.gov/programs-surveys/stc.html

and Massachusetts (8%). North Carolina had the lowest at 2.5% (Urban Institute 2023). According to the U.S. Census, the biggest user was New Hampshire, whose CIT accounted for 31% of its total tax revenue, compared with the national average of 7% in 2021.

Although CIT is a small share of state government revenue, it is very complicated and controversial (Brunori 2005; 2021). In the past decades, CITs have continued to be a target of state tax reforms driven by several forces. The first one is the lesson states learned from the Great Recession. The severe fiscal crisis pushed state governments to restructure their tax system, including CIT, to improve their fiscal stability. The second one is lawmakers' political and ideological beliefs. Numerous studies show that some wealthy and profitable corporations pay little to no CIT. Many see this as wrong and demand them to pay their fair share. On the other side of the spectrum are those who are calling to cut corporate taxes and even eliminate them, believing the tax hurts economic growth. Interstate competition is another factor that greatly influences state CIT policies. Using tax incentives as an economic development tool, states are always competing against each other to lower businesses' tax burden to attract or retain economic interests. Modern technology also imposes a challenge for CIT collections. It is easier for multistate and multinational corporations to operate across states and countries and easier for them to move profits. The debate about CIT and reforms reflects the impact of these different forces on state tax policy making. This chapter aims to examine how state CITs have changed in the past decades. It will also analyze whether and how the CIT reforms can contribute to state fiscal stability in the years to come.

State Corporate Income Tax Changes during 2008–2020

Table 7.2 is a summary of state CIT actions during 2008–2020. It shows the number of states that raised or cut CITs (Columns 2 and 3) and the overall net dollar impact (Column 4). A state is coded as one that reduces its corporate tax if its overall tax changes (e.g., rate changes, base changes, and any other changes) lead to a negative dollar amount and vice versa. Since tax changes can take the form of rate changes, base changes, or both, Table 7.2 also shows the number of tax rate changes (Columns 5 and 6) together with the number of tax base changes (Columns 7 and 8).

The Impact of the Great Recession on State Corporate Income Tax Reform

The data in Table 7.2 reveal several observations about state CIT changes. The first one concerns the impact of the Great Recession on state CITs. Similar to the effect on personal income tax (PIT) discussed in Chapter 6, the unprecedented fiscal crisis pressured state governments to restructure their CIT systems by raising the tax to generate the needed revenue. This is especially true in the years immediately after the Great Recession. However, with the fiscal crisis receding, the effort to cut CITs began to dominate.

In the years immediately after the Great Recession, states raised CITs. As shown in Table 7.2 (Columns 2 and 3), the number of states that raised CIT increased from 11 in 2008 to 20 in 2009, the highest number in recent history. The year 2009 is the only year that more states raised CITs than cut. The number of tax-raising states fell back to 11 in 2010 and stayed low after that. Table 7.2 (Column 4) shows net dollar tax increases in 2008, 2009, 2010, and 2012. The later years (i.e., 2014–2019) saw negative dollar amounts or only small positive numbers. The positive number for 2017 was mainly due to Illinois' increase of its CIT by $569 million.

This observation is also supported by the number of tax rates (Columns 5 and 6) and base changes (Columns 7 and 8). Again, in the years immediately after the Great Recession, there were more tax rate increases, as seen in 2008 and 2009, and more efforts to broaden the tax base, as seen in 2009 and 2015. Then the trend started to reverse.

During this period, the large tax-raising states (e.g., those that raised CIT by more than $100 million in the next year) included California, Connecticut, New Jersey, New York, Oregon, Pennsylvania, Massachusetts, Washington, Wisconsin, Delaware, Minnesota, and Illinois. In 2008, 2012, and 2013, California raised its CIT revenue by $1 billion to $2 billion by suspending net operating loss provisions, limiting and restructuring its tax credit programs, and raising tax rates. Connecticut also raised its CIT by imposing a temporary

State Corporate Income Taxes 139

TABLE 7.2 State Corporate Income Tax Changes: 2008–2020

Year (1)	Overall # States Net Raise (2)	Overall # States Net Cut (3)	Net $ Impact (Million) (4)	Tax Rate # of State Tax Actions Raise (5)	Tax Rate # of State Tax Actions Cut (6)	Tax Base # of State Tax Actions Broaden (7)	Tax Base # of State Tax Actions Narrow (8)	States with Big Tax Raise (cut)[a] (9)
2008	11	15	2347[b]	4	3	26	45	AL, CA, MA, MN, NY (MI)
2009	20	10	2014	10	2	34	27	CT, DE, NV, NY, OR, PA, WI (CA)
2010	11	11	494	2	1	26	30	PA, WA
2011	8	20	-804	2	8	13	45	IL (MI)
2012	4	13	822	0	2	7	32	CA
2013	8	17	82.1	2	6	25	47	CA, MN (TX)
2014	8	12	-1150	2	3	9	44	PA (CA, IL, IN, NY)
2015	9	13	-514	2	6	23	21	CT, LA, NV (IN, TX)
2016	5	20	-736	0	6	10	31	(IN, NM, WI)
2017	7	10	335	1	2	22	47	DE, IL (IN, TN)
2018	6	11	27.6	2	7	11	18	OR (CA, IN)
2019	8	11	-29	1	0	32	21	CA, MN (IL, IN)
2020	4	9	-1996	2	0	13	17	CA, NJ (AK, IN)
Total	109	172		30	46	251	425	

[a] States with big cuts or raises are those that increase or cut corporate income tax by more than $100 million in the next year.

[b] These numbers need to be interpreted with caution. In some years, the number is skewed by the changes in one or two states. For instance, in 2008, California corporate income tax increases of $1,955 million accounted for more than half of the total net dollar increase. The net negative dollar impact of 2011 was mainly due to Michigan's tax reform that involved cutting business taxes by over $1 billion as part of a major tax restructuring package.

Sources: Author's tally based on National Conference of State Legislature *State Tax Actions Database* by Waisanen and Haggerty (2010), Rafool and Haggerty (2011); Rafool (2013, 2014, 2015); NSCL (2009, 2012, 2016–2020).

corporate tax surcharge in 2009 and by limiting the use of the net operating losses rule in 2015. These increases occurred when states were facing extreme budget crises and were usually under Democratic leadership, but also occurred under Republican-controlled legislatures. For instance, when Kansas had severe financial trouble caused by earlier tax-cut efforts, even the Republican legislature was willing to reverse course.

Corporate Income Tax Rate Changes

The second observation is related to the CIT rate changes. Table 7.2 (Columns 4 and 5) shows that there were more tax rate cuts than hikes except in years immediately after the Great Recession. Table 7.3 shows that average CIT rates declined from 7.48% in 2008 to 6.87% in 2022. Twenty-two states reduced their CIT rates, while only five increased them.

The state often adopted multi-year tax cut packages, as with PIT cuts discussed in Chapter 6. Some also pursued several rounds of cuts. For instance, Indiana lawmakers voted for a rate reduction in 2011 and approved further reductions in 2014. As a result, the rate went down every year from

TABLE 7.3 Corporate Income Tax Rate Changes during 2008–2022

State	2008	2022	State	2008	2022
Arizona	6.968%	4.90%	Nebraska	7.81%	7.50%
Arkansas	6.50%	5.90%	New Hampshire	9.25%	7.60%
Colorado	4.63%	4.55%	New Jersey	9.00%	11.50%
Georgia	6.00%	5.75%	New Mexico	7.60%	5.90%
Idaho	7.60%	6.00%	New York	7.10%	7.25%
Illinois	7.30%	9.50%	N. Carolina	6.90%	2.50%
Indiana	8.50%	4.90%	N. Dakota	6.50%	4.31%
Iowa	12.00%	9.80%	Oklahoma	6.00%	4.00%
Kansas	7.35%	7.00%	Oregon	6.60%	7.60%
Kentucky	6.00%	5.00%	Rhode Island	9.00%	7.00%
Louisiana	8.00%	7.50%	Utah	5.00%	4.85%
Massachusetts	9.50%	8.00%	W. Virginia	8.75%	6.50%
Michigan	4.95%	6.00%	DC	9.975%	8.50%
Missouri	6.25%	4.00%			
Average Top Rates of All 45 States	7.48%	6.87%			

Source: Tax Foundation's *State Corporate Income Tax Rates* (2008, 2022). This table does not show those states whose corporate income tax rates stay the same.

TABLE 7.4 North Carolina's Corporate Income Tax Rates

2013	6.90%	2022	2.5%
2014	6%	2023	2.5%
2015	5%	2024	2.5%
2016	4%	2025	2.5%
2017	3%	2026	2%
2018	3%	2027	2%
2019	2.5%	2028	1%
2020	2.5%	2029	1%
2021	2.5%	2030	0%

Source: Loughead (2021b).

8.5% in 2011 to 4.9% in 2022. New Mexico implemented a five-year phase in of a CIT reduction from 7.6% in tax year 2013 to 5.9% by tax year 2018. Missouri, Arizona, and Ohio pursued similar reductions. Among those that cut rates, North Carolina stands out for being bold and controversial.

In 2013, Republican political leaders in North Carolina pushed through a major reform package and continued the efforts in 2014, 2015, and 2017. The CIT rate was cut from 6.9% to 3% (see Table 7.4). The law also imposes a tax trigger to further lower the corporate rate if state revenue meets certain thresholds (Kaeding and Horpedahl 2018). By 2021, the rate had dropped to 2.5%, the lowest in the nation. In the same year, North Carolina reduced its rate further with the goal of reaching 0% by 2030 (Loughead 2021b). Many proponents pointed to rapid economic growth in the last decades and deemed North Carolina's tax reform as a successful story for other states to follow (Hillis 2017). However, other commentators quickly pointed out other factors, such as skilled labor availability, highway access, and high-technology industries, contributing to North Carolina's economic growth (Francis 2016).

The Significance of Corporate Income Tax Base Changes

The third observation based on Table 7.2 concerns CIT base changes. Although tax rate changes attract much public attention, tax base changes are more prevalent and have a much greater impact on state revenue systems. State lawmakers have pursued more actions related to tax base changes than rate changes (Table 7.2, Columns 5, 6, 7, and 8). Among 752 observations during 2008–2020, 676 were concerned with tax base changes, and 76 were about tax rate changes. In addition, among tax base changes, the dominant efforts (i.e., 425) resulted in narrowing the tax base rather than broadening it (i.e., 251). In some years, the opposite is true. For instance, in 2009, 2015, and 2019, more actions led to broadening the tax base. The actions in 2009 and 2015 were direct responses to states' fiscal crisis. The actions in 2019 were the result of several states' efforts to conform to the federal Tax Cuts and Jobs Act (TCJA), which broadened the CIT base.

These observations are consistent with much of the findings of an empirical study conducted by Serrato and Zidar (2018) based on state CIT data from 1980 to 2010. Their analysis revealed more state tax actions leading to tax base narrowing than broadening, and there were much more frequent tax base changes than tax rate changes. Furthermore, Serrato and Zidar (2018) found that tax base changes have a larger role than tax rate changes in influencing tax revenue, and the impact of tax rate changes on revenue depends on the broadness of the tax base. That is, with a narrow base, a big tax rate increase will not be able to generate much additional revenue. With a broad base, a slight rate increase will bring in sizable revenue allocations. In addition, they also reveal that "the vast majority of tax base changes are not associated with tax rate changes" (p. 158). That means state legislatures tend to increase tax credits and change base rules without changing tax rates. In this current study, tax reforms (e.g., tax rate cuts) are sometimes accompanied by an effort to broaden the tax base. However, the extent to which this is done depends on the specific situation. For instance, North Carolina eliminated its generous film tax credits in its 2013 tax reform and later used a grant program. It also let several tax credits expire, including those for low-income housing, historic rehabilitation, and recycling oyster shells (Kaeding and Horpedahl 2018).

Serrato and Zidar's (2018) empirical findings and those in the current study have important policy implications. The most basic one is that policy debate should give due and adequate attention to tax base changes; they have a larger impact on state revenue and fiscal stability. Second, public debate should focus not only on tax rate changes but also on changing the tax base.

What Are the Tax Base Changes?

Given the significant impact of tax base changes on tax revenue production, this section will look further at how recent tax actions affected base changes. The author selected six years for a content analysis. The first two years, 2008 and 2009, were the Great Recession years. The years 2014 and 2015 were in the middle of this period under examination. The years 2019 and 2021 are more recent: one before the pandemic and one after the economy reopened. The results are presented in Table 7.5. They include only those that went through the legislative process. In other words, this review does not cover many existing base rules and tax credits that did not require legislative actions.

TABLE 7.5 State Corporate Income Tax Base Changes: Selected Years

	2008	2009	2014	2015	2019	2021	Total
Expanding Tax Base							
Combined Reporting	1	2	0	2	1		6
Suspend/Modify Operating Net Loss	1	2	2	2	1		8
Decoupling from the Federal Tax Code	2	2	0	2	0	1	7
REIT/Close Other Loopholes	3	2	0	0	0	0	5
Narrowing Tax Base							
Apportionment & Sales Factor	2	2	6	3	3	2	18
Favorable Net Loss Carry Forward/Backward						2	2
Conforming to Internal Revenue Codes							
Conforming to the Federal Tax Code	6	8	0	12	12	14	52
Tax Credits (Narrow Tax Base)							
Environmental	4	5	5	3	2	2	21
Social Purpose	4	0	9	3	1	8	25
Low-Income Housing	2	0	2	0	0	0	4
Historical Preservation	0	0	2	0	0	0	2
Healthcare	3	0	0	0	0	0	3
Economic Development	25	24	19	6	15	13	102
Total	53	47	45	33	35	42	255

Sources: Author's tally based on National Conference of State Legislature *State Tax Actions Database* by Waisanen and Haggerty (2010); Rafool (2015); NSCL (2009, 2016–2021).

Table 7.5 reveals several characteristics of state tax base actions. First, there are more activities in some years than in others. Facing the fiscal crisis immediately after the Great Recession, state legislatures took a great deal of actions in 2008 and 2009, including decoupling from the federal tax code such as bonus depreciation and bank debt write-off rules, closing or tightening real estate investment trust (REIT) loopholes, requiring combined reporting, and suspending or reducing net operating loss deductions for certain years. These efforts mostly expanded the tax base. For instance, California suspending the net operating loss generates close to $1 billion each year. During this time, states also started to scrutinize their tax credit programs and reduced the use of tax credits.

Second, the most dominating category in any year is economic development credits. This includes a wide range of credits provided to corporations for R&D, investment (e.g., angel investors), job creation (e.g., Enterprise Zones), filmmaking, industrial revitalization, and supporting certain industries. In the years after the Great Recession, some of the actions in this category aimed to broaden the base. For instance, Hawaii limited certain high-tech tax credits to 80% of the value with no carryover for two years; Kansas reduced various income tax credits by 10% for two years; California limited business credits to one-half of tax liability; and Maine repealed the educational attainment investment tax credit. Several states imposed limitations, caps, and reductions to Enterprise Zone tax credits.

Third, conforming to the federal tax codes takes sizable state actions. This is especially true when the federal government changes its tax policy. The 12 conforming actions in 2019 are responses to the 2017 federal tax reform. Some provisions in 2017 broadened the base; others did the opposite. The 14 actions in 2021 were responses to COVID-19 relief efforts such as Paycheck Protection Program (PPP) loans and continuing efforts to conform to the 2017 tax reform. The decoupling efforts are also responses to federal actions.

Fourth, there are a good number of environmental "green" tax credits. These encourage businesses to invest in and produce biodiesel fuel, alternative energy, renewable energy, solar energy development, and energy efficiency. Most of these years also witnessed new and expanded Brownfield tax incentive programs to clean up and rehabilitate the contaminated land in Michigan, Massachusetts, Florida, and Colorado. Connecticut is the only state that repealed its program in 2019.

Social tax incentives provide tax credits to businesses if they hire interns, disabled employees, veterans, and urban youth. Veteran hiring tax credits, known as Hire-A-Vet tax credits, were implemented in Alabama, New Mexico, Wisconsin, New York, and Massachusetts.

Other common tax incentive programs for states are low-income housing tax credits and historic preservation programs. During the years under examination, New York stood out by taking a series of actions to expand its low-income housing tax credits.

Table 7.5 provides a snapshot of tax base changes over several years. Again, these are only a small number of tax base rules and tax incentive programs. Most of the rules and tax incentive programs do not have sunset dates, do not undergo the annual legislative review, and are not reflected in Table 7.5.

Erosion of State Corporate Income Tax Bases

CIT as a percentage of nationwide gross state products (GSD) – a measure of statewide economic activity, was 0.5% in the 1980s and then declined to 0.33% in 2013 (Gardner et al. 2017). Bivens (2022) concludes that CIT revenue as a share of overall tax revenue for state and local governments fell by 2.8% points between 1979 and 2019 and that "corporate income tax erosion is the biggest factor in declining state and local revenues" (p. 11). Table 7.1 in this chapter also shows that CIT as a share of state total tax revenue has steadily declined except for in 2021. Tax literature has identified several causes for this shrinking tax base, including state CIT linking to the federal system, tax loopholes, states' generous use of tax incentives, and the rise of pass-through businesses.

Linking to the Federal Corporate Income Tax System

Like the case with PIT, states' corporate income tax systems also use the federal definition of "taxable income" as a starting point, though there are some deviations. This way, state tax agencies can save their administrative and compliance costs. However, any federal tax deductions, exemptions, and credits will also shrink the state corporate income tax base, even though the opposite is also true. Oregon has 185 tax expenditures related to personal and corporate income taxes. More than half are the results of Oregon's connection to the federal income tax code. Boddupalli, Sammartino, and Toder (2020) examined the state individual and corporate income tax expenditures in California, Massachusetts, Minnesota, and the Washington D.C. They found that 70%–85% of them were conforming to the Internal Revenue Codes. This current study also reveals that substantial state tax changes are to conform to the federal tax codes (see Table 7.5). Although the 2017 federal TCJA broadened the tax base in numerous provisions, most of the federal tax policy changes led state CIT bases to narrow, and some can be costly. For instance, the "bonus depreciation" enacted by the federal government in the early 2000s continued to very recently allows businesses to write off their investments in machinery and equipment faster than they would otherwise. The original estimated cost was $97 billion for the federal government and $14 billion for states. The Coronavirus Aid, Relief, and Economic Security Act (CARES) allows businesses to temporarily carry back losses and use them to reduce their 2020 taxable income to zero. Without timely decoupling, states will lose tax revenue. The favorable treatment of pass-through entities that contributes a great deal to the corporate income tax decline also comes from IRS tax codes, which will be discussed shortly.

Tax Loopholes and Corporate Tax Planning

The 44 states enact their corporate income taxes separately, creating a series of loopholes for corporations to explore. For instance, many big corporations have subsidiaries across the nation. Under the traditional "separate-entity taxation," state tax laws treat parents and subsidiaries as separate tax entities. A common tax sheltering strategy for corporations is shifting their profits from states where they have earned income to states with low tax rates. Under what is known as "a Delaware Holding Company," or a passive investment company (PIC), corporations such as Toys-R-Us can transfer their logo and other trademarks to their subsidiaries in Delaware and Nevada and then pay them royalties for the right to display the trademarks. Loyalties, as costs of doing business, are tax deductible, thus reducing parent corporate tax liability. The payment subsidiaries received is not taxed because of Delaware and Nevada's favorable tax shelter laws (Gardner et al. 2017).

Another tax avoidance technique similar to PIC is a captive REIT. A company such as Walmart can establish a REIT to transfer the ownership of all its stores to this REIT and then rent the stores. The rent Walmart pays the REIT resembles the loyalty for the PIC. Walmart can deduct it from its tax. The REIT that receives the rent will not pay corporate income tax because it is a tax-exempt entity under the federal tax law, and state governments follow the federal tax code. All the dividends of REITs will be allocated to owners who only pay PIT (Mazerov 2009).

Gardner et al. (2017) study how some corporations can hire well-trained accountants to exploit the tax codes and incentives to avoid their tax share. After examining 240 profitable Fortune 500 corporations between 2008 and 2015, they concluded that while the average statutory tax rate was 6.25%, these companies only paid 2.9% of their U.S. profit. If they had paid the 6.25% rate, that would have brought in $126 billion more in state CIT. Among the 240 companies, 92 did not pay any tax in at least one of the eight years under examination. Four did not pay any taxes in all the years.

The global economy that has arisen in recent decades imposes an even bigger challenge to state corporate income tax systems. An increasing number of multinational corporations have subsidiaries in other countries, allowing corporations to shift their profits (Toder and Viard 2016).

Tax Incentive Programs

As discussed above, state governments allow businesses to reduce their tax liabilities through tax exemptions, exclusions, deductions, credits, and preferential tax rates. Some of these programs are due to the link to federal tax codes, but states do establish a wide range of tax expenditure programs on their own to promote certain economic and social policies as discussed earlier.

While the exact dollar amount is not known, these programs cost states billions of dollars every year. Loughead (2021a) from the Tax Foundation states that in 2019, "altogether, state and local governments gave out an estimated $95 billion a year in business incentives" (p. 1) when corporate income tax revenue was only $66 billion. According to Boddupalli, Sammartino, and Toder (2020), who studied tax expenditure programs in California, Minnesota, Massachusetts, and the Washington D. C., the combined estimated cost of individual income tax and corporate income tax incentives ranged from 51% to 61% of total individual and corporate income tax. Among the incentives, the most prevalent and most expensive are those for economic development. For instance, in 2020, California's top programs include those for economic development, with the cost ranging from $150 million for California Competes credit to $1.7 billion for research and development credits.

Costly as they are, many studies have found many of these programs are ineffective and inefficient. For instance, the Maryland state auditor found that while the fiscal impact of its enterprise zone tax credits continues to rise, they did not effectively create job opportunities for enterprise zone residents (McConville, Ogden, and Rehermann 2022). The Missouri state auditor concluded that its historic preservation tax credit program and low-income housing tax credit program were both inefficient uses of state resources. Only 49–85 cents of every historic preservation tax credit dollar issued went toward rehabilitation costs. About 35 cents of every low-income housing tax credit went to the development of housing (Montee 2008; Schweich 2014).

Indeed, public finance scholars and commentators, both liberal and conservative, all criticize tax incentives as poor policy choices. As Brunori (2021) states, they "violate every principle of sound policy" (p. 24). They are costly and ineffective in promoting jobs and giving favors to some at the expense of others. However, pressured by interstate competition, state officials continue to use them. One incentive program that has received a lot of criticism from state tax experts is the states' adoption of a Single Sales Factor (SSF) apportionment formula. Traditionally, states used a three-factor apportionment method where equal weight was given to a corporation's payroll, property, and sales in calculating the share of multi-state corporation profit that a state should collect in its corporate income tax. In the past 20 years, more and more states have given more weight or all weight to sales in the calculation, arguing that counting property and payroll in the apportionment discourages businesses from maintaining a large payroll and physical plants. There is no empirical evidence to prove an SSF formula would encourage companies to expand their physical plants and hire more employees (Griffith 2014). SSF apportionment is also costly and further erodes the corporate income tax base. Taxpayers know how to game the sales factor, and the SSF formula can allow large and profitable companies with little to no sales in the state to end up paying no taxes.

The Increase of Pass-through Businesses, Particularly S-corporations

Pass-through businesses include sole proprietorships, partnerships, and S-corporations. Sole proprietorships have one single individual owner; partnerships have multiple owners; S-corporations can have up to 100 shareholders. While C-corporations pay the federal CIT at the entity level, and then shareholders pay PIT on capital gains and dividends, pass-through businesses do not pay the federal CIT. Instead, the owners report their income to federal personal income returns and are subject to federal income tax rates (Tax Policy Center 2020). To a large extent, state governments treat the pass-through entities the same way.

The number of pass-through businesses has almost tripled in the last three decades, from roughly 10.9 million in 1980 to 30 million in 2011 (Pomerleau 2015). In 2018, 95% of the companies in the United States were pass-through businesses that employed more than half of the workforce. The rise of pass-through entities has corresponded with C-corporations' decline in both numbers and the share of economic income (Krupkin and Looney 2017). Until the 1980s, C-corporations dominated the U.S. economy and generated four times more business income than pass-through businesses. By 2013, C-corporations' share had declined to 37% of aggregate state-level business income.

Several factors contribute to the growth of pass-through businesses. A major element is the favorable tax treatment of pass-through businesses relative to corporations. For instance, the Tax Reform Act of 1986 (TRA86) lowered the personal income top marginal tax rate from 50% to 28%, making it more profitable to run a pass-through business, leading more companies to shift to pass-through businesses. Another factor is federal and state legislation loosening limitations on the activities, financial structure, and ownership of S-corporations. For instance, the maximum number of shareholders allowed for S-corporations increased from 15 in 1980 to 100 in 2004, with all family members up to six generations counted as one person (Gale and Haldeman 2021; Krupkin and Looney 2017).

When more businesses shift from the traditional C-corporation to pass-through businesses, fewer businesses pay corporate income tax. A study by economists from the University of Chicago, the U.S. Treasury Department, and the University of California at Berkeley revealed that if pass-through businesses were taxed as C-corporations, the federal government could have collected $100 billion in 2011 and $790 billion between 2003 and 2012. They also concluded that pass-through preferential tax treatment causes enormous long-term revenue loss (Thornton and Duke 2016). "The U.S. Congressional Budget Office (CBO) recently estimated that about half of the projected decline in corporate income tax revenue in recent years was a result of C-corporations transferring to pass-through entities and thereby no longer paying any corporate income tax at all" (Thornton and Duke 2016, p. 4). Although CBO's study focuses on the impact on the federal government, it is not hard to see the significant revenue loss for state governments. Bivens (2022) stated that S-corporations are the major factor that contributed to the reduction of the effective rate of business-level taxation from 5.2% in 1989 to 2.6% in 2017, a 50% reduction. If the 5.2% effective rate had remained, state and local governments could have raised $57 billion in 2019.

Corporate Income Tax in Financing State Governments

Given its small and continually declining share (except in 2021), will corporate income tax hold an important role in state tax revenue systems? To many, the answer is no. Corporate income tax is often blamed for hurting the state economy. There are constant efforts to cut and even eliminate it. Judging from taxation theory, Brunio (2005) states that corporate income tax is not an effective tax. It never works well and never will. Critics claim it creates double taxation, the tax incidence is not certain, administrative and compliance costs are high, and the revenue generated is low.

However, proponents see the important role corporate income tax plays in state tax revenue systems and insist measures be taken to broaden the base. According to ITEP (2011), corporate income tax is the most progressive tax a state can impose. The shareholders are dominantly wealthy people. Research has generally confirmed that the tax burden falls on the stockholders and has found a weak link between corporate income tax rate cuts and wage increases for common workers (Serrato and Zidar 2016). When the corporate income tax was adopted in the early 1900s, one of the major reasons was to ensure that corporations would pay their fair share. This rationale still stands well today. A system will be perceived as unfair when it taxes ordinary people but not the profitable corporations that also use public services.

From a revenue stability perspective, corporate income tax has an interesting place. On one hand, it is the most volatile revenue among all taxes. On the other hand, eliminating it would cost states billions of dollars of revenue that is not easy to replace. Several states have proposed a gross income tax, but gross income tax is more distortionary than corporate income tax. Bivens (2022) states that even if another resource can be tapped, it cannot entirely offset the impact of lost corporate income tax collections because of the strong positive relationship between states' overall tax revenue and corporate income tax revenue. His analysis shows that one dollar collected in corporate income taxes is associated with more than one dollar in overall tax revenue. In the same logic, a one-dollar cut would lead states to lose more than one dollar in overall tax revenue. More importantly, keeping state corporate income tax will keep state tax systems diverse and broad, releasing pressure from personal income and sales taxes. As far as its volatility is concerned, states could structure their revenue system to incorporate a variety of taxes that respond to economic changes differently. Furthermore, CIT with a broad base can also mitigate the impact of its volatility.

State Fiscal Stability and Measures to Broaden the Tax Base

Since corporate income tax has an important role in state government finance, reform efforts could focus on broadening its base. Theoretically, the base could be broadened by decoupling from the federal corporate income tax system, closing the loopholes, reforming incentive programs, and reforming pass-through businesses. In reality, some of these actions are not politically feasible, but there are still some that elected officials are able to undertake and have pursued.

Decoupling from the Federal Tax

Many states have tried to decouple from the federal system to avoid costly federal tax provisions. For instance, more than half of corporate income tax states have passed measures not allowing the federal "bonus depreciation" and the federal special manufacturing tax breaks in their corporate tax. Those who could not decouple their tax system in a timely manner saw their base shrinking (Gardner et al. 2017). Another example concerns the federal "net operation loss carry back" provision. While every state allows corporations to carry their operating loss forward, the federal provision allows businesses to carry it back for two years. Many states have made efforts to decouple from the federal provision. Those who have not would have to allow corporations to apply their net operating loss to the prior two years even if businesses had done well then.

Closing Tax Loopholes

One significant corporate income tax reform is replacing "separate-entity taxation" with combined reporting. With more public awareness of corporate tax sheltering, combined reporting has received much support. In 1983, the U.S. Supreme Court upheld its validity (Mazerov 2009). Sixteen states had adopted it prior to 1985. Today, at least 28 states require combined reporting (Brunori 2023). Under combined reporting, the parent and subsidiaries are treated as one entity, not separate ones. The profits from all of them are combined, including those from Delaware and Nevada. For tax purposes, a state taxes a share of the combined profits. Proponents believe this effectively eliminated the loopholes created under the separate-entity taxation and helped stop the further erosion of state corporate income tax bases. Yet, critics point out that this imposes more burdens on businesses but does not bring as much revenue as promised (Brunori 2023). The revenue increase runs somewhere between 10% and 25%. Whether this number is significant depends on how it is perceived. The combined reporting, though not a penicillin that can cure all the flaws in the system, is a significant and influential move for improving the state CIT base and improving the fairness of the system.

Related to the combined reporting is the idea of "worldview" combined reporting or complete reporting. "Worldview" combined reporting is meant to address the concern that an increasing number of multinational corporations can shift their profits to offshore tax havens. The estimated tax revenue loss is $298.9 billion per year (Phillips and Proctor 2019, p. 3). Under "worldview combined reporting, all the subsidiaries in the U.S. and other parts of the world are included when calculating the profits earned and then "a formula based on business fundamentals is used to determine the portion of those profits that should be subject to a given state's corporate income tax" (Davis and Gardner 2023, p. 3). Worldview combined reporting has been discussed for several decades among those who want to reform CIT but with limited successful implementation.

States have also undertaken a few other measures to expand their corporate income tax base. One is the alternative minimum tax (AMT). That is, no matter how many loopholes a corporation uses, it has to pay a certain amount of tax. Several states utilized the federal AMT, but the rule is watered down. Gardner et al. (2017) recommend "rejuvenating the old federal AMT rules as an alternative-less loophole-prone tax regime" (p. 10).

Tax Expenditure Reforms

Tax expenditure programs should be reformed to broaden the corporate income tax base. State policy makers have made progress in this area in the past decades, but there is still a long way to go. The starting point is to generate tax expenditure reports so that the public and lawmakers can identify and analyze these programs. Most states require tax expenditure reporting, yet the quality and frequency differ. Some are more detailed, while others are not. The best practice requires that reporting be performed on a regular basis, ideally every year or every other year, and include information on the rationale behind the incentive, the desired outcome, who benefits, and metrics for rigorous effectiveness evaluation. Some state reports meet the criteria, but many do not (Boddupalli et al. 2020).

Two elements are critical for the reform to take place. First, there must be a process to have meaningful evaluations of the incentives. This requires states to establish a strategic plan for periodic evaluations using measures of their impacts to inform policy choices. The impact includes how the program influences business behaviors, affects the state budget and economy, and whether certain businesses benefit at the expense of others (Goodman and Chapman 2017). Second, the process must ensure that the legislature will study the evaluation results (such as by holding legislative hearings) and make incentive changes accordingly. This is critically important because changes can occur only when legislatures use the results.

For a long time, legislatures, in general, gave little scrutiny to incentive programs. They are usually permanent programs, written into tax codes, and do not go through regular review as other direct spending programs do (Goodman and Chapman 2017). While there were some concerns about the actual benefits of these programs, it was the financial crisis of the Great Recession that pushed lawmakers to look closely at these programs. From 2009 to 2016, 26 states adopted laws requiring regular evaluation to provide lawmakers with better information on tax incentives. Missouri and Washington, who had adopted these laws earlier, continue to improve their efforts (Goodman and Chapman 2017). State legislatures also tried to ensure lawmakers use the evaluation results. For instance, in 2021, the Colorado General Assembly used a legislative oversight committee to ensure lawmakers dedicate time to study the evaluation results.

Due to these efforts, many states cut or modified some major tax incentive programs. For instance, legislators in several states, including California, Florida, and Maryland, reformed their Enterprise Zone programs after evaluations showed the programs provided a much weaker return on states' investment than other programs and were not effective in creating jobs for enterprise residents. In Florida, legislators let the program expire in 2015 instead of continuing it with another multimillion-dollar investment (Goodman and Chapman 2017). The legislature replaced the Enterprise Zone program with several more comprehensive tax incentive programs in California. In Maryland, even though the legislature ignored the state auditor's evaluation and did not accept the recommendations, the 2021 re-evaluation did catch their attention, which led to a revision of the program (McConville, Ogden, and Rehrmann 2022).

The story of filmmaking tax credits also illustrates the impact of tax expenditure evaluations on state policy. This tax incentive started with Louisiana in 1992 and reached its peak in 2010 when 45 states adopted it. After the Great Recession, state governments began to scrutinize the program by evaluating its effectiveness. A common finding from various states was that "despite the positive anecdotal evidence that accompanies big film projects, such programs do not provide a substantial return on investment" (Brainerd and Jimenez 2022, p. 2). As a result, although the program was popular, the post-Great Recession years saw various states imposing limits, caps, reductions, and even terminations on the program, and this trend continued well into economic recovery. For instance, in 2008, Indiana placed a $5 million annual cap on its media production expenditure income tax credit. In 2009, Kansas suspended its film production income tax credit for two years. In 2010 and 2011, Kentucky and New Mexico capped film tax credits, respectively. In 2010, New Jersey added temporary limits to certain film tax credits. Alaska repealed its film production tax credit in 2016 and West Virginia in 2018 (Brainerd and Jimenez 2022).

Based on how well they evaluate their incentive programs, Pew Charitable Trusts rated the 50 states as leading, making progress, and trailing. There are 10 leading states, 17 states making progress, and 23 trailing states. The leading states are those that have a policy for periodic evaluation, effectively measure the incentives' impacts, and use evaluation results to inform policy choices. They are Washington, Minnesota, Nebraska, Oklahoma, Iowa, Indiana, Mississippi, Florida, Maine, and Maryland. Those making progress are those whose evaluation falls short of one or two tenets of the criteria. The trailing states are those that do not have an evaluation policy or have a policy in place but are ineffective in measuring impact or helping lawmakers improve program effectiveness (Goodman and Chapman 2017).

Tax incentive structures also deserve careful examination. Many incentive credits have no caps, and many are refundable and transferable. Refundable credits allow a business to claim a refund when their tax liability is smaller than the tax credits. Transferable credits allow a business to sell its extra tax credits to another company that owes state tax. All these designs can lead to runaway program costs and not necessarily desirable program results (Boender 2022). In Maryland's Enterprise Zone program, the state reimburses half of the local government's property tax credits. Since there is no upper limit, the fiscal impact increased from $2.4 million in fiscal 2019 to an estimated $26.2 million in fiscal year 2021, a 12.6% average annual growth rate (McConville, Ogden, and Rehrmann 2022). The Missouri Low-Income Housing Tax Credit Program and Missouri Historic Preservation Tax Credit are both refundable, transferable, and can be sold. The redemption credit costs run much higher than what was estimated when the programs were authorized (Montee 2008; Schweich 2014). Imposing caps can enhance the program's effectiveness and minimize fiscal risks.

There are several ways to impose caps. They can be applied to incentive authorization, the total approved for a business when it applies for the incentive, or to incentivize redemption when the actual credits are redeemed. According to Boender (2022), authorization caps should be used together with redemptions for greater short- and long-term cost certainty. "By capping the authorizations, the state limits their overall financial commitments, caps on redemptions, on the other hand, control what incentives can cost each year" (p. 3). The cap can be applied to all of a state's incentive programs as a whole or to each program. The former is more effective in containing the cost. Refundable and transferable credits sound poorly constructed, but there are certain situations wherein they are justified. For instance, for a startup business that does not owe much tax liability, a refundable and transferable credit will be attractive. If this is the choice made, caps should be used to avoid cost runoff (Boender 2022).

States often offer some generous deals to businesses. It is not uncommon for the tax credits to be carried forward and backward for certain years. In Hawaii, a tax incentive to high-tech companies allowed businesses to carry forward tax credits they earned indefinitely. Therefore, years after the program was terminated in 2010 due to its ineffectiveness, the state is still paying businesses millions of dollars under the program (Goodman and Chapman 2017). States should avoid this design.

It is encouraging to see that states have taken measures to reform their incentive programs. At the same time, it is still true that elected officials sometimes cannot resist political pressure from businesses and continue to enact popular tax incentives that lead to more base erosion. Let's return to the story about film tax incentives. Even though states restricted the incentive upon the general finding that the programs do not provide a substantial return on investment, lawmakers in some states have re-implemented it in the past few years. For instance, in 2021 Indiana created the state's first film tax credit program, Illinois raised the tax credit cap from $100,000 to $500,000, and West Virginia reinstated the program in 2021 with no annual cap on the amount of credits. State lawmakers do this because the film tax incentive is popular, and they do not want to lose the film industry to other states (Brainerd and Jimenez 2022).

In American federalism, states have been engaging in interstate competition by offering businesses more and more generous benefits to attract or retain those interests. Gardner et al. (2017) warn that "chasing after businesses by fighting over who can give the largest tax concessions is a zero-sum game. States should coordinate and agree to stop this futile, destructive competition" (p. 12).

Tax incentives, although seen as a poor policy choice, will not disappear. Many started with laudable purposes. But they always involve trade-offs and need to be appropriately designed, managed, and overseen. Lawmakers need to deliberate on the pros and cons of policy choices and have a full understanding that these incentives will reduce the tax base and affect tax revenue generation for years to come. They need to know what they really want to achieve with the incentives, whether the programs are cost-effective, and how they impact the whole corporate income tax system and even the state tax system. If the incentive programs are not effective, they need to be reformed.

Reforming S-corporations

To restore corporate income tax bases, policy makers need to address the issue raised by pass-through entities. They do not pay corporate income tax, and their effective tax rates are much lower than those of C-corporations. Critics point out that it makes sense to reduce the tax burden for small businesses, but many partnerships and S-corporations are large, profitable businesses, including financial firms, oil and gas companies, real estate businesses, and large multinational law and accounting firms. They account for the increasing number of pass-through entities. S-corporations have the fastest growth rate, from 545,000 in the 1980s to 4.15 million in 2001, a 660% increase (Pomerleau 2015). According to Thornton and Duke (2016), 70% of partnership and S-corporation revenue goes to big corporations, 70% of these businesses' income goes to the top 1% of the households, and 98% of business income goes to the top 5% of the income distribution.

In the past few years, 31 states have enacted a pass-through entity tax where partnerships and S-corporations can elect to file their state income tax at the entity level. Interestingly, these laws do not aim to reform pass-through entities but to bypass the $10,000 state and local tax (SALT) deduction cap stipulated in the federal TCJA of 2017. Because the cap only applies to individual filers, not entities, filers who choose to pay the entity tax can claim tax credits or reduce their taxable income when they pay their state PIT (CBIZ 2021). This arrangement gives pass-through business owners a tax cut at the federal government's expense. States do not lose any tax revenue. As pass-through entity tax is counted as corporate income tax, this may be one factor that push up 2021 state CIT revenue collection. If Congress allows the $10,000 SALT cap to expire as planned in 2025, this arrangement may fade away.

One idea to reform the pass-through entity tax is to require big and profitable pass-through entities to pay the entity tax as C-corporations do. Governments can use the level of profits, gross receipts, or assets to set specific thresholds beyond which corporate taxes will be applied. This threshold should be such that it includes a small number of wealthy owners whose income counts for a large share of pass-through revenue. Meanwhile, more targeted help should be provided to small businesses (Thornton and Duke 2016). Another idea is to impose either an employment tax or a net investment tax on higher earners. Not everyone supports these ideas, but the issue is real and deserves debate and continual searching for a solution (Greenberg 2017).

Conclusion

Corporate income tax is an important element in a state tax system, even though it is a small share of total state tax revenue. In addition to their progressive nature, CITs contribute to a state's financial system stability by bringing in a share of revenue that will not be easily replaced. Although the system contains a wide range of tax loopholes and incentive programs, lawmakers might try to address some of them and expand the tax base. Over the years, particularly in the post-Great Recession era, state lawmakers made various efforts to raise corporate income tax rates, broaden its base by closing some loopholes, and impose more scrutiny on tax incentive programs. Though rational analysis provides valuable insight for improving tax policy, tax policies are always political decisions and are affected by Ideological and political beliefs. In the absence of fiscal crisis, the pressure from businesses, communities, and interstate competition may cause state lawmakers to feel unable or unwilling to adopt the suggestions discussed above.

While state corporate income tax will remain controversial and complicated, what is clear is that a broadened tax base can afford lower tax rates and improve revenue production and fiscal stability. It is important for lawmakers to understand the long-term implications of policy choices and engage in full deliberation from the fiscal stability perspective. When making corporate tax policy decisions, state lawmakers should examine how that action affects the tax base, their preferred policy goals, and revenue stability. State policy makers would also consider how their choice might impact other taxes. When their policy choices result in a narrowed base and diminished revenue generation, this might force the increase of other state taxes, such as the general sales tax and PIT. This may be something that lawmakers do not want to see.

References

Bivens, Josh. 2022. "Reclaiming Corporate Tax Revenues." *Economic Policy Institute.*

Boddupalli, Aravind, Frank Sammartino, and Eric Toder. 2020. "State Income Tax Expenditures." Washington, DC: Urban-Brookings Tax Policy Center.

Boender, Khara. Khara Boender to Kirk Fulford, memorandum. (2022). "Resources on Improving Incentive Design and Administration, Particularly Through Evaluation Findings and Associated Study Committee/Commissions." The PEW Charitable Trusts. (May 2).

Brainerd, Jackson and Andrea Jimenez. 2022. "Brief Film Tax Incentives Back in the Spotlight." *National Conference of State Legislatures.*

Brunori, David. 2023. "Pennsylvania to Consider Combined Reporting…Again". *Tax Alert.* RMS. (January 26).

Brunori, David. 2021. "Essays on State Tax Policy – Rethinking State Corporate Income Taxation." *Journal of State Taxation,* 39 (2) (March), pp. 21–25.

Brunori, David. 2005. *State Tax Policy: A Political Perspective.* 2nd ed. Washington, DC: The Urban Institute Press.

CBIZ. 2021. "Pass-through Entities can Accrue State Taxes Anew, Who Knew?"

Davis, Carl and Matthew Gardner. 2023. "Far from Radical: State Corporate Income Taxes Already Often Look beyond the Water's Edge." *Institute on Taxastion and Economic Policy.* (November 7).

Francis, Norton. 2016. "State Tax Incentives for Economic Development." *Urban Institute.*

Gale, William G. and Claire Haldeman. 2021. "The Other 95%: Taxes on Pass-through Businesses." *Econofact.* (April 22).

Gardner, Matthew, Aidan Russell Davis, Robert S. McIntyre, and Richard Philips. 2017. "3 Percent and Dropping: State Corporate Tax Avoidance in the Fortune 500-2008 to 2015." *Institute on Taxation and Economic Policy.*

Goodman, Josh, and Jeff Chapman. 2017. "How States are Improving Tax Incentives for Jobs and Growth: A National Assessment of Evaluation Practices." *The Pew Charitable Trusts.*

Greenberg, Scott. 2017. "Pass-through Businesses: Data and Policy." Fiscal Fact No. 536. *Tax Foundation.* (January).

Griffith, Cara. 2014. "Single Sales Factor Apportionment May Be Inevitable, But It Is Fair?" *Forbes.* (September 18).

Hillis, Thom. 2017. "Senator Thom Tillis: Tax Reform Transformed North Carolina. Congress, Take Note." *Thom in the News.* (September 21).

Institute on Taxation and Economic Policy. 2011. "Guide to Fair State and Local Taxes." *Institute on Taxation and Economic Policy.*

Kaeding, Nicole, and Jeremy Horpedahl. 2018. "Help from Our Friends: What States Can Learn from Tax Reform Experiences Across the Country." *Tax Foundation.*

Krupkin, Aaron and Adam Looney. 2017. "9 Facts About Pass-through Businesses." *Brookings.*

Loughead, Katherine. 2021a. "Illuminating the Hidden Costs of State Tax Incentives." *Tax Foundation.*

Loughead, Katherine. 2021b. "North Carolina Reinforces Its Tax Reform Legacy." *Tax Foundation.* (December 3).

McConville, Mindy L., Brett Ogden, and Robert Rehrmann. 2022. *Evaluation of the Enterprise Zone Tax Credit.* Annapolis: Maryland Department of Legislative Services Office of Policy Analysis.

Mazerov, Michael. 2009. "A Majority of States Have Now Approved a Key Corporate Tax Reform – Combined Reporting." *Center on Budget and Policy Priorities.* (April 3).

Montee, Susan. 2008. *Tax Credit Analysis of Low-Income Housing Tax Credit Program.* Report No. 2008-23. Jefferson City: The Office of the Missouri State Auditor.National Conference of State Legislature (NCSL). 2009. *State Tax Actions 2008: Special Fiscal Report.* Denver, Colorado: National Conference of State Legislature.

National Conference of State Legislature (NCSL). 2012. *State Tax Actions 2011: Special Fiscal Report.* Denver, Colorado: National Conference of State Legislature.

National Conference of State Legislature (NCSL) (2016-2021). *State Tax Actions Database.* State Tax Actions Database.

Phillips, Richard, and Nathan Proctor. 2019. *A Simple Fix for a $17 Billion Loophole: How States Can Reclaim Revenue Lost to Tax Havens.* Washington, DC: Institute on Taxation and Economic Policy.

Pomerleau, Kyle. 2015. "An Overview of Pass-through Businesses in the United States." Report No. 2014-018. *Tax Foundation.*Rafool, Mandy and Todd Haggerty. 2011. *State Tax Actions 2010: Special Fiscal Report.* Denver, Colorado: National Conference of State Legislature.

Rafool, Mandy and Todd Haggerty. 2011. *State Tax Actions 2010: Special Fiscal Report.* Denver, Colorado: National Conference of State Legislature.

Rafool, Mandy. 2013. *State Tax Actions 2012: Special Fiscal Report.* Denver, Colorado: National Conference of State Legislature.

Rafool, Mandy. 2014. *State Tax Actions 2013: Special Fiscal Report* Denver, Colorado: National Conference of State Legislature.

Rafool, Mandy. 2015. *State Tax Actions 2014: Special Fiscal Report.* Denver, Colorado: National Conference of State Legislature.

Schweich, Thomas A. 2014. *Economic Development: Historic Preservation Tax Credit Program.* Jefferson City: The Office of the Missouri State Auditor.

Serrato, Juan Carlos Suarez and Owen Zidar. 2018. "The Structure of State Corporate Taxation and Its Impact on State Tax Revenues and Economic Activity." *Journal of Public Economics,* 167 (October), pp. 158–176.

Serrato, Juan Carlos Suarez and Owen Zidar. 2016. "Who Benefits from State Corporate Tax Cuts? A Local Labor Market Approach with Heterogeneous Firms." *American Economic Review,* 106 (9) (September), pp. 2582–2624.

Tax Foundation's *State Corporate Income Tax Rates* (Selected Years) (2008; 2022). https://taxfoundation.org/data/state-tax/?sort_order=date+desc&_sft_datamaps=state-corporate-income-tax-rates-and-brackets#results

Tax Policy Center. 2020. "Briefing Book: A Citizen Guide to the Fascinating (though often complex) Elements of the U.S. Tax System." *Urban-Brookings Tax Policy Center*.

Thornton, Alexander and Brenden Duke. 2016. "Ending the Pass-through Tax Loophole for Big Business." The Center for American Progress.

Toder, Eric and Alan Viard. 2016. "A Proposal to Reform the Taxation of Corporate Income." Urban-Brookings Tax Policy Center.

Urban Institute. 2023. "Corporate Income Taxes." *State and Local Backgrounders*. www.taxpolicycenter.org/briefing-book/how-do-state-and-local-corporate-income-taxes-workU.S. Census *Annual Survey of State Governments Tax Collection*. www.census.gov/programs-surveys/stc.html

Waisanen, Bert and Todd Haggerty. 2010. *State Tax Actions 2009: Special Fiscal Report*. Denver, Colorado: National Conference of State Legislature.

8
STATE SALES TAXES

How to Modernize Them for State Fiscal Stability?

Introduction

In the United States, 45 states and many local governments collect general sales tax. The exceptions are Alaska, Delaware, Montana, New Hampshire, and Oregon. Several states collect both general sales tax and gross receipts tax, including Nevada, Ohio, Tennessee, Texas, and Washington. Delaware collects gross receipts tax only. General sales tax is paid at the retail level by consumers on goods and services they purchase as a percentage of their retail prices. Gross receipts tax, also a sales tax, is imposed on all sales paid by sellers, typically taxing business-to-business (B2B) purchases. Thirty-eight states also allow local governments to collect general sales tax (Urban Institute No Date).

Sales tax rates vary from state to state, ranging from 2.9% in Colorado to 7.25% in California, with most states levying tax at 5%–7% rates. When a local government sales tax rate is added, total sales tax rates can easily reach over 7.25% for most states (Urban Institute No Date). Though different among states, gross receipts tax rates are nearly all well below 1%. The sales tax base also varies from state to state. According to a 2021 Tax Policy Center study, the amount of a purchase subject to the sales tax, including general sales tax and excise tax, ranges from 5% in Delaware to 36% in Vermont and 91% in Hawaii. This variation is mainly due to different treatment methods for services (Urban Institute No Date). Reliance on sales tax varies significantly from 13.4% of total state tax revenue in the Washington DC to 65.4% in South Dakota, depending on the mix of other taxes, rates, and the breadth of the sales tax base. Heavy users of sales tax states include Florida, Texas, Nevada, Washington, and Tennessee, each of whom collected 55% or more of their total state revenue from sales taxes (Walczak 2022).

Compared with income tax and property tax, the sales tax receives less opposition since the tax burden can be exported to nonresidents. It also has less impact on economic activity decisions and is easier to administer. However, the sales tax is a regressive tax, imposing a heavier burden on low-income households.

The sales tax is productive, generating more tax revenue for states than other taxes from 1947 through 2001, and in 2003 and 2004 (Mikesell and Kioko 2018). Even though personal income tax slightly surpasses sales tax, the sales tax still makes up roughly one-third of states' total tax revenue (see Table 8.1). According to the U.S. Census data, general sales and gross receipts taxes generated $337 billion in 2019, $342 billion in 2020, and $370 billion in 2021. Furthermore, the retail sales tax is less elastic and less volatile than the personal income tax (PIT). Therefore, general sales tax performance is critically important to state fiscal stability. According to Mikesell and Kioko, "Any challenges to the viability of the retail sales tax base translate into challenges for the finances of individual state governments" (Mikesell and Kioko 2018, p. 5).

The state sales tax system was a product of the Great Depression when state property tax revenue collapsed. While the sales tax has been a major tax revenue generator for state governments, over the past a few decades, the new service-based and technology-oriented economy has imposed serious challenges on the sales tax system. This chapter examines how states can modernize their sales tax systems for the sake of their fiscal stability. The discussion will first focus on sales tax changes in terms of tax rate and tax base in the past decades. Then, it will examine the challenges the sales tax faces and how state governments

TABLE 8.1 State General Sales and Gross Receipts Tax as a Percentage of State Total Tax Revenue: 2007–2021

Years	% of State Total Tax Revenue	Years	% of State Total Tax Revenue
2007	31.461	2015	31.282
2008	30.802	2016	31.502
2009	31.786	2017	31.851
2010	31.776	2018	30.971
2011	31.199	2019	30.849
2012	31.265	2020	32.023
2013	30.566	2021	29.171
2014	31.335		

Source: Author's calculation based on data from U.S. Census *Annual Survey of State Governments Tax Collection.* www.census.gov/programs-surveys/stc.html

have addressed and should address them. While political and ideological factors always affect any tax decisions, state sales tax reforms are more driven and complicated by the new and emerging forms of the economy and by the U.S. Supreme Court's jurisdiction over states' ability to tax remote sales.

State Sales Tax Changes during 2008–2020

While challenges and issues with state sales taxes existed long before the Great Recession, the event and subsequent serious revenue shortages pushed states to reform their tax systems, including the sales tax. This section will examine sales tax policy changes that states enacted in the years since the Great Recession in light of their impact on state fiscal stability.

The Data in Table 8.2 reveals four observations.

First, for those years under examination, state general sales tax experienced net dollar increases almost every year (see Column 4). Three years—2011, 2014, and 2017—saw negative dollar impacts, but two of them were the results of the expirations of temporary sales tax increases that some states adopted in the previous years. In 2011, California let expire a temporary rate increase approved in 2009, causing a $4.5 billion revenue loss. In the same year, North Carolina also allowed a 1% temporary sales tax rate increase to expire for a revenue reduction of nearly $1 billion. In 2017, the California sales tax increase approved by voters in 2012 under Proposition 30 faded away after four years as planned. All of these were not the results of intentional tax cuts.

The consistent overall net tax increases reflect the fact that the sales tax, a major source of state general revenue, is often an easy target for states to increase their revenue, especially when they face severe revenue shortages. This is clearly seen in California, New York, Connecticut, Kansas, North Carolina, and Maine during the Great Recession. In addition to shoring up states' general revenue, some states also turned to the sales tax to fund certain specific public programs, including school funding, transportation, Medicaid expansion, and others. Here are a few examples:

- In 2008, Minnesota used its increase to protect natural resources and preserve arts and cultural heritage.
- In 2009, Nevada increased its sales tax for school funding.
- Virginia increased its sales tax rate in 2013 from 5% to 5.3% to generate $800 million per year as part of its transportation funding reform (Bishop-Henchman 2013).
- Arkansas' voters, in 2012, approved a ten-year sales tax increase from 6% to 6.5% to fund roads and construction.
- Ohio increased its sales tax and property tax rates but cut income tax in 2013.

TABLE 8.2 State Sales Tax Changes: 2008–2020

Year (1)	Overall # States Net Raise (2)	Overall # States Net Cut (3)	Net $ Impact (Million) (4)	Tax Rate # of State Tax Actions Raise (5)	Tax Rate # of State Tax Actions Cut (6)	Tax Base # of State Tax Actions Broaden (7)	Tax Base # of State Tax Actions Narrow (8)	Sales Tax Holiday (9)	States with Big Tax Raise (Cut)[a] (10)
2008	6	13	685.6[b]	2	1	8	24	4	IN (MD)
2009	17	6	7,236.5	2	5	22	14	3	CA, MA, NY, NC, OH
2010	10	6	1,736.5	3	0	19	9	3	AZ, KS, NY
2011	7	12	−5,244.7[c]	1	2[c]	23	14	2	CT, HI, MD (MA, NY, NC)
2012	3	13	428.1	2	0	8	18	3	CA
2013	11	16	770.3	4	2	28	39	3	AZ, MD, OH, VA (TX)
2014	6	16	−420.4	0	0	6	30	4	(MN)
2015	11	11	151.5	1	0	14	34	5	CT, KS, LA, (FL, GA)
2016	6	15	788.6	2	2	9	26	4	LA, PA, SD (MI)
2017	11	15	−1,915.2[c]	0	2	11	37	4	OK, WA (CA, NJ, TN)
2018	14	11	817.3	1	3	15	20	4	GA, IL, KY, LA (WI)
2019	25	7	1,456.8	0	0	39	23	2	NM, NY OH, TX
2020	8	8	397.7	0	0	7	8	3	MA
Total				23	17	209	296	44	

[a] States with a big raise or cut are those that increased or cut their tax by more than $100 million the next fiscal year.
[b] These numbers need to be interpreted with caution. In some years, the number is skewed by changes in one or two states. The net sales tax increase in 2008 is due to Indiana's $937 million revenue increase resulting from its 1% general sales tax rate increase to offset a substantial local government property tax reduction.
[c] The negative amount resulting from the expirations of the earlier tax increase(s).

Sources: Author's tally based on National Conference of State Legislature *State Tax Action Database 2008–2021* by Waisanen and Haggerty 2010; Rafool and Haggerty 2011; Rafool 2013; 2014; 2015; NSCL 2009; 2012; NCSL 2016–2020.

Data in Table 8.2 reveal four observations.

- Utah voters approved a ballot measure to raise the sales tax for Medicaid expansion in 2020.
- South Dakota's $60 million additional sales tax revenue in 2023 was to give public school teachers a pay raise.

Second, among these years, the largest sales tax increases occurred in the years immediately after the Great Recession (i.e., 2008–2009), when states were desperate for funding during the financial crisis, and the years after the *Wayfair* decision (i.e., 2018 and 2019), when states were allowed to legally require remote sellers to collect sales tax. These years not only experienced significant net dollar increases but also more states that increased their tax rates than decreased them, and more states that broadened their tax base than narrowed them.

Third, in terms of tax rate changes, there are more rate increases than decreases. Several rate increases were temporary (e.g., California in 2009 and 2012, New York in 2011, and North Carolina in 2011), but many are permanent. Table 8.3 also shows that 18 states have a higher general sales tax in 2022 than in 2008. This is consistent with the sales tax rate increasing trend observed by Mikesell and Kioko (2018). States raise sales tax rates to compensate for a narrower tax base. Besides, raising the sales tax rates is easier than other taxes because the tax burden can be exported to nonresidents, and public opposition is less.

Table 8.3 shows that New Jersey is the only state that has a lower sales tax rate in 2022 than in 2008. In 2017, New Jersey adopted a two-step rate reduction plan, cutting its sales tax rate from 7% to 6.625% in 2018. This is part of New Jersey's broader tax reform package. Several states have more targeted rate cuts for a specific area of consumption. Mississippi reduced its sales tax rate on farm implements and parts in 2008. Several states have cut their sales tax on groceries and women hygiene products.

Fourth, compared with tax rate changes, there are much more tax base changes. Among the base changes, more actions contributed to tax base narrowing than base expansion. In some years, states have tried expanding their tax bases by eliminating existing tax exemptions and credits, looking into taxing digital goods, and including certain services. For instance, in 2011, Connecticut expanded its sales tax base to include services such as pet grooming, spa services, cosmetic surgery, motor vehicle towing, yoga classes, and nonprescription medicine. Rhode Island extended its sales tax to include previously exempt items, including nonprescription drugs, travel and tour company products, vehicle insurance proceeds, and prewritten downloaded software. North Carolina and Vermont expanded the sales tax on entertainment and other services, including digital download sales.

However, the pressure to keep and expand exemptions is always greater. For instance, in 2014, Minnesota reinstated several sales tax exemptions that were

TABLE 8.3 State General Sales Tax Rates: 2008–2022

State	2008	2022	State	2008	2022
Alabama	4.00%	4.00%	Nebraska	5.50%	5.50%
Arizona	5.60%	5.60%	Nevada	6.50%	6.85%
Arkansas	6.00%	6.50%	New Jersey	7.00%	6.63%
California	7.25%	7.25%	New Mexico	5.00%	5.13%
Colorado	2.90%	2.90%	New York	4.00%	4.00%
Connecticut	6.00%	6.35%	N. Carolina	4.25%	4.75%
Florida	6.00%	6.00%	N. Dakota	5.00%	5.00%
Georgia	4.00%	4.00%	Ohio	5.50%	5.75%
Hawaii	4.00%	4.00%	Oklahoma	4.50%	4.50%
Idaho	6.00%	6.00%	Pennsylvania	6.00%	6.00%
Illinois	6.25%	6.25%	Rhode Island	7.00%	7.00%
Indiana	6.00%	7.00%	S. Carolina	6.00%	6.00%
Iowa	5.00%	6.00%	S. Dakota	4.00%	4.50%
Kansas	5.30%	6.50%	Tennessee	7.00%	7.00%
Kentucky	6.00%	6.00%	Texas	6.25%	6.25%
Louisiana	4.00%	4.45%	Utah	4.65%	6.10%
Maine	5.00%	5.50%	Vermont	6.00%	6.00%
Maryland	6.00%	6.00%	Virginia	5.00%	5.30%
Massachusetts	5.00%	6.25%	Washington	6.50%	6.50%
Michigan	6.00%	6.00%	W. Virginia	6.00%	6.00%
Minnesota	6.50%	6.88%	Wisconsin	5.00%	5.00%
Mississippi	7.00%	7.00%	Wyoming	4.00%	4.00%
Missouri	4.23%	4.23%	DC	5.75%	6.00%
National Average Rates	5.44%	5.66%			

Source: Urban-Brookings Tax Policy Center (2024).

repealed in 2013. New York eliminated the sales tax exemption on clothing purchases of less than $110 in 2009, but in 2011, it reinstated it. States also continued to provide more exemptions related to groceries, clothes (in NY), diapers, and women's hygiene. Some states have enacted new exemptions for data centers and certain B2B purchasing. The exemptions of the last group, though further eroding the tax base, improve sales tax efficiency because they reduce tax pyramiding, where the sales tax is applied to the same item several times.

The most noticeable tax base expansion occurred in online sales. In recent years, particularly after the 2018 *Wayfair* ruling, every sales tax state has passed economic nexus rules and marketplace facilitator rules to require remote sellers to collect sales tax from online purchases and marketplace facilitators to collect sales tax from third-party sellers. More on this point will be discussed in a separate section.

Erosion of the State Sales Tax Bases

It is widely documented that states' general sales tax bases have eroded over the decades. According to Mikesell and Kioko (2018), state reliance on sales tax revenue (i.e., sales tax revenue as a percentage of total state tax revenue) remained relatively stable from 1970 to 2016 in a range between 32% and 36%. Yet, sales tax breadth (measured by sales tax as a percentage of personal income) has consistently declined from 49.0% in 1970 down to 37.3% in 2016 (Mikesell and Kioko 2018) and further down to 29.52% in 2020 and 29.71% in FY 2021 (Walczak 2022) (see Table 8.4). To compensate for the breadth decline, states have raised their tax rates. If not corrected, states will have to continue to raise their tax rates or shift to other taxes (Walczak 2022). Due to the recent efforts to extend sales tax to services and remote sales, the mean breadth has improved.

Sales tax base erosion comes from two sources: the state legislatures' actions and the new internet-based economy. State legislatures' actions contribute to a wide use of sales tax exclusions and exemptions. The new economy, such as e-commerce, the sharing economy, and the service-oriented economy, produces economic transactions that are outside the traditional scope of the sales tax, causing sales base shrinkage. This section will discuss each of these sources and explain how states have addressed these challenges.

Before we move on, it is necessary to highlight another issue with the sales tax base. That is, the sales tax also has the problem of its base being "too broad." In theory, the sales tax should be imposed on the final consumption of goods. However, sometimes it taxes intermediate goods or B2B purchasing. This leads to tax pyramiding, where taxes are imposed on the same final products a few times, distorting market efficiency. States with retail sales taxes generally exempt inventory but tax many other B2B purchases, and the degree to which this happens varies from state to state. According to Mikesell and Kioko (2018), B2B purchases comprise 40% of the sales tax base. In the past decades, state governments have made efforts to exempt some of B2B purchasing, thus reducing tax pyramiding, but it is still an issue.

TABLE 8.4 Sales Tax Breadth, Reliance, and Rates: 1970–2022

	1970	*2000*	*2016*	*2021*	*2022*
Mean Reliance	32%	35.29%	34.2%	29.52%	31.18%
Mean Tax rate	3.5%	5.16%	5.56%	6.00%	6.01%
Mean Breadth	49.0%	49.98%	37.3%	29.71%	34.78%

Sources: Mikesell and Kioko (2018); Walczak (2022); Walczak (2024).

Exemptions

Over the years, state lawmakers have enacted various exemptions for certain commodities, groups, or purchasing time periods. The common sales tax exemptions are those for daily necessities, including groceries, clothes, and prescription medicine. The rationale is that since low-income households spend a disproportionate share of income on these necessities, these exemptions will make the sales tax less regressive. According to Kaedling (2017), prescription medicine is exempt in all sales tax states except in Illinois, groceries are exempt in 32 states and Washington, DC and are taxed at a reduced rate in four states, and clothes are exempt in seven states.

The consensus among public finance scholars, conservative and liberal, is that blank exemptions are costly for governments but not effective in helping low-income families. For instance, Louisiana estimated that its grocery exemptions cost the state $424 million in FY 2016. When groceries are exempt, all taxpayers, regardless of their income, receive a break. Exemptions also muddle the system, increasing both administrative and compliance costs. Scholars insist an effective and efficient way to reduce the regressivity of sales tax is through more targeted relief measures such as an income tax credit or rebate (Kaedling 2017; Mikesell and Kioko 2018). Currently, five states (Maine, Kansas, Oklahoma, Idaho, and Hawaii) are using some form of tax credit system to refund sales taxes to low-income families (Mikesell and Kioko 2018).

State governments have also exempted other products, such as female hygiene products, flags, newspapers, and magazines. Pennsylvania also exempts youth sports programs (Kadling 2017). Many states also exempt gasoline and cigarettes and then tax them at a different and higher rate as selective taxes.

The sales tax holiday is a more recent and popular form of sales tax relief. It started in New York in 1997 and then spread to more than half of the states. The holidays can be for back-to-school shopping, natural disaster preparation, or Energy Star appliances. From 2008 to 2020, state governments enacted sales tax holidays 44 times, as shown in Table 8.2. Researchers have evidence that these sales tax holidays do not increase overall economic activities. Instead, they shift the time of purchasing and cost governments a significant amount of revenue. Several states, including Georgia and Massachusetts, have eliminated their sales tax holiday, but others are still adopting it.

Why do state governments continue these relief methods when they are known to be costly and ineffective? The answer is American interest group politics. Interest groups lobby elected officials for special tax treatments, and elected officials respond to gain their support in their next election (Mikesell and Kioko 2018). Interstate competition is another factor. States want to offer the preferential tax treatments if other states do it.

Services

A major exclusion from the sales tax is services. When the sales tax was adopted during the 1930s–1950s, state lawmakers imposed a sales tax on tangible personal properties, the dominant form of consumption (Mikesell and Kioko 2018). Consumption of services was small and hard to trace. It made sense to exclude them in tax laws. Over the past several decades, consumption of services has increased, and today it accounts for 70% of people's consumption. The exemption of services reduces revenue production and makes the system more regressive because high-income households' consumptions comprise a much larger share of services (Walczak 2018).

Extending the sales tax to services would broaden the sales tax base or at least stop further erosion. The current sales tax base is 20% narrower than that in 1970. If all household services are added back, the base would be 11% broader. If healthcare and education services are excluded and all other services are added, the base would only be 8% narrower than its 1970 level (Mikesell and Kioko 2018). The revenue potential from service sales is broadly estimated to be billions of dollars (Brainerd 2022).

States pursue different approaches to extend the sales tax to services: a) taxing services generally with exemptions for certain services, and b) taxing it selectively by applying the sales tax to each type of service one after another. Four states assume the general taxing approach (i.e., Hawaii, South Dakota, New Mexico, and West Virginia), and 38 states take the selective approach. The general taxing approach is better at expanding the sales tax base. Among those with a selective basis, states differ greatly in the set of services taxed. No state taxes the services the same (Avalara No Date; Mikesell and Kioko 2018).

According to Avalara (No Date), services can be classified into six categories:

1. Service to Tangible Personal Property: This includes services that improve or repair personal property, such as car repairs and carpentry. Many states tax this category.
2. Service to Real Property: This refers to the improvements to buildings and land, such as landscaping, lawn services, and janitorial services. Many impose sales tax on some of these services.
3. Business Services: This includes services provided to businesses, such as examination services, phone answering services, and credit reporting services. Most states tax this category.
4. Personal Services: This covers a range of services for self-improvement and personal grooming such as those provided by tanning salons, massages not performed by a licensed massage therapist, and animal grooming services. About half of the states tax personal services.

5 Professional Services: This refers to the services provided by licensed professionals such as attorneys, physicians, and accountants. These are the least taxed category.
6 Amusement/Recreation: This includes admission to amusement parks and entertainment events. Amusement and recreation services are the most taxed category.

Among these categories, no states tax professional services, except for Florida and New Mexico. The opposition from professional associations is too strong. The most taxed categories are services to tangible personal property and amusement/recreation services, followed by business services, which should be exempted to avoid tax pyramiding. Among each of these general categories, states differ dramatically in the specific services each one taxes (Avalara No Date). Delaware, Hawaii, New Mexico, and South Dakota, which tax services by default, tax the most services. Other states like Texas, Connecticut, and Minnesota have actively expanded service taxability. Still, others move more slowly.

According to the Council on State Taxation, over the past 30 years, more than a quarter of states have tried to enact sweeping sales tax reform to include most services into the tax base but have failed (Brainerd 2022). In some cases, like Florida, comprehensive reform was passed but repealed shortly thereafter. The American political process typically does not accommodate comprehensive reforms.

States have largely taken a piecemeal approach to taxing services. They often add certain services to the tax base as a part of a larger measure that provides relief from income tax. For instance, in 2022, Kentucky added 35 new services to its sales tax base in a tax package that also reduced PIT rate and established a 60-day tax amnesty program. Connecticut and Iowa also enacted modest expansions in 2018 and 2019 (Brainerd 2022).

Several issues make it difficult to apply the sales tax to services. The first one is the wide objection to taxation in general. Even though it is logical to extend the sales tax to services, there is strong opposition from elected officials, the public, and affected industries. In 2017 alone, bills to tax services were introduced and debated in 23 state legislatures, but none were enacted (Povich 2017). Conservative legislators in many states predominated and opposed the changes. Taxpayers do not welcome the changes. Voters in Missouri and Arizona passed constitutional amendments prohibiting base broadening to any service not already taxed in 2018 and 2019. This may set the trend for many other states (Walczak 2018). Affected industries and professional groups do all they can to stop the passage of these tax bills, fearing that the tax will reduce their competitiveness.

Second, there is also the concern that since many services are purchased by businesses, such as payroll processing and television advertising, taxing services could further worsen the problem of tax pyramiding. Along with this is the absence of a clear line between the worker-client relationship and the worker-employer relationship (Mikesell 2018). For instance, a business can use an accounting firm to perform accounting activities, but it can also use its accountants. The former is a service, and the latter is not. If the service is taxed, businesses may choose to use their employees to produce the service even if it is less efficient than an independent firm performs (Mazerov 2009).

Third, state tax laws on services can be complicated and confusing to taxpayers. In some cases, such as in North Carolina, state tax offices must write clarifying memos about what is and is not taxable. Roof repair is taxable but not roof replacement; repairs of air conditioning and heating, repairs of water pump motors, and unclogging a drain are taxable, but the construction of added bathrooms is not. Pennsylvania does not tax snow removal unless it is from gutters and downspouts (Povich 2017). This is not only confusing to taxpayers but also costly for state administration. This complexity of the state laws is the result of the piecemeal approach states have taken to expand their sales tax and the result of a messy legislative process.

It is hard to address the first issue, but public debate and dialogue may help. The second issue is a valid concern, and in general, B2B purchases of services should be exempted. To address the third issue and modernize the state sales tax, state lawmakers could consider pursuing a comprehensive and broad-based reform approach, not the piecemeal approach. More on this point will be discussed later in the chapter.

Challenges Imposed by the Internet-based Economy

The new and digital-based economy has imposed several challenges to the sales tax base. These challenges are outside the control of state tax authorities, and they are more difficult to address. The sales tax system, established with an economy based on manufacturing, does not work well when consumption shifts to remote sales, digital goods and services, or the sharing economy.

Sharing Economy

The sharing economy refers to the economic structure where peer-to-peer transactions of goods and services occur, such as Uber and Lyft for transportation and Airbnb for short-term rental. These transactions happen on a community-based platform, not through a formal business structure. The sharing economy has always existed, but online platforms are making it easier and more proliferate (Mikesell and Kioko 2018). Enforcing the sales tax on these sharing activities is challenging because existing sales tax laws do not consider the features of the new model. The sharing economy will add to sales tax base erosion if not addressed.

There are two main obstacles to addressing this challenge. First, the sharing economy predominantly involves services. As stated earlier, services are not broadly taxed. For state governments to extend the sales tax to the sharing economy, they need to enact legislation to tax that specific service, such as lodging and car sharing, before applying the tax to the same service in the sharing economy. It is not legal to pass legislation just targeting the service in the sharing economy. For example, in New York, taxi service has long been taxed, so the state legislature can also enact a law requiring Uber to collect the sales tax. However, in most states, taxi services are not taxed, and state legislatures cannot require Uber to collect the sales tax. Those states could pass a law taxing transportation services, but opposition from industry would be too great to overcome. The public is also against tax policy change (Peterson 2020). The second obstacle is who collects and remits the sales tax—the platform hosts or the individual service providers. All sales tax states have passed marketplace facilitator laws, but these laws apply to the platforms where the transactions involve tangible goods. It is easier if platform hosts assume responsibility for collecting and remitting the tax, just as marketplace facilitators do. Even though not all platform hosts are willing to, the most sensible solution is still for state governments to use the platform hosts to do the job (Mikesell and Kioko 2018; Craig 2022).

Online Sales and the Wayfair Decision

Online sales increased dramatically and rapidly with the Internet, eroding the sales tax base. For many years, under the U.S. Supreme Court ruling *Quill Corp. v. North Dakota* (1992), states could not require remote sellers to collect and remit sales tax unless remote sellers had a physical presence—having employees or property in the states. The rationale behind this is that the complexity of the state sales tax system—a system with so many different bases and rates across states and even within a single state—would impose an undue burden on interstate sellers.

State governments opposed the physical presence rule, insisting that it cost them billions in sales tax revenue and was outdated with the advancement of technology. According to Bruce and Fox's (2001) estimation, total e-commerce would result in a $13.3 billion revenue loss for state and local governments in 2001, $45.2 billion in 2006, and $54.8 billion in 2011. The 2011 number represents anywhere from 2.6% to 9.92% of total state tax collection, and states had to raise the sales tax rate between 0.83% and 1.72% points to make up for the total e-commerce losses.

The U.S. Government Accountability Office (GAO) (2017), using actual and estimated sales data for remote sellers, predicted that states in 2016 would have generated somewhere between $8.5–$13.4 billion in sales tax revenue, which represented 2%–4% of the total 2016 state and local government general sales and gross receipts tax revenue (GAO 2017, p. 1). Although GAO's number was moderate compared with Bruce and Fox (2001), it is seen as significant because most Supreme Court justices cited these numbers in their argument when ruling on *S. Dakota v. Wayfair*. The revenue impact differs from state to state. The average revenue gain could be about $200 million per state.

Over the years, states found creative, sometimes dubious, ways to expand the definition of physical presence, such as click-through, cookie nexus, or notice and reporting requirements for remote sellers (Walczak and Cammenga 2019). Finally, in 2016, South Dakota passed legislation developed by the National Conference of State Legislatures (NCSL), known as an economic nexus law, requiring remote sellers who, on an annual basis, sell more than $100,000 of goods or services into the state or engage in 200 or more separate transactions to collect and remit sales tax on all taxable sales into the state. An online retailer, Wayfair, challenged the law, arguing that it violated the existing rule of physical presence. Eventually, the case reached the U.S. Supreme Court.

State governments supported South Dakota. In their amicus curiae brief, 41 states and DC pointed to the fact that retailers' use of the internet is ubiquitous. They convincingly argued that "the very technology that makes online retailers so successful at targeting their customers also allows them to collect and remit the owed sales tax through an automated process that requires minimal effort" (Lindholm and Frieden 2018, p. 669).

In a split 5–4 decision, the Court ruled in June 2018 in favor of South Dakota, overturning its 50-year precedent, eliminating the physical presence rule, and letting the economic nexus law stand. The Court held that its prior rulings were outdated and effectively caused market distortions with modern technology, giving e-commerce and out-of-state retailers an advantage over dealers with in-state locations. Under the economic nexus law, state governments have the authority to demand remote retailers exceeding a certain volume of sales and/or transactions collect and remit sales taxes.

States' Adoptions of Economic Nexus Laws and Marketplace Facilitator Laws

State governments responded immediately to the ruling. Hellerstein (2020) stated that the ink was barely dry in the Court's opinion before the state legislatures and state tax administrators began to pass and enforce remote sales tax laws. As a matter of fact, even prior to the *Wayfair* case, several states, including New York, Connecticut, and Minnesota, had adopted economic nexus laws in anticipation of the Court's favorable ruling. One month leading up to the court decision, a dozen more states also did. By the end of 2019, only 18 months after the Court decision, all but three states (i.e., Kansas, Florida, and Missouri) passed economic nexus laws (GAO 2022). Eventually, the three "hold-out" states adopted their economic nexus legislations in the 2021 session (Fritts 2021).

Since the Supreme Court approved South Dakota's remote sales tax legislation, other states saw it as a model for their legislation. The state economic nexus laws contain certain common features:

1 Providing Safe Harbors: All 45 states and DC have adopted safe harbors for small sellers. The safe harbor provisions are one of the ways for states to avoid the unconstitutional burden on remote sellers, especially the small ones. It helps to "reduce the compliance and administrative costs and ensure the cost of collecting and remitting the tax will not exceed a company's net revenue from transactions within the state" (Walczak and Cammenga 2019, p. 9). Most states borrowed South Dakota's example by setting the threshold at $100,000 gross sales or 200 transactions. Walczak and Cammenga (2019) state that legally, it is more viable to eliminate the number of transaction requirements. The reason is that when transactions involve a small amount of gross sales (e.g., $1 for each transaction), the cost of compliance can exceed the net profit that small businesses make from these transactions. Another reason is that transactions may not be clearly defined in the statute. Those states that adopted the remote seller law in later days tend to rely only on the gross sales requirement. A few states set the threshold at a higher level, like New York ($500,000), Texas ($500,000), and California ($500,000). Since what constitutes a small business depends on the size of the state economy, a higher threshold makes sense for big states (Walczak and Cammenga 2019).
2 Waiving Retroactive Tax Collection: The Supreme Court noticed that South Dakota did not apply the sales tax retroactively. This became the standard practice for all states' remote sales laws. Retroactive tax collection can introduce several serious issues for remote sellers, making the law legally shaky. First, since remote sellers did not collect the tax in the first place, they have no way to go back to purchasers and collect the tax. Forcing the collection would create an undue burden for remote sellers. In addition, if remote sellers pay the tax themselves, this will impose a financial burden on the seller, while the sales tax should fall on purchasers (Walczak and Cammenga 2019). According to GAO (2022), all 45 states and DC waived retroactive tax collection.

Behind these shared elements, state economic nexus laws differ in numerous aspects (GAO 2022). Regarding the small business harbor, states use different types of sales. Some use total gross sales, while others use retail sales to determine their numeric thresholds. Furthermore, six states (i.e., Arkansas, Florida, Missouri, New Mexico, North Dakota, and Oklahoma) include only taxable sales, but others include part of or all the tax-exempt sales. What is exempt from the sales tax differs from state to state. State requirements also differ in when a business must register to collect the tax after exceeding a threshold. In some states (such as Maine, Mississippi, South Dakota, and Wisconsin), a business must register as soon as it completes the next transaction into the state after exceeding the threshold. Other states include the day the threshold is exceeded (California) or use the first of the month after it is exceeded (Hawaii and Maryland), the first of the second month after it is exceeded (South Carolina and Nebraska), or the first of January after it is exceeded (Alabama, Michigan, New Mexico, and Rhode Island) (GAO 2022).

Economic nexus laws generally go hand in hand with marketplace facilitator laws. Marketplace facilitator laws make marketplace facilitators (e.g., Amazon Marketplace, eBay, Etsy, and smartphone app stores like the App Store) responsible for collecting and remitting sales tax on behalf of their third-party sellers. As an increasing number of remote sales are facilitated by platforms, marketplace facilitator laws offer several advantages. They cut down on the administrative cost of taxing states and extend obligations to sellers who will not exceed the safe harbor. They also reduce sellers' compliance burdens by centralizing responsibilities in larger companies that are in a better position to handle the process. A few states enacted market facilitator laws before the *Wayfair* decision, but most of the laws were adopted in the post-*Wayfair* days. All 45 sales tax states and DC have broadened remote sales taxation with marketplace facilitator laws in place.

Fiscal Implications of Wayfair Decision for States

The fiscal implications of Wayfair are seen at three levels. First and foremost, the *Wayfair* ruling broadened states' sales tax base by adding the growing e-commerce sector and allowing states to generate more sales tax revenue from remote sales. Table 8.5 shows the result of a GAO (2022) survey sent to state revenue agencies regarding revenue gains from remote sellers between 2018 and 2021. In 2018, 21 states reported a revenue gain of $3.2 billion. This seemed to be a moderate number, but GAO (2022) recognizes that this report does not represent the entire picture because some states did not report their remote sales tax revenue data. The data also show that the total revenue gain and average amount per state increased every year during the study. In 2021, 33 states reported $23 billion in remote sales tax revenue, a dramatic increase over 2020 and nearly double GAO's 2017 estimate.

What happened during COVID-19 proves the importance of online sales tax revenue in state government finance. E-commerce sales skyrocketed in 2020, up 77% in May 2020 over May 2019, and the growth rate for the entire year of 2020 was 44% (Peterson, 2021). The quick adoption of economic nexus and market facilitator laws provided states with a much-needed cushion against falling tax

TABLE 8.5 State Remote Sales Tax Revenue Collection: 2018–2021 (in $million)

Year	Revenue from All Remote Sales			Revenue from Remote Sales via Marketplaces		
	Total Revenue	# of States Reporting	Average Amount Per State[a]	Total Revenue (% of all Remote Sales)	# of States Reporting	Average Amount Per State[a]
2018	$3,200	21	$152	$344 (11%)	5	$69
2019	$6,735	28	$240	$1,276 (19%)	12	$106
2020	$16,328	31	$526	$6,529 (40%)	20	$226
2021	$23,104	33	$700	$9,539 (41%)	20	$476

Source: GAO (2022) p. 14.

[a] The author's calculations are based on dividing total revenue by the number of states reporting.

revenues caused by the pandemic. Although not enough to prevent negative sales tax growth overall, the tax revenue on these online purchases gave a degree of stability to state finances at a critical time (Brainerd 2021, p. 2). In addition, experts believe people will continue to shop online, sustaining the remote sales tax revenue (Peterson 2021).

Second, the *Wayfair* ruling also gives state governments the authority to require remote sellers to collect and remit sales tax on digital product sales when the economic nexus is satisfied. A discussion of taxing digital goods and services will be provided shortly.

Third, the *Wayfair* decision's effects could go far beyond state sales and use taxes. States could undertake broader efforts to reform their tax codes by requiring remote sellers and marketplace facilitators to collect other taxes and fees. According to Gail Cole from Avalara,

> The *Wayfair* decision did not specifically authorize states to enforce economic nexus. All it did was to remove the barrier to enforce it – the physical presence rule. The Supreme Court did not reference other types of taxes, but it was likely inevitable that states would eventually broaden the scope of their economic nexus laws.
>
> *(Cole 2021, p. 1)*

Cole (2021) identified numerous fees and taxes that many states require remote sellers and marketplace facilitators to collect and remit. For instance, Texas already applied economic nexus laws to the franchise tax and Washington to the business and occupation tax. In Indiana, registered remote sellers are responsible for three additional fees: the fireworks public safety fee, the prepaid wireless service charge, and the waste tire management fee. This trend will continue (Cole 2021). In addition to generating revenues, these efforts are modernizing state remote sales taxation (Brainerd 2021).

In sum, the *Wayfair* decision and subsequent economic nexus laws and marketplace facilitator laws give states the authority to reach remote sales and collect certain other fees and taxes, thus bringing a rapidly increasing share of commerce into the state tax base. The legislation has moved the state sales tax in the right direction. However, the *Wayfair* decision only deals with the nexus issue associated with remote taxable goods and services. It says nothing about the root of problems with sales tax laws. These laws were narrowly construed and have become outdated with current consumption behaviors (Agrawal and Fox 2020)—consumption of services and digital goods and services. To modernize states' sales tax systems, state lawmakers must look broadly and modernize state tax laws. Further discussion will be provided later.

Sales Tax on Digital Products and Services

When states adopted sales tax, there was no computer software and few digital goods on the market. Yet, in the past 25 years, the digital economy has grown at a 9.9% annual rate in real terms (Bureau of Economic Analysis 2019). Software and software services have become ubiquitous and indispensable to nearly all entities, and the global cloud computing market will exceed $1.2 trillion by 2026 (Forrester 2022).

Taxing the consumption of digital goods and services has become one of the most important and contentious tax issues for state lawmakers. This taxation is essential to keep sales taxes fair and neutral. It is also crucial for the state government's long-term financial stability (Mazerov 2012; Agrawal and Fox 2020). According to Garrett and Nulle, "Whether these new delivery methods or digital solutions are treated as taxable goods or nontaxable services will augment, sustain, or erode state tax bases" (Garrett and Null 2020, p. 874). However, the unique nature of digital products and rapid technological evolution make this effort extremely challenging and complex.

Definitions and Categories of Digital Products

Digital goods and services refer to products delivered to or accessed by a consumer electronically over the Internet. It can be goods that existed previously in tangible form, such as books, films, or software. It can also be something that did not have a tangible counterpart, such as computer applications and digital information services. Although the sales tax on digital goods and services has attracted much attention among tax policy makers and experts, there is "no single legal definition of digital goods" (Hamer 2019, p. 1). The most authoritative and commonly used definitions are from the Streamlined Sales and Use Tax Agreement (SSUTA). As far as categories are concerned, the literature often mentions three categories of digital goods and services:

- Specified digital products
- Computer software
- Cloud computing

Specified Digital Products: SSUTA defines specified digital products, including digital audiovisual works (e.g., Netflix), digital audio works (e.g., iTunes), and digital books (e.g., Amazon Kindle). As most of this category has previously existed in tangible form, it is relatively easy to extend the sales tax to it. In 2022, 35 states taxed most of the digital products (Frieden, Nicely, and Nair 2022). They account primarily for business-to-consumer transactions.

Computer Software: SSUTA treats computer software as a separate category from specified digital products. It classifies computer software into prewritten computer software and custom software.

- Prewritten computer software is off-the-shelf and ready to use by anyone. It is specifically designated as a type of tangible personal property. As such, it is subject to sales tax.
- Custom software is developed for specific buyers and is considered a service. Sales of services are usually not taxable. Only 10 states tax it.

All 45 sales tax states and Washington, DC tax the transfer of prewritten computer software when they are loaded onto a CD, but among them, 36 states tax them whether they are in tangible form or electrical form. The other 12 states exempt them when the transfer is conducted electronically. The complexity does not stop here. If software is sold in conjunction with a service, the taxability is determined by its true object—whether "to obtain the work performed by a computer system" or "to obtain personal and professional service" (Avalara 2022, p. 44).

Cloud Computing: Cloud accessibility roughly equals Internet. The user can use cloud-based software when a computer is connected to the Internet. There are three different service delivery models (Beebe 2019; Le 2020): Software as a Service (SaaS), Infrastructure as a Service (IaaS), and Platform as a Service (PaaS).

The proliferation of cloud computing further complicates the taxability of software. The line drawn between different models is not always clear, and states do not always know how to handle newer services. Even for the same delivery model, the tax treatment varies from state to state. For instance, New York sees SaaS as the sales of prewritten software and taxable; Texas views it as a taxable

> **BOX 8.1 THREE CLOUD COMPUTING DELIVERY MODELS**
>
> - SaaS includes web-based email services, calendars, and digital photo applications. These services offer customers the ability to use software applications running on a cloud infrastructure.
> - IaaS includes web hosting and remote storage services. These services allow consumers to control operating systems, storage, and applications but not the underlying infrastructure.
> - PaaS can be used to create applications and games using programming languages, tools, and computing power supplied by a cloud service provider.

data processing service with 20% of revenue exempted from tax; Wisconsin treats it as a nontaxable data processing service.

Variations of State Digital Taxation

State governments have selected different approaches to extend the sales tax to digital products. Some states enacted new or amended legislation. For instance, Rhode Island passed a law expanding the sales tax base to computer software and streaming services (Le 2020). Other states still rely on their existing laws but reinterpret them in such a way as to cover digital goods and services. For instance, the Colorado Department of Revenue in 2020 interpreted tangible personal property to "include digital goods regardless of the method of delivery and application of the true object test" (Le 2020, p.2). The second approach can cause more legal challenges from the business community because digital goods and services do not often fit neatly into existing tax codes. For either approach, the most common way for states to extend the sales tax to certain digital items is to characterize them as "tangible personal property" because that is what the sales tax applies to. Arizona classified Netflix streaming services as rental of tangible personal property and Automatic Data Processing cloud-based software as tangible personal property. In both cases, the businesses challenged the classification, believing the characterization inappropriate (Beebe 2019).

Issues and Challenges with Taxing Digital Products

States' efforts so far have resulted in a maze of digital tax laws that are complicated, confusing, and uncertain. Taxing remote sales is complicated enough, but taxing digital goods and services adds another layer of complexity.

Several issues make digital tax efforts particularly complicated, controversial, and challenging.

Conceptual Issues

As with most taxes, taxing digital products involves political consideration. Some elected officials and interest groups may oppose extending sales tax to digital products and services. In addition, digital tax reform has its distinct conceptual issues. Many digital products are complex and not easy to define, characterize, or understand. This complexity will continue to increase as technology evolves quickly and "incorporates a wider range of components that are not easily distinguishable from a taxability perspective" (Beebe 2019, p. 6). Rapid technological evolution makes it difficult, if not possible, for lawmakers to catch up, leaving sales tax laws always behind technology.

Digital Products Sourcing

Sales tax sourcing refers to which sales tax rules should apply to the transactions. SSUTA recommends the destination-based sourcing rule—using the sales tax policy of the state where buyers reside or the products are first used or possessed. Destination-based sourcing is preferable because it discourages mobile cross-border shoppers (Agrawal and Mardan 2019) and better reflects the provision of benefits of public services (McLure 1998). SSUTA also provides that "the general sourcing provision applies to all sales regardless of the characterization of a product as tangible personal property, a digital good or a service" (Hamer 2019, p. 3). Most states follow this rule. Only 12 states use origin-based sourcing, where the sales tax policy of the state where the purchase takes place determines the tax rules. While sales tax sourcing is often an issue for e-commerce, sourcing rules for digital goods and services are even more complicated. What if a consumer from Washington purchases a digital book when he or she travels in Chicago and then opens it in New York? Which state's sales tax should be applied? Many computer software and services are delivered electronically and do not require a physical address. They can be downloaded or accessed anywhere and are shared by multiple users in different states for numerous purposes (Beebe 2019). Determining where sales happen can be difficult.

Inadequate Attention to B2B Exemptions

While states, in general, could further expand their digital tax base, they also overextend the base by including many B2B transactions. States' piecemeal approach to tax digital products fails to correct the cascading problem associated with the sales taxation of business inputs practice and causes further tax pyramiding. According to Friden, Nicely, and Nair (2022), among the states that tax some or most digital products, only one state (Iowa) provides broad exemptions to digital business input; three states (i.e., Maryland, New Jersey, and Washington) provide partial exemptions; one state (Connecticut) provides a reduced rate; and all other states provide no exemptions to business inputs (Frieden, Nicely, and Nair 2022).

Narrow and Piecemeal Approach to Reform Digital Sales Tax

States' digital tax reform efforts, as well as sales tax on services, so far have taken a narrow and piecemeal scope by adding additional transactions into the tax base. This can help states and taxpayers adjust to the changing economy and is valuable in modifying the sales tax base to reflect digital transactions. However, Thimmesch states that "narrowly focusing on known deficiencies in state's laws without a full understanding of the digital economy would lead to incomplete and potentially problematic reforms" (Thimmesch 2023, p. 1184). This piecemeal approach, together with the decentralization of the sales tax, has resulted in a lack of uniformity of digital tax rules, creating confusion and uncertainty among taxpayers and leading to inequity, distortion, and loss of revenue. Second, with technology continuing to evolve at a rapid pace, state tax laws and rules under this narrow scope will always fall behind, "leaving states in an endless cycle of legislative catch-up that will only benefit companies and tax advisers that can leverage gaps in state law for economic gain" (p. 1184). Third, the piecemeal approach also perpetuates and exacerbates tax pyramiding by including B2B transactions, as discussed above, because states tend to follow the existing pattern.

State Fiscal Stability and a Comprehensive Approach to Broaden the Sales Tax Base

There is no need to stress the importance of sales tax in state finance. As a general consumption tax, the sales tax can have a broad base. With its revenue accounting for over one-third of state tax revenue, sales tax wellbeing determines the health of state finances (Mikesell and Kioko 2018). The sales tax has been one of the major revenue sources for state governments for many decades, and it will remain so for years to come. In addition, the earlier section shows that in times of financial need, the sales tax is the major source that supports state government finance. Easier to raise than income tax, state governments often rely on the sales tax for additional revenue to maintain general-purpose services and support other important programs such as public education and transportation. Public finance experts also support sales taxation because it is relatively neutral for the economy and is a desirable tax policy (Agrawal and Fox 2020).

The challenges to states' sales tax systems are numerous, complex, and still forthcoming. The *Wayfair* decision and resulting economic nexus laws and marketplace facilitator laws have made a breakthrough towards modernizing state sales tax, but they "only affect states' ability to enforce taxation on a particular set of goods" (Agrawal and Fox 2020, p. 6), and they do not address major issues causing sales tax base erosion. "The digital economy has fundamentally [not slightly] changed many traditional market dynamics and structures" (Thimmesch 2023, p. 1184), and policy makers need to consider a broad and comprehensive approach to address the root cause of the problem as Thimmesch (2023) suggested. The root cause of the sales tax dilemma is not the digital economy or the service-oriented structure but the flawed tax system that was adopted long ago, narrowly construed, and covered only tangible personal properties.

Under a broader scope, policy makers and taxpayers could think broadly and "have a broad understanding of the digital economy and its scope and trajectory" (Thimmesch 2023, p. 1184) and then use tax principles to restructure the system. The system should be designed to "keep up with the economy and provide taxpayers with a tax system that makes sense" (Thimmesch 2023, p. 1184). Agrawal and Fox (2020) echo similar thoughts, suggesting state governments "could entirely restructure their sales tax laws to broadly tax consumption, which could generally incorporate new forms of consumption in the base" (p. 23). Comprehensive reforms are harder to accomplish. The American political system favors incremental changes, and voters never favor paying more taxes. There are conceptual and political issues, as mentioned earlier. Technology also evolves rapidly, making it difficult to forecast or understand.

Even so, serious thought and effort should be given to this broad-scoped, comprehensive tax reform. Such reform requires time and thoughtful dialogue among state lawmakers, policy consultants, experts, the affected industries, and all other stakeholders. The reform should follow the basic principles of a good consumption tax:

- Include all the final consumptions regardless of their delivery form.
- Exclude business inputs.
- Use destination-based sourcing.

A comprehensive reform would produce a broad-based consumption tax that would yield needed revenue. The tax system would be simple, neutral, and fair to all consumers when including all final consumptions regardless of their format (goods or services) and delivery form (download and accessed) without numerous tax exemptions. When the system is simple and business inputs are excluded, it will eliminate tax pyramiding, improve the efficiency of the system, and reduce administrative costs.

References

Agrawal, David R. and Mohammed Mardan. 2019. "Will Destination-based Taxes Be Fully Exploited When Available? An Application to the U.S. Commodity Tax System." *Journal of Public Economics*, 169 (January), pp. 128–143.

Agrawal, David R. and William F Fox. 2020. "Taxing Goods and Services in a Digital Era." CESifo Working Paper, No. 8708. Munich: Center for Economic Studies and Ifo Institute (CESifo).

Avalara. No Date. "A State-by-State Analysis of Charging Sales Tax on Services."

Avalara. 2022. "Tax Changes 2023: A Tax Compliance Guide for Businesses."

Beebe, Joyce. 2019. "The Current State of Sales Tax on Digital Products." Baker Institute Report no 08.07.19. Houston, TX: Rice University's Center for Public Finance in the Baker Institute for Public Policy.

Bishop-Henchman, Joseph. 2013. "Virginia Legislators Approve Increases in Sales Tax, Car Tax, Regional Taxes." *Tax Foundation* . (February 25).

Brainerd, Jackson. 2021. "The Wayfair Cushion: Internet Sales Tax Revenue Softened the Pandemic's Economic Blow." *National Council of State Legislatures.*

Brainerd, Jackson. 2022. "Brief Examining State Sales Taxes." *National Council of State Legislatures.* (October 7).

Bruce, Donald and William Fox. 2001. "State and Local Sales Tax Revenue Losses from E-Commerce: Updated Estimates." Knoxville, TN: Center for Business and Economic Research.

Bureau of Economic Analysis. 2019. "Measuring the Digital Economy: An Update Incorporating Data from the 2018 Comprehensive Update of the Industry Economic Accounts."

Cole, Gail. 2021. "States are Broadening Scope of Economic Nexus and Marketplace Facilitator Laws." *Avalara*. (May 10).

Craig, Sarah. 2022. "Why Getting Tax Right is Challenging with the Sharing Economy?" *TaxJar*. (April 18).

Frieden, Karl A., Frederick J. Nicely, and Priya D. Nair. 2022. "Down the Rabbit Hole: Sales Taxation of Digital Business Inputs." *Tax Notes State*, 105 (3) (July 18), pp. 265–279.

Fritts, Janelle. 2021. "Florida and Missouri, the Last Wayfair Holdouts, Consider Remote Sales Tax Bills." *Tax Foundation.*

Forrester. 2022. "Forester: Public Cloud Is Poised to Surpass $1 Trillion By 2016 – But Not Without Enduring Several Global Challenges." (December 13). www.forrester.com/press-newsroom/forrester-public-cloud-market-outlook-2022-to-2026/

Garrett, Natalia, and Grant Nulle. 2020. "Digital Goods and Services: How States Defines, Tax and Exempt These Items." *Tax Notes State*. (May 18).

Hamer, Brian. 2019. "Report Sourcing Digital Goods and Services." *Uniformity Committee Meeting.* Denver, CO: Multistate Tax Commission.

Hellerstein, Walter. 2020. "The Rapidly Evolving Universe of US State Taxation of Cross-border Online Sales after South Dakota v Wayfair, Inc., and Its Implications for Australian Businesses." *eJournal of Tax Research*, 18 (1), pp. 320–349.

Kaedling, Nicole. 2017. "Sales Tax Base Broadening: Right-Sizing a State Sales Tax. Fiscal Fact No. 563." *Tax Foundation.* (October).

Le, Tram. 2020. "The Digital Era: States to Expand Tax to Digital Goods and Services." *TaxOps*. (October 5).

Lindholm, Douglas L. and Karl A. Frieden. 2018. "After Wayfair: Modernizing State Sales Tax Systems." *State Tax Notes* (May 14), pp. 667–677.

Mazerov, Michael. 2009. "Expanding Sales Taxation of Services: Options and Issues." *Center on Budget and Policy Priorities*. (August 10).

Mazerov, Michael. 2012. "State Should Embrace 21st Century Economy by Extending Sales Taxes to Digital Goods and Services." *Center on Budget and Policy Priorities*. (December 13).

McLure, Charles E., Jr. 1998. "Economic Commerce and the Tax Assignment Problem: Preserving State Sovereignty in a Digital World." *State Tax Notes*, 14, pp. 1169–1181.

Mikesell, John. 2018. *Fiscal Administration: Analysis and Application for the Public Sector*. 10th ed. Boston, MA: Cengage Learning.

Mikesell, John L. and Sharon N. Kioko. 2018. "The Retail Sales Tax in a New Economy." *Municipal Finance Conference (July 16–17, 2018)*.

National Conference of State Legislature (NCSL). 2009. *State Tax Actions 2008: Special Fiscal Report*. Denver, Colorado: National Conference of State Legislature.

National Conference of State Legislature (NCSL). 2012. *State Tax Actions 2011: Special Fiscal Report*. Denver, Colorado: National Conference of State Legislature.

National Conference of State Legislature (NCSL) (2016-2020). *State Tax Actions Database*. State Tax Actions Database.

Peterson, Scott. 2020. "Insight: Sales Tax and the Sharing Economy." *Bloomberg Tax: Daily Tax Report: State*. (January 17).

Peterson, Scott. 2021. "Online Sales Tax Collections Proving Essential for Many State and Local Governments during COVID-19." *American City and County*. (February 19).

Povich, Elaine S. 2017. "Why States Are Struggling to Tax Services." *Stateline*. (June 27).Rafool, Mandy and Todd Haggerty. 2011. *State Tax Actions 2010: Special Fiscal Report*. Denver, Colorado: National Conference of State Legislature.

Rafool, Mandy and Todd Haggerty. 2011. *State Tax Actions 2010: Special Fiscal Report*. Denver, Colorado: National Conference of State Legislature.

Rafool, Mandy. 2013. *State Tax Actions 2012: Special Fiscal Report*. Denver, Colorado: National Conference of State Legislature.

Rafool, Mandy. 2014. *State Tax Actions 2013: Special Fiscal Report* Denver, Colorado: National Conference of State Legislature.

Rafool, Mandy. 2015. *State Tax Actions 2014: Special Fiscal Report*. Denver, Colorado: National Conference of State Legislature.

Thimmesch, Adam. 2023. "The Scope of Digital Sales Tax Reform." *Tax Notes State* 107 (13), pp. 1181–1186.

U.S. Census Bureau. "Annual Survey of State Government Tax Collections" (STC). https://www.census.gov/programs-surveys/stc/data/tables.html

U.S. Government Accountability Office (GAO). 2017. *Sales Taxes: State Could Gain Revenue from Expanded Authority, but Businesses Are Likely to Experience Compliance Costs*. GAO-18-114. www.gao.gov/products/gao-18-114

U.S. Government Accountability Office. 2022. *Remote sales tax: Initial Observations on Effects of States' Expanded Authority*. GAO-22-106016.

Urban-Brookings Tax Policy Center. 2024. "State Sales Tax Rates: 2000-2023." (June 27).

Urban Institute. No Date. "General Sales Taxes and Gross Receipts Taxes." *Briefing Book.*Waisanen, Bert and Todd Haggerty. 2010. *State Tax Actions 2009: Special Fiscal Report.* Denver, Colorado: National Conference of State Legislature.

Waisanen, Bert and Todd Haggerty. 2010. State Tax Actions 2009: Special Fiscal Report. Denver, Colorado: National Conference of State Legislature.

Walczak, Jared. 2018. "Tax Trends Heading into 2019." Fiscal Fact: No. 628. Washington, DC: Tax Foundation. (December).

Walczak, Jared. 2022. "State Sales Tax Breadth and Reliance, Fiscal Year 2021." Fiscal Fact No. 792. Washington, DC: Tax Foundation. (May 4). State Sales Tax Breadth and Reliance, FY 2021 | Tax Foundation

Walczak, Jared. 2024. "State Sales Tax Breadth and Reliance, Fiscal Year 2022." *Tax Foundation.* (July 23).

Walczak, Jared and Janelle Cammenga. 2019. "State Sales Taxes in the Post-Wayfair Era." Fiscal Fact No. 680. Washington, DC: Tax Foundation. (December). State-Sales-Taxes-in-the-Post-Wayfair-Era-PDF..pdf

9
STATE SIN TAXES
Are They Stable Enough for State Fiscal Stability?

Introduction

State governments collect sin taxes—excise or selective taxes imposed on certain consumptions or activities considered harmful to consumers and communities. The traditional sin taxes are taxes on tobacco, alcohol, and gambling. Adding to the list are a few new ones: taxes on vaping and e-cigarettes, marijuana, and sugar-sweetened beverages (SSB). Sin taxes share certain similarities in their tax structure. They are largely based on the quantity of consumption, not the price of the products. These taxes also serve dual and conflicting goals. They are designed to deter people from engaging in harmful products and activities, but at the same time, governments want revenue to flow from them (Dadayan 2019; Haile 2009). If the taxes successfully accomplish the first goal, governments cannot fulfill the second goal, or vice versa.

Sin taxes can trace their origins to the 17th century. Massachusetts implemented an ad valorem tax—a tax based on price—on imported goods such as wine, sugar, tobacco, and liquor. Shortly after the nation was founded, Alexander Hamilton proposed a whisky tax to generate revenue to pay for the debt incurred during the Revolutionary War, which eventually "helped spark the Whisky Rebellion" (Huh, Levin, Murphy, and Zhang 2018, p. 4). Adam Smith also supported taxes on alcohol and tobacco products, given their wide consumption (Huh et al. 2018). Gambling is an old activity, but regulating and taxing it started only in the early 20th century.

Similar to other taxes, sin tax policies also involve value trade-offs. Lawmakers should consider how the tax affects equity, revenue collection, economic activities, and tax administration. A main concern with sin taxes is

DOI: 10.4324/9781003494324-9

their regressivity, leaving a larger burden on low-income individuals who tend to consume harmful products disproportionately. Among them, tobacco taxes are the most regressive. Roughly 25% of those living under the poverty line smoke, as compared with just 14% of those at or above the poverty line. "About 28 percent of [Medicaid] recipients and 27 percent of the uninsured smoke, while only 11 percent of people on private insurance and 9 percent of non-Medicare recipients do" (Huh et al. 2018, p. 10). As a result, lower-income families pay a higher percentage of their income on tobacco taxes.

Moreover, research shows that in the last two decades, tobacco consumption has become more concentrated among those at or below the poverty line. Conlon, Rao, and Wang (2021) conclude that the sin tax burden is highly concentrated among a small portion of the population: "with 10% of households paying more than 80% of taxes on alcohol and cigarettes" (p. 1). For cigarette taxes, 8% of households are responsible for virtually all purchases, and they are usually low-income, less educated, and between ages 55 and 64. They also point out that the sin tax burden is further concentrated because these households purchase multiple categories of sin goods. This is particularly true for smokers, who buy not only highly taxed tobacco products but also larger quantities of SSB, as well as beer and spirits, than the typical household.

Sin tax revenues make up a relatively small share of state tax revenues. However, these taxes often become easy targets for state and local governments to raise needed revenue, especially during fiscal crises. They are politically popular because they tax sinful consumption and do not affect 90% of households that do not engage in these "sinful" consumptions, as Conlon et al. (2021) explained.

Sin taxes are often considered as budget fixers, but are they reliable revenue sources for state government in the long run? This chapter examines state tobacco, alcohol, and gambling taxes. The discussion will examine the tax structures, revenue trends, and the role of these taxes in contributing to state long-term fiscal stability. Chapter 10 discusses marijuana taxes due to their rapid and significant development in recent years. The tax on SSB, also known as soda taxes, is levied by an increasing number of cities, with rates ranging from one cent per ounce in four California cities to two cents per ounce in Boulder, Colorado (Urban Institute No Date d). Several states (i.e., Connecticut, Hawaii, and Washington) proposed adopting state-wide soda taxes, but none have passed the legislation (Boesen 2021b). Therefore, this chapter does not extend any further discussion of soda taxes.

Tobacco Taxes

As stated earlier, tobacco is one of the first consumption products to be taxed in North America. For a long time, taxes on tobacco served solely to generate revenue due to its widespread consumption. It has been a part of the federal tax system since the Civil War, with its revenue rising during wartime and falling in peace periods. Cigarette taxes at the state level started in Iowa in 1921. North Carolina was the last state to adopt these taxes in 1969 (Institute of Medicine (U.S.) Committee on Preventing Nicotine Addiction in Children and Youths 1994).

All fifty states and the Washington D.C. levy cigarette taxes. Ten states allow their local governments, approximately 650 cities, to tax cigarettes. In addition, 40 states impose taxes on other tobacco products like cigars, chewing tobacco, snuff, and pipe tobacco. Yet cigarette taxes comprise the lion's share of all tobacco-related taxes. For example, in North Carolina, cigarette taxes accounted for 80% of tobacco tax revenue (Urban Institute No Date b).

States use different methods to tax different types of tobacco products. Taxes on cigarettes are based on the quantity (per pack) paid by producers and wholesale sellers, which is assumed to be passed down to consumers at the retail level. All other tobacco products are taxed as a percentage of the price (Urban Institute No Date b). Table 9.1 shows that cigarette tax rates differ widely among states, ranging from $0.17 per pack in Missouri to $4.50 per pack in D.C. In September 2023, New York raised its rate to $535 per pack. The national average rate was $1.93 per pack in 2023 (Erb 2023). On average, taxes comprise nearly half of the retail price of cigarettes. State tax rates for non-cigarette products range from 5% of the manufacturers' price in South Carolina to 95% of the wholesale price in Minnesota. Tax rates appear to be related to the importance of tobacco in local economies. Those tobacco-producing states tend to impose lower tax rates than non-tobacco-producing states. For instance, in 1992, the average cigarette tax in tobacco-producing states was 19 cents lower than in non-tobacco-producing states (Institute of Medicine (U.S.) Committee on Preventing Nicotine Addiction in Children and Youths 1994).

Tobacco Tax Revenue Trends

Brainerd (2020) states that "it is rare to find a truly popular tax, but the tobacco tax comes pretty close" (p. 1). State governments often rely on tobacco taxes to fund programs ranging from infrastructure to education and to address revenue shortages. During 2000–2018, "48 states increased cigarette tax rates about 133 times" (Dadayan 2019, p. 11). Seven of them raised it at least five times: Connecticut, Hawaii, Minnesota, New Hampshire, New Jersey, Rhode Island, and Vermont. Missouri and North Dakota are the only states that did not increase their tobacco taxes (Dadayan 2019). Many of the hikes occurred during economic downturns. The 2001 recession witnessed more than half of states raising their cigarette taxes. This came after the 1998 Master Settlement Agreement when states focused their attention on the adverse effects of cigarettes (Dadayan 2019). Based on the *State Tax Actions Database*, 18 states raised their tobacco tax rates in 2009, generating over $1.8 billion in new tax revenue to close their large budget gaps. Since the Great Recession, every year except 2014,

TABLE 9.1 State Excise Tax Rates on Cigarettes (January 1, 2023)

State	Tax Rate (¢ Per Pack)	Rank	State	Tax Rate (¢ Per Pack)	Rank
Alabama (a)	67.5	41	Nebraska	64	42
Alaska	200	19	Nevada	180	25
Arizona	200	19	New Hampshire	178	26
Arkansas	115	36	New Jersey	270	14
California	287	13	New Mexico	200	19
Colorado	194	24	New York (a)	435	2
Connecticut	435	2	North Carolina	45	48
Delaware	210	17	North Dakota	44	49
Florida (b)	133.9	33	Ohio	160	29
Georgia	37	50	Oklahoma	203	18
Hawaii	320	8	Oregon	333	7
Idaho	57	46	Pennsylvania	260	15
Illinois (a)	298	12	Rhode Island	425	4
Indiana	99.5	39	South Carolina	57	46
Iowa	136	32	South Dakota	153	30
Kansas	129	34	Tennessee (a) (c)	62	43
Kentucky	110	37	Texas	141	31
Louisiana	108	38	Utah	170	27
Maine	200	19	Vermont	308	9
Maryland	375	5	Virginia (a)	60	44
Massachusetts	351	6	Washington	302.5	11
Michigan	200	19	West Virginia	120	35
Minnesota (d)	304	10	Wisconsin	252	16
Mississippi	68	40	Wyoming	60	44
Missouri (a)	17	51			
Montana	170	27	District of Columbia (e)	450	1
			U.S. Median	193	

Source: Compiled by FTA from state sources. https://taxadmin.org/wp-content/uploads/resources/tax_rates/cigarette.pdf. Permission granted.

(a) Counties and cities may impose an additional tax on a pack of cigarettes: in Alabama, 1¢ to 25¢; Illinois, 10¢ to $4.18; Missouri, 4¢ to 7¢; New York City, $1.50; Tennessee, 1¢; and Virginia, 2¢ to 15¢.
(b) Florida's rate includes a surcharge of $1 per pack.
(c) Dealers pay an additional enforcement and administrative fee of 0.05¢ in Tennessee.
(d) Minnesota also imposes an in-lieu cigarette sales tax determined annually by the Department. The current rate is 69.2¢ through December 31, 2023.
(e) In addition, the District of Columbia imposes an in-lieu cigarette sales tax calculated every March 31. The current rate is 52¢.

there have been states raising their tobacco tax rates. The public often supports substantial rate increases, particularly when the revenue is earmarked for specific purposes such as deficit reduction or healthcare financing. Although the situations behind the increases vary, two primary motives prevail: "advancing public health by making tobacco use more costly and collecting revenue from those who do not give up the habit" (Huh et al. 2018, p. 2). Although there is concern that tax hikes increase tax burdens on low-income households, the experts point to the larger health benefits flowing to this group from smoking withdrawal.

Even though tobacco taxes are attractive revenue options, they play a minimal role in state government financing, and this role has become increasingly smaller over the decades. Table 9.2 shows that tobacco-related tax revenues accounted for 2% of total state tax revenue in 2008 and only 1% in 2022. States do vary in their reliance on tobacco taxes. In 2022, the largest share was 5% of state tax revenue in New Hampshire and 3% in Rhode Island, while the lowest shares were in Hawaii, Kansas, and Massachusetts, with 0.9% based on the U.S. Census Bureau data.

Moreover, inflation-adjusted tobacco tax revenues declined substantially from $16,068 million in 2008 to $13,454 million in 2022, or a 16% decline (see Table 9.2). Dadayan (2019) examined tobacco tax revenues with data from 2008–2017, providing more insight into tobacco tax trends. Although inflation-adjusted tobacco tax revenue grew by 0.8% between FY 2008 and FY 2017, or a 0.1% compound annual growth rate, that was skewed by a $946 million

TABLE 9.2 Tobacco Taxes Revenue: 2008–2022

	Current Dollars (in Million)	Inflation-adjusted (in Million) (2008 Dollars)	As % of Total State Revenue
2008	16,068	16,068	2.0%
2009	16,690	16,749	2.3%
2010	16,858	16,645	2.4%
2011	17,276	16,536	2.2%
2012	17,195	16,125	2.1%
2013	17,092	15,797	2.0%
2014	16,913	15,381	1.9%
2015	17,744	16,118	1.9%
2016	18,089	16,227	1.9%
2017	18,663	16,393	1.9%
2018	19,376	16,613	1.8%
2019	18,776	15,812	1.7%
2020	18,559	15,439	1.7%
2021	19,145	15,212	1.5%
2022	18,287	13,454	1.3%
% Change 2008–2022		−16.2%	
Compound Annual Growth Rate		−1.26%	

Source: U.S. Census Bureau "Annual Survey of State Government Tax Collections" (STC).

tobacco tax increase in Florida, largely due to rate hikes on cigarettes and other tobacco products. If Florida is excluded, inflation-adjusted tobacco tax revenues for the rest of the nation decline by 3.1% between 2008 and 2017. Her analysis shows that among 34 states that raised tax rates, 22 saw revenue increase, but 12 observed decreases. For all other states that did not raise rates, tobacco tax revenue declined. This declining trend has continued even more rapidly in recent years when looking at the numbers for 2018–2022 shown in Table 9.2.

Various factors have contributed to the overall declining trends. Two major ones are the tax structures and declining consumption. As cigarettes are taxed by quantity of consumption, the prices and inflation bear no impact on overall revenue collections. For tax revenue to increase, consumption and rates must be sustained. However, tobacco consumption per capita has declined significantly over the decades, starting in the 1980s (see Figure 9.1) and continuing after that. From 2008 to 2017, cigarette consumption in the median state declined from 55.9 packs per capita to 40.6 packs per capita (Huh et al. 2018). The decline was driven by higher federal and state tax rates and individual shifts to other tobacco products or e-cigarettes. Research has confirmed that raising cigarette taxes leads to a decline in smoking behaviors. For instance, the American Lung Association estimates that when price increases by 10%, adult smokers would drop by 4%, and kids who smoke drop by 7% (Erb 2023). The anti-smoking campaigns have

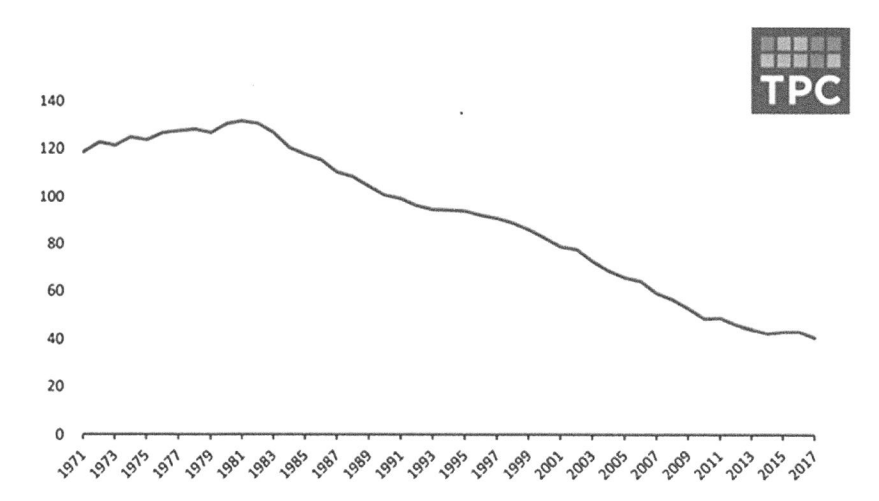

FIGURE 9.1   Steady Decline in Cigarette Consumption since the 1980s; Per Capita Sales of Taxed Cigarette Packs.

Source: Orzechowski and Walker. "The Tax Burden on Tobacco, 1970–2017." Reused with permission from Lucy Dadayan. 2019. "Are States Betting on Sin? The Murky Future of State Taxation." *Urban-Brookings Tax Policy Center.* www.taxpolicycenter.org/publications/are-states-betting-sin-murky-future-state-taxation.

raised public awareness of the negative health impacts of smoking. The decline has been so significant that some states that raised tax rates still see revenue declines.

In addition, significant variations among state tobacco tax rates lead to smuggling and tax evasion, and high taxes can motivate black market activities (Boesen 2021a). In 2019, New York, a state with one of the highest rates in the nation, had an inbound smuggling rate of 52.2%, followed by California (43.4%), Washington (42.6%), and New Mexico (37.2%). Previous state experiences have enough evidence to show cigarette tax rate increases inevitably lead to significant declines in expected tax collections and a concomitant rise in tax avoidance strategies (Guppy and Hansen 2010).

Tobacco product consumption and tax revenues are expected to decline in years to come. Besides the factors discussed above, federal regulations will further restrict the legal sales of tobacco products. In 2022, the U.S. Food and Drug Administration proposed a ban on flavored cigars and menthol cigarettes. With menthol cigarettes accounting for 37% of the cigarette market, such a ban would decrease cigarette tax collection by at least $6 billion annually (Hoffer 2023a). The FDA may also require a very low nicotine product standard by limiting the nicotine levels reflected in tobacco. Such a standard "could be a de facto prohibition on cigarettes" (Hoffer 2023a, p. 2). The impact on state tobacco taxes can be greater than any other FDA tobacco regulations.

Taxes on E-cigarettes

Entering the U.S. market in the mid-2000s, vapes or e-cigarettes became an established category of product. In the absence of federal regulation, states started to regulate and tax these items. Minnesota was the first state to tax e-cigarettes in 2012 by classifying them into an "other tobacco products" category. By January 2023, 30 states and the District of Columbia had collected this tax. Research has shown that youth vaping has increased, and more states are expected to tax vaping products and increase rates on currently implemented taxes (Cole 2022).

Taxes on vaping can be based on quantity (e.g., a certain amount of tax per ounce of vaping liquid) or price (e.g., a percentage of price). Taxing as a percentage of price is more common and desirable. Proponents believe this method discourages product consumption, while taxes based on quantity can result in greater consumption. The rates vary from 7% of the sale price in Georgia to 95% of the wholesale price in Minnesota. Some of these states treat vaping products as "other tobacco products and subject them to other tobacco product rates. States with volume-basis taxes have their rates varying between 5–40 cents per milliliter of liquid" (Urban Institute No Date b).

Although vaping has become common, tax revenue on vaping products remains a small portion of tobacco-related taxes. For example, North Carolina collected $5 million from vaping products in 2020, which is only 2% of the state's tobacco-related revenue (Urban Institute No Date b). Hoffer (2023b) from the Tax Foundation states that "substantial revenue is unlikely in the short run" (p. 1). There is concern that high taxes on vaping products will discourage smokers from shifting to vaping, which is believed to be less harmful than traditional combustible tobacco products (Hoffer 2023b). However, the opposite view argues the low rate will encourage young people to use these products to seek out nicotine. How vaping products and e-cigarettes are taxed will depend on whether these products "are seen as a device to help people stop smoking or as an alternative product" (Dadayan 2019, p. 17). Similar to the case of cigarette taxes, the wide difference in tax rates for vapor products and e-cigarettes can fuel smuggling and tax evasion operations. High rates could also lead to a larger black market. Ultimately, all these factors show that revenue from this source will not be substantial.

Tobacco-related Taxes and State Fiscal Stability

How much can tobacco-related taxes contribute to state fiscal stability? The history of sin taxes shows that these revenue sources have deteriorated over time. Tobacco tax revenue will continue to decline due to the continuing decline in cigarette consumption. Raising cigarette tax rates may accrue sizable revenue in the short run and be a useful tool to support public health objectives. However, they are not a reliable long-term revenue source and cannot build state fiscal stability.

Even if cigarette tax collections were stable, they do not serve as a sustainable source for state government finance. Haile (2009) states that reliance on sin taxes creates an ethical dilemma for state governments. He states that "when states become dependent on sin tax revenues to fund essential government services, they develop an interest in maintaining sales of the 'sinful' product. Consequently, the states' financial interest may conflict with the interest in protecting their citizens' health" (Haile 2009, p. 1). Although the debate over sin taxes usually does not emphasize this conflict of interest, the issue is clearly present, especially when sin tax revenues are used to finance essential government services or programs unrelated to consumption, such as school construction. Haile (2009) also shows that in the $200 billion Master Settlement Agreement between states and major tobacco manufacturers, state financial interest aligns with that of the manufacturers because the payments to states depended on the continuing increase of tobacco sales. As explained, sin taxes serve paradoxical purposes. If policy makers use sin taxes to deter harmful consumption, they cannot expect them to be an effective way of raising substantial revenue on a consistent basis.

Alcohol Taxes

State governments collect revenue from alcohol sales in two ways. Thirty-three states levy selective taxes on sales, usually at the production and wholesale stages. The tax is calculated based on the quantity of sales, a certain amount per ounce. Revenue collection depends on consumption and tax rates similar to cigarette taxes. Price increases and inflation impose no impact on tax collections. Dadayan (2019) refers to these states as "license states" because the buyers and sellers at the wholesale stage must obtain a license to operate their stores and must pay license fees.

In the remaining 17 states, state governments control spirit sales and, in some cases, wine. Dadayan (2019) refers to them as control states. They operate state-run liquor stores like private businesses, set uniform or minimum shelf prices, and engage in sales operations. States collect revenues mainly from price markups, various taxes, fees, and net profits. Most of these states allow private businesses to sell beer and wine, in some cases, through the license system, and states subsequently collect taxes (Huh et al. 2018).

In 2020, state and local governments collected $7.5 billion in alcohol taxes or 0.2% of general revenue, with no state collecting more than 1%. Local taxes comprise a tiny portion of revenue collections. Those states with state-owned liquor stores collected $11.3 billion in revenue through various taxes, fees, price markups, and net profits. States also collected $0.9 billion from license taxes for the manufacturing, importing, wholesaling, and retailing of alcohol. This is less than 0.1% of state and local general revenue (Urban Institute Na Date a).

Tax rates differ depending on the product type and the alcohol percentage inside the product. Liquor bears higher tax rates than wine, and wine higher than beer (Urban Institute No Date a). Tax rates vary considerably across states. In 2023, the rates per gallon for wine are $0.20 in California and $2.50 in Alaska (see Table 9.3). The rate for liquor runs from $2.5 in Missouri and Maryland to $14.27 in Washington. Many states impose multiple taxes on the same units of alcohol. A state's tax rate on an alcoholic beverage can include fixed-rate per-volume taxes, wholesale taxes, distributor taxes, retail taxes, case or bottle fees, and a sales tax" (Dadayan 2019, p. 6).

Alcohol Tax Revenue Trends

Compared with tobacco taxes, states were less likely to raise alcohol tax rates after the Great Recession. Between 2008 and 2022, only 14 states raised the rates on beer and/or wine: California, Connecticut, Delaware, Illinois, Indiana, Louisiana, Maryland, New Jersey, New York, North Carolina, Oregan, Rhode Island, Tennessee, and Washington (Waisanen and Haggerty 2010; Rafool and Haggerty 2011; Rafool 2013; 2014; 2015; NSCL 2009; 2012; NCSL 2016–2022).

TABLE 9.3 State Alcohol Excise Tax Rates as of January 1, 2023

State	Control State	Beer ($ Per Gallon)	Rank	Wine ($ Per Gallon)	Rank	Distilled Spirits ($ Per Gallon)	Rank
Median		$0.200		$0.73		$3.77	
Alabama	X	$0.533	6	$1.700	5	n/a/	n/a
Alaska		$1.070	2	$2.500	1	$12.800	2
Arizona		$0.160	12	$0.840	21	$3.000	23
Arkansas		$0.230	23	$0.750	23	$2.500	26
California		$0.200	26	$0.200	47	$3.300	20
Colorado		$0.080	46	$0.280	44	$2.280	30
Connecticut		$0.240	22	$0.790	24	$5.940	10
Delaware		$0.260	19	$1.630	6	$4.500	13
Florida		$0.480	7	$2.250	2	$6.500	4
Georgia		$0.320	14	$1.510	7	$3.790	17
Hawaii		$0.930	3	$1.380	11	$5.980	7
Idaho	X	$0.150	35	$0.450	35	n/a	n/a
Illinois		$0.231	24	$1.390	10	$8.550	3
Indiana		$0.155	40	$0.470	34	$2.680	25
Iowa	X	$0.190	28	$1.750	3	n/a	n/a
Kansas		$0.180	29	$0.300	40	$2.500	26
Kentucky		$0.080	45	$0.500	32	$1.920	32
Louisiana		$0.400	11	$0.760	22	$3.030	22
Maine	X	$0.350	13	$0.600	28	n/a	n/a
Maryland		$0.090	43	$0.400	37	$1.500	33
Massachusetts		$0.110	41	$0.550	29	$4.050	15
Michigan	X	$0.200	25	$0.510	31	n/a	
Minnesota		$0.148	36	$0.300	40	$5.030	12
Mississippi	X	$0.4268	8	$0.350	38	n/a	
Missouri		$0.060	49	$0.420	36	$2.00	31
Montana	X	$0.140	38	$1.020	13	n/a	
Nebraska		$0.310	15	$0.950	16	$3.750	18
Nevada		$0.160	32	$0.700	26	$3.600	19
New Hampshire	X	$0.300	16	$0.300	40	n/a	n/a
New Jersey		$0.120	39	$0.875	19	$5.500	9
New Mexico		$0.410	10	$1.700	4	$6.060	6
New York		$0.140	37	$0.300	40	$6.440	5
North Carolina	X	$0.6171	5	$1.000	15	n/a	n/a
North Dakota		$0.160	32	$0.500	32	$2.500	26
Ohio	X	$0.180	29	$0.300	39	n/a	n/a
Oklahoma		$0.400	11	$0.720	25	$5.560	8
Oregon	X	$0.080	44	$0.670	27	n/a	n/a
Pennsylvania	X	$0.080	46	n/a	n/a	n/a	n/a
Rhode Island		$0.110	41	$1.400	9	$5.400	10
South Carolina		$0.770	4	$0.900	18	$2.720	24
South Dakota		$0.270	17	$0.930	17	$3.930	16
Tennessee		$1.290	1	$1.210	12	$4.400	14
Texas		$0.194	27	$0.204	46	$2.400	29
Utah	X	$0.4226	9	n/a	n/a	n/a	n/a
Vermont	X	$0.265	18	$0.550	29	n/a	n/a

(*Continued*)

TABLE 9.3 (Continued)

State	Control State	Beer		Wine		Distilled Spirits	
		($ Per Gallon)	Rank	($ Per Gallon)	Rank	($ Per Gallon)	Rank
Virginia	X	$0.2565	21	$1.510	7	n/a	n/a
Washington		$0.260	20	$0.870	20	$14.27	1
West Virginia	X	$0.180	31	$1.000	14	n/a	n/a
Wisconsin		$0.060	48	$0.250	45	$3.250	21
Wyoming	X	$0.020	50	n/a	n/a	n/a	n/a

Sources: Data from "State Tax Rates on Distilled Spirits," "State Beer Excise Tax Rates," and "State Wine Excise Tax Rates." *Federation of Tax Administrators.* Accessed October 12, 2023. https://taxadmin.org/search/

Five of these states did so in 2009, together with New Hampshire, which reduced the off-premises liquor discount. In recent years, three states reduced rates (i.e., Kentucky, North Dakota, and Connecticut). After adjusting for inflation, the median tax rates in 2016 were lower than those in the 1980s (Huh et al. 2018).

Despite the stable rates, the overall state alcohol tax collection and liquor store revenues increased by 14% after adjusting for inflation in the 2008–2017 period. According to Dadayan (2019), this marks a steady and strong growth compared with the overall state tax growth of 5.5%. When additional years are included, alcohol tax revenue increased by 15.9% during 2008–2022 (see Table 9.4).

The primary contributor to this growth is the increase in alcohol consumption during the past decades. For instance, overall alcohol consumption increased by 1.3% from 2.31 gallons per capita in 2008 to 2.34 gallons per capita in 2017. However, the growth is uneven across the different types. "Per capita consumption of wine and spirits rose 13.2% and 15.1%, respectively, between 2008 and 2017, whereas per capita consumption of beer declined by 11.7% during the same period" (Dadayan 2019, p. 8). As spirits and wine carry higher rates, the consumption increase in these categories led to the overall growth of tax revenue collections. The revenue growth is unequal across the states. The control states experienced 26.2% growth during 2008–2017, but the license states had 2.9% decline. In Overall, 38 states, the total inflation-adjusted alcohol revenue increased. Usually the big increases occurred in states that also raised the tax rates (Dadayan 2019).

Alcohol Tax and State Fiscal Stability

Although alcohol taxes perform better than cigarette taxes, they contribute little to state long-term fiscal stability. First, revenue performances are uneven, and some states have seen revenue decline in real terms. Second, alcohol revenue is

TABLE 9.4 Alcohol Tax Revenues[a]: 2008–2022

	Current Dollar (in Millions)	Inflation-adjusted (Million) (2008 $)	As % of Total State Revenue
2008	5,744	5,744	0.73%
2009	5,778	5,776	0.81%
2010	5,961	5,886	0.84%
2011	6,180	5,916	0.81%
2012	6,430	6,030	0.81%
2013	6,753	6,242	0.80%
2014	6,760	6,148	0.78%
2015	7,032	6,387	0.77%
2016	7,265	6,517	0.78%
2017	7,259	6,376	0.76%
2018	n/a[b]	n/a[b]	n/a[b]
2019	n/a[b]	n/a[b]	n/a[b]
2020	7,578	6,304	0.71%
2021	8,316	6,608	0.65%
2022	9,052	6,660	0.62%
% Change 2008–2022		15.9%	
Compound Annual Growth Rate		0.09%	

Source: U.S. Census Bureau "Annual Survey of State Government Tax Collections" (STC).

[a] This includes only alcohol beverage sales tax and alcohol beverage license revenue. It does not include state-owned liquor stores' revenues.
[b] The Census Bureau does not have data for 2018 and 2019.

a small share of total state tax revenue, and the share increased from 0.07% in 2008 to 0.84% in 2010 and then declined to 0.6% in 2022. Third, since alcohol taxes are mainly based on volume, not responding to price increases, its revenue growth depends on consumption increases. Although overall consumption has increased, consumption per capita is down from the 1980s' peak of 2.8 gallons to 2.3 gallons in 2015. In addition, alcohol consumption tends to be cyclical, changing with societal trends and consumer attitudes. Fourth, more consumption is not desirable from public health and safety perspectives. All these factors make it uncertain for long-term alcohol tax revenue gains. Therefore, Huh et al. (2018) state that "policymakers should therefore not rely on alcohol tax revenue for long-term budget commitments" (p. 11).

Gambling Taxes

Forty-seven states collect gambling taxes. The three states that do not are Alaska, Hawaii, and Utah. State-sanctioned gambling includes lotteries, casinos, parimutuel wagering, sports betting, and online games (i.e., video poker). States' gambling tax revenue as a share of the total state revenue varies greatly from 10.2% in Nevada, 7.9% in Rhode Island, and 6.9% in West Virginia and Louisiana to 0.1% in Wyoming and North Dakota, and 0.8% in California in 2015 (Huh et al. 2018).

States legalize and expand gambling activities mainly because of their difficult fiscal situations. When states face fiscal crises, lawmakers hope gambling taxes can bring in revenue without raising income and sales taxes. Fifteen states authorized lottery operations during the 1980s when the economy experienced a double-dip recession. The expansion of casino and racino operations since the 1990s was "partly in response to the prior three recessions" (Dadayan 2016, p. 24). States also legalized casinos and racinos in hopes of stimulating economic development in certain distressed areas, but studies do not show consistent evidence of economic development. Interest groups such as casino industries represent another factor in pushing for expansion. States usually respond to interstate competition by expanding gambling options to retain residents and gambling taxes (Dadayan 2016).

Lottery

Lottery operations are legal in 45 states and Washington D.C. Alabama, Alaska, Hawaii, Nevada, and Utah are no-lottery states. New Hampshire was the first state to authorize lotteries in 1964. Many other states followed suit in the 1970s, 1980s, and 1990s. The most recent state to join was Mississippi in 2018. Nationally, lotteries account for roughly two-thirds of gambling revenues, with the remainder coming from casinos and racinos. In 18 states, lotteries represent 95% of the gambling revenues (Dadayan 2019). As state governments administer lottery operations, a certain share is retained, ranging from 20% to 30% of lottery sales, to state funds. After this, the remaining shares are used for the prize and lottery administration (Urban Institute No Date c). States usually dedicate lottery revenue to specific programs, including public education, environmental protection, natural resources, and veteran services. Almost one-third of these states also use revenue for general funds (Dadayan 2019).

Casino and Racino

As of March 2023, 25 states authorized casino gambling. Some are commercial casinos, and some are racetracks, riverboats, and other facilities where casino betting is permitted. Nevada and New Jersey are the only states that authorized commercial casinos before the 1990s. Nevada still sponsors over 50% of commercial casinos today. Governments impose taxes on casinos (as well as racinos, parimutuel wagering, sports betting, and video games) by levying a certain percentage of operator profits. The tax rates vary "from 0.25% in Colorado to 62.5% in Maryland" (Urban Institute No Date c, p.6). Some states impose a flat tax rate, while others use graduated rates. In most states, tax rates for table games are lower than for other forms of gambling such as slot machines. The rates are lower in early adopting states such as New Jersey and Nevada than in later adopters (Urban Institute No Date c).

Sports Betting

Sports betting is the latest authorized gambling activity. Although gambling has been a part of American culture, it was not until the 1940s that Nevada began to regulate it. In 1992, the federal government passed the Professional and Amateur Sport Protection Act (PASPA), prohibiting sports betting, and banned states from further regulation. Delaware, Montana, and Oregon retained their rights to operate sports lotteries. New Jersey officials challenged the law, arguing it was unconstitutional because it did not treat all the states the same. Eventually, the U.S. Supreme Court invalidated the law in 2018, permitting states to regulate sports betting as another potential revenue source. States acted quickly, and as of March 2023, more than half of the states (i.e., 28 states) and Washington D.C. authorized sports betting and collected taxes from the operators (Urban Institute No Date c).

There are two forms: mobile and retail betting. Most sports betting states allow both forms, but few only allow retail betting. Evidence suggests that online gaming brings in more revenue. Tax rates vary widely from 50%–51% of gross sports gaming revenue (GGR) in Delaware, New Hampshire, New York, and Rhode Island to about 6.75% in Nevada (Ruddock 2022). Most states set their rates between 6.75% and 20%. The rates are usually the same for mobile and retail betting in most states, with a few exceptions. States also require operators to obtain licenses. The license fee can be a sizable amount in some states. For example, the one-time license fee was $10 million per license in Pennsylvania (Auxier 2019).

Gambling Tax Revenue Trends

Although gambling taxes are grouped into sin taxes, their purpose is not to discourage certain behaviors as cigarette taxes do but to generate revenue. State governments promote and encourage sanctioned gambling activities. This is particularly true when facing fiscal crises, as discussed. More states turned to gambling taxes in the years during the Great Recession and the subsequent years to generate more revenue.

Total gambling revenue in 2021 was $35 billion for both state and local governments, or 1% of their general revenue. It is concentrated in the populous states, including New York (11% of the total gambling tax revenue), Pennsylvania (8.2%), Florida (6.3%), Illinois (5.3%), and California (5.3%). In terms of per capita, Rhode Island led the nation with $428 per capita, while Nevada is second at $381 per capita. From 2008 to 2017, the cumulative gambling revenue increased after being adjusted with inflation by 6%, but 19 states observed a decrease. Per capita spending declined in 29 states, leading to a 3.1% nationwide decline (Dadayan 2019).

Revenue from Lotteries

As stated earlier, lotteries account for most of the gambling tax revenue. According to Dadayan (2019), from its conception in 1967 to 2018, lotteries generated $576 billion for state governments. The revenue increase is related to the number of states adopting lotteries. For instance, aggregate revenue increased from $3 billion in 1980 to over $13 billion in 1990, more than four times, because 15 more states started to operate lotteries during this period.

TABLE 9.5 State and Local Lottery Revenue: 2008–2021

	Dollar (in Million)	*Constant Dollars (in Million)*	*As % of Total State Revenue*
2008	20,671	20,671	1.6%
2009	20,218	20,290	1.6%
2010	20,409	20,151	1.6%
2011	20,902	20,007	1.6%
2012	22,326	20,936	1.6%
2013	23,211	21,452	1.6%
2014	23,874	21,713	1.6%
2015	23,837	21,653	1.5%
2016	26,149	23,457	1.6%
2017	25,574	22,463	1.5%
2018	26,501	22,722	1.5%
2019	28,424	23,937	1.5%
2020	26,647	22,167	1.4%
2021	30,379	24,138	1.4%
% Changes			
(2008–2020)		7%	
(2008–2021)		16%	
Compound Annual Growth Rate			
(2008–2020)		0.58%	
(2008–2021)		1.1%	

Sources: State and local lottery revenue data are collected from the Urban-Brookings Tax Policy Center. Total state and local tax revenue data are from the U.S. Census Bureau. "Annual Survey of State Government Tax Collections."

However, revenue growth was not stable in the past decade. Table 9.5 shows state and local lottery revenue during 2008–2021. Between 2008 and 2018, revenue growth stagnated or even declined in some years. The spike in 2019 was related to "the boost in sales from $1.5 billion Mega Million jackpot won in October 2018" (No Author 2019). This was followed by a drop in 2020 due to economy shutdown and then another increase in 2021 when many states reopened. Inflation-adjusted lottery income increased by 7% from 2008 to 2020, with a compound annual growth of 0.58%. If 2021 data are included, the overall revenue increased by 16% with a compound annual growth rate of 1.1%. However, this increase is unsustainable since it is reactionary to a specific event.

In addition, Dadayan (2019) shows that lottery revenue growth is uneven across states. During 2008–2017, inflation-adjusted lottery revenue declined in 19 states. Many of them are in the New England and Midwest regions, and they are the early operators. The largest declines happened in Oklahoma (34.7%), Montana (26.9%), New Mexico (18.9%), Rhode Island (17.8%), Maryland (13.3%), and West Virginia (16.3%). The states with the largest revenue increases were North Carolina (56.3%) and South Carolina (35.3%). In terms of real revenue per adult, lottery revenue declined in 29 states during 2008-2018 with -2.6% growth rate nationwide. The stagnation or decline was due to increasing interstate lottery competition. The proliferation of other forms of gambling activities may also have taken customers away from lottery schemes.

Casino and Racino Tax Revenues

With the inflation-adjusted lottery revenue stagnant or declining, state governments became more interested in tapping revenue from casinos, racinos, and sports betting, especially in recession periods. Eight states have legalized casino operations, and three states have legalized racino operations since 2008. The total number of casinos and racinos increased, but aggregated total tax revenue was relatively stagnant in the past decade. According to Dadayan (2019), from 2008 to 2017, casino and racino revenue collection in real dollars grew slightly from $8.4 billion to $9.0 billion in real terms, or a 6.8% growth rate. Yet, revenue collection for the earlier states that adopted casinos before 2008 declined by 9.3% over the years, or 1.1% annually. Among these 20 older casino/racino states, 15 experienced negative growth, ranging from 52% in New Jersey, 40.5% in Illinois, and 36%–39% in Delaware, Indiana, Mississippi, and West Virginia, to 5% in Colorado and Louisiana (see Table 9.6).

In terms of per adult, the casino and racino tax revenue decline was steeper, dropping from $89.4 after adjusted with inflation in 2008 to $75.9 in 2017, or a 15% decline. The annual growth rate was –0.3%. Among the older casino/racino states, New Jersey's annual growth rate is –8.2%, Illinois' –5.9%, and –5.5% for Indiana (see Table 9.6).

200 State Tax Systems

TABLE 9.6 Casino and Racino Revenues (Inflation-adjusted) Per Adult Resident Declined Despite Overall Growth: FY 2008–FY 2017

State	Real Revenues ($millions)				Real Revenue Per Resident Age 18+ ($)		
	FY 2008	FY 2017	% Change 2008–2017	CAGR (%), 2008–2017	FY 2008	FY 2017	% Change 2008–2017	CAGR (%), 2008–2017
United States	$8,453	$9,026	6.8	0.7	36.8	36.0	(2.4)	(0.3)
"Older" Casino/racino States	$8453	$7,669	(9.3)	(1.1)	89.4	75.9	(15.1)	(1.8)
Colorado	123.7	117.4	(5.1)	(0.6)	33.6	27.0	(19.6)	(2.4)
Delaware	243.6	150.8	(38.1)	(5.2)	359.5	200.1	(44.3)	(6.3)
Florida	137.9	192.2	39.4	3.8	9.5	11.5	20.6	2.1
Illinois	798.4	475.3	(40.5)	(5.6)	83.2	48.1	(42.3)	(5.9)
Indiana	936.5	596.9	(36.3)	(4.9)	194.6	117.3	(39.7)	(5.5)
Iowa	356.9	317.6	(11.0)	(1.3)	155.8	131.7	(15.5)	(1.9)
Louisiana	728.0	685.7	(5.8)	(0.7)	218.8	192.4	(12.1)	(1.4)
Maine	23.3	54.0	131.4	9.8	22.3	49.9	124.1	9.4
Michigan	353.7	290.2	(17.9)	(2.2)	47.0	37.2	(20.8)	(2.6)
Mississippi	394.1	252.9	(35.8)	(4.8)	180.2	111.1	(38.3)	(5.2)
Missouri	490.2	442.8	(9.7)	(1.1)	109.0	93.7	(14.1)	(1.7)
Nevada	1,120.7	874.8	(21.9)	(2.7)	562.9	381.8	(32.2)	(4.2)
New Jersey	441.8	212.5	(51.9)	(7.8)	66.6	30.7	(53.9)	(8.2)
New Mexico	76.7	60.3	(21.4)	(2.6)	51.2	37.6	(26.5)	(3.4)
New York	491.6	933.0	89.8	7.4	33.1	60.3	81.9	6.9
Oklahoma	12.3	20.7	68.4	6.0	4.5	7.0	56.2	5.1
Pennsylvania	883.5	1,375.2	55.7	5.0	90.2	135.8	50.5	4.6
Rhode Island	338.5	306.8	(9.4)	(1.1)	410.3	361.1	(12.0)	(1.4)
South Dakota	18.2	15.8	(13.1)	(1.5)	30.4	24.1	(20.8)	(2.6)
West Virginia	483.6	293.6	(39.3)	(5.4)	333.5	202.8	(39.2)	(5.4)

"New" Casino/racino States		
	$1,358	**63.4**
Kansas	100.2	45.6
Maryland	601.6	128.5
Massachusetts	77.6	14.1
Ohio	578.2	63.8

Notes: CAGR = computed annual growth rate. States that opened the first casino/racino facilities after fiscal year 2008 are classified as "new" casino"/racino states.

Source: Dadayan (2019, p. 40).

The casino/racino revenue increased for those states that adopted casino/racino after 2008. For instance, in 2017, Kansas collected $100 million ($45.6 per capita), Maryland $601 million ($128 per capita), Massachusetts $77.6 million ($14.1 per capita), and Ohio $578.2 million ($63.8 per capita). However, even though newly legalized casinos and racinos often spur new activities, the proliferation of gambling options can cannibalize state revenue collections. Instead of adding new gamblers to the pool, a new casino will draw customers away from existing casinos, both within and across states. As a result, new states or new operations will experience revenue increases in the short term, but older casinos and earlier-adopting states will experience revenue declines (Huh et al., 2018; Urban Institute No Date c). When Maryland and Pennsylvania legalized casinos, neighboring New Jersey, which started to operate its casinos in 1976, saw its gambling revenues decline by 54% in real terms from 2008 to 2015. Atlantic City was on the brink of bankruptcy due to heavy reliance on declining casino tax revenues. When five new casino states (i.e., Florida, Kansas, Maryland, Ohio, and Pennsylvania) that added over 30 casinos during 2006–2018 experienced a 164% revenue increase, 18 older casino states saw their revenue decline by 16% during 2008–2015 (Huh et al. 2018). As Huh et al. (2018) state, "While casinos do offer short-term padding for budgets, these funds often come at the expense of neighboring states and other casinos in the state. Policymakers should also expect casinos and racinos to taper off as their numbers expand" (p. 14).

Sport Betting Revenue

With the authority to legalize sports betting, states see another potential revenue source. Indeed, "the potential revenue has been a big selling point for legalizing sports betting in many states" (Brainerd 2021, p. 1). Some elected officials promised to use the revenue for a wide range of programs, including general funds and public education. This growth of sports betting tax revenue in the past few years is related to the number of states legalizing such operations. In 2022, sports betting generated $1.5 billion in tax revenue for 28 states. The largest users are Pennsylvania, $144 million, and New York, $691 million. The smallest user is South Dakota, which has less than $1 million in tax revenue.

The $1.5 billion figure appears impressive, yet it is "only a fraction of total casino gambling revenue" (Brainerd 2021, p. 1) and 20 times less than lottery revenue. Due to its brief history, the performance of sports tax revenue is still being determined. Experts predict that sports betting tax revenue will always be relatively volatile and insignificant (Auxier 2019; Dadayan 2019). Sports betting is a relatively low-margin industry (Auxier 2019; Brainerd 2021). The average hold (or gaming revenue divided by the total amount wagered) was 7.2% in

2020 (Brainerd 2021). Bookkeepers can only retain a small share of the total amount wagered, implying the tax base is narrow. They need to pay prizes to winners and then pay all other operating expenses, which can be as much as 60% of gaming revenue (Auxier 2019). Any tax on gaming revenue will further reduce the remaining profits. If states raise the tax rates, there is the danger of driving sports betting to the black market or bankrupt operators. There is also the poaching issue, in which sports betting will affect other gambling options, and new sports betting states will draw customers away from early operators. Hill (2018) suggested that when people spend more on gambling, they have less to spend on other sales. That could affect the sales taxes, which depend on consumption.

Gambling Tax and State Long-term Fiscal Stability

Gambling taxes represent a small share of total state tax revenue. In 2017, gambling tax revenues represented roughly 2.2% of state own-source general funds. State reliance on gambling taxes varies. Among the 47 states that legalize gambling, only 10 have gambling tax revenues that comprise more than 5% of state own-source revenues. The shares in the other 33 states are less than 3%.

Moreover, the share has declined in some states, though increased in others. The overall trendline shows that the expansion of gambling activities produced some initial bursts of revenue, but these were not long-lasting. Their growth does not align with that of the overall economy or tax collection.

The increasing number of gambling options will cannibalize the revenues, as discussed, drawing customers away from existing gambling activities and sites. Though it is appealing to designate gambling taxes for some important programs, the revenue may not be adequate in the long term. Similar to all other sin taxes, gambling taxes raise similar ethical issues. Gambling activities are not socially desirable, and their addiction is a valid concern. It is destructive to personal financial decision-making and harmful to families (Auxier 2019).

Conclusion

This chapter examines several sin taxes: the tobacco tax, alcohol tax, and gambling tax—their tax structures, revenue trends, and contributions to state long-term fiscal stability. The overall discussion shows that these taxes have their limitations, and states cannot depend on these taxes to build their long-term fiscal capacity.

Sin taxes are politically popular. State officials often view them as budget fixers. Polls show the public supports substantial increases, especially if they are

TABLE 9.7 Inflation-Adjusted Sin Taxes Revenue as Share of State Tax Revenue

Year	Tax Revenue (in Constant $millions)			As % of Total State Revenue		
	Tobacco Tax	Alcohol Tax	Lottery[a]	Tobacco Tax	Alcohol Tax	Lottery
2008	16,068	5,744	20,671	2.06%	0.73%	1.6%
2021	15,212	6,608	24,138	1.51%	0.65%	1.4%

Source: The U.S. Census Bureau. Annual Survey of State Government Tax Collections.

[a] The lottery data are collected from the Tax Policy Center.

earmarked for such programs as public education and healthcare. Intermittently, revenue may be spurred when rates are increased and new activities are introduced. The sizable revenues that are generated can be helpful in supporting certain public health objectives, but they tend to be short-lived. These taxes contribute little to the state's long-term fiscal stability. First, they represent a small share of total state revenue. Altogether, they comprise no more than 4% of total state tax revenue in 2021 (see Table 9.7). Second, all tax shares have declined (see Table 9.7). Third, their tax structures usually rely heavily on quantity rather than price, thus limiting long-term revenue growth potential. Revenue growth requires increases in both tax rates and consumption. As discussed, cigarette consumption has declined steadily and significantly, and alcohol consumption, though increasing per adult, has declined, attributable to consumption changes with societal trends and consumer attitudes. Gambling taxes will continue to experience greater competition. The expansion and proliferation of gambling activities will cannibalize state collections. Fourth, as said several times, state governments should not rely heavily on sin taxes because that reliance will induce states to encourage harmful consumption and activities.

Sin taxes are typically earmarked for some important programs ranging from education to homelessness, public health programs, and general funds. Politicians tend to overestimate revenues and overpromise outcomes. The fact is that sin taxes are a small portion of state tax revenue. Even if revenue is earmarked for these programs, the amount is only a minimal component of the revenue needed for that program (Auxier 2019). These programs often increase faster than sin tax revenues, thus adding more pressure to state structural imbalances.

Based on historical experiences with sin taxes, states must carefully assess long-term fiscal revenue performances to avoid structural budget challenges. If long-term performance is not certain or dwindling, states should not use these taxes to fund ongoing budget commitments and recurring expenditures (Dadayan 2019). When considering adopting a new sin tax, lawmakers should be mindful of the potential pitfalls in using new revenue for any permanent programs.

References

Auxier, Richard C. 2019. "States Learn to Bet on Sports: The Prospects and Limitations of Taxing Legal Sports Gambling." *Tax Policy Center*.(May 14).

Boesen, Ulrik. 2021a. "Cigarette Taxes and Cigarette Smuggling by State, 2019." *Tax Foundation*. (December 2).

Boesen, Ulrik. 2021b. "Sugar Taxes Back on the Menu." *Tax Foundation*. https://taxfoundation.org/blog/sugar-taxes/ (February 18).

Brainerd, Jackson. 2020. "A Quick Take on Traditional and Electronic Cigarette Taxes." *National Conference of State Legislatures*. (March 2).

Brainerd, Jackson. 2021. "The Early Bets Are In: Is Sports Betting Paying Off?" *National Conference of State Legislature*. (ncsl.org) (March 1).

Cole, Gail. 2022. "Vape Tax by State: 2023 E-cigarette Tax Guide." *Avalara*. (December 15).

Conlon, Christopher, Nirupama Rao, and Yinan Wang. 2021. "Who Pays Sin Taxes? Understanding the Overlapping Burdens of Corrective Taxes." NBER Working Paper No. w29393.

Dadayan, Lucy. 2016. "State Revenues from Gambling: Short-Term Relief, Long-Term Disappointment." *The Nelson A. Rockefeller Institute of Government*. (April).

Dadayan, Lucy. 2019. "Are States Betting on Sin? The Murky Future of State Taxation." *Tax Policy Center, Urban Institute & Brookings Institution*.

Erb, Lelly Philips. 2023. "New York State Cigarette Tax Just Went up to $5.35 a Pack – The Highest in the Nation." *Forbes*. (forbes.com). (September 5).

Federation of Tax Administrator. "State Excise Tax Rates on Cigarettes (January 1, 2023)." https://taxadmin.org/wp-content/uploads/resources/tax_rates/cigarette.pdf

Guppy, Paul and Betsy Hansen. 2010. "Lawmakers Cannot Count on Sin Taxes for Budget Relief." *Washington Policy Center*. (January).

Haile, Andrew J. 2009. "Sin Taxes: When the State Becomes the Sinner." Temple Law Review, Forthcoming, Elon University Law Legal Studies Research Paper No. 2009-05. (June 25).

Hill, Misha. 2018. "Lottery, Casino and Other Gambling Revenue: A Fiscal Game of Chance." *Institute on Taxation and Economic Policy (ITEP)*. (June).

Hoffer, Adam. 2023a. "Compare State Tobacco Tax Data in Your State." *Tax Foundation*. (May 24).

Hoffer, Adam. 2023b. "Vaping Taxes by State, 2023." *Tax Foundation*. (August 29).

Huh, Kil, Adam Levin, Mary Murphy, and Alexsandria Zhang. 2018. "Are Sin Taxes Healthy for State Budgets?" *The Pew Charitable Trusts*. (July 19).

Institute of Medicine (U.S.) Committee on Preventing Nicotine Addiction in Children and Youths; Lynch B. S., Bonnie R. J., editors. 1994. *Growing Up Tobacco Free: Preventing Nicotine Addiction in Children and Youths*. Washington, DC: National Academies Press (U.S.).

National Conference of State Legislature (NCSL). 2009. *State Tax Actions 2008: Special Fiscal Report*. Denver, Colorado: National Conference of State Legislature.

National Conference of State Legislature (NCSL). 2012. *State Tax Actions 2011: Special Fiscal Report*. Denver, Colorado: National Conference of State Legislature.

National Conference of State Legislature (NCSL) 2015–2022. *State Tax Actions Database*. State Tax Actions Database.

No Author. 2019. "La Fleur's Fiscal 2019 Report." *La fleur's*. (September 9). https://lafleurs.com/magazine-feature/2019/09/09/la-fleurs-fiscal-2019-report/

Rafool, Mandy and Todd Haggerty. 2011. *State Tax Actions 2010: Special Fiscal Report.* Denver, Colorado: National Conference of State Legislature.

Rafool, Mandy. 2013. *State Tax Actions 2012: Special Fiscal Report.* Denver, Colorado: National Conference of State Legislature.

Rafool, Mandy. 2014. *State Tax Actions 2013: Special Fiscal Report* Denver, Colorado: National Conference of State Legislature.

Rafool, Mandy. 2015. *State Tax Actions 2014: Special Fiscal Report.* Denver, Colorado: National Conference of State Legislature.

Ruddock, Steve. 2022. "Comparing Sports Betting Taxes by State." *Gambling.com.* (December 20).www.gambling.com/us/news/comparing-sports-betting-taxes-by-state-3775500

U.S. Census Bureau. "Annual Survey of State Government Tax Collections" (STC). www.census.gov/programs-surveys/stc/data/datasets.html

Urban-Brookings Tax Policy Center. No Date. "Statistics: Lottery Revenue 1977–2021." HYPERLINK "https://taxpolicycenter.org/statistics/lottery-revenue" Lottery Revenue | Tax Policy Center

Urban Institute. No Date a. "Alcohol Taxes." *State and Local Government Backgrounders.* Urban Institute.

Urban Institute. No Date b. "Cigarette and Vaping Taxes." *State and Local Backgrounders.* Urban Institute.

Urban Institute. No Date c. "Lotteries, Casinos, Sports Betting, and Other Types of State-Sanctioned Gambling." *State and Local Government Backgrounders.* Urban Institute.

Urban Institute. No Date d. "Soda Taxes." *State and Local Government Backgrounders.* Urban Institute.

Waisanen, Bert and Todd Haggerty. 2010. *State Tax Actions 2009: Special Fiscal Report.* Denver, Colorado: National Conference of State Legislature.

10
MARIJUANA TAX
Is This New Revenue Source Reliable?

Background of Legalizing Recreational Marijuana

Before 1938, marijuana was a legal substance in the United States prescribed for labor pains, nausea, and other conditions. It became illegal with the passage of the Marijuana Taxation Act of 1938. In 1970, under the Controlled Substance Act, marijuana was classified as a Schedule 1 substance "with a high potential for abuse and little known medical benefits" (Hansen, Miller, and Weber 2017, p. 7).

Marijuana is still illegal under federal law, but state marijuana laws have evolved dramatically in the last decade. An increasing number of states have permitted medical and/or recreational marijuana use. This marijuana movement started with California, the first state to legalize medical marijuana, in 1996. As of May 2, 2024, 38 states and Washington D.C. (Sacco, Lampe, and Sheikh 2024) allowed the medical use of the substance. Sales of medical marijuana have not raised much revenue because these sales are just subject to the general sales tax or even exempt from the general sales tax with no excise tax being levied.

In 2012, Colorado and Washington took one step further by legalizing recreational marijuana. The momentum for recreational legalization is sustained by increasing public support. Two-thirds of the public believe marijuana should be legalized (NCSL 2021). From 2012 to 2020, nearly all recreational marijuana legalization was conducted through voter initiatives. In the last few years, more legalization efforts came from the state legislature. As of May 2, 2024, 24 states and DC had legalized recreational marijuana (see Table 10.1) and established functional recreational marijuana markets with actual sales.

DOI: 10.4324/9781003494324-10

TABLE 10.1 State Legalizing Recreational Marijuana: Year and Way of Approval

Year	State Legislature	Ballot Measures
2012		CO, WA
2014		AK, DC, OR
2016		CA, ME, MA, NV
2018	VT	MI
2019	IL	
2020		AZ, MT, NJ
2021	CT, NM, NY, VA	
2022	RI.	MD, MO
2023	DE, MN	OH

Source: Matthews and Hickey (2024).

There are several rationales behind legalizing recreational marijuana. The primary one is to generate tax revenue to fund government services (Hansen et al. 2017). Under this purview, legalization will bring "the illegal trade into a legal marketplace" (Boesen 2020, p. 22). Advocates argue that taxing marijuana consumption can capture new and untapped revenue sources. Therefore, the legalization can bring additional revenues for state and local governments to provide a wide range of services (Philips 2015). This is attractive to state and local officials who constantly face difficult budgets and who are always looking for new revenue sources. In addition, state and local governments can save hundreds of millions of dollars every year, which they would otherwise have spent on enforcing the prohibition. Criminal justice is another consideration for marijuana legalization. As minorities have been disproportionately impacted by marijuana enforcement during the War on Drugs, proponents argue that legalizing recreational marijuana will improve the justice for these groups.

Tax Designs

As marijuana becomes legalized in more and more states and as sales increase, it is essential to discuss how to tax the sales. Although forty-five states collect a general sales tax, an appropriate marijuana tax policy is not simply extending the sales tax base to cover marijuana. Marijuana is intoxicating, causing behavior changes and long-term adverse health effects. Its consumption will impose negative externalities on the community. Therefore, an excise tax with a high rate, like other sin taxes, should have a role in the marijuana tax design to better capture the negative externalities.

However, there is a black market for recreational marijuana. Marijuana excise tax policy must balance the need to tax products at a sufficient rate to dissuade consumption and raise revenues to offset social costs, but not perceived as too high that it "results in widespread tax evasion and black market marijuana sales" (Philips 2015, p. 2). A solution to this dilemma suggested by Boesen (2020 and 2021) and Davis, Hill, and Philips (2019) is to keep the tax rate "low enough to allow legal markets to undercut, or at least gain price parity with the illicit market" (Boesen 2021, p. 4) in the early stage of market development. After the legal market is fully developed, the rates can and should go high.

As states transition to legalizing marijuana, they have imposed various taxes on marijuana use and products. Those with general sales tax have extended this tax on the use. Furthermore, they also have established an excise tax on marijuana with different tax methods and rates that apply either at the retail or wholesale level or at both levels. Many states also authorized their local governments to extend general sales and excise taxes to marijuana sales (see Appendix G). For example, in California, if a marijuana business needs to purchase marijuana flowers from a grower to sell or manufacture a cannabis product, the state government will impose a $9.25 tax for each ounce. Once the products are sold to customers, the state will collect a 15% excise tax on the retail prices, together with the general sales tax of 7.25%. Simultaneously, local governments can impose their own general sales tax or excise tax on purchases. In Washington state, marijuana businesses do not pay taxes at the wholesale level. Instead, consumers pay 37% of the retail prices along with the 6.5% general sales tax. Local governments can also collect the general sales tax up to a 3.1% limit.

In constructing their marijuana excise taxes, states employ one of the three methods. The most used strategy is the price-based method, followed by weight-based methods. Only three states use a potency-based method. Some states use more than one of these methods (see Table 10.2). The following section will explain the benefits and issues of each method from the perspectives of tax equity and revenue stability. In the context of the marijuana tax, equity requires a system that can minimize the negative externalities caused by marijuana consumption, as mentioned above. In considering revenue stability, Boesen (2021) states that "taxes should be designed to offer stable revenue in the short term regardless of potential price declines" (p. 4) because revenue volatility imposes extra difficulties for practical public budgeting.

Tax on the Prices of the Product

This method mirrors the general sales taxes but is typically set at higher rates. The tax is a certain percentage of the retail price, and most states levy it during the retail transaction (i.e., the consumer pays the tax in addition to the product's cost at the cash register). Some states collect the tax at the wholesale transaction paid by cultivators or distributors, hoping to pass it along to consumers at the

TABLE 10.2 Types of Cannabis Taxes by State as of November 2023

State	Percentage of Prices State	Percentage of Prices Local	Weight-based	Potency-based	General Sales Tax State	General Sales Tax Local
Alaska		x	x			x
Arizona	x				x	x
California	x	x			x	x
Colorado	x		x			x
Connecticut		x		x	x	
Delaware	x					
Illinois	x	x		x	x	x
Maine	x		x			
Maryland	x					
Massachusetts	x	x			x	
Michigan	x				x	
Minnesota	x				x	x
Missouri	x	x			x	x
Montana	x	x				
Nevada	x		x		x	x
New Jersey		x	x		x	
New Mexico	x				x	x
New York	x	x		x		
Ohio	x				x	x
Oregon	x	x				
Rhode Island	x	x			x	
Vermont	x				x	x
Virginia	x	x			x	x
Washington	x				x	x

Source: Tax Policy Center analysis of state government website. "How Do State and Local Cannabis (Marijuana) Taxes Work?" *Tax Policy Center Briefing Book*, last updated January 2024. Permission granted.

retail stage. Some states also allow local jurisdictions to levy a percentage of the price-based excise tax, but usually with a maximum rate limit.

The price-based method is simple and straightforward but has shortcomings. Several sources predict the falling of marijuana prices, although they are unsure of the extent. Since the tax rate is fixed at a certain percentage of the purchase price, tax revenues will drop, and the tax deterrent effect will diminish, resulting in an unstable and unsustainable revenue source together with marijuana overconsumption. As prices have no connection to the negative impact of marijuana consumption on the communities, this method is not considered equitable (Philips 2015; Davis, Hill, and Philips 2019; Boesen 2020; 2021).

Tax on the Weight of the Product

Excise taxes are typically applied to per unit of consumption. Just as cigarettes are taxed at $2.5 per pack, this method taxes marijuana can be taxed based on the weight (per pound or per ounce) of the product. Alaska, New Jersey, and Maine have adopted this approach (Philips 2015; Davis et al. 2019; Boesen 2020; 2021).

The weight-based tax is usually levied on the wholesale transaction. The cultivator and distributor pay the tax that is presumably passed to consumers at the final stage. Collecting taxes at the early stage of the production process has several advantages. The number of entities needed to pay tax is reduced, making the collection and auditing easier. At the same time, it leads to more accurate tax collection on edible products whose marijuana elements vary (Davis et al. 2019). Taxes per unit of weight should also yield relatively stable revenue, as government revenue is not affected by expected marijuana price drops (Boesen 2020).

One concern with this approach is that a flat weight does not take into consideration the potency of the marijuana, and producers will have more incentives to cultivate stronger marijuana, which will sell at a higher price but carry the same amount of tax. There is evidence these circumstances have occurred. Orens, Light, Lewandowski, Rowberry, and Saloga (No Date) found a substantial increase in the tetrahydrocannabinol (THC) content in both marijuana flower and trim in Colorado since its legalization. Taxing based on weight also complicates the tax system, as governments must distinguish weights for different products and establish different rates. For instance, a tax on one pound of flower should be different than from one pound of trim. In California, marijuana flowers were levied at $9.65 per ounce; marijuana leaves at $2.87 per ounce; and fresh plant material at $1.35 per ounce. Colorado has seven categories for weight: bud, trim, bud allocated for extraction, trim allocated for extraction, immature plants, wet whole plants, and seeds. As the variety of available products increases, a system based on weight (and potency) will become more complicated. As a result of this complexity, California dropped its weight-based cannabis tax and adopted a price-based method to make the system simpler and less burdensome for cannabis businesses (Auxier and Airi 2022). However, the weight-based system is more equitable than a price-based system as it can better account for the harmful impacts consumption imposes on the community.

Tax on the Potency of the Product

Similar to the alcohol tax whose rate varies according to alcohol content, the marijuana tax can be based on THC, the primary psychoactive compound in marijuana plants. This method allows the excise tax to most directly account for the negative externalities associated with marijuana consumption and could potentially encourage consumers to move away from more potent products (Boesen 2020). Illinois, Connecticut, and New York are the only states using this method. In Illinois, the tax rate is 25% of the retail price for marijuana products with a THC content of more than 35%, 10% for a THC content of 35% or less, and 20% for all marijuana-infused products (e.g., edibles).

This tax format is ideal. Potency-based methods, not affected by price changes, will generate stable revenue. It is also equitable since it targets harm-generating products, allowing market participants to incorporate any external effects into their decision-making and discourage consumption. However, it may be burdensome for both compliance and administrative purposes. The value of potency is not readily available, as is the price or the weight. The state government must find a reliable means to assess and measure potency consistently. This is not easy, particularly for raw plant materials. Another concern is that the THC measures may not be a reliable indicator of potency (Davis et al. 2019).

Tax Design Recommendations

While each method has its advantages and disadvantages, from equity and revenue stability perspectives, policy makers should move away from a price-based system despite its simplicity. This is the consensus among researchers who studied marijuana taxes (Davis, Hill, and Philips 2019; Boesen 2020). The excise tax based on weight or potency neutralizes the system and provides a sustainable revenue stream for state governments. To prevent erosion in the real value over time, Davis, Hill, and Philips (2019) recommend indexing tax rates with inflation. The weight-based and potent-based methods are preferable, given their ability to capture externalities.

Although the price-based method is the dominant method and is still adopted by newly legalizing states, states are engaging in new experimentations to design excise tax systems that are equitable and revenue-stable. Illinois is the first state to use a potency-based method, adopted in 2019. After legalizing marijuana, New York also designed its tax based on potency levels. Although adopting a price-based method, New Mexico establishes rates per a steady raising schedule. This facilitates tax revenue stability for the state and preserves the deterrence effect.

New Jersey is embracing an innovative approach by linking its weight-based tax to marijuana price ranges (Davis 2021b) (also see Appendix G). This design offers additional benefits by keeping after-tax prices steady. During the early stages of legal market development, prices are usually high, and the tax rate per ounce is low. This allows the legalized market to compete with illegal operations by charging a lower tax on consumers. At the point when the legal market is fully developed and prices decline, the tax rate is higher. This will accumulate revenue collections over time and preserve the tax as a deterrent to overconsumption and youth consumption. These outcomes align with expert recommendations. That is, starting with low tax rates to keep legal businesses competitive with the illicit market during the early stages and then raising it over time when the legal market is well established.

There are several challenges to marijuana taxation design. The first obstacle is that marijuana markets have not generated a standardized product. While tobacco can be taxed by stick or pack, marijuana products take a wide range of forms, and new ones are still emerging. THC-containing products assume different appearances, from brownies to sparkling water and more to come. The intoxicating ingredient (i.e., THC) is not easily measured like alcohol content. According to Boesen (2021), "any tax system should either be nimble enough or updated frequently enough to capture new products as they enter the market" (p. 5). All of these add more complexity to the weight-based or potency-based tax system.

The second challenge posed to taxation designs is the coexistence of medical marijuana and recreational marijuana. There is enough reason to believe that tax rates should differ between the two categories. However, this distinction can foster significant tax evasion, as Colorado's experience demonstrates. Consumers will be incentivized to seek out medical recommendations to purchase marijuana at a discount rate. This causes a large share of the marijuana tax base to disappear and "adds downward pressure on recreational marijuana tax rates" (Philips 2015, p. 5).

Marijuana Tax Revenue Trends and Prospect

The first legal taxable sales of recreational marijuana occurred in Colorado and Washington in 2014. In the past ten years, marijuana tax revenues have dramatically increased in those states that permit such sales (see Table 10.3). Marijuana tax revenue from those states exceeded $1 billion for the first time in 2018, rivaling the total excise tax revenue from all forms of alcohol ($1.16 billion). The amount was doubled in 2020, tripled in 2021, and remains at that level after that.

Even back in 2018, Colorado's marijuana excise tax revenue surpassed its tobacco tax revenue. In addition, general sales taxes on cannabis also raised substantial revenues of $300 million total in California, Colorado, Nevada, and Washington. The total recreational marijuana tax revenues from both the general sales and excise taxes for 2018 were $1.4 billion, about 2.5 times the amount in 2016 (Davis, Hill, and Philips 2019).

The dramatic increases are due to several reasons. With more states taxing marijuana products, the revenue increases. The expansion of the markets inside the states generates more revenue. For instance, in 2020, California alone collected $1 billion due to its large population and relatively new market

TABLE 10.3 Marijuana Tax Revenue for State Governments (in $million)

State	2014	2015	2016	2017	2018	2019	2020	2021	2022	2023	Total through 2023
24 States Total	68	264	530	736	1,308	1,749	2,856	3,934	3,817	4,188	19,456
Alaska			0.3[a]	6	16	22	27	29	29	28	156
California					398	638	1,031	1,361	1,116	1,082	5,706
Colorado	46	105	167	221	243	279	362	396	305	257	2,381
Illinois							216	509	562	522	1,840
Massachusetts					0.6[a]	66	112	227	250	263	920
Michigan						1[a]	81	210	326	473	1,092
Nevada				43[a]	120	149	172	225	196	178	1,086
Oregon			60[a]	69	94	116	158	178	150	148	973
Washington	22[a]	159	303	397	437	477	614	630	529	532	4,103

[a] These revenue collections cover a few months, not the entire year.

Note: Recreational marijuana is also taxed in 15 other states that have already started a marijuana tax or will start soon.

Source: MPP, "Marijuana Tax Revenue in States That Regulate Marijuana for Adult Use." Cannabis Tax Revenue in States that Regulate Cannabis for Adult Use (mpp.org).

continuing to gain a foothold. Significant increases also occurred in states with more developed markets, like Colorado, Washington, Oregon, and Alaska. The COVID-19 pandemic also increased sales and tax revenue (Davis 2021a).

Table 10.3 shows marijuana tax revenue for the nine states that first taxed recreational marijuana. Table 10.4 shows the annual growth rates. Tax collections were booming in the first two or three years after the collection started and remained high until after COVID-19. With its large population, California represents the largest market, followed by Washington, Colorado, and Oregon, which initiated their legal sales earlier.

Even though revenue amounts are impressive and meaningful, these figures will not be transformative for two major reasons (Davis et al. 2019). First, these amounts represent approximately 1% of total state tax collections. It is about 1% of state general revenue for Colorado, Alaska, and Washington and less than 1% for all other states. Second, the revenue booms that are observed are not sustainable. Table 10.3 shows that after the COVID-19, the tax revenue collections declined in each of the states in 2022 and 2023. Table 10.4 displays the annual tax revenue growth rate for the nine states. The growth rate was highest for the first full year and still relatively high in the second or third full year as their markets matured. After that, the annual growth stagnated or declined. The growth rates for some states in 2020 bounced back due to the stay-home orders issued during the pandemic. Eventually, when economy return to a pre-COVID-19 period and markets fully develop, growth rates will remain stagnant at best.

In the near future, marijuana tax revenues are expected to rise as more states legalize recreational marijuana and as the legal market becomes more fully developed. However, in the long term, the revenue prospect will be different. Coupled with the slower or even negative growth rates discussed above, several other factors will also affect marijuana tax revenue collections.

Factors Affecting Marijuana Tax Revenue

One factor affecting marijuana tax revenue is the predicted falling prices of marijuana products. As many states tax recreational marijuana on the basis of prices either at retail or wholesale, their tax revenue will most likely experience a decline. There are several downward pressures on prices. With more states legalizing marijuana, people will not cross the state borders to buy the products as they used to. As competition increases, businesses need to reduce prices. In its peak selling year, recreational marijuana price in Colorado was $2,007 per pound in 2015. The price fell to $782 per pound in 2019. A study by RAND Corporation estimated $227 per pound as a conservative estimate in the long term (Davis et al. 2019). Additionally, future federal marijuana policy changes, to be discussed shortly, will accelerate ongoing negative revenue trends. When prices

TABLE 10.4 Annual Marijuana Tax Growth Rates for Selected States

States	2015–2016	2016–2017	2017–2018	2018–2019	2019–2020	2020–2021	2021–2022	2022–2023
24 States Total	100%	36%	76%	34%	57%	46%	-2.9%	9%
Alaska			166%	37%	23%	7%	0%	-3%
California				60%	61%	32%	-18%	-3%
Colorado	59%	32%	10%	15%	30%	9%	-23%	-16%
Illinois						136%	10%	-7%
Massachusetts					70%	103%	10%	5%
Michigan						159%	55%	45%
Nevada				24%	15%	30%	-12%	-9%
Oregon			36%	23%	36%	13%	-15%	-1.3%
Washington	91%	31%	10%	9%	29%	3%	-16%	0.5%

Source: Author's calculation with data from MPP.

decline, their revenue "will collapse" (Davis 2021a, p. 3). This is particularly troublesome for the states that utilize a price-based format.

The amount of consumption will affect tax revenue as well. There is an expectation that legalization may invite many new consumers, but the Cato Institute predicts that "new consumers under legalization are most likely to be 'casual users' whose spending on cannabis will remain modest" (Davis et al. 2019, p. 27). The bulk of marijuana tax revenue derives from heavy users, who are only about one-third of total marijuana users. It is highly probable that turning the sales from the illicit market to the legal market "will generate an unambiguous revenue gain for states" (Davis et al. 2019, p. 27). However, when the new customers are casual customers, they are not likely to spend all their limited leisure budget on recreational marijuana.

Future actions by the federal government in addressing cannabis will significantly affect states collecting tax revenue. Currently, under the federal tax code in Section 280E, businesses that engage in trafficking-controlled substances are not allowed to deduct business-related costs, resulting in a high effective income tax rate of 70% for state-sanctioned marijuana businesses. If this code is relaxed or terminated, it would significantly reduce business costs, leading businesses to reduce the prices of marijuana products.

Second, since marijuana usage is still illegal under federal law, the cannabis industry can only operate within state boundaries. If the federal government allows shipments across state lines, businesses will be able to consolidate, realizing the economies of scale, and prices will be cut as a result. At present, federal law blocks banking services to the cannabis industry, and marijuana businesses operate almost exclusively on cash supply. If the federal government permits banking services, the sector will improve its financial standing, and state governments will improve their tax enforcement. Consequently, these changes would produce price falls and tax revenue declines for state governments that use price-based excise taxes (Davis et al. 2019).

The Use of Marijuana Tax Revenue

Given that marijuana tax revenue is a small portion of the entire state budgeting and that the tax is volatile and uncertain, state lawmakers need to be cautious as to how to spend the revenue collection (Chapman, Levin, Murphy, and Zhang 2019). Although many lawmakers perceive legalizing marijuana as a feasible strategy to generate revenue, experts have constantly warned against using it as a general revenue measure, as a primary source of funding programs, particularly those programs that demand ongoing budget commitments, and as the sole funding source for a program (Zaretsky 2018, p. 4). Instead, marijuana tax revenue should be directed to support programs to cover the societal cost resulting from consumption and to compensate the communities targeted by past punitive drug policies (Boesen 2021). After that, the additional funds can be used to shore up savings (Chapman et al. 2019).

Appendix H shows how state governments use their tax revenues. To a significant extent, their uses are consistent with experts' suggestions. First, states often dedicate a certain amount of marijuana tax revenues to fund the administration and enforcement of marijuana statutes. Second, many states utilize the funds to support programs closely associated with marijuana consumption. As stated earlier, marijuana consumption creates negative externalities, and revenue should be dedicated to correcting these impacts. Examples include programs to study marijuana use impacts and programs for drug education, prevention, and reduction. Furthermore, programs can incorporate youth substance abuse education, drug treatment, crime prevention, and supporting public safety and healthcare programs. Third, there is an overwhelming usage of earmarks for marijuana tax revenue. Almost all legal-marijuana states direct revenues for specific programs. Though Alaska is the only state that allows revenues to be placed in the general revenue fund, it creates, within the general revenue fund, two programs—recidivism reduction and health education, receiving 75% of marijuana tax revenue.

Some use of earmarking makes good sense, such as directing revenue toward programs that offset negative externalities caused by marijuana consumption stated above. Still, some do not, such as school capital construction and public education. Lawmakers and the public need to be aware of earmark limitations. Even though the earmarking process is politically popular, according to Davis et al. (2019), "it is not necessarily an effective budget policy" (p. 33). Examples include when marijuana tax revenue is earmarked for school capital construction and public education (Colorado), afterschool programs (Michigan), kindergarten programs, and transportation purposes. Advocates often use these popular programs to gain public support, yet "state revenue is typically fungible between different spending areas" (Philips 2015, p. 6). In other words, state policy makers can and often do shift current revenue away from earmarked services, leaving total spending levels unchanged. Even in the case that total expenditures increase, earmarking can still hinder the effective usage of tax dollars. When funds are committed regardless of policy priority changes, lawmakers lose the flexibility for determining how to use funds. To address this concern, lawmakers should evaluate the use of earmarking periodically. Another risk is that lower-than-expected marijuana tax revenue collection will leave these programs insufficiently funded.

Lastly, marijuana tax revenue does go to the general fund, but this has happened only in a few states and as a small proportion of the revenue. There is always the temptation to use marijuana tax and other sin tax to fill the budget gaps, but lawmakers must understand they cannot rely on it for major projects and cannot count on it to solve their long-term fiscal problems.

Conclusion

The marijuana tax is a sin tax. It differs from other sin taxes in that its market is still developing, its products are not standardized, and it operates under a unique legal environment where the federal government still prohibits consumption. As a new and untapped revenue source, marijuana taxes are appealing to state governments that often struggle to balance their budget. This chapter discussed the various marijuana tax designs. From state revenue stability and equity perspectives, state governments should employ weight-based or potency-based excise taxes and move away from the price-based system. Several pressures will push down marijuana prices, and if the tax is based on prices, tax revenue will be reduced. Price-based methods cannot capture the negative impact consumption has on individuals and communities.

This chapter also reviews the revenue collection in the past decade and how states use them. As one of the hottest trends in state taxation, marijuana taxes have brought and will continue to bring impressive tax revenue to state governments. States collected over $4 billion in marijuana tax in 2023. If all states legalized recreational marijuana, it could have generated $8.5 billion annually (Hoffer 2023). However, marijuana tax cannot serve as a solution for the long-term fiscal problems that states have faced for decades. First, the marijuana tax is a relatively new tax with a developing market and facing many uncertainties and volatility. New information about the impact of drug usage and the changes in federal policies will affect market development and revenue collections. Second, although the tax revenue collected is impressive, it is roughly 1% or less of state tax revenue. For instance, in 2023, Alaska's 1.34% of tax revenue came from marijuana tax, the highest ratio among the 24 states. On the lowest end is New York, which has only 0.03% of its revenue from marijuana tax (Lange 2024). Third, as stated earlier, the robust revenue collection that states experienced in the first few full years is not sustainable when the market faces more competition. Fourth, given that the marijuana tax is a sin tax, the revenue should not go to the general fund. Instead, it should be first appropriated to address the external harms created by marijuana consumption (Hoffer 2023), including public safety, youth drug use education, and cessation programs.

References

Auxier, Richard and Nikhita Airi. 2022. "The Pros and Cons of Cannabis Taxes." *Tax Policy Center: Urban Institute & Brookings Institute*. (September 29).

Boesen, Ulrick. 2020. "A Road Map to Recreational Marijuana Taxation." *Tax Foundation*. (June).

Boesen, Ulrik. 2021. "How High are Taxes on Recreational Marijuana in your State?" *Tax Foundation*. (March).

Chapman, Jeff, Adam Levin, Mary Murphy, and Alexandria Zhang. 2019. "Forecasts Hazy for State Marijuana Revenue." *The Pew Charitable Trusts.* (August).

Davis, Carl, Misha E. Hill, and Richard Philips. 2019. "Taxing Cannabis." *Institute on Taxation and Economic Policy.* (January).

Davis, Carl. 2021a. "State and Local Cannabis Tax Revenue Jumps 58%, Surpassing $3 Billion in 2020." *Institute on Taxation and Economic Policy.* (March 15).

Davis, Carl. 2021b. "New Jersey Leads by Example with its New Cannabis Tax." *Institute on Taxation and Economic Policy.* (January 12).

Hansen, Benjamin, Keaton Miller, and Caroline Weber. 2017. "The Taxation of Recreational Marijuana: Evidence from Washington State." Working paper 2332. *National Bureau of Economic Research.* (August).

Hoffer, Adam. 2023. "Cannabis Taxation: Lessons Learned from U.S. States and Blueprint for Nationwide Cannabis Tax Policy." *Tax Foundation.* (April).

Lange, Tony. 2024. "These 23 States, D.C. Collected $2.9 Billion in Cannabis Excise Tax Revenue in 2023." *Cannabis Business Times.* (April 4).

Marijuana Policy Project (MPP).No Date. *Marijuana Tax Revenue in States That Regulate Marijuana for Adult Use.* Marijuana Tax Revenue in States That Regulate Marijuana for Adult Use (mpp.org).

Matthews, Alex Leeds and Christopher Hickey. 2024. "More U.S. States Are Regulating Marijuana. See Where It's Legal across the Country." *CNN.* (April 19).

National Conference of State Legislature (NCSL). 2021. *State Cannabis Taxation.* (January 7).

Orens, Adam; Miles Light, Brian Lewandowski, Jacob Rowberry, and Clongton Saloga. No Date. "Market Size and Demand for Marijuana in Colorado: Prepared for the Colorado Department of Revenue." *Colorado Department of Revenue.*

Philips, Richard. 2015. "Issues with Taxing Marijuana at the State Level." *The Institute on Taxation & Economic Policy.* (May).

Sacco, Lida, Joanna R. Lampe, and Hassan Z. Sheikh. 2024. "The Federal Status of Marijuana and Policy Gap with States." *Congressional Research Service.*

The Tax Policy Center. No Date. "How Do State and Local Cannabis (Marijuana) Taxes Work?" *Tax Policy Center Briefing Book: State and Local Tax Policies,* https://www.taxpolicycenter.org/briefing-book/how-do-state-and-local-cannabis-marijuana-taxes-work

Zaretsky Renu. 2018. "High Hopes and Altered States: Choices, Marijuana, and Tax Revenue." *Tax Vox: State and Local Issues.* (August 1).

11
USER FEES AND CHARGES, GASOLINE TAXES, AND HEALTHCARE PROVIDER TAXES

Introduction

This chapter analyzes three revenue sources. It first discusses user fees and charges, followed by fuel taxes and healthcare provider taxes. They are joined into one chapter because gas taxes and healthcare provider taxes resemble user charges to a certain extent. The National Conference of State Legislatures (NCSL) lists some healthcare provider taxes under the fee category in its *State Tax Actions Database*. The gasoline taxes are the best example of a tax based on the benefits taxpayers receive from using the services.

User Fees and User Charges

User charges and fees are always part of governmental finance. Tollways were common in Ancient Rome. Later, tolls were imposed on bridges to support bridge construction in the Middle Ages (FasterCapital 2023). The United States Postal Services (USPS), the first federal service-delivery agency, sells stamps to customers before delivering the mail. The inception of the National Parks system and state parks endorsed a user-payment system to support park operations. Over the years, user fees and charges have evolved to meet the needs of the time, becoming diverse and complicated, applying to a significant range of activities, and generating a substantial amount of revenue for state and local governments.

User fees and charges appear interchangeable, but they are different. Mikesell (2018) gave the following definitions:

> User fees are derived from government sale of licenses to engage in otherwise restricted or forbidden activities;
> User charges, or prices charged for voluntarily purchased, [are for] publicly provided services that, although benefiting specific individuals or businesses, are strongly associated with basic government responsibilities.
>
> *(p. 571)*

Payments for licenses and franchises constitute user fees. They are assessed on the licenses as a condition for holders to exercise a business or nonbusiness privilege. A person cannot operate a business or drive a vehicle without a license. Franchise fees give the holders sole rights and responsibilities to serve the entire population in the servicing area at a specified rate for specific quality conditions. While licenses can be issued to many individuals or entities, franchises are limited to one. All licenses generate revenue, but some are regulation licenses, and others are revenue licenses. Regulation licenses apply controls and are difficult to obtain. Revenue licenses serve to collect revenue without requiring the government to inspect businesses or merchandise and are never denied. In 2014, states collected $51.1 billion from licenses, of which 46% came from motor vehicle licenses and 11% from state corporate licenses (Mikesell 2018).

User fees do not purchase specific products or services, but user charges do. Visitors pay a charge to enter a state park to enjoy its natural beauty and aesthetics. Drivers pay tolls to drive on the tollway. College students pay tuition to receive education services. The user charges constitute an exchange of services and can be avoided if they choose not to use the service.

Both user fees and charges relieve governmental burdens from its general revenue system by requiring identifiable beneficiaries to contribute full or partial funding for specific services. User fees are used to compensate governments for incurring costs when issuing licenses and should be related to the overall cost. User charges are considered the prices paid for services and products (Mikesell 2018) and should reflect the costs of services, but often at discounted rates.

Imposing charges requires two related conditions, "benefit separability and chargeability" (Mikesell 2018, p. 578), both of which are missing in pure public goods. First, there must be a way to separate users from non-users before charges can be imposed. If the benefit flows to an entire community, the service should be funded by a tax source. Second, there must be "an economic method fro excluding from service benefits those who do not pay for the service" (Mikesell 2018, p. 578). Otherwise, there is no way to impose charges on users. Furthermore, services and benefits should be gauged with meters, fences, and other structures so that the level of payment is based on the amounts of services received (Mikesell 2018).

The Increasing Role of User Fees and Charges in State Government Finance

Over the past decades, user fees and charges have become increasingly important for state and local government finance. According to the data compiled by the Urban-Brookings Tax Policy Center (No Date), state and local government nontax revenue[1] per capita has grown from $213 in 1977 to $1,930 in 2007 to $2,569 in 2020. Local governments collect a larger share of user fees and charges than state governments. In 2008, user charges accounted for 25% of local general revenue, compared with 14% for state government. One reason is that local governments provide more beneficiary services to residents, including utilities and sewage. The other reason is that local governments face more tax restraints and are under more pressure to search for additional nontax revenues (Urban Institute No Date a). For state governments alone, user charges as a share of state general revenue from own sources increased from 12% in 1995 to 14% in 2008 and 19% in 2019 (U.S. Census Bureau).

Different forces are behind the increasing usage of charges and fees by states. Governments impose user fees on a wide range of licenses to regulate these professions and activities to protect the public interest. From an economic theory perspective, user charges, when applicable, can improve the efficiency and equity of public services, which will be further discussed later. However, the dominant force pushing governments toward fees and charges is their fiscal struggle and effort to search for nontax revenue. The tax revolt movement that began in the late 1970s led to the enactment of Tax and Expenditure Limitations (TELs) in many states, restraining state government authority to raise taxes (Hager 2011). At the same time, the public continues to demand more services. User fees and charges provide an appealing alternative revenue source that does not burden most taxpayers. State government fiscal struggles are exacerbated during economic downturns, and raising user fees and charges is less burdensome than increasing taxes. Technological changes erode some of the existing tax base. The fuel tax is a prominent example. The proliferation of alternative fuel motor vehicles forced states to raise motor vehicle-related fees and search for alternative transportation user fees to generate funds.

State User Charges

User charges generate substantial revenue for state governments. In 2021, current charges amounted to $243 billion or 18% of state general revenue. Charges and miscellaneous general revenue were $421 billion in 2021, or 31%. As a comparison, states collected $369 billion in general sales tax revenue and $89 billion in corporate income tax revenue that year. Only the individual income tax ($503 billion) outperformed charges and miscellaneous revenue (U.S. Census Bureau).

As shown in Table 11.1, among the charges, the largest shares derive from education services, particularly higher education, accounting for 7% of state general revenue in 2008, increased to 9% in 2019 before the pandemic, and then declined to 7.9% in 2021. The second largest user charge stems from hospital services, increasing from 3.4% in 2008 to 6.6% in 2021. The third largest charge is from highways, comprising 0.6% in 2008 and 0.8% in 2021, followed by natural resources. Payments to higher education institutions primarily derive from tuition and payment spent on dormitories, athlete contests, and book materials. Hospital charges include payments made from insurance companies, patients, and public insurance programs like Medicare. Highway charges are collected from the tolls on toll roads (Urban Institute No Date b). Several categories have declined, including school lunch sales, housing, community development, and solid waste management.

In constant dollars, from 2008 to 2019, charges and miscellaneous general revenue increased by 18%, and user charges increased by 33% (see the last column in Table 11.1). Growth rates vary from service to service. Sewage charges experienced the largest increase of 131%, although, in dollar amount, it is less than 0.1% of state general revenue. Charges for hospital services had the second largest growth of 80%–90%, followed by highway at 66%, sea and inland port facilities at 49%, and parking facilities at 38%. Higher education service charges increased by 17%. The COVID-19 pandemic impacted user charge revenues. In almost every category, inflation-adjusted charges declined due to the stay-at-home orders during 2020–2021.

Some states relied on user charges more than others. In 2021, the national average of state user charges as a percentage of their general revenue was 14%. The highest ratios were 29% in Utah and 27% in South Carolina, Kansas, and Alabama. Meanwhile, the lowest ratio was at 7% in Wyoming, Illinois, Minnesota, and Nevada. Only seven states and Washington, DC had charges accounting for less than 10% of their general revenue. Together with Wyoming, Illinois, Minnesota, and Nevada, the other three states are Tennessee 8.5%, Connecticut 9%, and New York 9.6% (U.S. Census Bureau).

State User Fees

How did states employ user fees to shore up revenue in the past decades? To find out, the author reviewed the NCSL *State Tax Actions Database*. The Database contains information about states' adoption of new fees, increases or decreases of existing fees, and the net fiscal impact. It also includes some tuition charges on several occasions. The results are presented in Table 11.2.

TABLE 11.1 Current Charges and Miscellaneous General Revenue and as a Percentage of State General Revenue from Own Sources (in Constant $million)

	2008	2019	2021	% Changes 2008–2021	% Change 2008–2019
General Revenue from Own Sources	1,067,648	1,252,125	1,338,146	25.3%	17.3%
Charges and Miscellaneous General Revenue	287,927	338,578	334,987	16.3%	17.6%
Current Charges	153,863	204,435	193,512	25.8%	32.9%
Education	83,716	97,918	85,910	2.6%	17.0%
% of Gen Revenue from Own Sources[a]	7.8%	9.1%	8.0%		
Higher Education Institution	82,557	97,044	85,206	3.2%	17.5%
School Lunch Sales (Gross)	31	29	6	−80.4%	−5.3%
Hospitals	37,123	66,858	70,547	90.0%	80.1%
% of Gen Revenue from Own Sources	3.4%	6.2%	6.6%		
Highways	6,574	10,898	9,335	42.0%	65.8%
% of Gen Revenue from Own Sources	0.6%	1.0%	0.8%		
Air Transportation (Airports)	1,326	1,675	1,036	−21.9%	26.3%
Parking Facilities	19	26	20	2.4%	37.8%
Sea and Inland Port Facilities	1,221	1,814	1,859	52.2%	48.5%
Natural Resources	2,543	3,059	2,477	−2.6%	20.3%
Parks and Recreation	1,593	1,587	1,208	−24.2%	0.0%
Housing and Community Development	802	795	892	11.2%	−0.9%
Sewage	388	896	894	130.3%	130.7%
Solid Waste Management	520	209	201	−61.3%	−59.8%
Other Charges	18,038	18,700	19,134	6.1%	3.7%
Miscellaneous General Revenue	134,064	134,143	141,474	5.5%	0.1%
Interest Earnings	47,689	33,768	28,796	−39.6%	−29.2%

(*Continued*)

226 State Tax Systems

TABLE 11.1 (Continued)

	2008	2019	2021	% Changes 2008–2021	% Change 2008–2019
Special Assessments	631	17	16	–97.4%	–97.3%
Sale of Property	1,049	1,032	1,138	8.5%	–1.6%
Other General Revenue	84,695	99,326	111,524	31.7%	17.3%
Current Charges and Miscellaneous General Revenue as % of State Revenue from Own Sources					
Charges and Miscellaneous General Revenue	26.9%	31.7%	31.3%		
Current Charges	14.4%	19.1%	18.1%		
Miscellaneous General Revenue	12.5%	12.6%	13.2%		

Source: U.S. Census Bureau, *Annual Surveys of State and Local Government Finances.* Percentages are the author's calculations based on *Annual Surveys.*

[a] The charges from education, hospitals, and highways are also expressed as percentages of general revenue. The percentages of all charges are not provided because they are all small, usually less than 0.01%.

Table 11.2 shows that states constantly enacted new fees and raised existing fees. More states have enacted new fees and raised existing fees than reduced them. All the years except 2014 witnessed net dollar fee increases. The net reduction in 2014 was due to Florida's reduction of a series of fees, including approval of many tuition waivers and exempt identification card fees for low-income persons. Table 11.2 also shows that fee increases are substantial in most fiscal years, particularly in the years during and immediately after the Great Recession. In some years (e.g., 2008 and 2019), the net dollar amounts from fee increases are comparable to those from major tax increases. For instance, in 2008, new fees and fee increases generated a net revenue increase of $584 million. As a comparison, the general sales tax increase collected an additional $688 million, and personal income tax changes resulted in a $254 million loss for states.

Some states relied heavily on fee increases to restore their revenue during the Great Recession. In 2009, Florida raised an additional $1.2 billion from a range of fee increases. In the same year, Colorado and Illinois generated an additional $200 million and $332 million, respectively, by increasing fees on motor vehicle registration and other vehicle fines and charges. The last column in Table 11.2 shows the states with major fee increases. While state legislators may have to raise major taxes in some years, they also reduce them in other years. As a contrast, they always adopt new fees and fee increases from year to year.

TABLE 11.2 States Fee Changes: FY 2008–FY 2020

Fiscal Year	# States with New Fees and Fee Increases	# of States with Fee Decreases	States' Net Amount (in $million)	States with Fee Changes Larger Than $100 Million
2008	18	0	$584	FL $136.80—Court Fee
2009	22	0	$3,350	AZ $134.00—Tuition
				CO $200.00—Motor Vehicle
				$122.20—Tuition
				FL $797—Vehicle License
				$195—Court Fees
				$108—Tuition
				IL $332—Vehicle License
				NY $220—Tuition
				$115—Water Bottle Deposit
				OR $130—Tuition
2010	12	0	$698	AZ $102.00—Tuition
				OH $200—Casino License
2011	18	3	$1,078	CA: $300—Vehicle Registration
				$200—Fire Prevention Fee
				FL $182—Tuition
				OR $105—Tuition
2012	12	0	$229	**None**
2013	12	2	$69	TX -$121—Eliminate a Specific Utility Fee
2014	9	1	$–11	FL -$307—Eliminate a Highway Safety Fee
				PA $227 Motor Vehicle Fees
2015	15	4	$116	TX -$125—Eliminate Professional Fee
2016	15	5	$297	MI $158—Motor Vehicle
2017	20		$1,038	CA $726—Transportation Improvement Fee
				GA $310—Hospital Provider Fee
				PA $200—Gaming Revenue
2018	13	4	$670	AZ $91–$182—Vehicle Registration
				MD $280—Health Insurance Provider Fee
				VA $215—Healthcare Provider Fee
2019	22	3	$1,067	IL $465—Vehicle Registration
				$152—Certificate of Title
				MD $105—Health Insurance Provider Fee
				WI $114—Vehicle Title
Total	188	22		

Sources: Author's calculation based on NCSL *State Tax Actions Database* ; Waisanen and Haggerty (2010); Rafool and Haggerty (2011); Rafool (2013, 2014,; 2015); NSCL (2009, 2012, 2016–2020).

The new fees and fee increases cover a wide range of activities. They fall into several categories.

- **Motor Vehicle-related Fees:** The most dominant type is the fees related to motor vehicles and transportation. At least half of the states increased vehicle registration fees, title fees, driver license fees, new or high fees for alternative fuel vehicles, and vehicle-related fines. At least eight states have authorized a hefty fee of $200 or more on electronic vehicles (Kindy 2023). Several states (i.e., California, South Carolina, Indiana, and Colorado) established a Transportation Improvement Fee. The reason states frequently target motor vehicle-related activities is that the motor fuel tax is not aligned with transportation funding needs. In 2011, California generated $300 million in revenue by raising car registration fees. In 2017, the Transportation Improvement Fee enacted by California, ranging from $25 to $175 based on the market value of the vehicle, together with the motor vehicle registration fee, collected an additional $726 million in revenue. In 2019, Illinois raised $646 million by increasing the electric vehicle registration fee from $35 to $248 and the passenger vehicle registration fee from $98 to $148. Illinois also increased the registration fee for trucks, buses, and trailers and the fee for certificate of title.
- **Healthcare-related Fees:** Several states enacted a new fee or increased existing fees on healthcare providers to generate revenue to pay for states' share of Medicaid funding. In 2018, in response to its Medicaid expansion, Virginia lawmakers authorized an assessment imposed on private acute care hospitals. The assessment would be used to pay for the non-federal share of Medicaid expanded coverage. In 2017, Louisiana authorized the increase of the per-bed per day fee charged to nursing facilities. In 2019, Maryland enacted a health insurance provider fee assessment of 2.75%, expecting to increase the revenue by $280 million in FY 2019. The second section of this chapter discusses healthcare-related fees.
- **Recreational Activities:** Numerous states enacted new fees or increased fees for recreational activities. Minnesota and Alaska both raised fees for fishing, hunting, and trapping. Rhode Island and South Carolina enacted beach preservation fees. In 2017, Montana established an aquatic invasive species prevention pass, requiring individuals to obtain a pass for a fee before applying for a fishing license.
- **Court Fees and Fines:** Many states also raised their court fees and fines. For instance, Florida, Kentucky, Kansas, and Vermont raised their court fees in 2008.
- **Occupational License:** Some states also raised their license and occupational license fees. Nevada raised the business license fee to $500 per year for

corporations. California created an application fee for a debt collection licensure in 2021.
- **Higher Education:** In the area of higher education, several states raised tuition rates for their public universities.
- **Others:** States also adopted a wide range of other fee increases, including fees on tax preparation, landfill tipping fees, 9-1-1 fees on wireless phones and prepaid wireless and landlines, record retention fees, and mutual fund and broker registration fees. Moreover, fees are imposed per ton of air pollutants, facility usage, and oil and petroleum production owners. There is a service fee for credit/debit cards used in the payment of fees, a hotel/motel fee for all lodging, and an annual registration fee for captive insurers.

In reviewing the NCSL *State Tax Actions Database*, the author also noticed the impact of COVID-19 on state fee decisions. Several states reduced certain fees or suspended some license renewal fees to make it easier for businesses to operate. For instance, Washington authorized temporary waivers of liquor licensing renewal fees required from certain businesses and suspended the collection of child-care license fees. California waived several license renewal fees.

User Fees and Charges in State Government Financial Stability

User fees and charges are important to state government finance and financial stability. As Table 11.1 shows, their shares of state general revenue have increased over the decades. The constant dollar amounts of most categories increased steadily. Over the past decades, states have enacted new fees and increased existing ones. User fees and charges have also established their continuing and prevalent role in state finance for the following reasons.

Wide Support among Public Finance Experts

Finance experts have broad support for using fees and charges toward government finance. The Government Finance Officers Association (GFOA) (No Date) recommends that when certain services benefit a particular group, governments should utilize fees and charges as a funding method. Mikesell (2018) echoed a similar message. The wide support for user fees and charges comes from the numerous advantages associated with their use. First, the additional and substantial revenues that these items generate relieve pressure from the states' general revenue systems. This is appealing to state governments whose tax powers are restrained, particularly after the 1980s, as discussed earlier. At the same time, user fees and charges diversify government revenue sources and reduce revenue structure volatility (Hager 2011).

Second, user fees and charges can improve the efficiency of public services. User charges mimic a private market business model where users determine their service demands by calculating and comparing marginal costs and benefits. Without a charge, the demand can be excessive. For example, if water usage is not metered, one has no incentive to conserve it, resulting in unnecessary consumption. Governments will have to build more water towers to avoid the suboptimal allocation of public funds. User charges can also improve operating efficiency because agency staff must respond to customers' demands. Poor service will cause them to lose customers, as reflected in the current marketplace dynamics (Hager 2011; Mikesell 2018).

Third, user charges also improve the equity of public services because those who use the service pay for the service. General revenue is not used to subsidize the service that does not benefit the entire community. Furthermore, user fees and charges can correct two other less noticeable but equally significant equity problems associated with services consumed by nonresidents and services used by tax-exempted entities. The absence of user charges allows nonresidents and tax-exempted entities to impose financial burdens on governments they do not financially support. When nonresidents pay a charge to attend a cultural event, and when a charitable organization pays a charge for water usage, they contribute funding to the received service instead of imposing the cost on the general tax-paying public (Mikesell 2018).

Potentially Increasing Use in the Future

User fees and charges contribute to state fiscal stability because, in some areas, user charges can better serve revenue needs than tax. Transportation is a good example. The rapidly growing number of highly efficient fuel and electric vehicles has reduced fuel tax revenue—the traditional source of infrastructure funding. The engineering firm CDM Smith estimated that states will lose approximately $87 billion of fuel tax revenue by 2050, widening an already large revenue gap for states to construct and maintain their highways (NCSL 2023).

States have turned to alternative transportation user fees such as tollways and Road Use Charges (RUC) to replace or supplement the fuel tax to generate transportation revenue. Tollways have expanded significantly in many states in the past two decades, and the trend will continue in the years to come (Schaper 2018). Many states in the Northeast and Midwest, as well as California, have implemented plate reading systems such as E-ZPass on their toll roads to reduce collection costs and ease travel difficulties. Sensors read the plates as vehicles pass toll gates, wherein the system can monitor travel miles, and a subsequent bill is sent to vehicle owners at certain intervals (Mikesell 2018).

Since the early 2000s, states have led the discussion on RUCs. Many view RUC as a viable alternative to the motor fuel tax. Under this system, the driver pays a fee based on the number of miles driven. Oregon was the first state to pilot the system in 2006 and 2012, thereafter launching a voluntary program in 2015 (NCSL 2022; Boardman and Oregon Department of Transportation 2023). Oregon's RUC system contains the following major elements:

- "Participants sign up with an account manager, select a mileage reporting option, and are billed for reported miles with a credit for the fuel tax paid on fuel used to drive taxable miles" (Boardman & Oregon Department of Transportation 2023, p. 2).
- "Participants may choose a GPS-based option in which they are automatically not billed for out-of-state miles, or they can choose a non-GPS-based option, wherein all miles are presumed to have been driven in Oregon" (Boardman & Oregon Department of Transportation 2023, p. 2–3).

The Oregon Department of Transportation is working with transportation departments in 20 other states, forming the Western Road Usage Charge Consortium, later known as RUC America. This association aims to develop RUC policy and explore existing and potential RUC programs. In Utah, residents can enroll and pay an RUC rather than paying an enhanced registration fee if the vehicle uses alternative fuel such as electricity (North Carolina 1st Commission 2020). California and Washington also started their pilot programs. The trend will continue. The Infrastructure Investment and Jobs Act included a provision directing the U.S. Department of Transportation to design and conduct a national per-mile RUC program. This will encourage more states to explore their own RUC project, further advancing RUC research and policy (Boardman and Oregon Department of Transportation 2023; NCSL 2022). Implementing a large-scale RUC is an integral component of modernizing the transportation system and financing.

There are numerous challenges in implementing an RUC system. One is educating the public about the need to replace the motor fuel tax with an RUC. Another challenge is the high collection cost associated with the program. While the fuel tax is collected at the pumps, collecting RUC fees requires installing technology to enroll users, conducting electronic billing, processing credit card and bank fees, and performing enforcement activities. The collection cost for motor fuel taxes is 1%, whereas RUC's is estimated to be 5%–13%. These costs need to be reduced to make the program feasible. Technological challenges also involve how to deal with users who do not have bank accounts and credit cards. For the program to be mandatory, mechanisms will need to be developed to allow for cash and other forms of payment. Protecting users' privacy is also another concern (North Carolina 1st Commission 2020; NCSL 2022).

Limitations and Issues

While user fees and charges have become an important part of state government finance, their usage has limitations and drawbacks. First, most public services cannot be financed with user charges because they benefit the public or exhibit positive externalities. Examples are public safety, fire services, and public education, wherein the benefits are not separatable or chargeable, or the benefit flows beyond the users (Hager 2011; Mikesell 2018). For other services, even though beneficiaries can be individually identified, such as income transfer and social services programs, charges cannot be applied because that contradicts the original intentions of those programs.

Second, user charges are often criticized as being regressive, imposing a higher burden on low-income families (Hager 2011). Mikesell (2018) argues that this is not entirely accurate. For instance, user charges will not affect low-income families if they do not use the services. In case they do use services such as admission to swimming pools in the summer, vouchers and seasonal passes can be issued to mitigate any impact.

User fees and charges, usually designated to support specific fee-related services, should not be diverted to general funds. This is a basic legal principle that state and local governments must follow. In 2010, the Oklahoma State Supreme Court struck down court fees as unconstitutional because the state uses them to pay for non-court-related expenses (Peteritas 2013). NCSL warned a decade ago that if user fees and charges were not separated from the general fund or if the charges exceeded the cost of providing the services, "governments are vulnerable to a court ruling that such charges are taxes" (Hager 2011, p. 4). Taxes are subject to much stricter court scrutiny. Tax increases may be subject to voters' approval or require a supermajority of votes from state legislators.

Furthermore, public tolerance for user charges is limited. In August 2013, Californian voters passed Proposition 26, which required two-thirds of legislators to vote for any new fees to be enacted. Public groups and activists also often challenge the imposition of fees in court.

Another prominent issue with user charges and fees is how to set the right prices. GFOA (No Date) states that "well-designed charges and fees not only reduce the needs for additional revenue source but promote service efficiency" (p. 1). Establishing the system is essential but can be extremely complex. GFOA provides the following guidelines to invite government officials to consider various elements in the design. See Box 11.1.

In setting fees and charges, state and local governments need to choose whether they should gain full cost recovery or partial cost recovery. The full cost recovery approach sounds logical but may not be applicable because it can render the service too expensive. Building a new public transportation system requires

BOX 11.1   GFOA BEST PRACTICES ON ESTABLISHING GOVERNMENT CHARGES AND FEES

1. Consider applicable laws and statutes [regarding charges and fees] before the implementation of specific fees and charges.
2. Adopt formal policies regarding charges and fees. The policy should
   a. Identify the factors (affordability, pricing history, inflation, service delivery alternatives, and available efficiencies) to be taken into account when pricing goods and services.
   b. State whether the jurisdiction intends to recover the full cost of providing goods and services and set forth under what circumstances the jurisdiction might set a charge or fee at more or less than 100 percent of the full cost. [If less than the full is collected, provide the explanations.]
3. Calculate the full cost of providing a service in order to supply a basis for setting the charge or fee. Full costs include direct and indirect costs such as operations, maintenance, overhead, and the charges for using capital facilities.
4. Review and update charges and fees periodically based on factors such as the impact of inflation, other cost increases, adequacy of cost recovery, use of services, and the competitiveness of current rates.
5. Utilize long-term forecasting in ensuring that charges and fees anticipate future costs in providing the services.
6. Provide information on fees and charges to the public.

Source: GFOA (No Date), pp. 2–3.

land acquisition, long-term planning, labor, and construction. Fees based on full cost recovery deter many people from using the services. In many cases, "partial cost recovery is a more appropriate approach, where the fee is set to cover all or most of the ongoing operational costs, or a fixed percentage of costs" (Hager 2011). This is especially true for services that can benefit a broader community, such as public transit. However, this does not undermine the importance of accurately calculating the full cost because the full cost provides the basis for setting the price, as GFOA states. It provides government officials with crucial information to decide whether to approve fees and how many subsidies need to be provided. A full cost calculation also informs the public of the true cost of services. Regardless of which approach is used, governments should ensure the process is transparent to the public, be clear about what is included in the calculation, and identify the rationales behind the calculations.

Government agencies should also conduct regular reviews to ensure prices reflect the costs of services. More frequent reviews are warranted in sudden and dramatic changes in the marketplace. However, in practice, public agencies do not have the discretion to adjust the prices quickly. Existing statutes often limit fee and charge structures. Adjusting fee levels requires public agencies to follow a rule-making process that can be time-consuming (Hager 2011). This further underlines the need for regular reviews to maintain an adequate price and retain service efficiency.

Conclusion

User fees and charges are important for state government finance. Their increasing use is mainly driven by states' fiscal struggle to find additional revenue to provide public services and public aversion to paying more taxes. They are appealing to policy makers as they can generate more revenue but not impose financial burdens on taxpayers. User charges can improve the efficiency and equity of public services and have the potential to serve as a more viable technique to generate needed revenue for transportation. At the same time, user fees and charges are effectively limited to those services wherein beneficiaries are identifiable, which is not an attribute of most public services. Ultimately, these items can serve as a reasonable supplement to states' major tax revenue systems.

State Motor Fuel Taxes

Motor fuel taxes are the best example of a benefit-based tax that links tax payment to the use of public goods. Those who drive will buy fuel, and the fuel tax revenue is used to build and maintain transportation infrastructure (Mikesell 2018). The motor fuel tax also captures the negative externality associated with using petroleum-powered vehicles.

All states and the District of Columbia levy motor fuel taxes. Oregon was the first state to impose a fuel tax, one cent per gallon, in 1919. All other states and Washington D.C. followed suit in the following decade. The federal government started to levy fuel taxes in 1932 (Boesen 2020).

Motor fuel taxes are imposed on gasoline, diesel, and gasohol (a mixture of unleaded gasoline and ethanol). The rate varies from state to state, ranging from 9.0 cents per gallon in Alaska to 77.9 cents in California (as of July 1, 2023). Five other states have rates below 20 cents. They are Arizona (19.0 cents), Hawaii (8.95 cents), Mississippi (18.40 cents), Missouri (17.47 cents), and New Mexico (19.00 cents). The highest rate states after California are Illinois (66.5

cents), Pennsylvania (62.20 cents), Indiana (54.4 cents), and Washington (49.4 cents). These rates combine state excise taxes on gas and any related taxes and fees that the consumer pays at the pump (Hoffer and Dobrinsky-Harris 2023).

Motor fuel tax is one of the major revenue sources for transportation infrastructure. In 2018, it accounted for 27% of highway and road spending. Fees, including tollway fees, account for another 12%. The remaining 61% comes from other sources (i.e., federal funding) (Urban Institute No Date b). Among state infrastructure revenues, motor fuel tax revenue usually accounts for half or more than half of the revenue (Boesen 2020).

For a long time, the fuel tax had a fixed rate. All states except Kentucky imposed fixed cents per gallon. In 2011, 36 states exclusively relied on the fixed rate; in 2024, 23 states still do. Their rates were not indexed to inflation or construction costs. In addition, as vehicles become more fuel efficient and people, especially the younger generations, drive less, the gas tax revenue has stagnated over the decades.

State lawmakers should have updated their gas tax rates along the way, but they seldom do because raising taxes is always politically unpopular. According to Carl Davis (2021), 14 states and Washington, D.C. kept the same rate for over a decade without raising it; 10 states kept the same rate for over two decades, and five states over three decades. At the same time, the building material prices have increased significantly. As a result, the gas tax purchasing power is declining. For instance, the inflation-adjusted gasoline tax value was $45.8 billion in 2007, higher than the value in 2014 ($45.4 billion). A study by the Institute on Taxation and Economic Policy (ITEP) (2011) found that states' failure to update their gas tax rate to the transportation cost growth resulted in a $10 billion loss for states. "After adjusting for transportation cost growth, gas tax rates in 2011 are about 17% lower than they were in the 1990s and about 14% lower than they were in 2000" (ITEP 2011, p. 3). Therefore, the Congressional Budget Office reported that even though nominal spending on infrastructure increased 44% since 2003, "the real spending is down 9%" (NCSL 2024b, p. 1).

Fuel Tax Reforms

There is a consensus that the gas tax is not adequate in the short run and not sustainable over the long run. The gas tax revenue cannot keep up with transportation funding needs. This inadequacy leads to falling bridges and dams and crumbling roads. Take Michigan as an example. Its roads were so poorly maintained that they became a state joke. There were contests to find the worst pothole. "Michigan pothole" was used as the name for an ice cream. The cracks and potholes were so bad on a segment of Interstate 75 in suburban Detroit that the state had to close a 10-mile segment even though it was the state's most heavily trafficked stretch. One study finds that Michigan roads need an annual investment of $2.5 billion (Eggert 2019).

Based on the American Society of Civil Engineers (ASCE) infrastructure assessment, America earned a cumulative GPA of D or D+ for every report card from 1998 to 2017. The bridge category received a grade of C– to C+ and road D– to D+. The cost to improve ranged from $1.3 trillion in 2001to $4.59 trillion in 2017 (ASCE 2021). The deteriorating infrastructure has serious economic consequences. For instance, ASCE (2017) states that failure to address the infrastructure investment gap will lead to

- $3.9 trillion in losses to the U.S. GDP by 2025;
- $7 trillion in lost business sales by 2025; and
- $2.5 million in lost American jobs in 2025.

Facing the big and urgent infrastructure fund need and pressure from business communities, state governments started to reform their fuel tax systems in the years after the Great Recession. Nearly all of them aim to create more sustainable funding sources for the transportation infrastructure. Since 2010, 36 states have raised their fuel tax rates either through legislative action or automatic formulas that regularly adjust them. This includes those who had done nothing about their gas taxes for decades, including Illinois, Alabama, Iowa, Massachusetts, Maryland, Montana, New Hampshire, New Jersey, Oklahoma, S. Carolina, and Tennessee. According to NCSL (2024b), 33 states and DC enacted legislation to increase their gas tax between 2013 and 2024. Based on the NCSL *State Tax Actions Database* (Rafool 2014; NCSL 2016–2020), state fuel tax actions resulted in significant fuel tax revenue increases, particularly in the years after 2014. The fuel tax increases in 2015 ($1,120 million) and 2019 ($2,492 million) were the largest among all tax categories, even more than personal income and sales tax increases. The fuel tax revenue increase in 2017 ($2,762 million) was the second largest one, only after personal income tax.

Although conservative state lawmakers have made a series of efforts to cut income tax in recent years, they have realized and decided it is time to push for tax increases to fix roads. They support business development, which depends on good and efficient transportation. Many Republican-lean groups are advocates for increasing fuel taxes (Eggert 2019). Interestingly, unlike other taxes that are clearly influenced by partisan politics, the fuel tax increase is not. Fuel tax increases happen under both Democratic and Republican or split-party control.

Types of Reforms and the Future of American Highway Funding

These gas tax changes take several forms. In addition to raising the tax rates, what is more noticeable and significant is that 24 states and Washington, D.C. have adopted variable rate structures where gas tax rates automatically change without regular legislative actions (NCSL 2024a). Some states already used this method before the Great Recession. For example, Kentucky and Connecticut linked their gas tax with gas prices in 1980 and 1990. Florida linked their gas tax with the Consumer Price Index. In the past decade, more states came to use this method.

These fuel tax actions take different forms (NCSL 2024b). Appendix I presents which states have adopted which form, the year of the adoption, and the year of the last change.

1. Raise the gas tax rate. For example, in 2021, Missouri raised its per gallon rate of 17 cents per gallon by 2.5 cents every July until it reached 25 cents per gallon. This is straightforward and simple, but it requires legislative action to raise it again in the future, which may add political difficulty.
2. Tie the gas tax rate to the gasoline price. This is done in 11 states and Washington D.C., where the tax rate is partially linked with the price. When the gas price goes up, the rate goes up, thus bringing in more revenue. However, the risk is that the revenue will decline when the price goes down. This is the experience of Kentucky and North Carolina. Lawmakers added a tax rate floor in Kentucky to prevent a dramatic revenue decrease. In North Carolina, lawmakers changed the link to population and inflation growth.
3. Link the gas tax rate to inflation or population. Maryland was the first state to adopt this method. In 2013, it raised its gas tax rate to 27 cents and indexed the tax rates with inflation. A more effective way is to link the rate with the state consumer price index, like in California starting on July 1, 2020. This automatic rate increase will guarantee more gas tax revenue even with less consumption. Nine other states also used this method.
4. Apply the state general sales tax to the gas tax. Two states (Hawaii and Indiana) do this. However, gas tax revenue may decline if the price is down or if the state cuts the sales tax rate.
5. Use other formulas. Some states use other formulas to automatically update the tax rates. Nebraska links its gas tax to appropriation decisions. The Georgia legislature is the first to tie its gas tax to motor vehicle efficiency standards. Minnesota and Colorado link the rate with the highway construction cost index.
6. Use other revenue sources. Many states use toll roads to directly shift the funding burden to consumers. States' tollway charges were $10.5 billion in 2008 and increased to $18.5 billion in 2018, a 76% increase compared with a 10% increase in gas taxes over the same period.
7. Tax vehicle miles traveled (VMT) instead of gasoline tax. VMT is a sound method to fund road repair and construction by linking the use directly with the funding. Oregon, Utah, and an increasing number of states are running pilot programs. The U.S. Department of Transportation is also funding more

programs of the same nature in several other states. This method will also provide more stable gas tax revenue because it may solve the problems caused by fuel-efficient vehicles and the increasing use of electric vehicles. The problem with this method is how to measure VMT (see the discussion on RUC in the section on "User Fee and Use Charges").

Among the various reform efforts, the traditional tax rate increases are only short-term fixes, not long-term solutions. In comparison, a variable rate structure is a more effective method to insure against the inevitable increases in the cost of construction. Different variable rate designs have different long-term implications. Those indexed with inflation or population and even construction costs are closely related to gas consumption. However, the biggest challenge to fuel tax adequacy comes from technological changes resulting in little or no gas consumption. As fuel efficiency continues to improve and more people use electric vehicles, the gas tax base will continue to erode. The revenue loss is estimated to be as much as $87 billion by 2050 (NSCL 2023). To address such a challenge, experts recommend using other options to generate infrastructure revenue. One such option is VMT that taxes actual road usage, not how much gas was consumed. Therefore, it is an effective method to capture the cost of using and maintaining the roads and the externality they cause. Long supported by many economists, VMT should be a more sustainable choice compared with the current gas tax. VMT has certain issues with its implementation, which are discussed in the User Fees and Charge section. Another option to address falling gas tax revenue is to charge users of public EV charging stations based on how much energy they consume to charge the vehicle's batteries.

Some states tried other methods to find revenue for highway construction outside motor fuel taxes. For instance, since 2012, Arkansas has dedicated part of the general sales tax levy (0.5% of the rates) to roads and bridges. Virginia earmarked part of the sales tax increase (from 5% to 5.35%) on all taxed goods for transportation funding. While good for generating more funding for transportation projects, these funding mechanisms reduce the link between the need to use the road and the funds to provide it. The tax cannot measure and affect the externalities that road consumption causes. In addition, state governments, in general, rely heavily on sales tax to support their general fund responsibilities, and they often struggle to have enough revenue. Therefore, this route of reform may not serve the purpose well in the long run (ITEP 2011, Auxier 2014).

Conclusion

The gas tax is a good application of the benefit-received tax principle, as the payment is linked to highway use. This principle should be kept when reforming the gas tax. Until VMT is fully implemented, gas tax reform through variable rate tax will play a major role in applying the benefit-received principle to transportation infrastructure finance, but eventually, VMT and other similar reforms will offer more promise.

Healthcare Provider Taxes

Provider taxes are "the health care-related fee, assessment, or other mandatory payment for which at least 85% of the tax revenue burden falls upon health care providers" (Congressional Research Service 2016, p. 3). These payments blur the line between taxes and fees. When they originated, provider taxes were voluntary donation programs. If not for federal regulation, providers who pay the assessments would benefit from higher reimbursement rates. This section will discuss the conception of provider taxes and federal regulations, states' increasing use of this tax, and its role in state financial stability.

The Concept of Healthcare Provider Tax and Federal Regulations

The conception and use of provider taxes are directly related to Medicaid financing. The Medicaid program is jointly funded through federal and nonfederal shares. State governments can finance their nonfederal share with either the general revenue or any other sources. The federal government will match whatever states decide to spend on the program. This open reimbursement creates an incentive for states to seek out any non-general revenue source that can be used as part of their share of Medicaid expenditures (Blasé 2016).

Provider taxes are an ideal source for such a purpose. They allow states to generate new in-state funds, which will be used to leverage additional federal matching dollars. Then, states can reimburse providers with a higher Medicaid reimbursement rate for patient treatment and services. State governments are borrowing providers' funding to accrue more federal funding and to raise the reimbursement rate for providers. Indeed, provider taxes are unique in that their taxpayers support, lobby, or even initiate these taxes instead of opposing them, as in all other tax cases (Blasé 2016). Aside from supporting Medicaid, state governments can also use provider taxes for other state purposes.

As provider taxes artificially raise state shares for Medicaid, they create contention between federal and state lawmakers. Provider taxes are cited as a factor causing high federal Medicaid costs. This is particularly true when some states aggressively implement these taxes. To restrict usage, Congress passed the Medicaid Voluntary Contribution and Provider-specific Tax Amendment (MVCPSTA) in 1991 to ensure the provider tax is a tax, not a mechanism for drawing federal Medicaid funds. Under federal rules, provider taxes must be broad-based and uniform. "Broad-based" means that the tax must be applied to all healthcare providers in given classes of the healthcare industry,[2] including those who do not provide Medicaid services. Before the enactment of the law, the tax was applied only to Medicaid providers. "Uniform" means the same tax rate or the same tax amount for all covered providers in each class. However, the Secretary of the Department of Health and Human Services can waive these rules if the tax is "generally redistributive" and the amount of tax is not directly correlated to Medicaid payments (Blasé 2016). Many states apply for these waivers. Between 2008 and 2012, 29 states were granted such waivers (CRS 2016).

Federal law prohibits states from pursuing "hold-harmless" arrangements with providers. "Hold-Harmless" refers to a situation where providers will receive at least as much money back from the state (in the form of a higher Medicaid reimbursement) as the tax amount they paid (Congressional Research Service 2016). Three tests are used to determine whether the tax holds providers harmless. The primary test is that states cannot guarantee that providers will receive back the tax. However, the federal government set a "safe harbor" exception allowing states to establish harmless arrangements if tax rates do not exceed a certain threshold (CBO 2022). This threshold has remained at 6% of net patient revenue except for the years 2008–2011, when the threshold was reduced to 5.5%. The second test is that state governments cannot directly or indirectly pay providers "a non-Medicaid payment in an amount that is positively correlated to either the tax amount or the difference between their Medicaid payment and the tax amount" (CRS 2016, p.5). Third, states cannot allocate Medicaid payments to providers based only on the amount of paid taxes (Kaiser Commission on Medicaid and the Uninsured 2011; CRS 2016).

The Center for Medicaid and Medicare Services (CMS) is responsible for determining whether states are complying with federal rules and regulations regarding the provider tax. If a provider tax fails to meet the criteria, states cannot count it as part of their non-federal share.

The Increasing Use of Healthcare Provider Tax

Healthcare provider taxes started in the mid-1980s when states asked providers to pay a tax or donations to help fund their Medicaid program. In some situations, Medicaid providers initiate these arrangements because they know they would be held harmless with higher Medicaid reimbursement rates from states (Congressional Research Service 2016, p. 2). Florida was the first state to adopt a healthcare-related tax in 1984 when the state legislature imposed a 1.5% assessment fee on the annual net operating revenues to be deposited to the Public Medical Assistance Trust Fund (PMATF) (Congressional Research Service 2016). In 1985, West Virginia established the first provider donation program where providers can voluntarily make payments to state or local governments. By 1990, six states had established tax and donation arrangements. The increasing use of provider taxes is related to states' inability to fund their Medicaid programs. For instance, the recession in the early 1990s caused severe revenue shortages and growing Medicaid enrollment in states. To obtain more federal matching grants, 39 states had adopted a provider tax by 1992. Together with donation programs, these taxes were estimated to bring states approximately $8 billion in revenue (Blasé 2016).

After the passage of MVCPSTA, the number of states using provider taxes declined. However, when states faced dire fiscal situations during the Great Recession, provider taxes became attractive for states to direct federal funding to support their Medicaid programs. During this time, the federal government also temporarily increased the Federal Medical Assistance Percentage (FMAP) and provided states with an additional $87 billion for their Medicaid programs (Blasé 2016).

Table 11.3 shows the number of states that used provider taxes from 2004 to 2019. By 2013, all states, except Alaska and Washington, DC, collected at least one type of provider tax. Among the various provider taxes, nursing home taxes were the most widely used (44 states as of 2015). These were adopted earlier than other provider taxes because, historically, nursing homes received about one-third of the revenue generated from Medicaid payments. From 2008

TABLE 11.3 Number of States with Medicaid Provider Taxes, 2004–2019

	Hospital Tax	*Nursing Home Tax*	*Intermediate Care Facility Tax*	*Any Tax*
2004	12	22	16	35
2007	18	30	22	41
2008	20	33	29	44
2009	23	35	28	45
2010	29	37	33	46
2011	34	39	33	47
2012	38	42	36	49
2013	39	44	37	50
2014	40	44	37	50
2015	39	44	37	50
2016	40	44	36	50
2017	42	44	36	50
2018	42	44	36	50
2019	43	45	35	50
Changes during 2007–2019	+25	+15	+13	+9

Source: Kaiser Family Foundation (No Date).

to 2019, the largest increase was with the hospital tax. About 25 more states adopted this tax. The hospital tax was underutilized before the Great Recession, making it an attractive target for state lawmakers during that period. Thirteen more states implemented a tax on intermediate care facilities (ICF) during the same period. ICFs are long-term facilities "designed to provide custodial care for those who are unable to care for themselves because of mental disability or declining health" (Connected Risk Solutions 2018).

States typically implement multiple provider taxes. GAO (2014) revealed that 47 states enacted 159 provider taxes in 2012. According to the Kaiser Family Foundation (2022), 38 states collected three or more provider taxes in 2022. Only four states (i.e., Nevada, North Dakota, South Dakota, and Virginia) imposed one provider tax.

There is no complete data concerning provider tax rates. According to GAO (2014), many tax rates are not expressed as a percentage of net patient service revenue or measurement that CMS employs to establish the safe harbor threshold. Instead, rates are often expressed as a certain dollar amount per bed per day. For a small number of taxes (65 out of 831) that were expressed as a percentage of net patient service revenue, most are within 1% point of the hold-harmless threshold.

Federal safe harbor thresholds restrain provider tax rates. Within that restraint, states tend to raise tax rates when facing tight budgets (Blasé 2016). Table 11.4 shows that the years 2007–2015 witnessed more tax rate increases than decreases. States raised the three major provider tax rates 150 times but cut the rates only 49 times. More than half of the cuts happened in 2008. That was the year when

TABLE 11.4 Number of States That Changed Medicaid Provider Tax Rates: 2007–2014

Increasing Taxes

	2007	2008	2009	2010	2011	2012	2013	2014	Total
Hospital	2	2	6	5	13	18	7	5	58
Nursing Home	2	4	3	7	11	23	8	4	62
ICF	1	2	1	3	3	14	4	2	30
Total	5	8	10	15	27	55	19	11	150

Decreasing Taxes

	2007	2008	2009	2010	2011	2012	2013	2014	Total
Hospital	1	3	3	0	2	1	1	3	14
Nursing Home	0	11	3	0	1	0	2	2	19
ICF	0	14	1	0	0	0	1	0	16
Total	1	28	7	0	3	1	4	5	49

Source: Blasé (2016, p. 18). Permission granted.

TABLE 11.5 States' Provider Tax Changes: 2008–2020

Fiscal Year	# of States Increasing Tax	# of States Decreasing Tax	States' Net Amount (in $ million)	Provider Tax Increase Larger than $100 million
2008	2	4	$237	PA $237
2009	12		$2,535	ID $101; NY $482; PA $528; OH $441; WI $157; AL $200; CO $336; OR $187
2010	12		$1,298	NY $242; GA $229; TN $286; WA $352
2011	15	1	$1,956	IN $475; CT $403; MD $279 OH $245; OK $152; OR $214
2012	6	1	–$394	CA -$436
2013	5		$475	CA 107; GA $242
2014	3	1	$521	MI $502
2015	5	1	$312	CT $244
2016	4	1	$1,349	CA $1,100; LA $244
2017	6	3	$530	OR $144; CT $344
2018	2	1	–$3.8	
2019	5	0	$663	IL $530
2020	5		1472	AL $112; CA $394; NJ $103; NC $115; TN $748

Sources: Author's calculation based on NCSL *State Tax Actions Database*; Waisanen and Haggerty (2010); Rafool and Haggerty (2011); Rafool (2013, 2014, 2015); NSCL (2009, 2012, 2016–2020).

the federal government temporarily lowered the safe harbor threshold from 6% to 5.5%. State governments were forced to adjust their rates to avoid violating federal regulations. Blasé (2016) offered two explanations for the large number of tax rate increases in 2011 and 2012. The safe harbor threshold returned to 6.0%, and states responded to the federal reverse of its FMAP to the original level after earlier rate elevation. With the normal FMAP level, states needed to raise provider taxes to regain federal Medicaid funds (Blasé 2016).

Table 11.5 shows states' increasing use of a provider tax in dollar amounts. It shows the net fiscal impact of state provider tax actions for that fiscal year and the states whose provider tax changes result in more than $100 million for the subsequent year. The overall net changes may be attributed to a tax rate increase, the expansion of the current tax, or the enactment of a new tax.

Table 11.5 shows that almost every year, the number of states that increase provider taxes exceeds the number of states that decrease taxes. From 2008 to 2020, states raised provider taxes every year except 2012 and 2018. The net decrease of $393.9 million resulted from California's massive cut of $436 million in 2012 when the state discontinued its tax on Medi-Cal managed care plans effective July 1, 2012. The California legislature did not intend to cut its provider taxes but had to conform to CMS's ruling that such a tax must apply to all managed care plans, not just those serving Medicaid enrollees (NCSL 2017). In 2016, California passed a new law to establish the same programs again. The net decrease in 2018 was primarily due to Washington's decision to provide tax exemptions for Accountable Community of Health Funds.

Furthermore, provider taxes raise substantial new revenue for state governments. In several years, the additional revenue that provider taxes raised was comparable to those from major tax sources (i.e., personal income and sales tax). During 2009–2011, the provider tax raised $4.8 billion in new revenue for state governments at a time when states faced stringent budgets. Comparatively, the state generated $2.7 billion in new general sales tax revenue during the same time period. In 2011, 15 states raised their provider taxes, resulting in an additional $1.9 billion revenue increase for states to support their increasing Medicaid costs, giving this category the second largest increase that year. Personal income tax increases generated $2.9 billion in revenue, and sales tax changes resulted in a $5.2 billion loss. Some states raised more revenue from sales or personal income tax changes in some years. However, it is interesting that state governments attempted to cut the personal income tax and sales tax for numerous years, but they raise provider taxes almost every year.

GAO (2014) distributed a questionnaire to state Medicaid officials regarding how states used the new Medicaid provider taxes adopted from 2008 to 2012. Results show several uses, including "increasing the Medicaid provider payment rates (34 times), Disproportionate Share Hospital (DSH) payments (13 times), non-DSH supplemental payments (31 times), avoiding Medicaid benefit cuts (27 times), expanding Medicaid benefits (11 times), and to fund part or all of the Affordable Care Act (ACA) Medicaid expansion starting in FY2017" (p. 49). The DSH program funds hospitals that care for the most vulnerable populations.

Why States Are Increasing the Use of Provider Taxes

Studies have been conducted to explain why states adopt provider taxes. State fiscal conditions and healthcare provider associations are repeatedly found to be the best indicators. For instance, Miller and Wang (2009) studied factors leading to 18 states' adopting nursing home taxes during 2000–2004. They found that the best predictors are the lobbying strength of nursing home industries, a greater percentage of nursing home residents receiving services paid by Medicaid or Medicare, and broader Medicaid eligibility. Other indicators included weak state fiscal conditions and nursing home supply restrictions. According to GAO (2020), several state Medicaid officials state that "They implemented provider taxes to maintain or increase Medicaid provider payments when budget constraints limited their states' use of state general revenue funds to finance the nonfederal share" (p. 22). Officials from four healthcare provider associations told GAO that their members support states' use of provider taxes to avoid the possible reduction of Medicaid payments when states face revenue shortages. The discussion above also shows that states increase their reliance on provider taxes during recessions. State Medicaid officials' response to the GAO (2014) questionnaire revealed that the major purpose of their expansion was to finance payments, not expand benefits or services.

Role of Healthcare Provider Tax in State Financial Stability

The exact total healthcare provider tax revenue is unknown, partly due to state underreporting (Blasé 2016). Given what is known, the amount is considerable and has increased over time. In 2015, states were estimated to raise more than $22 billion from provider taxes, doubling the amount in 2008 after being adjusted for inflation (Blasé 2016). Federal Medicaid spending in real dollars increased by 59% during that time period. In 2018, states collected a total of $36.9 billion from provider taxes (Medicaid and CHIP Payment and Access Commission 2021). Indeed, provider taxes have become an integral source of Medicaid financing.

Due to the increase in provider taxes, states reduced their general revenue contributions to support Medicaid expenditure (see Table 11.6). The state general revenue portion was 95% in 1990. It declined to 80.7% in 2008 and continued diminishing to 68.8% in 2018 (see the last column in Table 11.6). At the same time, other sources (mainly provider taxes and local government funds) steadily increased. Local government funds are derived from county nursing homes or state university hospitals. States collect these funds also to leverage federal matching grants just as provider taxes do. Other sources were 21% in

TABLE 11.6 Provider Tax and State General Revenue Funds as a Percentage of Nonfederal Share of Medicaid Payments: 2008 and 2018 ($billion)

Fiscal Year	Provider Taxes	Local Government Funds — Intergovernmental Transfers	Local Government Funds — Certified Public Expenditures	Provider and Local Government Total	State General Fund
2008	7.0% ($10)	9.0% ($13)	6.0% ($8)	21.0% ($31)	80.7%
2012	10.4% ($18.8)	10.1% ($18)	5.4% ($9.7)	26.0% ($47)	76.5%
2018	17.0% ($37)	10.0% ($22)	2.0% ($4)	28.0% ($63)	68.8%

Sources: GAO (2014; 2020); NASBO (2008; 2012; 2018).

2008 and 28% in 2018. This increase is primarily due to the big jump in provider taxes. The figures were $10 billion or 7% of total state shares in 2008, eventually increasing to $37 billion or 17% in 2018.

The extent to which states rely on provider taxes and local government funds varies. In 2008, among the 48 states that responded to GAO's questionnaire, 13 states obtained over 30% of their nonfederal shares from provider taxes and local funds, with Missouri having the highest percentage at 53%, followed by Alabama at 46.3%. On the other end, South Dakota had less than 1%. Between 2008 and 2012, 36 out of the 47 states reported an increase in the percentage of using provider taxes and local funds to finance state shares. Only 11 reported percentage decreases (GAO 2014). Among the former group, Idaho's percentage increased from 1% in 2008 to 19% in 2012.

Even though provider taxes have served an irreplaceable role in state finance, their overall usage is limited, and their future is uncertain. Federal regulations restrict the use of provider taxes. The safe-harbor threshold definitively establishes a cap for tax rates. Although states can expand the tax to other classes of services, they must comply with the same federal rules. Health policy experts, both conservative and liberal, oppose the utilization of provider taxes because they have several issues with the tax. First, as stated earlier, this type of tax artificially raises the state's share of Medicaid spending, resulting in higher federal matching grants. As a result, it is blamed as a factor contributing to significant federal Medicaid spending. At the same time, this funding mechanism "violates the intent of the statutory federal-state Medicaid cost-sharing formula" (Blasé 2016, p. 5) by raising the federal share without any real state Medicaid contribution (Blasé 2016).

Second, the provider tax also reduces the transparency of Medicaid financing since the real state spending level is obscured and, subsequently, total Medicaid spending is elevated, particularly the federal component (Blasé 2016). Third, the use of provider taxes raises concern about fairness. Heavy-user states can leverage more federal spending than those of minimal-user states. Providers that serve many Medicaid enrollees inside state confines will benefit more than non-Medicaid providers. The tax will result in higher Medicaid payment rates and supplemental payments. But non-Medicaid providers who pay provider taxes do not partake in higher Medicaid payment rates. Non-Medicaid providers often lobby to terminate or reduce provider taxes (Blasé 2016). GAO (2020) found that for the increase of the federal share of net Medicaid payment, a greater increase occurred with certain payment types and in some states.

Over the years, there has been bipartisan support at the federal level to reform provider taxes. The reforms focus on reducing the safe-harbor threshold or the maximum rates that provider taxes can levy without violating federal requirements. In 2006, the Bush administration proposed cutting the threshold from 6% to 3%, which was estimated to produce $10 billion in savings over the next 10 years. In his 2013 budget, President Obama proposed to reduce the rate from 6% to 3.5% during FY 2015 and FY 2017, with an estimated federal saving of $22 billion over the subsequent decade. The National Commission on Fiscal Responsibility and Reform, whose mission is to examine how to reduce the federal budget deficit, recommends eliminating the tax to save the federal government $44 billion during 2015–2020 (Blasé 2016; CRS 2016). The CBO (2022) discussed alternative options to change the thresholds. Eliminating the tax would save the federal government $542 billion in outlays over the next 10 years. These proposals are naturally incremental and do not address systemic issues. To address the root causes, the federal government needs to change the funding mechanisms of the Medicaid program. Blasé (2016) stated that fixing Medicaid payments to states would render provider taxes obsolete.

Even for these incremental reforms, strong opposition from industry lobbies, state governors, and beneficiary advocates was successful in blocking reform proposals. The threshold was only reduced during 2008–2011 from 6% to 5.5%. In addition, some federal lawmakers are also concerned that reducing or eliminating provider taxes would force states to provide fewer medical services to low-income families. With less funding, state governments may constrain Medicaid expenditures by reducing reimbursement rates, limiting benefit packages, or restricting eligibility. These program changes may affect the access and quality of Medicaid services. This is a risk the federal lawmakers did not want to assume (CRS 2016). During COVID-19, a lot of people, especially low-income families, could not afford to lose access to healthcare services. Therefore, any major reform is unlikely to occur soon, and the provider tax will remain an integral source for state Medicaid financing.

Conclusion

States have increased their use of provider taxes to fund nonfederal shares for Medicaid programs. Every fiscal year, provider taxes generate billions of dollars in state revenue.

> In almost all states, the policy decisions tied to these taxes affect health policy as well as fiscal policy. In particular, the rate of taxation and the allocation or earmarking of the revenue can have far-reaching impacts on state health programs and overall state budgets.
>
> *(NCSL 2017, p. 1)*

However, provider taxes face several limitations and uncertainties. Safe harbor thresholds limit the degree to which states can raise additional revenue. Various concerns regarding usage exist, and federal policy makers have proposed numerous legislative initiatives to reform or eliminate these taxes. Although no major reform is likely to occur soon and provider taxes will continue to support states' Medicaid programs, the future of provider taxes is overshadowed by underlying uncertainties.

Other Minor Taxes

States also collect several minor taxes, including property taxes, insurance taxes, severance taxes, and estate and gift taxes. These minor taxes generate insignificant tax revenue for states (see Table 11.7), except for the severance tax for several states.

Property tax

This old tax is imposed on "real property" (e.g., land and buildings) or personal property (e.g., motor vehicles, equipment, and inventories). As the tax base does not fluctuate very much, it is a stable revenue source. Economists also favor this tax over income tax and sales tax because they have relatively little impact on the economy as real property is immovable, and they closely adhere to the benefit principle in public finance, where the revenue is used to finance projects benefiting taxpayers (Loughead 2022). Though states used to collect more than half of tax revenue from property tax before the Great Depression, the share has become smaller and smaller after that, with only $20 billion in 2021, or 1% of state general revenue ("How do state and local property taxes work?"). States have shifted to sales tax and income taxes and no longer collect real property tax, and many do not even collect personal property tax, leaving property taxes the major revenue generator for local governments (cities, counties, and school districts).

Insurance Tax

Instead of paying corporate income tax, insurance companies pay insurance taxes. The tax is imposed on premiums on life, property, and casualty insurance,

TABLE 11.7 Minor Tax Collections as a Percentage of Total State Tax Revenue in Selected Years

	2008	2010	2014	2016	2018	2020	2022
Property Tax	1.6%	2.0%	1.6%	2.0%	1.9%	2.0%	1.7%
Insurance Premiums Tax	2.0%	2.2%	2.1%	2.2%	2.2%	2.3%	1.9%
Death and Gift Tax	0.7%	0.6%	0.5%	0.6%	0.5%	0.5%	0.5%
Severance Tax	2.3%	1.6%	2.1%	0.8%	1.2%	1.1%	1.7%

Source: U.S. Census Bureau. "Annual Survey of State Government Tax Collections Datasets."

and all 50 states and DC collect this tax. The tax base is the total amount of direct written premiums an insurance company receives within a state. The rates vary from state to state, with an average of around 2.5%. The seemingly low rate can generate a substantial amount because the tax is on gross premiums rather than profits. It is roughly 2% of the state's total tax revenue (see Table 11.7). Measured in revenue per capita, Delaware collected the most and Nebraska the least.

Severance Taxes

These taxes are imposed on the extraction of natural resources, including oil, natural gas, coal, and nonfuel minerals. Most states have natural resources, but some do not levy or levy only a little tax on them. Overall, severance tax is a small portion of the state revenue stream, generating only 1%–2% of state total tax revenue (see Table 11.7). Yet, they are the major revenue generators for the natural resource-rich states, particularly Alaska, North Dakota, and Wyoming. For instance, in 2022, Alaska had 69% of its tax revenue from severance tax, followed by North Dakota with 53%, and Wyoming with 31%. Several other states (e.g., Montana, New Mexico, Texas, and West Virginia) collected over 10% of revenue from severance taxes.

The severance tax base is the values of oil, coal, natural gas, and nonfuel minerals production (Gordan, Auxier, and Iselin 2016). As the energy prices (or the value of the commodities) fluctuate a great deal, the severance tax is inherently volatile. The drop in the crude oil price in 2016 saw the severance tax share drop to 37.5% in Alaska and 41.7% in North Dakota. Another concern with severance tax is the finite supply of the natural resources. They will be used up someday. It is important for state officials, particularly those who rely heavily on severance taxes, to design programs to address these issues, aiming for long-term stability. The Pew Charitable Trust (2016) studied the use of severance tax and recommended that states establish "sovereign wealth funds to deposit a portion of the revenue in an investment account intended to generate returns that will be used to achieve specific public purposes or a set of goals" (p. 2). Alaska, West Virginia, and five other states have established such long-term savings funds with the intention to "transform this volatile, finite tax stream into more permanent, revenue-generating assets" (p. 3).

Estate Tax, Inheritance Tax, and Gift Tax

Estate taxes are collected on the transfer of property after death. Some states impose an inheritance tax on the heirs of the deceased and an estate tax on the deceased person's estate. Gift taxes are levied on property transfers during life. The purpose is to prevent people from evading inheritance taxes by transferring property before death (Gordon, Auxier, and Iselin 2016).

Before 2001, all 50 states and Washington D.C. had estate taxes because the federal estate tax provided a credit for state taxes. States collect a share of the federal estate tax, which is equal to the federal credits, without raising the tax burden on taxpayers. However, the federal tax reform in 2001 phased out the credit by 2005. As a result, nearly half of the states let the tax disappear. Twenty-one states decoupled from the credits and established their own estate tax. As of June 2021, only 17 states and Washington, DC still levy an estate or inheritance tax. These 17 states are Connecticut, Hawaii, Illinois, Iowa, Kentucky, Maine, Maryland, Massachusetts, Minnesota, Nebraska, New Jersey, New York, Oregon, Pennsylvania, Rhode Island, Vermont, and Washington (McNichol and Waxman 2021).

Opponents of the estate and gift taxes argue that the tax would drive wealthy people out of the states and, therefore, hurt the state economy. There is no solid evidence to support the claim. In addition, this tax affects only a few wealthy people because of the exemption threshold, typically running from $2 million to $5 million per estate. The tax rates range from 1% to 16%. On average, fewer than 3% of estates—the very large ones owned by the wealthiest individuals—pay estate taxes. As so many states have given up estate taxes, they generated $5 billion in 2022 or 0.05% of state tax revenue.

Again, the revenues from these taxes are small. They do not significantly change the fiscal landscape of state finance. Severance taxes are important for resource-rich states, and policy makers need to be aware of their inherent volatility and address them to gain fiscal stability.

Notes

1. This includes user fees and charges and lottery revenue.
2. There are 19 classes of health providers that are permissible by the law, including inpatient hospital services, outpatient hospital services, nursing facilities service, services of intermediate care facilities for individuals with intellectual disabilities, physicians' services, home healthcare services, outpatient prescription drugs, services of Medicaid managed care organization ambulatory surgical centers, dental services, podiatric services, chiropractic services, optometric/optician services, psychological services, therapist services, nursing services, laboratory and X-ray services, emergency ambulance services, and other healthcare items or services for which the same has enacted a licensing or certification fee.

References

American Society of Civil Engineers. 2017. *2017 infrastructure report card.* www.infrastructurereportcard.org/wp-content/uploads/2016/10/2017-Infrastructure-Report-Card.pdf

American Society of Civil Engineers. 2021. *2021 Report card History.* https://infrastructurereportcard.org/making-the-grade/report-card-history/

Auxier, Richard C. 2014. "Reforming State Gas Taxes: How States Are and Are Not Addressing an Eroding Tax Base." *Urban Institute*. www.urban.org/sites/default/files/publication/49811/413286-Reforming-State-Gas-Taxes.PDF (November).

Blasé, Brian C. 2016. "Medicaid Provider Taxes: The Gimmick That Exposes Flaws with Medicaid Financing." *Mercatus Center: George Masson University*. www.mercatus.org/system/files/Blase-Medicaid-Provider-Taxes-v2.pdf

Boardman, Scott and Oregon Department of Transportation. 2023. "Road User Fee Task Force Report to the Oregon Legislative Assembly."

Boesen, Ulrik. 2020. "Who Will Pay for the Roads?" *Tax Foundation*. (August). https://files.taxfoundation.org/20200824160626/TaxFoundation_FF7251.pdf

Congressional Budget Office. 2022. "Limits State Taxes on Health Care Providers." (December 7).

Congressional Research Service. 2016. "Medicaid Provider Taxes." (August). www.everycrsreport.com/files/20160805_RS22843_3182f2d592fac73742c8139104802cac88f05f43.pdf

Connected Risk Solutions. 2018. "What Is an Intermediate Care Facility?" https://connectedrisksolutions.com/what-is-an-intermediate-care-facility/ (January 31).

Davis, Carl. 2021. "Years since Last Gasoline Tax Increase." *Institute on Taxation and Economic Policy*. https://itep.org/how-long-has-it-been-since-your-state-raised-its-gas-tax/ (March).

Eggert, David. 2019. "GOP States Discover a Tax Hike They Have to Like: For Roads." *AP*. https://whyy.org/articles/gop-states-discover-a-tax-hike-they-have-to-like-for-roads/ (April 4).

FasterCapital. 2023. "Usage Based: The Future of User Fees: Embracing Usage Based Pricing Models." (October 12).

Gordon, Tracy., Richard Auxier, and John Iselin. 2016. "Assessing Fiscal Capacities of State: A Representative Revenue System – Representative Expenditure System Approach, Fiscal Year 2012." *Urban Institute*. (March).

Government Financial Officer Association (GFOA). No Date. "Establishing Government Charges and Fees."

Hager, C. J. Eisenbarth. 2011. "User Fees: The Hidden, 'Other' Tax." *Arizona State University Morrison Institute for Public Policy*. (January).

Hoffer, Adam and Jessica Dobrinsky-Harris. 2023. "How High Are Gas Taxes in Your State?" *Tax Foundation*. https://taxfoundation.org/data/all/state/state-gas-tax-rates-2023/ (August 15).

"How Do State and Local Property Taxes Work." *Urban-Brookings Tax Policy Center Briefing Book*. www.taxpolicycenter.org/briefing-book/how-do-state-and-local-property-taxes-work

Institute on Taxation and Economic Policy (ITEP). 2011. Building a Better Gas Tax: How to Fix One of the State Government's Least Sustainable Revenue Sources. https://itep.sfo2.digitaloceanspaces.com/bettergastax/bettergastax.pdf (December).

Kaiser Commission on Medicaid and the Uninsured. 2011. "Medicaid Financing Issues: Provider Taxes." *Kaiser Family Foundation*. (May). https://www.kff.org/medicaid/fact-sheet/medicaid-financing-issues-provider-taxes/

Kaiser Family Foundation. 2022. "How the Pandemic Continues to Shape Medicaid Priorities: Results from an Annual Medicaid Budget Survey for State Fiscal Years 20022 and 2013." (October 25).

Kaiser Family Foundation. No Date. "State Health Facts – States with a Nursing Facility Provider Tax in Place." *KFF*.

Kindy, Kimberly. 2023. "GOP States Raise Fees on Electric Cars as Gas Tax Revenue Falls." *The Washington Post* (October 16).

Loughead, Katherine. 2022. "Unpacking the State and Local Tax Toolkit: Sources of State and Local Tax Collections (FY 2020)." *Taxation Foundation*, No. 797. (August).

McNichol, Elizabeth, and Samantha Waxman. 2021. "State Taxes on Inherited Wealth." *Center on Budget and Policy Priorities*. (June 17).

Medicaid and CHIP Payment and Access Commission. 2021. "Health Care-Related Taxes in Medicaid." *MACPAI*. (May).

Mikesell, John. (2018). *Fiscal Administration*. Boston, MA: Cengage Learning.

Miller, Edward Alan and Lili Wang. 2009. "Maximizing Federal Medicaid Dollars: Nursing Home Provider Tax Adoption, 2000–2024." *Journal of Health Politics, Policy and Law*, 24 (1). (December).

National Association of State Budget Officers. 2008. *State Expenditure Report: Fiscal 2007–2009*.

National Association of State Budget Officers. 2012. *State Expenditure Report Fiscal 2011–2013*.

National Association of State Budget Officers. 2018. *State Expenditure Report: Fiscal 2017–2019*.

National Conference of State Legislature (NCSL). 2009. *State Tax Actions 2008: Special Fiscal Report*. Denver, Colorado: National Conference of State Legislature.

National Conference of State Legislature (NCSL). 2012. *State Tax Actions 2011: Special Fiscal Report*. Denver, Colorado: National Conference of State Legislature.

National Conference of State Legislatures (NCSL). 2016-2019 *State Tax Action Database*.

National Conference of State Legislatures (NCSL). 2023. "NCSL Alternative Transportation User Fees Foundation Partnership." (June 19).

National Conference of State Legislatures (NCSL). 2017. "Healthcare Provider and Industry State Taxes and Fees." www.ncsl.org/research/health/health-provider-and-industry-state-taxes-and-fees.aspx

National Conference of State Legislatures (NCSL). 2022. "Report NCSL Road Usage Charges Summit Report." (October 3).

National Conference of State Legislatures (NCSL). 2024a. "Fuel Tax Legislation." www.ncsl.org/transportation/recent-legislative-actions-likely-to-change-gas-taxes (March 22).

National Conference of State Legislatures (NCSL). 2024b. "Variable Rate Gas Taxes." www.ncsl.org/research/transportation/variable-rate-gas-taxes.aspx (February 9).

North Carolina First Commission. 2020. "Mileage-based User Fees." *Issue Brief: Edition 12*. (June).

Peteritas, Brian. 2013. "The Risks of Relying on User Fees." *Gov*. (March 28).

Pew Charitable Trusts. 2016. "From Volatile Severance Texas to Sustained Revenue: Key Recommendations to Improve State Sovereign Wealth Funds." *The Pew Charitable Trusts*. (October 16).Rafool, Mandy and Todd Haggerty. 2011. *State Tax Actions 2010: Special Fiscal Report*. Denver, Colorado: National Conference of State Legislature.

Rafool, Mandy and Todd Haggerty. 2011. *State Tax Actions 2010: Special Fiscal Report*. Denver, Colorado: National Conference of State Legislature.

Rafool, Mandy. 2013. *State Tax Actions 2012: Special Fiscal Report.* Denver, Colorado: National Conference of State Legislature.

Rafool, Mandy. 2014. *State Tax Actions 2013: Special Fiscal Report* Denver, Colorado: National Conference of State Legislature.

Rafool, Mandy. 2015. *State Tax Actions 2014: Special Fiscal Report.* Denver, Colorado: National Conference of State Legislature.

Schaper, David 2018. "More States Turning to Toll Roads to Raise Cash for Infrastructure." *NPR.org*. (January 18).

United States (U.S.) Census Bureau. Annual Survey of State Government Tax Collections Tables (census.gov).

United States Department of Health and Human Services, Office of Inspector General. (2018). *Although Hospital Tax Programs in Seven States Complied with Hold-Harmless Requirements, the Tax Burden on Hospitals Was Significantly Mitigated.* https://oig.hhs.gov (November).

United States Government Accountability Office (GAO). (2014). *Medicaid Financing: States' Increased Reliance on Funds from Health Care Providers and Local Governments Warrants Improved CMS Data Collection.* https://www.gao.gov/assets/d14627Errata.pdf. (July).

United States Government Accountability Office (GAO). 2020. *Medicaid, CMS Needs More Information on States' Financing and Payment Arrangements to Improve Oversight.* https://www.gao.gov/assets/gao-21-98.pdf (December).

Urban-Brookings Tax Policy Center. No Date. "State and Local Nontax Revenue, Per Capita: 1977-2021."

Urban Institute. No Date a. "Charges." *State and Local Backgrounders*. *Urban Institute.*

Urban Institute. No Date b. *Motor Fuel Taxes.* www.urban.org/policy-centers/cross-center-initiatives/state-and-local-finance-initiative/state-and-local-backgrounders/motor-fuel-taxes

Waisanen, Bert and Todd Haggerty. 2010. *State Tax Actions 2009: Special Fiscal Report.* Denver, Colorado: National Conference of State Legislature.

12
STATE TAX POLICIES DURING THE COVID-19 PANDEMIC

Introduction

With the economic shutdown in early 2020 as a response to the unprecedented Coronavirus pandemic, state budgets were on the brink of collapse. Their tax revenue was falling fast, at a steep and drastic rate, but the costs to cope with the pandemic were rising sharply. Aggregate state tax revenue for the second quarter (April to June) of 2020 was 25% lower than the same quarter of the previous year, representing the steepest single-quarter decline in 25 years (Theal and Fall 2023). Thanks to the quick and substantial federal financial assistance and the rapid economic recovery, states emerged out of the pandemic unexpectedly financially strong. Their revenue collections were record-breaking, and they ran historically high year-end surpluses. How have states handled such favorable fiscal conditions? What tax policies have they adopted? Will these policies contribute to states' long-term fiscal stability? This chapter will examine these questions.

States' Unprecedentedly Strong Fiscal Conditions

States' financial performances were remarkable in FY 2021, FY 2022, and FY 2023. Their revenue collections were record-breaking, and year-end surpluses were historically high. According to NASBO's data, state revenue collections exceeded original estimates in 49 states in FY 2021 and again in FY 2022, and 45 states in FY 2023. Each fiscal year, states ended with large and widespread budget surpluses, well over 20% of total general fund spending. For many states, these surpluses are considered the largest in state history. Table 12.1

DOI: 10.4324/9781003494324-12

shows revenue collection growth at double-digit rates in FY 2021 and FY 2022. Such growth is unprecedented and extraordinarily high compared with the real average annual growth rate of 1.7% during the 1979–2022 period. Some of the revenue collected in 2021 was the 2020 tax revenue that was shifted to FY 2021 due to the postponement of the tax filing deadline to 2021. Even accounting for that, revenue growth in 2021 was robust, and FY 2022 continued to express similar strength (NASBO 2022; 2023).

Table 12.1 also shows that state rainy-day funds grew from $77 billion in 2020 to $164.3 billion in 2022, more than doubling as states deposited part of their surpluses to the funds. Although the total rainy-day fund balance in FY 2023 was slightly lower than that of FY 2022, 35 states saw their funds increased. The total balances (i.e., rainy-day funds and general fund end balances) was 37.3% of state general fund spending in 2022 (NASBO 2023) (see the total balance column in Table 12.1).

State general fund expenditures also grew at a record-setting rate of double digits in 2022 and 2023. Even after adjusting for inflation, growth rates were 8.1% in 2022 and 4.4% in 2023. By comparison, the average annual inflation-adjusted spending growth was 1.7% from 1979 to 2022.

Three factors contributed to the unexpected and unprecedented state revenue growth. The first was the federal government's large and quick response to the pandemic. Several rounds of stimulus checks were distributed to households, and a substantial amount of financial aid was given to businesses. Unemployment compensation checks were expanded, and advanced child tax credit (CTC) payments were sent out. This financial assistance reduced unemployment rates, boosted personal income and sales tax revenues, and helped the national economy turn around quickly and the stock market recover faster than expected. The second factor was the unequal economic impact of the pandemic. The major implications fell on low-income workers who were employed in factories and service industries. High-income professionals could continue to work

TABLE 12.1 State Fiscal Conditions: FY 2020–FY 2023

Fiscal Year	General Fund Spending Nominal Growth (Real Growth)	General Fund Revenue Collection Growth (Real Growth)	Rainy-day Fund in Billion Dollars (as % of General Fund Expenditure)	Total Balance in Billion Dollars (as % of General Fund Expenditures)
2020	4.0% (2.4%)	−0.6% (−2.2%)	77.0 (8.6%)	111.2 (12.4%)
2021	2.5% (−1.4%)	16.6% (12.7%)	121.8 (10.3%)	241.3 (26.4%)
2022	16.8% (8.1%)	16.3% (7.6%)	164.3 (15.4%)	398.8 (37.3%)
2023	12.6% (4.4%)	−0.3% (−8.5%)	154.9 (13.2%)	349.6 (29.0%)

Source: NASBO (2023). *The Fiscal Survey of States: Spring 2023.* P. 45, 57, 68, and 73.

remotely and pay their income taxes. The third factor that contributed to state revenue growth involved consumer behavior changes during the pandemic. The economic shutdown shifted the consumption of services, often untaxed, to taxable tangible personal property. The dramatic increase in online purchases and quick implementation of economic nexus laws after the *Wayfair* decision allowed state governments to collect more in sales tax revenues (Auxier and Weiner 2023).

The federal government also provided $800 billion in direct, pandemic-related grants to state governments during the pandemic. While the CARES Act enacted in March 2020 designated much of its funds for COVID-19-related expenses, states were given significant flexibility in how to spend funds from the American Rescue Plan Act (ARPA) of 2021. States could spend these funds any way they wanted with few restrictions. The large amount of federal funds also reduced the need for states' general fund spending (Mackellar and Jimenez 2022). Although states were forbidden from using relief funds to subsidize tax cuts directly, one of the few restrictions attached to ARPA, many state governments were able to navigate this rule without violating it (Rappeport 2022, p. 1). Overall, the unprecedented level of state revenues and surpluses resulted from the combined effects of enormous federal financial assistance and strong economic growth spurred by federal aid. It is important to point out that these factors are not long-lasting, nor are the strong state financial conditions.

State Tax Policies during the Pandemic—A Wave of Big Tax Relief

Historically, when the economy is doing well and states have budget surpluses, lawmakers provide tax relief to taxpayers. This time was no exception. Several states raised their income taxes (e.g., California, New York, and Minnesota) in 2023[1], but they were overshadowed by the large tax-cut wave across the nation. In the face of record-setting revenue surpluses, the most prominent theme in state capitals was tax relief. Tax relief efforts were widespread, taking place in every state, regardless of which political party was in charge; the theme was recurring, year after year for three years; and the relief was significant, in hundreds of millions or even billions of dollars for each tax relief measure. As many governors claimed, these were the largest tax cuts in states' histories. Both personal and corporate income taxes were the major relief targets, but relief was extended to other taxes such as sales, property, and fuel taxes.

States pursued different approaches to deliver income tax relief (see Table 12.2). More than half of the states reduced income tax rates. At least 13 states provided relief through one-time tax rebates. Some states undertook tax cuts together with tax rebates. Many also provided targeted tax credits such as retirement income exemptions, CTCs, earned income tax credits (EITCs), and other tax breaks, including property tax credits. For many states, lawmakers used a combination of these measures to provide relief to their people.

Cutting Tax Rates

States embraced another round of major tax cuts during 2021–2023 (see Appendix J). The Institute of Taxation and Economic Policy called it "tax cut fever"—with at least 43 states cutting tax rates. The most noticeable cuts fell in the income taxes. At least 13–14 states enacted legislation to cut income taxes each year. Some did it multiple times, often accelerating or building upon the rate reductions adopted in previous years. At least 26 states reduced personal income tax rates, and 14 cut corporate income tax rates. Several states reduced both personal income tax and corporate income tax (see Table 12.2 and Appendix J). In many states, these rate reductions were paired with other structural changes to their income tax base, such as consolidating brackets to create a more neutral structure, eliminating state deductions for federal taxes paid, or conforming to the federal government's generous standard deduction.

States took various approaches to cut income tax rates. Some cut all rates, and at least 22 states reduced or eliminated the top rates (Loughead, Jaros, and Johnson 2023). Many collapsed the number of brackets, and six states transformed their graduated rates into flat rates. The effective dates varied. Some started immediately, others would begin the following year, and some were retroactive. As a result of the cuts, the median top rate declined from 5.4% in 2020 to 5.0% in 2023. The average top rate dropped from 5.36% to 5.24% in 2023 (Walczak 2023).

There were also proposals to eliminate personal income tax. Although not materialized in most states, income tax will be phased out in a few states. New Hampshire will phase out its limited version of income tax (tax on interest and dividends) by 2027. Kentucky will use a revenue trigger to reduce its personal income tax each year when the threshold is met. Theoretically, this will eliminate the state's income tax. Mississippi will continue to phase out its 3% income tax rate. Among the current tax-cut arrangements, observers point to two trends. The first one is the flattening of the tax structure. The second is the increasing use of revenue triggers and phase-in arrangements. These trends were present before the pandemic (see discussion in Chapter 6), but their use is more prevalent with this recent wave of tax cuts.

Using Triggers and Phasing-in Mechanics

As of March 2023, 14 states had adopted provisions "that could lower their personal or corporate income tax through an automatic phase-in or a trigger mechanism" (ITEP 2023, p. 1). At least eight states (i.e., Arizona, Georgia,

258 State Tax Systems

TABLE 12.2 State Tax Relief Measures: FY 2021–FY 2023

	PIT Rate Reduction			CIT Cut	Tax Rebate	Child Tax Credit	EITC	Retirement Income Relief	Property Tax Relief	Others[a]
	2021	2022	2023							
Alabama	X									
Arizona		X			X			X	X	X
Arkansas			X	X				X	X	
California					X		X			
Colorado		X		X	X		X		X	
Connecticut			X			X	X	X		X
Delaware					X					X
Florida										X
Georgia		X			X			X		X
Hawaii					X		X			
Idaho	X	X		X X	X					X
Illinois					X		X			X
Indiana		X	X				X			X
Iowa	X	X		X				X		
Kansas										X
Kentucky		X	X							X
Louisiana	X			X						
Maine					X		X			X
Maryland						X	X	X		
Massachusetts					X					X
Michigan			X							
Minnesota						X	X			
Mississippi		X								
Missouri	X									

Montana	X			X		X		
Nebraska		X					X	X
New Hampshire	X		X	X X				
New Jersey				X X		X	X	
New Mexico					X	X	X	X
New York		X				X		
N. Carolina							X	
N. Dakota			X					X
Ohio	X							
Oklahoma	X		X	X X		X	X	
Oregon								
Pennsylvania				X				X
Rhode Island							X	
S. Carolina		X			X			
Tennessee						X	X	X
Utah		X		X		X	X	X
Vermont					X	X	X	X
Virginia					X	X		
W. Virginia			X					
Wisconsin	X		X		X			

[a] This includes grocery and gasoline tax cuts, among others.

Sources: National Conference of State Legislatures. *State Tax Actions Database* (2021; 2022); Vermeer (2022); Loughead and Walczak (2021); Loughead (2023); Brainerd (2022); Davis (2023); Auxier and Weiner (2023).

Indiana, Kentucky, Louisiana, New Hampshire, N. Carolina, and West Virginia) adopted or used previously adopted triggers in the current round of tax cuts. For instance, in 2023, West Virginia passed a law that reduced all bracket rates and included a trigger for further cuts based on general fund revenue performance. Several states implemented phased-in tax cuts. For example, Mississippi will reduce its flat rates year after year until 2026. South Carolina will decrease its top rate every year from 7% to 6% by 2027. North Carolina will reduce the PIT flat rate from 5.25% to 3.99% by 2026 and phase out the corporate tax altogether by 2028.

Chapter 6 discusses the pros and cons of using tax triggers and phasing in. Proponents see it as a way to hold the government fiscally responsible, but critics point to several pitfalls, including denying future lawmakers real-time decision-making power since the tax-cut decision is made beforehand and based on a trigger.

Flat Tax Revolution

By 2022, 13 states had opted for a flat rate (see Table 12.3). The first state that implemented a flat tax was Massachusetts in 1917. It took over a century for another three states to switch their graduated rates to flat rates. Then, in FY 2022, five more states passed legislation to transform their graduated income tax rates into flat rates, launching what Walczak called "the flat rate revolution"

TABLE 12.3 States with Flat Income Tax

State	PIT Adopted	Flat as of	Constitutional
Arizona	1933	2024	
Colorado	1937	1987	X
Georgia	1929	2024	
Idaho	1931	2023	
Illinois	1969	Always	X
Indiana	1965	Always	
Iowa	1934	2026	
Kentucky	1936	2019	
Massachusetts	1917	Always (reverted to graduate rates in 2023)	X
Michigan	1967	Always	X
Mississippi	1912	2023	
N. Carolina	1912	2023	
Nebraska	1968	Not specified	
Pennsylvania	1971	Always	X
Utah	1971	2007	

Source: Walczak and Loughead (2024, p. 4).

(Walczak and Loughead 2024, p. 1). In addition, lawmakers in Oklahoma and Missouri also discussed the possibility to turn their nearly flat tax structure into a single rate. Four states (i.e., Montana, Ohio, S. Carolina, and North Dakota) consolidated their income tax rates into fewer brackets, making their income tax much flatter. Among all the flat income tax states, five states also enshrined a flat rate into their states' constitutions, making it difficult to change (Walczak and Loughead 2014).

Proponents maintain that the simplicity of the flat rate system makes it easy for taxpayers to figure out their tax liability and easy for governments to project revenue and administer the tax. Furthermore, a flat tax will eliminate the uncertainty associated with graduated rates because the next marginal rate will not affect one's economic decision (e.g., investing, working, and relocating) (Walczak and Loughead 2024). Opponents are concerned about the lack of progressiveness and the certain loss of revenue in flat rates (Byerly-Duke and Davis 2023). Kansas' Governor vetoed the state FY 2023 tax-relief package, which contained a flat income tax rate, insisting the change would favor the rich and cause government revenue to decrease (Lysen and Mesa 2023). Byerly-Duke and Davis (2023) also point out numerous pitfalls for flat income taxes. For instance, when the stock market surges, flat rates will collect investment profits, usually concentrated in top income earners, at the same rate as wages and salaries earned by middle-low-income families. Governments cannot collect that part of revenue at a higher rate, which is important for building states' long-term fiscal capacity (Byerly-Duke and Davis 2023). Also, recall the discussion in Chapter 6 regarding tax progressiveness and state fiscal stability. Chernick, Reimers, and Tennant (2014) found that the higher tax burden for the 80th–95th percentiles in a graduated rate system could provide a cushion for state revenue decline during a recession.

Although the number of flat income tax states increased, graduated rates still dominate, with two-thirds of income tax states using it. Massachusetts, the first state to adopt a flat rate, has converted to a graduate income tax with a higher bracket for those over $1 million after the voters approved it in a ballot measure in November 2022 (Byerly-Duke and Davis 2023).

Tax Rebates and Other Relief Programs

Tax rebates are another means to provide tax relief. The number of states with tax rebates differs from author to author. Brainerd (2022) from the National Conference of State Legislatures (NCSL) identified at least eight states that enacted new one-time income tax rebates in 2022. Auxier and Weiner (2023) reported 18 states. It is common for state governments to refund taxpayers when their revenue exceeds certain limits. Yet, there has been no time in history when so many states rebated their taxpayers as in 2022. Three states authorized rebates in 2021. A few more did that again in 2023. Some states provided tax rebates multiple times or in multiple years, as New Mexico did. Some states also combined rate cuts with tax rebates and increased tax credits. The cost for most rebate programs ranged from several hundred million dollars to over one billion dollars. South Carolina's 2022 tax rebate cost $1 billion; Colorado's $900 million; Maine's $682 million; Idaho's $359 million; Minnesota's nearly $1 billion; Delaware's $230 million (Brainerd 2022); and Georgia's $1.1 billion (Lieb 2022).

Rebate eligibility and the amount differed among states. Some states distributed the rebate to all tax filers with a tax liability (e.g., Georgia, Arkansas, Delaware, Massachusetts, South Carolina, and Virginia). Others were limited to filers with children (e.g., Rhode Island) or filers who could claim CTC or EITC (e.g., Oregon). Many states, including Arkansas, California, Hawaii, Illinois, Maine, and New Mexico, established upper limits for household income. The rebates amounted from $50 per single filer with no child in Illinois to $1,500 for married couples in New Mexico. The distributional effects differed as well (Auxier and Weiner 2023). The states that sent rebates to all tax filers distributed the benefits widely, but low-income households who did not file a tax return would not receive the benefit. For other rebates with some eligibility restrictions, the benefits were concentrated among those needing assistance. For instance, Connecticut's rebate was for those filers with a child on their tax return and who earned less than $100,000 or $200,000 (for a couple). Only 19% of Connecticut households received that rebate. Delaware's eligibility includes all taxpayers who filed a tax return the previous year. Although the rebate sizes were similar for the two states ($220 million for Delaware and $160 million for Connecticut), those who received the benefit in Connecticut received more than those in Delaware (Auxier & Weiner 2023). The eligibility also affected total state revenue costs.

States have also provided relief through tax credit programs. Among the numerous programs, several stand out. One is retirement income relief, where states exempt social security benefits or retirement income. In some states, these benefits target specific groups, such as military retirees in Arizona, Virginia, and North Carolina, as well as teachers in Connecticut. However, in most states, these programs are available to all. These credits tend to benefit high-income individuals and will not be sustainable with our aging population (Davis 2023). The following are a few examples of retirement income relief programs enacted in FY 2022.

- Connecticut's existing law exempts certain groups whose income falls under certain AGI thresholds. The new law accelerates the 100% exemption for certain pension and annuity earnings starting from 2022 instead of 2025.

- Iowa exempts retirement income for people aged 55 and older.
- Maryland modified its retirement income subtraction for public safety employees and has created a new retiree tax credit.
- Nebraska accelerated the phase-out of income tax on social security.
- Utah and Vermont have expanded eligibility for social security benefits by increasing the threshold for the income-based phase-out.

Ten states have either enacted or improved the CTC, and 17 states have established or expanded the EITC (Davis 2023). These two credits can be either refundable or nonrefundable. Nonrefundable credits only offset tax liability, while refundable credits allow taxpayers to receive cash back if their tax liability is less than the credits. State EITC programs are usually set as a share of the federal EITC. In the past few years, some states, such as Connecticut and Maine, increased their matching rates. Maine increased the rate from 12% to 25%. Some states like Hawaii and Virginia have shifted their credits from nonrefundable to refundable, which benefits low-income families more (Auxier and Weiner 2023). States' CTCs can be a flat dollar amount per child or as a percentage of the amount offered under the federal program. In 2022, 12 states had CTC programs. Among them, three (i.e., New Mexico, New Jersey, and Vermont) are newly established and are all refundable credits. The EITC and CTC, particularly the refundable credits, provide more targeted help to low-income and middle-class families than other income levels (Auxier and Weiner 2023).

Several states have also established or expanded property tax relief programs. In 2022, Colorado "reduced property tax assessment rates and taxable valuations for the 2023 and 2024 tax years" (Brainerd 2022, p. 4). The estimated cost was $700 million over the next two years. Connecticut "increased property tax credits from $200 to $300 "per family (Brainerd 2022, p.4). Idaho" expanded the circuit breaker tax exemption"; Illinois "approved a property tax rebate", costing the state $475 million; and Nebraska established "a refundable income tax credit for community college taxes paid. New York created a $2.2 billion property tax rebate credit" (Brainerd 2022, p. 4). Voters in Texas "approved two ballot measures that would reduce property tax revenue by $2.3 billion from 2023 through 2026" (Brainerd 2022, p. 4).

A wide range of other tax incentives were also provided to individuals and businesses. Examples are Kansas establishing "a new $800 million investment incentive program for specific industries," Ohio's $2.1 billion incentive package targeted toward Intel Corporation," (Brainerd 2022, p. 5). Oklahoma's $698 million incentive programs, and new or expanded film tax subsidies in at least several states (Brainerd 2022). At least ten states have created entity-level taxes for S-corporations to fully deduct their state and local income taxes from the federal income tax (Brainerd 2022).

Sales Tax Relief and Fuel Tax Relief

FY 2022 saw at least fourteen states proposing to cut tax rates in the area of sales tax. Only New Mexico passed legislation to lower the gross receipts tax rate from 5.125% to 4.875% over two years (Brainerd 2022). In 2023, South Dakota, which does not have an income tax, temporarily dropped its sales tax rate from 4.5% to 4.2%, effective July 1, 2023, to 2027 (Loughead 2023). Groceries are taxed only in 13 states, and FY 2022 saw several more states reducing or eliminating their grocery taxes, even though this is not an effective way to help low-income families, as discussed earlier. Both Kansas and Virginia will eliminate their grocery tax. Illinois suspended its grocery sales taxes for one year. Tennessee provided a one-month food tax holiday for its residents. Most of the deductions are estimated to cost states millions of dollars in tax revenue (Brainerd, 2022).

In 2023, Florida enacted a series of changes to its sales tax base by "creating permanent sales tax exemptions for many products, including baby products" (Brainerd 2023, p. 2) and authorizing more sales tax holidays. This includes two 14-day "back to school" sales tax holidays, one three-month holiday for recreational items, "a seven-day holiday for skilled worker tools, and a one-year exemption on certain Energy Star appliances and gas ranges/cooktops" (Brainerd 2023, p. 2).

Regarding fuel taxes, at least 20 state legislatures proposed to provide fuel tax relief in 2022 in response to high inflation. Six of these states delivered relief through temporary fuel tax holidays ranging from one month to six months. "Illinois suspended gas tax inflation adjustments" (Brainerd 2022 p. 3). The costs for these reforms ranged from $90 million in Connecticut to $585 million in New York (Brainerd 2022).

Impact on State Fiscal Stability

Several rationales motivated widespread tax relief efforts. First, as indicated, tax relief is expected when states have record-setting budget surpluses. Second, this wave continued the tax-cut movement that had started in the 1970s. Elected officials, particularly Republicans, advocated cutting taxes to please their constituents, especially in an election year and at a time when high inflation reduced people's spending power (Lieb 2022; Rappeport 2022). Third, state lawmakers believed cutting taxes would make their state more competitive and boost economic growth (Fragassi 2023), which is not totally supported by the empirical findings.

Tax Cuts v. Tax Rebates: Different Impacts

Although Republicans and Democrats both pushed for tax relief measures, politics make a difference as to which approaches to select. Republicans preferred the tax cut option, and Democrats tended to use tax rebates. Among the 26 states that cut income taxes, Republicans controlled all those states except New York, where "Democrats accelerated the timetable for a previously approved tax rate reduction" (Lieb 2022, p. 2) for middle- and low-income families. At least 15 states approved one-time rebate programs in 2022, with 10 of them being led by Democratic governors and legislatures and one—Virginia—with split partisan control. The other four (Georgia, Indiana, Idaho, and South Carolina) were led by Republicans, but their rebate programs were on top of tax rate cut measures (Lieb 2022).

Partisan politics affect the choices because different approaches impact state budgets and income distributions differently. The tax cuts would permanently reduce the tax, while the rebate was a one-time deal without any future commitment. To many Republican lawmakers, a tax rebate without a tax cut was not acceptable. For instance, Missouri Governor Mike Parson vetoed a $500 million tax rebate program in 2022 because "he wanted a bigger, longer-lasting tax cut" (Lieb 2022 p. 1). The most aggressive tax cutter in 2022 was Georgia Governor Brian Kemp, who was running one of the most competitive gubernatorial re-election races against Democratic contender, Stacey Abrams. He enacted a permanent income tax cut and a $1.1 billion tax rebate. The tax cut reduced the top rate from 5.75% to 4.99% in 2019 through a trigger and then turned the graduated income tax rate to a flat rate. He also proposed an additional $2 billion in income and property tax rebates and extending the gas tax break (Lieb 2022).

Tax rebates, while usually refunding taxpayers, tended to target low-income households, as discussed earlier. Tax cuts usually benefit high-income families much more than low-income households. For instance, the top rate was reduced in Mississippi, and a flat rate replaced a graduated rate. Although no one pays a higher tax, the benefit distribution is uneven. The higher the household income, the more they benefited from the tax-cut (Auxier and Weiner 2023). In the current round of tax reform, many states cut the top marginal rates, eliminated the top rates, or flattened the structure. Minimal assistance goes to low-income families since their tax liability is low to nonexistent. Refundable income tax credits such as the CTCs and EITCs benefit low-income households.

Impacts on State Long-Term Fiscal Stability

How will these tax relief programs affect states' long-term fiscal stability? States face numerous fiscal challenges in the short and long term. Among other things, they are responsible for funding a series of fundamental and expensive programs such as public education, public safety, healthcare, infrastructure, and preparing for frequent natural disasters. Have the tax policies enacted in the past three years put states in a sound fiscal position to address these challenges?

The proponents of tax cuts are positive about the trends, insisting that the flattening of income tax structures, low rates, phase-in, and triggers make the system simple and stable. More importantly, they believe the changes have made the tax systems more conducive to economic growth and less burdensome to taxpayers. Yet, opponents offer equally sound counterarguments, some of which have been reviewed in the previous section.

While the discussion on tax policy and its impacts is always subjective, there are valid concerns that the current wave of massive tax cuts might not help build state long-term fiscal capacity and stability. First, the enormous budget surplus from the COVID-19 pandemic recovery is temporary and will not last, but these tax cuts are significant and permanent. According to Tharpe (2023, p. 5), the tax cuts will cost states tens of billions of dollars in revenue when fully implemented, and revenue losses cannot be easily reversed. Furthermore, the triggers and phase-in mechanisms automatically commit more tax cuts in the future without giving policy makers opportunities to assess the situation at that time. The state government budget is facing several uncertainties in the upcoming fiscal years. The major federal relief measures will be used up. The expiration of the 2017 federal Tax Cuts and Jobs Act (TCJA) in 2025 will affect state revenue collection as the state tax system is deeply intricated with the federal system (Tharpe 2023). The persistently high inflation rates have pushed up service costs. A possible economic recession can hit the revenue collection directly. The COVID-19 pandemic has shown that something unprecedented and highly costly could happen at any time. Federal assistance is not always guaranteed and is at the mercy of future administrations and Congress. Indeed, how these tax cuts affect state government revenue collection in the short and long term is still unknown and concerning. In this sense, tax rebates are preferable and more fiscally responsible since they will not involve future tax revenue losses.

Second, tax policy history raises concerns about these cuts affecting state fiscal capacity and stability. Similar tax-cut efforts, although on a much smaller scale, were made in the 1990s when state governments used temporary revenue streams to fund permanent tax cuts. When the recession hit, states had to make substantial cuts to a wide range of services and programs. Raising taxes is always difficult, especially in some states, such as Missouri, where voters must approve any major tax increase.

The argument that cutting taxes will improve state economic competitiveness and generate more income and tax revenue is not entirely supported by empirical and academic research conducted by economists (Leachman and Mazerov 2015), which has been reviewed in Chapter 6. Tax policy is one of the numerous factors that influence businesses' and individuals' decisions to relocate.

Tax productivity or revenue adequacy requires a tax system to have a broad base and reasonably low rates. The recent tax relief largely undermines these basic principles. First, these changes have not broadened the tax base. Instead, they continue to narrow it with more exemptions such as retirement income, high deductibles, and tax credits such as CTCs and EITCs. Studies have found that the exemption of retirement income, a stable and ordinary income, is associated with tax revenue volatility. In the area of sales tax, there are more exemptions and more and longer tax holidays. These tax breaks have good intentions, but lawmakers need to decide how much of a tax base a state can afford to surrender and how to replenish it with expansion in other areas. For tax rates, even though no theoretical standard can be used to determine what rate is reasonable, the race to the bottom and temptations to eliminate the rates are concerning. Personal income tax is the most important tax revenue for state governments (41 states and Washington, DC). Cutting it significantly or eliminating it will endanger state fiscal capability because no other tax can easily replace it. The more personal income tax is cut, the more pressure will be placed on the sales tax, the second largest and most productive tax revenue source for state governments. Any tax whose rates are too high tends to experience more distortions. Furthermore, sales tax has a problem with its base. The tendency is always there to exempt more items from the sales tax, and state lawmakers have difficulties extending their sales tax to the consumption of the rapidly increasing digital economy.

Tax policy is always political and involves trade-offs between different values. State lawmakers need to evaluate the impact of their tax policy actions and clearly understand how their actions will affect state fiscal stability and income distribution before pursuing further action in both the short and long terms.

Note

1 In 2023, "Minnesota added a 1 percent tax on high-earners investment income, becoming the first state with a broad-based income tax to tax long-term capital gains income at a higher rate than wages" (Davis 2023, p. 1). This will bring in $1 billion in new revenue. It also strengthened the tax on multinational corporations. Together with other changes, the reform makes Minnesota's tax system equitable (Davis 2023).

References

Auxier, Richard C. and David Weiner. 2023. "Who Benefited from 2022's Many State Tax Cuts and What Is in Store for 2023?" *Tax Policy Center*. (January 19).

Brainerd, Jackson. 2022. "States Pursue Tax Relief in 2022." *National Conference of State Legislature*. (June 28).

Brainerd, Jackson. 2023. "2023 Mid-year State Tax Actions Update." *National Conference of State Legislature*.

Byerly-Duke, Eli and Carl Davis. 2023. "Pitfalls of Flat Income Taxes." *Institute on Taxation and Economic Policy*. (January 17).

Chernick, Howard, Cordelia Reimers, and Jennifer Tennant. 2014. "Tax Structure and Revenue Instability: The Great Recession and the States" *IZA Journal of Labor Policy*, 3 (3).

Davis, Aidan. 2023. "The Highs and Lows of 2023 State Legislative Sessions." *Institute on Taxation and Economic Policy.* The Highs and Lows of 2023 State Legislative Sessions – ITEP.

Fragassi, Selena. 2023. "Tax Cuts: 50% of States Are Pushing for Reductions or Eliminating Texas Altogether." *Yahoo!neews.* (June 20).

Institute of Taxation and Economic Policy (ITEP). 2023. "Which States Have Tax Cut Triggers or Phase-ins?" *Institute on Taxation and Economic Policy.* (March 7).

Leachman, Michael, and Michael Mazerov. 2015. "State Personal Income Tax Cuts: Still a Poor Strategy for Economic Growth." *Center on Budget and Policy Priorities.* (May 14).

Lieb, David A. 2022. "States Tapping Historic Surpluses for Tax Cuts and Rebates." *Associate Press.* (August 31).

Loughead, Katherine and Jared Walczak. 2021. "State Respond to Strong Fiscal Health with Income Tax Reforms." *Tax Foundation: Fiscal Fact No. 774.* (July 2021).

Loughead, Katherine. 2023. "State Tax Reform and Relief Trend Continues in 2023." *Tax Foundation.* (June 8).

Loughead, Katherine, Benjamin Jaros, and Zachary E. Johnson. 2023. "State Tax Changes Taking Effect July 1, 2023." (June 28).

Lysen, Dylan and Blaise Mesa. 2023. "Kansas Governor Vetoes a Huge tax Relief Plan, Saying Its Flat Tax Favors the Rich." *NPR.org.* (April 24).

Mackellar, Erica and Andrea, Jimenez. 2022. "State Fiscal Conditions Are Strong, but Uncertainty Looms." *National Conference of State Legislatures.* (September 19).

National Association of State Budget Officers (NASBO). 2022. *The Fiscal Survey of States: Fall 2022.* Washington, DC: National Association of State Budget Officers.

National Association of State Budget Officers (NASBO). 2023. *The Fiscal Survey of States: Spring 2023.*

National Conference of State Legislatures. *State Tax Actions Database.* FY 2021 and FY 2022.

Rappeport, Alan. 2022. "States Turn to Tax Cuts as Inflation Stays Hot." *New York Times.* (May 10).

Tharpe, Wesley. 2023. "1 in 5 States Slashed Income Tax Rates in 2023, Deepening Already Worrisome Trend." *Center on Budget and Policy Priorities.* (June 20).

Theal, Justin and Alexandre Fall. 2023. "State Tax Revenue Growth Approaches Possible Inflation Point." *The Charitable Trust.* (February 14).

Vermeer, Timothy. 2022. "State Tax Reform and Relief Enacted in 2022." *Tax Foundation.* (July 13).

Walczak, Jared. 2023. "There's Still Room for Responsible State Income Tax Relief in 2023." *Tax Foundation.* (February 1).

Walczak, Jared and Katherine Loughead. 2024. "The State Flat Tax Revolution: Where Things Stand Today." *Tax Foundation.* (February 15)| https://taxfoundation.org/blog/flat-tax-state-income-tax-reform/

13
CONCLUSION
Have State Tax Policies Improved Their Fiscal Stability?

Introduction

State governments are responsible for providing the most direct services to the public. To do so, they need a stable and sustainable tax system. Though revenue stability is not the only goal of state tax policy, it is important to ensure the continuous flow of public services and to promote economic development.

This research examines a series of state tax systems: personal income tax, corporate income tax, general sales tax, tobacco tax, alcohol tax, gambling tax, sports betting tax, marijuana tax, fuel tax, healthcare provider tax, and user fees and charges. The discussion focuses on the issues of taxes and changes that have taken place in the past decades, particularly in the post-Great Recession era. Specific attention is on how the issues and reforms affect the tax base, which is critical for revenue generation and state fiscal stability. This research also analyzes the dynamics behind the tax policy changes through five case studies and state tax policies during the COVID-19 pandemic.

State Tax Policy Reforms and State Fiscal Stability

States vary significantly in their tax structure and tax mix. A few rely on one or two taxes, like Alaska on oil tax, Florida on sales tax, and Oregon on income tax, while the majority covers diverse sources. Each state's unique political, social, and economic context plays a major role in shaping its tax policy and the reforms it pursues. At the same time, they are also affected by some of the same forces: the Great Recession, the COVID-19 pandemic, and the overwhelming unified Republican control in many states. In addition, the interstate competition

DOI: 10.4324/9781003494324-13

within the American federalist system tends to induce states to look at each other and adopt similar policies.

The discussion in the previous chapters support several general statements about state tax policy changes and their impact on state fiscal stability. First, in the post-Great Recession era, state lawmakers have taken many tax actions and made efforts to diversify their tax system and broaden the tax base. This includes the following:

- Many states expanded their tax bases to income and sales taxes in the years immediately after the Great Recession.
- Numerous states increased rates for their major taxes and other taxes in the years immediately after the Great Recession.
- The breakthrough in sales tax is that states have gained the ability to collect taxes from remote sales. States have also made efforts to extend sales tax to some services and started to reach new digital goods and services.
- Many states have expanded gambling options, and many have instituted taxes on sports betting and recreational marijuana consumption.
- States have adopted more user fees and charges.
- Many states have expanded the uses of healthcare providers' taxes.

Second, even though state legislators have taken many tax actions dealing with various taxes, they have not transformed the tax system yet. The Great Recession provided urgency and pressure for state lawmakers to reexamine their tax systems and program structures, and they did make efforts to reform, as highlighted above. However, with the fiscal crisis receding, state lawmakers lost their drive to make fundamental changes. Tax politics remains the same, where the dominant theme is to cut taxes and use taxes as a policy tool to address social and economic issues. Several underlying factors explain this. First, the interest group politics inside the American political system makes any significant changes difficult. Second, the public opposition to taxation makes major tax reform politically risky. It is not likely to pass unless there is a fiscal crisis. In other words, a dire fiscal crisis is a condition for lawmakers to raise taxes and make major reforms. Without it, political and ideological beliefs prevail in tax policies. Third, the overwhelming unified Republican control in many state governments pushes for tax cuts.

Third, income and general sales taxes are the backbones of the state general revenue system, and their performance affects state fiscal stability. While diversifying and broadening all taxes' bases are important, state lawmakers should pay special attention to income and sales tax issues, challenges, and designs. To a large extent, state income and sales taxes still face similar issues and challenges as during the Great Recession. Their performances are still closely related to the economic cycle. Some states have implemented various mechanisms to reduce the volatility of income tax revenue, including setting aside traditionally volatile revenue into rainy-day funds and flattening the tax structures. The results remain to be seen and will be tested in the next recession. For income taxes, elected officials in many states have reduced personal and corporate income tax rates. At the same time, they have not broadened but narrowed the base with more tax expenditure programs. States tend to raise sales tax rates because the tax burden can be exported to nonresidents, making it easier to get support. Another reason is that the eroded tax base needs a higher rate to generate the same amount of revenue. States have made great efforts to extend the sales tax to remote sales, services, and digital goods, but many challenges remain.

Fourth, as discussed in various chapters, the tax bases for all the taxes have shrunk either by the political process or economic and technological changes. The best examples to show the influence of the political process are the tax expenditure programs existing with all taxes, particularly with the major taxes—income and sales taxes. Studies show that many of them are not effective in achieving their policy goals, and state officials made efforts to reform them. Yet, in recent years, state-elected officials, both Democrats and Republicans, tend to provide more tax incentives for promoting economic development and helping certain taxpayers.

It is important to understand the different roles of new technology in affecting different tax bases. New technology usually creates new wealth and adds to the income base. The erosion of the income tax base was primarily due to the political process in which elected officials granted preferential treatment to one group after another. On the other hand, new service- and technology-based economies significantly erode the tax bases for sale tax and fuel tax, and complicate corporate income tax collection. The best illustration is the general sales tax. Established in the industrial era, the sales tax system was designed to apply to tangible goods, not services, online sales, and digital goods. The *Wayfair* decision gave states the green light to collect tax from remote sales. Yet, various issues need to be resolved before sales tax can be applied to the digital economy in a wide manner. The piecemeal changes that most states have taken so far will not solve the problem's root. Instead, fundamental changes are warranted, and government officials should consider undertaking them.

Fifth, though state lawmakers tend to use sin taxes as a budget fixer, sin taxes are small as a percentage of state revenue and unstable. Some bases (e.g., tobacco's) have shrunk, and others are uncertain. Even if states have implemented new sin taxes (e.g., marijuana tax and sports betting), their revenue potential is unpredictable, usually earmarked for specific programs and not for general fund spending.

Sixth, user fees and charges have taken on a more significant role in state government finance, mostly due to their ability to promote efficiency and equity. In the area of highway finance, user fees and charges present a viable alternative to the traditional fuel tax, and more uses are expected. Yet, user charges and fees are usually earmarked for specific programs closely related to the fees, and they cannot contribute much to general fund revenue, just like sin taxes. This also shows the importance of income tax and sales tax in maintaining state fiscal stability.

Lastly, tax cuts are always politically popular. The efforts to cut taxes permanently, as seen during the pandemic years, always drown the efforts to expand the tax base and to restructure the state fiscal system deliberately. This highlights the difficulty of major tax reforms and the importance of communication with the public about the restructuring.

Have States Improved Their Fiscal Stability?

A stable finance system requires a broad and diversified tax base, as discussed in Chapter 1. Have states broadened their tax bases? To a large extent, they have not, as highlighted above. The bases for personal and corporate income taxes, fuel tax, and cigarette tax are eroded. In the area of sales tax, state governments have extended the sales tax to some services, e-commerce, and certain digital goods, but a large part of the new economy is still left out. Sales tax also contains more exemptions and credits.

Revenue diversification requires states to use various tax sources, such as personal income tax, corporate income tax, sales tax, selective taxes, and fees and charges, not relying on any of them. Over the years, many states have instituted new gambling options and new fees and charges, and nearly half of states have established reached recreational marijuana taxes. These efforts have diversified tax revenue, but the revenue they bring in is limited. At the same time, several states made attempts to eliminate personal income tax and corporate income tax. If these efforts succeed, they will significantly reduce the revenue diversity, pushing states to rely too much on sales tax.

Although state governments have made limited progress in diversifying and broadening their tax system, they have improved their fiscal stability in other ways. First, many states have instituted measures to set aside portions of the volatile revenue sources, such as capital gains and dividends, into reserves to be used during economic downturns. Second, states significantly expanded rainy-day funds to mitigate the impact of revenue shortfalls during the recession, which will be discussed shortly.

Have States Improved Their Fiscal Sustainability?

Though no hard data can answer this question, the discussion in various chapters has revealed that states are still facing challenges in meeting their long-term fiscal responsibilities. First, "restricted expenditures"—those already committed by the existing laws and other legal arrangements—discussed in Chapter 2 account for roughly 70% of state expenditures (Gordon, Randall, Steuerle, and Boddupalli 2019). They reduce flexibility for the current budgets and impose fiscal burdens on future ones. Similarly, the discussion of state expenditure trends and the cost drivers in Chapter 2 also shows state program expenditures always rise and will continue to rise. On the revenue side, the three sources to restrain revenue highlighted in Chapter 1 are still very much at work: economic and technological changes, the anti-tax attitude of the public, and constant tax-cutting efforts by elected officials. The last two factors are intertwined with American political culture.

Even though some efforts were made to address the fiscal imbalance in the years immediately after the Great Recession, they were not able to correct the structural imbalance. Data in Table 13.1 show the gap between revenue growth and expenditure growth. Between 2008 and 2019, state total expenditures grew at a higher rate than the tax revenues. This is also true for the entire period of 2008–2022. Though the tax revenue annual growth rate was greater than the expenditure during 2019–2022, that period was an anomaly. Table 13.1 also shows that the "All Others" annual growth rate is higher than any other program. This is not surprising because it contains various restricted spending programs. After that, Medicaid is the leading growing program, followed by elementary and secondary education. When looking at the personal income tax and sales tax, the major sources of states' general fund revenue, their annual growth rates are lower than those for elementary and secondary education, higher education, and corrections, whose spendings mainly come from states' general funds.

This is consistent with findings from other studies, which point to a state fiscal imbalance. For instance, Gordon et al. (2016) found large gaps between state revenue capacity and expenditure need. Even with the large amount of federal grants, "26 states still had a gap between how much they could raise and how much they would need to spend to [replicate national average]" (p. 48). The simulation conducted by GAO (2019) suggests that in the coming 50 years, state and local governments will likely face an increasing difference between expenditures and revenues, with the expenditure growing faster than its revenue.

Rainy-day Fund and State Fiscal Stability

In addition to tax structure (e.g., diversifying and broadening the tax base), maintaining an adequate revenue balance is critical to mitigate tax revenue volatility and maintain fiscal stability, as highlighted in Chapter 1. This is also the consensus among practitioners and those who study state budgeting. As indicated above, the development of rainy-day funds represents a bright spot in

TABLE 13.1 State Expenditure and Tax Revenue: Annual Growth Rates*

Expenditure	FY 2008–FY2019	FY 2019–FY 2022	FY 2008–FY 2022
Total Expenditure	1.715%	5.317%	2.476%
Medicaid	3.81%	4.58%	5.03%
Elementary and Secondary Education	2.86%	0.66%	4.52%
Higher Education	2.16%	1.47%	(0.30%)
Corrections	1.81%	0.25%	(2.22%)
Transportation	1.66%	1.42%	0.20%
Public Assistance	(1.76%)	(1.55%)	(0.84%)
All Others	4.02%	0.02%	8.64%
Tax Revenue			
Total Tax	1.46%	5.83%	2.38%
PIT	1.98%	5.89%	2.80%
CIT	(0.16%)	28.39%	5.53%
General Sales Tax	1.45%	3.88%	1.97%
Selective Sales Tax	1.75%	(0.44%)	1.27%
Licenses	0.14%	(0.25%)	0.05%

Note: All tax revenue and expenditure data are converted into 2019 dollars before calculating the annual growth rate.

Sources: U.S. Census Bureau's "Annual Survey of State Government Tax Collections." NASBO (2009; 2020b; 2023). *State Expenditure Report.*

the state fiscal landscape because state governments have significantly increased their fund reserves in the post-Great Recession period.

Reserve balances include rainy-day funds and general fund reserves. State governments have recently strengthened both areas (see Table 13.2). NASBO (2024) reports that "the median rainy-day fund balance as a percentage of general fund expenditures has grown every year since the aftermath of the Great Recession in fiscal 2011, and states are expecting to continue this streak" (p. 65). In addition, states' general fund ending balances have also seen tremendous growth primarily due to the record revenue collection in recent years (i.e., FY 2021, FY 2022, and FY 2023). The total balance grew from $111.2 billion in FY 2020 to $402.1 billion in FY 2022. Even though in FY 2023, the total balance was expected to decline, it did not. Instead, it had another increase due to the revenue exceeding expectations in most states, ending the fiscal year at $425.9 billion.

The total balance as a percentage of state general fund expenditures increased from 4.8% in 2009 to 37.4% in 2023. The rainy-day fund as a share of state

TABLE 13.2 States' Rainy-day Fund Balance and Total Fund Balance: 2007–2024

Fiscal Year	RDF Balance (in $billion)	RDF Balance (% of Gen Fund Expenditure)	Median RDF Balance (% of Gen Fund Expenditure)	Total Balance	Total Balance (% of Gen Fund Expenditure)
2024	147.7	11.9%	15.0%	297.3	23.2%
2023	174.8	15.4%	12.3%	425.9	37.4%
2022	167.3	15.8%	10.8%	402.1	37.9%
2021	121.8	13.3%	10.3%	241.3	26.4%
2020	77.0	8.6%	8.4%	111.2	12.4%
2019	79.1	9.1%	7.9%	121.6	14.0%
2018	68.1	8.3%	6.5%	98.9	12.0%
2017	55.7	6.9%	5.6%	79.4	9.8%
2016	52.0	6.6%	5.3%	81.8	10.4%
2015	48.2	6.4%	4.9%	82.5	10.9%
2014	48.1	6.6%	4.4%	74.0	10.2%
2013	41.8	6.0%	3.6%	74.4	10.7%
2012	36.9	5.5%	2.4%	55.8	8.4%
2011	29.0	4.5%	1.8%	46.0	7.1%
2010	27.4	4.4%	2.0%	32.1	5.2%
2009	29.4	4.4%	2.6%	31.6	4.8%
2008	33.2	4.8%	4.8%	60.1	8.7%
2007	31.1	4.8%	4.7%	69.2	10.6%

Sources: NASBO (2024, pp. 68, 71).

general fund expenditures grew from 4.4% in 2010 to 15.4% in 2023 (see Table 13.2). The fall in the 2024 total balance was due to the estimated decline of the general fund ending balance as a result of states spending down large unanticipated surpluses, as expected, on one-time investments such as debt payments and transferring the money to other funds (NASBO 2024). These spendings, not making ongoing commitments, are consistent with routine budget practices.

States maintain different levels of reserves, ranging from 0.6% of state expenditure in New Jersey to 69.8% in Wyoming in 2024. "This variation is related to differing rainy-day fund structure, policy decisions, revenue volatility levels, fiscal conditions, and other factors" (White 2023, p. 4). For instance, those states that rely on inherently volatile revenue sources typically have high fund balances. Even with the variation, rainy-day fund balance growth was widespread and significant. As shown in Table 13.3, an increasing number of states have held rainy-day fund balances greater than 10% of general fund spending over the years, and a decreasing number of states have balances below 5% (NASBO 2024).

TABLE 13.3 Number of States with Rainy-Day Fund and Total Balance as a Percentage of State General Fund Expenditure: Selected Years

Percentage	Rainy-Day Fund Balance Number of States					Total Balance Number of States				
	2010	2015	2019	2023	2024	2010	2015	2019	2023	2024
Less Than 1%	22	5	3	1	1	12	2	1	0	0
>1% but < 5%	14	19	12	2	2	14	10	4	0	0
>5% but <10%	8	16	18	13	14	14	16	8	3	4
10% or More	6	7	17	34	31	10	22	37	47	45
N.A.	0	0	0	0	2	0	0	0	0	0

Sources: NASBO (2011; 2016; 2020a; 2024).

What Contributes to the Significant Improvement of Rainy-day Funds?

State rainy-day fund balances and general fund end balances are four times those during the Great Recession. Two major factors contribute to the overall significant improvement. The first one is the robust tax revenue collection during 2021–2022 from quick economic recovery and the federal stimulus grants, as explained in Chapter 12. Many states put part of the huge surpluses into the rainy-day fund. The second factor is that states have made deliberate policy changes to strengthen their reserves. State governments learned the lesson from the Great Recession and understand the critically important role that healthy reserves play in fiscal responsibility and stability.

These policy changes take several forms. Those states (i.e., Kansas, Arkansas, and Montana) that did not have budget stabilization funds have established the funds in the past few years. By 2021, all 50 states and D.C. had maintained at least one rainy-day account for the first time in history. Some states have set up multiple rainy-day funds for different programs. In addition to budget stabilization funds helping the general fund expenditure, some states also have a reserve dedicated to K-12 education funding, higher education, or Medicaid spending (Murphy, Loiaconi, and Bailey 2018). Some states have deliberately changed deposit rules to strengthen the fund balances (NASBO 2020a). In 2019, 20 states had some rules tying their deposits directly with revenue volatility. Here are a few examples. Connecticut, California, and Massachusetts set aside excessively volatile revenue sources (e.g., capital gains and dividends) into rainy-day funds. Virginia deposits the excessive amount of general fund revenue into its rainy-day fund. Texas, Alaska, and Wyoming capture oil and gas revenue above a certain level. Maryland sets aside its non-withholding income tax revenue to its savings when it exceeds the 10-year average (White 2022; Murphy et al. 2018).

States use different formulas based on their economic and fiscal context, but the idea is the same. By tying deposit policy to revenue volatility, "states can put aside extraordinary or unexpected revenue increases, save more in high-growth years," and then use the reserve during economic downturns (Murphy et al. 2018, p. 2). Some states also made other policy changes to the rainy-day funds structure, including increasing the minimum size required and maximum size limit to bolster reserves.

Politics, Information, and Tax Policies

Talking about budgetary reform, Aaron Wildavsky (1961) stated, more than half a century ago, that "a normative theory of budgeting is Utopian in the fullest sense of that word" (p. 44). Government is about politics, and public budgeting reflects what the government chooses to do and for whom. In the same manner, it is not possible to remove politics from tax policies, one of the most important public policies through which elected officials allocate the costs and benefits of public services. Political ideologies heavily influence tax policies. Elected officials often push and adopt tax policies that go along with their beliefs. Taxpayers always demand less tax, no matter how many services they use.

Yet, elected officials have obligations to fulfill their legislative responsibility and are held accountable for the state's long-term financial interest, and many do desire to be good stewards for taxpayers. Fiscal structural imbalance and disruptive government services also cause real issues for the public and elected officials. Therefore, elected officials should strive for sound tax and expenditure policies to achieve fiscal stability.

A sound tax policy is one that is fair, generates adequate revenue, interferes little with the economy, and incurs reasonable collection costs. Not all the goals are consistent, and equity conflicts with others. Yet a broad and diverse base is the key to revenue adequacy, reasonable collection costs, and economic efficiency. Murray et al. (2011) discussed the essential role of broadening and diversifying the tax base in building fiscal stability and long-term fiscal structure for states. Brunori (2005) states:

> Policymakers and political leaders should demand a tax system with stability, where the rules of the game rarely change. Leaders should demand diverse revenue sources to end undue reliance on any one particular tax. They should demand a broad tax base with a minimum of exemptions, deductions, credits, and other loopholes. Broadening the tax base will lower tax rates for everyone.
> *(p. 126)*

Improving Decision-making by Providing Quality Information

In addition to diversifying and broadening the tax base, Brunori (2005) and Murray et al. (2011) discussed the key role that information and information sharing play in making good tax policies. With the rapid economic evolution, it is imperative for states to conduct regular reviews of the performance of taxes. The elected officials, the media, and the public need to know which tax works, which does not, and what should be changed (Brunori 2005). This also applies to the tax incentive programs, which will be discussed shortly. Even if politics heavily drive tax policies, good information will help improve the quality of the decision-making process. Elected officials should not only know this information but also use it in their tax proposals and understand the impact on the tax base and tax collection.

For any major tax and expenditure policy changes, careful studies should be conducted, and the information should be provided to lawmakers and the public. It is important for them to know how each of their actions affects revenue collection and budget in the short run and the long run. The long-term projections can be difficult and unreliable, "but the process of discovery associated with developing such projections can inform the policy debate and keep the electorate informed" (Murray et al. 2011, p. 16). For any real and projected fiscal conditions, quality information should be available to lawmakers, together with policy options and the consequences of different action choices. This will allow lawmakers to engage in candid conversations and make informed decisions.

The budget processes and data should be available to the public and easy for them to understand. Educating the public is important not only because the budget and tax policies affect them but also because taxpayers in many states use ballot measures to enact tax and budget policies. Transparency will allow the public to learn about the issues and policy choices.

Elected officials should also communicate with the public about the need for a major reform of the sales tax, whose base does not align well with the digital economy. It is easier to pursue incremental changes, but that does not address the root of the problem.

Reforming Tax Expenditure Programs

Since one of the major reasons for tax base erosion is the proliferation of tax expenditure programs, particularly with the major taxes, broadening the tax base requires states to reform their tax expenditure programs. First, states should have good information about the cost and benefits of these programs. As discussed above, states should conduct regular and quality reviews of tax incentive programs. States do publish tax expenditure reports, but some do not provide good cost estimates and narratives to explain the rationale. Good reports should be provided on an ongoing basis to allow the public and lawmakers to observe the short-term and long-term consequences (Murray et al. 2011). Also, see the discussion in Chapter 7.

To prevent further erosion of the tax base, particularly CITs, states should cooperate, not compete. Within the American federalist system, competition among states is inevitable and can help promote innovation and efficiency, but "they cannot preclude interstate cooperation" (Brunori 2005, p. 125). When states compete fiercely to offer businesses larger and larger tax incentives, no state wins, and all lose. States must work together to restore their tax base and to address other tax issues associated with CIT and all other taxes. This is particularly true given the increasing mobility of corporations.

Following the Basic Good Budgetary Practices

All of the above actions require substantial self-discipline from elected officials. Though hard to enforce, self-discipline is essential in materializing the efforts. Elected officials should stay informed and carefully consider and deliberate about any tax and expenditure proposals. They should follow basic, good budget practices. First, be cautious about permanent tax cuts. Second, if permanent tax cut is the policy choice, it should be accompanied by permanent changes in expenditures. Third, tax rate cuts should be accompanied by broadening the tax base. Low tax rates can be affordable only with a broad and diverse tax base. Fourth, diversify the tax system and avoid overburdening any specific tax. A tax system with personal income tax, corporate income tax, and sales tax can produce more stable collection and reduce revenue volatility than a system that just relies on sales tax.

Limitations of This Study

States vary in revenue capacity, tax structure, expenditure needs, and other policy choices. The discussion in this book focuses on general practices and trends and may not give adequate attention to the variations. If so, this note serves to remind readers of the enormous variations across states in all fiscal matters, including fiscal stability. This variation results from the American political system, in which states possess significant autonomy in deciding their tax and budgetary policies. Their history, local preferences, geography, economics, and demographics all affect their choices (Gordon, Auxier, and Iselin 2016).

Second, the federal tax system and its reforms influence state tax systems and reforms. Federal intergovernmental grants, accounting for more than one-third of the state total revenue, play a substantial role in state finance. The discussion in this book is brief on these topics.

While the discussion in this book tends to focus on individual categories of taxes, the fiscal stability of a state depends on its entire revenue system—the whole tax package. Even if one revenue is volatile, other stable sources can reduce this volatility. In addition, revenue stability is dynamic, not static. Boyd (2022) introduced a useful and interesting perspective on tax volatility based on tax portfolios. "Differences across states in the volatility of total tax revenue depend on the mix of taxes imposed, the structure of those taxes, and the structure of state economies, all of which vary across states and can change over time" (Boyd 2022).

This book examines state tax systems from a fiscal stability perspective. Again, fiscal stability may not always be the top policy priority for state lawmakers. Still, understanding how tax structures, the issues with each tax, and policy changes contribute to fiscal stability will help state lawmakers build a stable and sustainable fiscal system.

References

Boyd, Don. 2022. "State Tax Revenue Volatility and Its Impact on State Governments." *The Pew Charitable Trusts.* (June 30).

Brunori, David. 2005. *State Tax Policy: A Political Perspective*. 2nd ed. Washington D.C: The Urban Institute Press.

Gordan, Tracy, Megan Randall, Eugene Steuerle, and Aravind Boddupalli. 2019. "Fiscal Democracy in the States: How Much Spending Is on Autopilot?" *Urban Institute.* (July).

Gordon, Tracy, Richard Auxier, and John Iselin. 2016. "Assessing Fiscal Capacities of States: A Representative Revenue System-Representative Expenditure System Approach, Fiscal 2012." *Urban Institute.* (March).

Murphy, Mary, Airlie Loiaconi, Steve Bailey. 2018. "How States Can Balance Saving for a Rainy Fay and Other Priorities: The Case for Rules Tied to Revenue Volatility." *The Pew Charitable Trusts.* (December 4).

Murray, Matthew, Sue Clark-Johnson, Mark Muro, and Jennifer Vey. 2011. "Structurally Unbalanced: Cyclical and Structural Deficits in California and the Intermountain West." *Brookings Mountain West.* (January).

National Association of State Budget Officers (NASBO). 2009. *State Expenditure Report.* (Spring).

National Association of State Budget Officers (NASBO). 2011. *State Fiscal Survey.* NASBO. (Spring).

National Association of State Budget Officers (NASBO). 2016. *State Fiscal Survey.* NASBO. (Spring).

National Association of State Budget Officers (NASBO). 2020a. *State Fiscal Survey.* NASBO. (Spring).

National Association of State Budget Officers (NASBO). 2020b. *State Expenditure Report.*

National Association of State Budget Officers (NASBO). 2023. *State Expenditure Report.*

National Association of State Budget Officers (NASBO). 2024. *State Fiscal Survey.* NASBO. (Spring).

United States Government Accountability Office (GAO). 2019. *State and Local Governments' Fiscal Outlook: 2019 Update*. (December 19).

White, Kathryn. 2022. "State Budget Processes Spotlight: Rainy Day Funds." *National Association of State Budget Officers.* (February 3).

White, Kathryn. 2023. "Rainy Day Funds Reaches Historic Levels, Leaving States More Prepared Than Ever for a Future Downturn." *National Association of State Budget Officers.* (January 25).

Wildavsky, Aaron. 1961. "Political Implications of Budgetary Reform." In Hyde, Albert. 2002. *Government Budgeting: Theory, Process, and Politics*. 3rd ed. Toronto, Canada: Nelson Thomson Learning, pp. 44–51.

Appendices

APPENDIX A

Major Specific Tax Actions in California: 2009–2018

Tax Actions	Fiscal Impact ($million) Next Year
2009	
Personal Income Tax (PIT)	
Raise the personal income tax rate by 0.25%.	$3,658.0
Reduce the dependent credit against the income tax.	$1,440.0
Corporate Income Tax (CIT)	
Create corporate income tax credits.	($363.0)
Sales and Use Tax (SUT)	
Increase the sales tax by 1 cent.	$4,553.0
Increase vehicle license fees by 0.5%.	$1,692.0
2010	
PIT	($14.0)
Conform personal and corporation income tax laws to the federal code.	
CIT	
Continue and modify the suspension of businesses' ability to deduct net operating losses adopted in 2008 for an additional two years.	$1,200.0
Exempt some firms from the corporate tax understatement penalty.	($117.0)
Reverse recent changes to sales apportionment rules.	($31.0)

Appendix A **283**

Tax Actions	Fiscal Impact ($million) Next Year
2011	
PIT	
Allow the temporary income tax rate increase (adopted in 2009) of 0.25% to expire.	($1,343.0)
Allow the temporary reduction of the dependent exemption credit to expire.	($1,371.0)
Revise the state's child and dependent care expenses tax credit to be nonrefundable.	$75.0
SUT	
Allow the temporary sales tax increase (adopted in 2009) to expire.	($4,520.0)
CIT	
Expand the definition of retailer engaged in business to include certain internet retailers, thereby compelling them to collect and remit sales or use taxes on sales of tangible personal property.	$200.0
2012	
PIT	
Proposition 30: Increase PIT on annual earnings over $250,000 for 7 years. An additional rate of 1% is imposed on joint filers with income between $500,000 and $600,000. Furthermore, an additional 2% marginal tax rate on joint filers making between $600,000 and $1 million and a 3% for joint filers making over $1 million.	$4,300.0
CIT	
A ballot measure requires multistate businesses to calculate their California income tax liability using a single sales factor apportionment formula.	$1,000.0
SUT	
Proposition 30: Increase the sales and use tax by 1/4 cent for four years.	$607.0
Healthcare	
Let the temporary 2.35% tax on Medi-Cal managed care plans expire on July 1, 2012.	($436.0)
2013	
CIT	
Eliminate the enterprise zone program as part of a package of reforms. Create new tax expenditure programs and sales tax exemptions.	$170.0
Create two tax credits for new hiring by businesses in certain areas and targeted businesses.	($7.0)
Healthcare	
Change the gross premiums tax on managed care organizations to a sales tax. The rate changed from 2.35% on gross premiums to 3.9375 on sales of plans.	$107.0

Tax Actions	Fiscal Impact ($million) Next Year
2014	
PIT Extend the exclusion of mortgage forgiveness debt relief for an additional year.	($4.0)
CIT Modify current capital investment incentives for local governments and allow corporate tax credits in support of Lockheed Martin's efforts to win the bidding for the advanced strategic aircraft program. This incentive will generally impact property taxes. The legislative analysis indicates a potential net $345 million general fund reduction over 15 years with some potential offsets.	n.a.
Increase the annual film incentive program to $330 million.	n.a.
Implement new tax credits approved in the California Competes package.	($32.0)
Create a new tax credit for certain hires in former enterprise zones or areas with high unemployment and poverty rates.	($14.0)
Exempt qualified manufacturing and research and development equipment from the state sales tax. This is part of a tax package enacted in 2013 that eliminated enterprise zones and authorized new credits.	($491.0)
2015	
PIT Adopt a new EITC equal to 85% of the federal credit.	($380.0)
2016	
PIT Proposition 55: Extend by 12 years, the temporary personal income tax increases enacted in Proposition 30. The extension will not take effect until the tax year 2019.	
CIT Reduce income-related taxes on certain healthcare plans. Specified income excluded from gross income for purposes of corporate income taxation. This is part of the state's Managed Care Organization (MCO) tax package, passed during a special session in early 2016. This reduction is set to expire on June 30, 2019.	($90.0)
SUT Proposition 64: Give exemptions to certain sales of medical marijuana from state sales taxes.	($30.0)
Healthcare Enact a tax on certain Managed Care Organization (MCO) providers. The tax contained various taxing tiers and per enrollee amounts. Set to expire on June 30, 2019.	$1,100.0

Tax Actions	Fiscal Impact ($million) Next Year
Tobacco Proposition 56: Increase the cigarette tax by $2.00 per pack, with an equivalent increase on other tobacco products and electronic cigarettes containing nicotine. The estimated revenue increase was $1.4 billion in FY 2018, and $24 million would come from taxes on electronic cigarettes.	$368.0
2017	
PIT Expand the Earned Income Tax Credit to provide the credit across a broader income range and include self-employment income.	($140.0)
SUT Effective January 1, 2017, let the temporary state sales tax rate established in Proposition 30 of 2012 expire and the sales tax rate fall back to 3.94%. Expand and extend partial sales tax exemption for equipment. Effective January 1, 2018.	($1,600.0) ($22.0)
Motor Fuel Increase the gasoline excise by 12 cents per gallon, the diesel excise tax by 20 cents, and the diesel swap sales tax.	$1850.0
2018	
PIT and CIT Extend the EIT credit. Extend the California Competes Hiring Credit and reduce the credit amount.	($60.0) ($180.0)

Sources: National Conference of State Legislature (NCSL) (2016–2020). *State Tax Actions Database.*

National Conference of State Legislature (NCSL). 2009. *State Tax Actions 2008: Special Fiscal Report.* Denver, Colorado: National Conference of State Legislature.

National Conference of State Legislature (NCSL). 2012. *State Tax Actions 2011: Special Fiscal Report.* Denver, Colorado: National Conference of State Legislature.

Rafool, Mandy and Todd Haggerty. 2011. *State Tax Actions 2010: Special Fiscal Report.* Denver, Colorado: National Conference of State Legislature.

Rafool, Mandy. 2013. *State Tax Actions 2012: Special Fiscal Report.* Denver, Colorado: National Conference of State Legislature.

Rafool, Mandy. 2014. *State Tax Actions 2013: Special Fiscal Report* Denver, Colorado: National Conference of State Legislature.

Rafool, Mandy. 2015. *State Tax Actions 2014: Special Fiscal Report.* Denver, Colorado: National Conference of State Legislature.

Waisanen, Bert and Todd Haggerty. 2010. *State Tax Actions 2009: Special Fiscal Report.* Denver, Colorado: National Conference of State Legislature.

APPENDIX B

Major Specific Tax Actions in New York: 2009–FY 2018

Tax Actions	Fiscal Impact ($million) Next Year
2009	
PIT	
Increase the top rate of the personal income tax.	$3,948.0
Limit itemized deductions for high-income taxpayers.	$140.0
Create a non-LLC partnership filing fee.	$50.0
Four other changes to expand the tax base.	$0.0
CIT	
Reclassify the HMO tax from corporate franchise profits to insurance premiums.	$150.0
Eliminate the credit for the purchase of fuel cells and transportation improvements.	$2.0
Require "captive insurance companies" to combine financial reports with parent company.	$33.0
Reduce Empire Zone benefits.	$90.0
Raise the Metropolitan Transportation Authority payroll tax.	$1,000.0
Change the film tax credit.	$0.0
Increase the low-income housing credit.	($54.0)
SUT	
Six other changes to expand the sales tax base.	$9.0
Expand the definition of "vendor."	$626.0

Tax Actions	Fiscal Impact ($million) Next Year
Healthcare Change the hospital assessment tax; Change the home care assessment; Raise the hospital surcharge; Adjust a covered lives assessment (insurance surcharge).	$496.2
Tobacco Raise the tax on cigars and tobacco products.	$10.0
Alcohol Increase beer and wine rates.	$14.0
2010	
PIT Limit personal income tax deductions for charitable donations for taxpayers who earn more than $10 million a year. Three other changes to expand the PIT base.	$100.0 $66.0
CIT Require taxpayers with more than $2 million in aggregated business tax credits to defer the amounts above $2 million until 2013. Conform bank tax deductions for bad debts to IRC calculations. Make permanent REIT and regulated investment company captive provisions adopted in 2008. Increase the cap for film credits.	$100.0 $15.0 $0.0 $0.0
SUT Eliminate three sales tax exemptions, including clothing purchases of less than $110. Require online travel companies to collect sales tax on hotel rooms.	$370.0 $13.0
Healthcare Tax Increase the assessment of hospitals, home care, healthcare, and nursing homes. Expand the surcharge of 9.63% on hospital services to surgical and radiological services provided in private ambulatory surgery centers, physician's offices, and urgent care settings.	$215.6 $26.6
Tobacco Tax Raise the cigarette tax from $2.75 per pack to $4.35 per pack. Raise the tax on other tobacco products and on moist snuff and expand the definition to include small cigars.	$260.0 $30.0
2011	
PIT Let the temporary income tax surcharge (adopted in 2009) expire on December 31, 2011, as planned. The rate for high-income earners goes from 8.97% to 6.85%.	($1,700.0)

Tax Actions	Fiscal Impact ($million) Next Year
CIT Extend four tax credits with no change in taxpayer liability.	
SUT Authorize a sales tax exemption for clothing items under $55 until March 31, 2012, when the exemption amount goes up to $110.	
Motor Fuel Exempt for a one-year alternative motor fuel from all fuel taxes (also includes sales taxes).	($0.8)
2012	
PIT Restructure personal income tax brackets for tax years 2012 through 2014. Tax rates in most tax brackets were reduced, although rates in the upper brackets increased from the pre-2009 rate but were lower than the previous temporary surcharge.	($1,183.5)
CIT Reduce the corporate income tax rate for manufacturers from 6.5% to 3.25% for three years. Approve a youth jobs credit of $500 per month per employee for one year. Approve two other tax credits. Increase the amount allotted for low-income housing and reinstate the credits for a brewery that produces 60 million or fewer gallons of beer in NY.	($25.0) ($15.0) $0.0
2013	
PIT Authorize and extend four tax credits or exemptions.	$0.0
Extend the limit on charitable income tax deductions for two more years.	$70.0
CIT Approve a corporate tax rate reduction for manufacturers to be phased in over three years. Authorize two new tax credits. One for hiring veterans and one for increasing the minimum wage for teens. Approve new tax-free zones for new or expanded businesses. Extend two other tax credits: film tax credit and youth tax credits. Extend the 17% business tax surcharge for the metropolitan transportation authority.	$0.0 $0.0 $0.0 $0.0 $0.0
Healthcare Extend the 6% gross receipts tax on nursing homes for two years.	$595.0
2014	

Tax Actions	Fiscal Impact ($million) Next Year
PIT	
Approve a property tax freeze in the form of a personal income tax credit for homeowners for two school years. The credit will be implemented as a rebate check based on taxes imposed by local governments.	$400.0
Approve circuit breaker credit for property owners in New York City for 2 years.	$0.0
Adopt a measure that closes the resident trust income tax loophole.	$75.0
CIT	
Eliminate the bank tax and restructure the corporate franchise tax so that both corporations and banks would be taxed under one article of law. Also eliminate the alternative minimum tax calculation and phase out the capital base calculation.	$0.0
Eliminate the net income tax on manufacturers under the corporate franchise tax.	($193.0)
Repeal the agricultural cooperative tax as part of the tax reform measure.	n/a
Approve three new tax credits: for manufacturer's property tax, for hiring developmentally disabled, and for musical and theatrical productions.	n.a
Enhance three tax credits, including alternative fuel tax exemptions.	($4.0)
SUT	
Extend or increase two exemptions for alternative fuel sales tax and for vending machine sales.	($7.0)
Motor Fuel	
Extend the alternative fuels tax exemption.	($2.0)
2015	
PIT and CIT	
Extend two tax credits and increase the cap for urban youth jobs.	$0.0
SUT	
Approve three exemptions: for aviation aircraft on vessels with a purchase price over $230,000 and for vendors and purchasers covered companies within the Dodd-Frank Protection Act.	($10.0)
2016	
PIT	
Adopt legislation that will give middle-class taxpayers a permanent 20% rate reduction over eight years. Reduce the rate from 6.85% to 5.5% and 6%. The annual fiscal impact is $4.2 billion when fully effective.	$0.0
Approve a refundable tax credit to replace the existing STAR property tax exemption for new applicants. The changes will have an overall neutral revenue impact because the savings and spending are accompanied by a reduction in revenue.	($98.0)
Extend for five years the Clean Heating Fuel Tax Credit.	$0.0

Tax Actions	Fiscal Impact ($million) Next Year
CIT Create the farm workforce Retention Credit to allow farm employers to claim a refundable tax credit for each of their employees.	$0.0
Approve an additional amount for two tax credits: low-income housing credits and urban Youth Tax Credit.	$0.0
Extend three tax credits: Hiring a vet, Empire State Commercial Production Tax Credits, and Purchasing or upgrading a for-hire vehicle by disabled individuals.	$0.0
Expand eligibility for Economic Transformation and Revitalization program credit to psych centers.	$0.0
SUT Approve a sales tax exemption for the purchase of fuel cells.	($4.0)
Motor Fuel Extend the alternative fuel tax exemptions.	n. a.
Alcohol Approve an Alcohol Beverage Production credit to extend to wine, cider, and liquor, including a sales tax exemption for alcoholic beverages used for tastings.	($1.0)
2017	
PIT Create a personal income tax credit to replace the STAR program rate reduction.	n/a
Extend the millionaire's tax for two years.	$683.0
Extend the current limitations on itemized deductions for those with income over $1 million.	$0.0
Enhance Child and Dependent Care tax credit.	$0.0
Allow for the full deduction of union dues.	$0.0
CIT Extend three tax credits: film production, alternative fuel electric vehicle recharge property tax credits, and youth works.	n. a.
Create two tax credits: Empire State Apprenticeship and farmer credits for making donations to food pantries.	n. a.
Close two loopholes: in the sales of Co-Ops and in non-resident asset sales.	$20.0

Tax Actions	Fiscal Impact ($million) Next Year
Healthcare	
Extend Healthcare Facility Cach Assessment rate for hospitals and home care providers.	$400.0
Extend the assessment rate for nursing homes to 6.8%.	$600.0
Continuation of hospital reimbursement.	$3,300.0
Extend the collection of the covered lives assessment.	$1,100.0
Extend the current assessment of inpatient revenue in hospitals.	$424.0
2018	
PIT	
Extend three tax credits: Hire-A-Vet; the theater production; and Historic Rehabilitation Credit.	$0.0
Create an optional payroll tax for employees making over $40,000 at a company that has chosen to participate in the tax. The tax rate will be 1.5% in year one, 3% in year two, and 5% in year three and going forward.	n. a.
Decouple the Empire Child Credit from the federal Child Credit.	n. a.
CIT Modify the definition of CFC income to reflect federal changes without addressing GILTI.	Prevent a $2 Billion Revenue Loss

Sources:

National Conference of State Legislature (NCSL) (2016-2020). *State Tax Actions Database.*

National Conference of State Legislature (NCSL). 2009. *State Tax Actions 2008: Special Fiscal Report.* Denver, Colorado: National Conference of State Legislature.

National Conference of State Legislature (NCSL). 2012. *State Tax Actions 2011: Special Fiscal Report.* Denver, Colorado: National Conference of State Legislature.

Rafool, Mandy and Todd Haggerty. 2011. *State Tax Actions 2010: Special Fiscal Report.* Denver, Colorado: National Conference of State Legislature.

Rafool, Mandy. 2013. *State Tax Actions 2012: Special Fiscal Report.* Denver, Colorado: National Conference of State Legislature.

Rafool, Mandy. 2014. *State Tax Actions 2013: Special Fiscal Report* Denver, Colorado: National Conference of State Legislature.

Rafool, Mandy. 2015. *State Tax Actions 2014: Special Fiscal Report.* Denver, Colorado: National Conference of State Legislature.

Waisanen, Bert and Todd Haggerty. 2010. *State Tax Actions 2009: Special Fiscal Report.* Denver, Colorado: National Conference of State Legislature.

APPENDIX C

Major Specific Tax Actions in Connecticut: 2009–FY 2018

Tax Actions	Fiscal Impact ($million) Next Year
2009	
PIT Raise the PIT rate from 5% to 6.5% for high earners.	$594.0
CIT Impose a surcharge of 10% over $100 million or more in annual gross revenue.	$74.1
SUT Reduce the SUT rate from 6% to 5.5%.	($129.0)
Sin Taxes Increase cigarette tax from $2.00 to $3.00 per pack as of 10/1/09.	$99.3
2011	
PIT Increase the number of marginal rates and tax brackets from three (3%, 5%, & 6.5%) to six (3%, 5%, 5.5%, 6%, 6.5%, and 6.7%).	$564.8
Phase in 5% as the lowest rate, starting with taxpayers with AGIs over $100,500 for joint filers.	$159.4
Create a "benefit recapture" mechanism that increases the effective income tax rate of filers at a certain income level.	$110.6
Reduce the maximum property tax credit from $500 to $300 and change the phase-out schedule.	$150.5
Establish an EITC equal to 25% of the federal level.	($91.8)

Tax Actions	Fiscal Impact ($million) Next Year
CIT	
Raise the 10% surcharge to 20% and impose a 20% surcharge for 2012–2013 (renewed two more times).	$23.0
For businesses that created jobs in 2011 and 2012, waive the statutory 70% limit on the amount of credits that can be claimed to reduce tax liability.	($7.9)
SUT	
Raise sales and use tax from 6.0% to 6.25%.	$138.7
Raise the sales tax rate on luxury items to 7.0%.	$3.6
Increase the short-term **car** rental from 6.35% to 8.35%.	$3.8
Expand the tax base with 12 changes.	$169.7
Healthcare Tax	
Establish a quarterly tax on hospital net revenue.	$349.9
Increase the cap on nursing home resident user fees from 5.5% to 6.0%.	$37.9
Establish a new resident day-use fee for intermediate care facilities.	$16.9
Sin Tax	
Increase the alcoholic beverage tax by 20%.	$9.9
Increase cigarette tax from $3.00 to 3.40 per pack.	$44.6
Increase the excise tax on the current inventory of cigarettes for one year.	$3.6
Increase the tax on other tobacco products from 27.5% to 50%.	$3.5
Increase the snuff tax from $0.55 to $1.00 per ounce.	$1.4
Fuel tax	
Increase the base diesel tax by three cents to 29 cents per gallon.	$8.5
2015	
PIT	
Raise the top rate from 6.7% to 6.9% and establish a new top rate of 6.99%.	$151.5
Increase tax credits for teachers' pension income.	($11.8)
Increase tax credits for military pension income from 50% to 100%.	($6.0)
Reduce the property tax credits from $400 to $200.	$52.0
Reduce the state's EITC from 30% to 27.5% of the federal credit for two years.	$11.0
CIT	
Extend the phase out CIT surcharge of 20%. The rate was 10% in 2018 and will be completely phased out in 2019.	$44.4
Restrict the use of net operating losses to 50% of net income (eased in December Special Session).	$156.3
Establish mandatory combined reporting for corporate income (eased during the December Special session).	$14.9
Restrict the use of corporate tax credits from 70% of pre-credit tax liability to 50% (eased in December Special Session).	n/a

Appendix C

Tax Actions	Fiscal Impact ($million) Next Year
SUT Increase the sales tax rate on luxury items from 7% to 7.75%. Apply a 1% sales tax rate on luxury items from 7% to 7.57%. Expand the tax base with 5 changes.	$6.2 $7.8 $161.5
Healthcare Tax Increase the health provider tax rate and update the base. Restrict the use of tax credits against the health provider tax. Extend the health provider tax to ambulatory surgical centers.	$207.0 $2.8 $15.0
Tobacco Increase the cigarette tax from $3.50 per pack to $3.65 per pack in FY 2016 and then $3.90 per pack in FY 2017.	$24.5
2017	
PIT Temporarily limit eligibility for the $200 Property Tax Credit for tax years 2018 and 2019. Reduce the state EIT from 30% to 23% of the federal credit. Expand Social Security income tax exemption. Approve an exemption for pension and annuity income from income tax for certain filers.	$55.3 $35.0 ($7.9) ($8.2)
CIT Allow a phase out of the 20% corporate income tax surcharge on the 7.5% rate. Limit three tax credits.	($22.5) $26.7
Sin Tax Increase the cigarette tax rate from $3.90 to $4.35 per pack and the tax rate on snuff from $1.00 per ounce to $3.00 per ounce.	$35.0
Healthcare Tax Amend the hospital provider tax by creating a formula for calculating the tax rate on inpatient and outpatient hospital services based on the amount of tax revenue specified for the given fiscal year.	$343.9

Sources:
National Conference of State Legislature (NCSL) (2016-2020). *State Tax Actions Database.*
National Conference of State Legislature (NCSL). 2009. *State Tax Actions 2008: Special Fiscal Report.* Denver, Colorado: National Conference of State Legislature.
National Conference of State Legislature (NCSL). 2012. *State Tax Actions 2011: Special Fiscal Report.* Denver, Colorado: National Conference of State Legislature.
Rafool, Mandy and Todd Haggerty. 2011. *State Tax Actions 2010: Special Fiscal Report.* Denver, Colorado: National Conference of State Legislature.
Rafool, Mandy. 2013. *State Tax Actions 2012: Special Fiscal Report.* Denver, Colorado: National Conference of State Legislature.
Rafool, Mandy. 2014. *State Tax Actions 2013: Special Fiscal Report* Denver, Colorado: National Conference of State Legislature.

Rafool, Mandy. 2015. *State Tax Actions 2014: Special Fiscal Report.* Denver, Colorado: National Conference of State Legislature.
Waisanen, Bert and Todd Haggerty. 2010. *State Tax Actions 2009: Special Fiscal Report.* Denver, Colorado: National Conference of State Legislature.

APPENDIX D

Major Specific Tax Actions in Kansas: 2008–2018

Tax Actions	Fiscal Impact ($million) Next Year
2009	
PIT	
Tighten the individual income tax statute of limitations to clarify the three-year limit.	$3.0
CIT	
Suspend the film production income tax credits for two years.	$1.0
Reduce various income tax credits by 10% for two years.	$9.2
Continue the corporation tax phase-out enacted in 2007.	($26.0)
SUT	
Reduce the statute of limitations for sales and use tax refunds from three years to one year.	$13.7
Other Taxes	
Repeal $55.3 million in local property tax relief payments (to help offset the narrowing of the tax base from 2005 legislation).	$55.3
Repeal $13.5 million in general local property tax relief payments.	$13.5
Phase out the estate tax.	($25.0)

Tax Actions	Fiscal Impact ($million) Next Year
2010	
PIT Expand the personal income tax credit for sales taxes paid on food. Expand the EITC from 17% to 18% of the federal credit for three years. **SUT** Increase the sales tax rate by 1% from 5.3% to 6.3%. Rate falls to 5.7% in three years. **Healthcare** Create a new assessment on skilled nursing facilities. Approve a tax amnesty program from September 1, 2010 to October 15, 2010.	($10.9) ($4.1) $339.1 $15.3 $8.0
2011	
PIT Adopt a new state personal income tax deduction provision. **CIT** Adopt new state corporate income tax deduction provisions. Repeal the corporate income tax credit for property taxes paid on business machinery and equipment. **SUT** Repeal various business-related sales tax exemptions.	($1.5) ($4.5) $0.0 $8.9
2012	
PIT Rate reduction: collapse the current three rates (3.5, 6.25, and 6.45) into two brackets (3.0 and 4.9); Exempt certain non-wage business income of "pass-through" entities and raise the standard deduction for head of household and married taxpayers filing jointly; Repeal several income tax credits.	($249.2)
2013	
PIT Change itemized deductions allowed against PIT; Repeal deduction for certain gambling losses; and reduce most other deductions. Reduce the standard deduction level for married taxpayers filing jointly and for single heads of household to $7,500 and $5,500, respectively. Cut the PIT bottom rate from 3.0% to 2.7% and the top rate from 4.9% to 4.8%; the rate will continue to be reduced each year through 2018. **SUT** Partially restore the food sales tax rebates that were repealed in 2012. Reduce the sales tax rates from 6.30 to 6.25. Under current law, the rate was scheduled to fall to 5.7 for an increase of $193.2 million.	$114.6 Unknown ($35.2) ($20.0) ($64.4)

Tax Actions	Fiscal Impact ($million) Next Year
2014	
PIT	
Restore two personal income tax credits (repealed in 2012).	($1.6)
Approve an income tax deduction for the net gain of the sale of any cattle or houses used for draft, breeding, dairy, or sporting purposes.	($2.6)
Expand the rural opportunity zone income tax exemption program.	($0.8)
SUT	
Exempt certain animal production aquaculture businesses for the purchase of materials, machinery, and equipment for the purpose of constructing or remodeling the businesses.	($2.0)
2015	
PIT	
Slow down the scheduled rate cuts and repeal itemized deductions with a few exceptions. Eliminate income tax liability for low-income taxpayers.	$149.8
SUT	
Raise the sales and use tax rate from 6.15% to 6.5%.	$164.2
Cigarette tax	
Increase the cigarette tax rate by $0.25 per pack (from 0.79 to $1.29).	$40.4
Create a new tax on electronic cigarettes at a rate of 0.20 per milliliter.	n/a
2017	
PIT	
Repeal the exemption for non-wage business income, restore the third income tax bracket, and increase the rates of each bracket to 2.9%, 4.9%, and 5.2%, respectively.	$591.0
Expand the tax credit for low-income students' scholarship program.	($9.0)
Postpone the effective date and cut the rate of tax on electronic cigarettes.	($1.6)
Reduce insurance premium taxes due to a change in law providing that a privilege fee on HMOs will no longer be deposited in the State General Fund.	n/a
2018	
PIT	
Authorize personal income tax reform in 2017 that contains a series of phase-ins. Increase several itemized deductions.	$633.0
SUT	
Approve a three-year sales tax exemption for cash rebates granted by a manufacturer to a buyer or lessee of a new motor vehicle.	($3.3)

Sources:

National Conference of State Legislature (NCSL) (2016-2020). *State Tax Actions Database.*

National Conference of State Legislature (NCSL). 2009. *State Tax Actions 2008: Special Fiscal Report.* Denver, Colorado: National Conference of State Legislature.

National Conference of State Legislature (NCSL). 2012. *State Tax Actions 2011: Special Fiscal Report.* Denver, Colorado: National Conference of State Legislature.

Rafool, Mandy and Todd Haggerty. 2011. *State Tax Actions 2010: Special Fiscal Report.* Denver, Colorado: National Conference of State Legislature.

Rafool, Mandy. 2013. *State Tax Actions 2012: Special Fiscal Report.* Denver, Colorado: National Conference of State Legislature.

Rafool, Mandy. 2014. *State Tax Actions 2013: Special Fiscal Report* Denver, Colorado: National Conference of State Legislature.

Rafool, Mandy. 2015. *State Tax Actions 2014: Special Fiscal Report.* Denver, Colorado: National Conference of State Legislature.

Waisanen, Bert and Todd Haggerty. 2010. *State Tax Actions 2009: Special Fiscal Report.* Denver, Colorado: National Conference of State Legislature.

APPENDIX E

Major Specific Tax Actions in Missouri: 2008–2018

Tax Actions	Fiscal Impact ($million) Next Year
2009	
CIT Start to phase out franchise tax. By 2016, the tax rate will be 0. Create a few credits.	($7.0) ($35.0)
2010	
PIT Voters approved a measure prohibiting local governments from instituting an earned income tax.	$0.0
2011	
CIT Phase out the corporate franchise tax for a loss of $87.5 million in FY 2016.	$0.0
2013	
CIT Approve a tax credit package, worth $1.7 million, to Boeing over 23 years to expand its facilities in St. Louis and build its 777X passenger Jet.	$0.0

Tax Actions	Fiscal Impact ($million) Next Year
2014	
PIT (SB 509) When the previous year's net general revenue collected exceeds $150 million in any of the three years prior to that year, 1) cut the rate from 6% to 5.5% by 0.1% increment, starting in 2017; and 2) deduct certain business income by 25% over a period of years starting in 2017 by 5% increments	n. a.
Continue phasing out the corporate franchise tax.	($16.5)
2015	
CIT Implement the final phase down of the corporate franchise tax, and the rate was 0.	($16.5)
2016	
CIT Continue to phase in an income tax reduction of the top bracket to 5.5% from 6% by 0.1% increments annually. Continue phase-in of a 25% deduction of business income by 5% increments annually. Increase personal exemption by $500 for Missouri adjusted gross income less than $20,000.	($72.5)
Enact exemptions for payment from agriculture disaster programs.	($12.0)
Authorize an exemption for income from individuals in active-duty military service.	($3.0)
50% deduction for costs related to business relocation and expanded Brownfield tax credit.	($0.8)
SUT A ballot measure prohibits a new state/local sales & use tax or other similar tax on any service or transaction.	$0.0
Extend for 10 years the 0.1% sales and use tax used for soil and water conservation and for state parks and historic sites.	$90.0
2017	
PIT Lower the tax rate from 6.0% to 5.9%.	($80.0)
Deduct 50% of the net capital gain from the sale or exchange of employer securities of a Missouri corporation to an ESOP.	($10.3)

Tax Actions	Fiscal Impact ($million) Next Year
2018	
PIT	
HB 2540: Reduce the top rate even further from 5.5% gradually to 5.1% if the revenue trigger kicks in. Create an individual income tax deduction for business income and phase it in.	($240.0)
Modify the income tax deduction for federal tax liability paid by indexing the amount that may be deducted from the taxpayer's Missouri AGI.	n/a.
Modify the individual income tax deduction by reducing the maximum from 25% to 20%.	n/a
CIT	
SB 884: Reduce the rate from 6.25% to 4%.	n/a
Adopt a single receipt factor to calculate corporate income.	n/a
Fuel tax	
Phase in a 10-cent fuel tax increase.	

Source:
National Conference of State Legislature (NCSL) (2016-2020). *State Tax Actions Database.*
National Conference of State Legislature (NCSL). 2009. *State Tax Actions 2008: Special Fiscal Report.* Denver, Colorado: National Conference of State Legislature.
National Conference of State Legislature (NCSL). 2012. *State Tax Actions 2011: Special Fiscal Report.* Denver, Colorado: National Conference of State Legislature.
Rafool, Mandy and Todd Haggerty. 2011. *State Tax Actions 2010: Special Fiscal Report.* Denver, Colorado: National Conference of State Legislature.
Rafool, Mandy. 2013. *State Tax Actions 2012: Special Fiscal Report.* Denver, Colorado: National Conference of State Legislature.
Rafool, Mandy. 2014. *State Tax Actions 2013: Special Fiscal Report* Denver, Colorado: National Conference of State Legislature.
Rafool, Mandy. 2015. *State Tax Actions 2014: Special Fiscal Report.* Denver, Colorado: National Conference of State Legislature.
Waisanen, Bert and Todd Haggerty. 2010. *State Tax Actions 2009: Special Fiscal Report.* Denver, Colorado: National Conference of State Legislature.

APPENDIX F

State Personal Income Tax Rate Changes: 2008–2020

States	Tax Rate Increase Or Tax Rate Cuts	Rate Increase Effective Years	Rate Cut Phasing in Period
Arkansas	*2013: Cut the rates and reduce the number of brackets over multiple years.* *2015: Middle class tax relief: Lower rates (7% to 6% and 6% to 5%), Increase the capital gains exemption, and adjust rates for inflation.*		*A few years*
California	2009: Increase 0.25% to all brackets. 2012: Prop. 30 Add three new brackets (10.3%, 11.3%, and 12.3%) on income above $1 million for 7 years.	2009–2011 2012–2019	
Connecticut	2011: Raise the top marginal rate Phase out the lowest brackets.		
Delaware	2009: Increase the personal income tax rate by 1% on incomes over $60,000.	2009–2011	
Georgia	*2018: Double the standard deduction/cut the top rate from 6% to 5.5%.*		
Hawaii	2009: Add new brackets of 9%, 10%, and 11% for top earners. These brackets were reauthorized in 2018.	2009–2015 2018–2023	
Idaho	*2018: Lower all rates.*		

States	Tax Rate Increase Or Tax Rate Cuts	Rate Increase Effective Years	Rate Cut Phasing in Period
Illinois	2011: Increase flat rate from 3% to 5%. 2017: Increase the flat rate from 3.75% to 4.95%.	2011–2014 2017	
Indiana	*Cut the rate from 3.4% to 3.23%.*		2014–2017
Iowa	*2018: Cut top rate from 8.98% to 8.53%. A new tax system is effective if two triggers are met; the earliest possible year is 2023.*		
Kansas	*2012: Collapse 3-bracket structure of 3.5%, 6.25%, and 6.45% into 2-bracket structures of 3.0% and 4.9%, exempt certain non-wage businesses income, and increase the standard deduction. 2015: Slow down rate reduction. 2017: Reverse the cut. 2018: Repeal the exemption for non-wage business income.*		
Kentucky	*2018: Collapse the current brackets (2% and 6%) into a flat rate of 5%.*		
Louisiana	*The rate was cut to the 2001 level in 2008.*		
Maine	2009: Reinstate 8.5% for those with income of $19,950 or more for single filers. *2011: Replace current rates of 2%, 4%, 5%, and 7% with new rates of 0 and 6.5%, reducing the top rate from 8.5% to 7.95%. 2019: Reduce the rate from 7.95% in 2015 to 7.15%.*	2010–2011	
Maryland	2008: Add 4 new income tax brackets, including a top rate of 6.25% for income over $1 million. 2012: Enact the top rate of 5.75% on income above $250,000.	2008–2011 2012–present	
Massachusetts	*Trigger met/incremental rate reduction in 2015*		
Michigan	*The rate was cut from 4.35% to 4.25%, raising personal exemptions.*		
Minnesota	Millionaire tax: Add a new top bracket of 9.85%. *2019: Cut 2nd-tier tax rate from 7.05% to 6.8%. Modify the starting point of the 4th tier.*	2013–present	
Mississippi	*2016: Phase out rate on the 1st $5,000 of taxable income from 3% to 0% over a 5-year period.*		5 years

States	Tax Rate Increase Or Tax Rate Cuts	Rate Increase Effective Years	Rate Cut Phasing in Period
Missouri	2014: Approve a personal income tax reduction package that cuts the top rates from 6.0% to 5.5%, beginning in 2017 if a trigger is met.		A few years
Nebraska	2012: Reduce the rates across all brackets.		
New Jersey	2009: Enact a millionaire tax. 2018: Add a new permanent top rate of 10.75% on incomes above $5 million. 2020: Apply 10.75% on income above $1 million.	2009–2010 2018	
New Mexico	2019: Add a new top income bracket of 5.9% starting at $210K for single, $315K for married filing jointly, effective in FY 21. 2008: Continue multi-year cuts.	2021–present	Several Years
New York	2009: Raise the top rate to 8.97%. 2012: Replaced with a new top rate of 8.82%. 2012: Cut most rates.	2009–2011 2012–present	
N. Carolina	2008: Add 3% surtax. 2013: Approve a tax reform measure to broaden the base and lower the rate. The rate was changed to a flat rate of 5.8% in 2014 and 5.75% in 2015 and thereafter. 2017: Cut rate from 5.499% to 5.25% from 2019.	2008–2011	2014–2015 2019 -
N. Dakota	2011: Cut the highest rate from 4.8% to 3.99%. 2015: Reduce rate by 10%.		
Ohio	2008: Continue the cut adopted in 2005 (21% rate reduction spread over five years, TY 2005 through TY 2009). The nine bracket rates previously ranged from 0.618% to 6.24% and were changed to 0.587%–5.987%. 2009: Delay the cut. 2010: Resume the phasing in of rate deduction. 2013: Approve a PIT rate reduction of 8.5% for 2013, 9% in 2014 and 10% for 2015. 2017: Eliminate the bottom two tax brackets. 2019: Modify PIT brackets and lower the top rate from 4.997% to 4.79%.		2005–2009 2014–2015 2019–
Oklahoma	2013: Cut top rate from 5.25% to 5% in 2015 and then to 4.85% in 2016, contingent upon a certain revenue trigger.		2015–2016

Appendix F

States	Tax Rate Increase Or Tax Rate Cuts	Rate Increase Effective Years	Rate Cut Phasing in Period
Oregon	2009: Measure 66: Create new brackets of 10.8% and 11%. 2012: Merge the two rates into a single new top rate of 9.9% on incomes above $125,000 for single/$250,000 for joint filing. 2012: Reduce the top rate from 10.8% to 9.9%.	2009–2011 2012–present	
S. Carolina	2012: Phase down the income tax rate on active trade or business income over three years, from 5% to 3% over 3 years.		2012–2014
Tennessee	2016: Eliminate PIT over 6 years by 2022.		6 years
Wisconsin	2009: Raise the top rate from 6.76% to 7.75% and then *reduce it to 7.65% in 2013.* *2013: Merge 3rd and 4th brackets; Reduce rates for all brackets.* *2014: Lower the bottom marginal rate from 4.4% to 4.0%.*	2009–2013	

Sources:

National Conference of State Legislature (NCSL) (2016-2020). *State Tax Actions Database.*

National Conference of State Legislature (NCSL). 2009. *State Tax Actions 2008: Special Fiscal Report.* Denver, Colorado: National Conference of State Legislature.

National Conference of State Legislature (NCSL). 2012. *State Tax Actions 2011: Special Fiscal Report.* Denver, Colorado: National Conference of State Legislature.

Rafool, Mandy and Todd Haggerty. 2011. *State Tax Actions 2010: Special Fiscal Report.* Denver, Colorado: National Conference of State Legislature.

Rafool, Mandy. 2013. *State Tax Actions 2012: Special Fiscal Report.* Denver, Colorado: National Conference of State Legislature.

Rafool, Mandy. 2014. *State Tax Actions 2013: Special Fiscal Report.* Denver, Colorado: National Conference of State Legislature.

Rafool, Mandy. 2015. *State Tax Actions 2014: Special Fiscal Report.* Denver, Colorado: National Conference of State Legislature.

Waisanen, Bert and Todd Haggerty. 2010. *State Tax Actions 2009: Special Fiscal Report.* Denver, Colorado: National Conference of State Legislature.

APPENDIX G

State Marijuana Tax System as of 2021

States	Excise Tax		General Sales Tax	Local Excise/ General Sales Tax
Legalization Date (Sales Start Date)	Wholesales Excise Tax	Retail Excise Tax (% of Price)	General Sales Tax	Local Excise/ General Sales Tax
Alaska Nov 2014 (Oct 2016)	$50/oz: Mature bud/flower $25/oz: Immature bud/flower $15/oz Trim $1.29/oz: Clones		n/a	Excise: 0%–5% General Sales: 0%–7.5%
Arizona Nov 2020 (2021)		16%	5.6%	General Sales: Can apply.
California Nov 2016 (Jan 2018)	$9.65/oz: Flower $2.75/oz: Leaves $1.29/oz: Fresh cannabis plant	15%	7.25%	Excise: 0%–20% General Sales: 0%–2.5%

States	Excise Tax		General Sales Tax	Local Excise/ General Sales Tax
Colorado Nov 2012 (July 2014)	15%	15%	2.9%	General Sales:0%–7.5% a retail and/ or cultivator tax.
D. C.				
Illinois 2019 (2020)	7% of gross receipts.	10% of purchase price— Flower or products with THC at or below 35%; 20%— cannabis-infused products (i.e., edibles); 25%—any product with a THC level above 35%.	6.25%	General Sales: Can apply.
Maine Nov 2016 (Oct 2020)	$335/ lb: Flower or mature plant $94/lb: Trim $1.50/ lb: Immature plant or seedling $0.35/lb: Seed	10%	5.5% Sales Tax; 8% prepared food tax on edibles.	
Massachusetts Nov 2016 (Nov 2018)	n/a	10.75%	6.25%	Excise: 0%–3%
Michigan Nov 2018 (Dec 2019)	n/a	10%	6%	
Montana Jan 2021		20%	n/a	

States	Excise Tax		General Sales Tax	Local Excise/ General Sales Tax
Nevada Nov 2016 (July 2017)	15%	10%	6.85%	General Sales: 0%–1.25%
New Jersey Nov 2020		Up to $10/oz, if the average retail price ≥$359/oz; Up to $30/oz, if the average retail price is $350–$250; Up to $40/oz, if the average retail price is $250–$200; Up to $60/oz, if the average retail price < $200.	6.625%	General Sales: 0%–2%
New Mexico June 2021		12% till July 2025. The rate will rise by 1% point each subsequent year until the rates reach 18% in 2030.	5.125 to 8.6875% of state gross receipts tax.	Subject to local gross receipts tax.

States	Excise Tax		General Sales Tax	Local Excise/ General Sales Tax
New York April 2021	0.5 Cent/mg of THC for flower 0.8 cent/mg THC for concentrates 3 cents/mg of THC for edible.	9%	8.5% for both state and local.	Excise: 4%
Oregon Nov 2014 (Oct 2015)	n/a	17%	n/a	Excise tax: 0%–3%
Vermont Jan 2018		14%	6%	General Sales: May apply.
Washington Nov 2012 (July 2014)	n/a	37%	6.5%	General Sales: 0.5%–3.1%.
Virginia July 2021		21%	5.3%	Excise: 0%–3%. General Sales: May apply.

Sources: Boesen, Ulrik. 2021. "Recreational Marijuana Taxes by State, 2021." *Tax Foundation.* (March 31); Urban Institute. No Date. "Marijuana Taxes." *The State and Local Finance Initiative.* The Urban-Brookings Tax Policy Center. No Date. "How Do Marijuana Taxes Work?"

APPENDIX H

Marijuana Tax Revenue Use in States

State	Share	Earmarked Programs/General Fund
Alaska	50%	Recidivism reduction fund within GF
	25%	Health education within GF
	25%	General Fund
Arizona	33%	Community College (within Smart and Safe Arizona Fund or SSAF)
	31.4%	Local law enforcement and fire departments (SSAF)
	25.4%	State and local transportation programs (SSAF)
	10%	Public health and criminal justice programs (SSAF)
	0.2%	Arizona Attorney General enforcement costs (SSAF)
California	As incurred	Regulatory and administrative costs
	60%	Youth education, prevention, early intervention, and treatment account
	20%	Environmental restoration and protection account
	20%	State and local government law enforcement account
Colorado	100%	Public School Capital Construction Assistance Fund

State	Share	Earmarked Programs/General Fund
Illinois	As incurred	Administrative costs
	35%	General revenue fund
	25%	Reinvestment program
	20%	Substance abuse prevention and mental health programs
	10%	Budget Stabilization fund
	8%	Transfers to local governments
	2%	Drug treatment education campaigns and research
Maine	50%	Public health and safety programs
	50%	Law enforcement training programs
Massachusetts	As incurred	Administrative costs
	Subject to appropriations	Public and behavioral health
		Public safety
		Municipal police training
		Prevention and Wellness Trust Fund
		Restorative justice, jail diversion, workforce development, and other assistance program for those impacted by enforcement of marijuana laws
Michigan	35%	K-12 education
	35%	Repair and maintenance of roads and bridges
	15%	Transfers to city governments
	15%	Transfers to county governments
Montana	Subject to appropriation	Conservation
		Substance abuse prevention and treatment
		Veteran's services
		Healthcare
		Transfers to local governments
		General Fund
		Expungement and resentencing training, further impact zone investments, General Fund
Nevada	As incurred	Administrative costs
	Remainder	Education programs
New Jersey	70%	Impact zone reinvestment
	30% or as appropriated	Administrative costs, law enforcement training, further impact zoner investments, general fund
New Mexico	2%	Local government transfers
	Subject to appropriation	Regulatory costs, tax administration costs, public safety, and expunging past cannabis-related offenses
	Remainder	General fund

State	Share	Earmarked Programs/General Fund
New York	40%	Lottery grants for school districts
	20%	Drug treatment and public education
	40%	Community grants reinvestment fund
Oregon	40%	Schools
	20%	Drug prevention and treatment and mental health programs
	15%	Oregon State Police
	5%	Oregon Health Authority
	20%	Transfers to local governments
Rhode Island	Subject to appropriation	Program administration
		Revenue collection and enforcement
		Substance use disorder prevention
		Education and public awareness campaigns
		Treatment and recovery support services
		Public health monitoring, research, data collection, and surveillance
		Law enforcement training and support
		Other related uses
Vermont	100%	After-school and summer learning programs
Virginia	40%	Pre-kindergarten programs
	30%	Reinvestment in communities affected by prior drug law enforcement
	25%	Drug prevention and treatment programs
	5%	Public health education programs
Washington	50%	Basic health
	31%	General fund
	13%	Other
	4%	Transfers to local governments
	3%	Drug education and prevention
	Less than 1%	Research

Source: Auxier, Richard and Nikhita Airi. 2022. "The Pros and Cons of Cannabis Taxes." *Turban-Brookings Tax Policy Center*. pp. 41–42.

Note: The revenue only includes marijuana tax revenue generated from state excise taxes. They do not include marijuana tax revenue from general sales tax and from local government collections.

APPENDIX I

States with Variable Gas Tax

State	Fixed Rate	Variable Rate Structure	Year of Last Increase
Alabama	X	Tax is indexed annually to the National Highway Construction Cost.	2019
Alaska	X		
Arizona	X		
Arkansas	X	Tax is linked to the average wholesale price of gas and diesel, with a floor (to prevent the tax from dropping if the 12-month average wholesale price of fuel is less than the previous year) and a ceiling (limits the increase to no more than 0.1 CPG).	2019
California	X	Tax varies with inflation (enacted in 2010)[a] 2017 legislation stipulates that tax varies with state inflation.	2020 (per 2017 legislation)
Colorado	X	Beginning in fiscal year 2032–2033, the 8-cent road user fee, which is imposed on gasoline, will be indexed to Highway Construction Cost Index inflation.	2032 (per 2021 legislation)
Connecticut	X	Tax varies with gas prices (enacted in 1980).	2013

State	Fixed Rate	Variable Rate Structure	Year of Last Increase
Delaware	X		
Florida	X	Tax varies with CPI (enacted in 1992).	2015
Georgia	X	Tax varies with vehicle fuel efficiency and CPI.	2015
Hawaii	X	Using general sales tax.	
Idaho	X		
Illinois	X	Tax varies with CPI.	2019
Indiana	X	Tax varies with inflation, and general sales tax applies to gas.	2017
Iowa	X		
Kentucky		Tax varies with gas price (enacted in 1980).	2015
Louisiana	X		
Maine	X		
Maryland	X	Tax varies with gas price and CPI.	2013
Massachusetts	X		
Michigan	X	Tax varies with inflation.	2022 (per 2015 legislation)
Minnesota	X	Tax varies annually with increase in the Minnesota Highway Construction Cost Index. The rate will be 28.3 cents in 2024.	2023
Mississippi	X		
Missouri	X		
Montana	X		
Nebraska	X	Tax varies with gas prices and appropriation decisions (enacted in 2009).	2016
Nevada	X		
New Hampshire	X		
New Mexico	X		
New Jersey	X	Tax varies with gas prices and revenue collection.	2016
New York	X	Tax varies with gas prices.	2013
North Carolina	X	Tax varies with population and CPI.	2015
North Dakota	X		

State	Fixed Rate	Variable Rate Structure	Year of Last Increase
Ohio	X		
Oklahoma	X		
Oregon	X		
Pennsylvania	X	Tax varies with gas prices.	2015
Rhode Island	X	Tax varies with CPI.	2015
South Carolina	X		
Tennessee	X		
Texas	X		
Utah	X	Tax varies with gas prices and CPI.	2015
Vermont	X	Tax varies with gas prices.	2015
Virginia	X	Tax varies with CPI (enacted in 2013).	2020
West Virginia		Tax varies with gas prices.	2017
Wisconsin	X		
Wyoming	X		
D.C.	X	Tax varies with CPI (enacted in 2013).	2020

Source: National Conference of State Legislatures (NCSL) (2024). "Variable Rate Gas Taxes". pp. 2–4. www.ncsl.org/research/transportation/variable-rate-gas-taxes.aspx (February 9).

Institute on Taxation and Economic Policy (ITEP). 2011. Building a Better Gas Tax: How to Fix One of the State Government's Least Sustainable Revenue Sources. https://itep.sfo2.digitaloceanspaces.com/bettergastax/bettergastax.pdf (December).

[a] Fifteen states already had variable tax rates by 2011. The enaction year was noted here. The last column shows the last tax increase. For all other states, the year shown in the last column is also the year to enact the change.

APPENDIX J

State Income Tax Rate Cuts: 2021–2023

	2021 *(10 states)*	*2022* *10 states*	*2023[a]*
Alabama			
Arizona	Consolidate 4 rates to 2 by 2024. Reduce tax rates (a trigger can further lead to a flat rate).	Due to the trigger, tax rates will be reduced 2.55%/2.98% to 2.53%/2.75% in 2023.	
Arkansas		Graduated reduction to PIT; combine lower and middle tax tables with cliff adjustments.	Cut top PIT rate from 4.9% to 4.7%. Cut CIT from 5.3% to 5.1%.
Colorado	Prop 116: Reduce PIT and CIT rate from 4.63% to 4.55%.	Reduce the flat rate for PIT and CIT from 4.63% to 4.55%.	
Connecticut			Cut the two bottom tax rates.
Georgia		Turn graduated rates to a flat rate of 5.49%. Reduce the flat rate to 4.99% by 2029 if the trigger is met.	

	2021 (10 states)	*2022* 10 states	*2023*[a]
Idaho	Cut top rate: 6.925% to 6.5%. Consolidate 7 rates to 5; Reduce other rates; Tax rebate. CIT rate: 6.935% to 6.5%.	Consolidate 5 rates to 4 6.5–> 6 3.1–>3.0 Reduce CIT 6.5% to 6%.	
Indiana		Reduce the flat rate from 3.23% to 3.15% and then to 2.9% by 2029 if triggers are met.	Expedites the phase in of the tax cut enacted in 2022.
Iowa	Expedite cut adopted in 2018 by removing the revenue triggers to allow 9 rates consolidated to 4 and reduce the top rates from 8.53% to 6.5%; Taking effect in 2023. Phase out inheritance tax by 2025.	Graduate rate to flat rate by 2026. Reduce the current 9 rates to 4 rates in 2023, to 3 rates in 2024, and 2 rates in 2025. Reduce the top CIT marginal rate from 9.8% to 5.5% over the years.	
Kentucky		Use trigger to reduce PIT by 0.5% points in years in which the triggers are met. Theoretically this can lead to the phase out of PIT.	Cut rate from 4.5% to 4.0%, accelerating a rate reduction approved by 2022.

	2021 (10 states)	*2022* 10 states	*2023*[a]
Louisiana	Cap the top individual income tax rate at 4.75% from the current 6%. Consolidate the tax brackets and reduce the rates; Further rate reduction if the trigger is met. CIT: Consolidate 5 rates to 3 and reduce the rates.	Lower rate and eliminate certain large deductions.	
Michigan			Reduce the flat rate from 4.25% to 4.05% due to a tax trigger enacted in 2015.
Minnesota	Reduce the top PIT rate.		
Mississippi	Continue to phase out of the 3% income tax rate.	Eliminate the lower rates to establish a flat rate of 5% in 2023. The flat rate will be reduced to 4.7% in 2024, 4.4% in 2025, and 4% in 2026.	
Missouri	Adopt economic nexus and use the revenue to cut PIT; The revenue trigger adopted in 2014 is used to reduce the top rate.		

	2021 *(10 states)*	*2022* 10 states	*2023*[a]
Montana	Reduce the top rate from 6.9% to 6.75% and again to 6.5% by 2024; Consolidate 7 rates to 2: 6.5% and 4.7%.		Cut marginal rate from 6.5% to 5.9%.
Nebraska	CIT: Reduce the higher of the two top rates from 7.81% to 7.5% to 7.25% in 2023.	Reduce the top rate from 6.84% to 5.84% by 2027. Reduce the top CIT rate to 5.8% as well.	Accelerate 2022 cuts. Cut PIT and CIT from 5.84% in 2024 to 3.99% in 2027.
New Hampshire	Phase out its interest and dividends income tax by 2027. CIT: Reduce rates.		
New York		Accelerate tax rate cuts for low and middle earners originally passed in 2016.	
N. Carolina		Previously legislated (2021 session)—multi-year tax rate reduction.	
N. Dakota			Eliminate the top rate; Consolidate the remaining 4 tax brackets into 2 and reduce rates.
Ohio	Consolidate 5 rates to 4 and reduce each of the rates.		
Oklahoma	Reduce the rate by 0.25% across the board. CIT: Reduce rate from 6% to 4%.		

	2021 (10 states)	*2022* 10 states	*2023*[a]
S. Carolina		Reduce the top rate: 7% to 6.5%; Consolidate 6 rates into 3. The top rate will decrease by 0.1% each year till 6% in 2027.	
Utah		Reduce its flat rate from 4.95% to >4.85%.	Reduce rate: 4.85% to 4.65%.
W. Virginia			Reduce the top rate from 6.5% to 5.12%. Reduce all the rates and include a trigger for further reductions based on general fund revenue performance.
Wisconsin	Reduce the 2nd highest PIT rate from 6.27% to 5.3%.		

Sources: National Conference of State Legislature. *State Tax Actions Database* (FY 2021 and FY 2022); Vermeer, Timothy. 2022. "State Reform and Relief Enacted in 2022." *Tax Foundation.* (July 13); Loughead, Katherine and Jared Walczak. 2021. "State Respond to Strong Fiscal Health with Income Tax Reforms." *Tax Foundation: Fiscal Fact No. 774.* (July); Loughead, Katherine. 2023. "State Tax Reform and Relief Trend Continues in 2023." *Tax Foundation. (June 8)*; Brainerd, Jackson. 2022. "States Pursue Tax Relief in 2022." *National Conference of State Legislature.* (June 28); Davis, Aidan. 2023. "The Highs and Lows of 2023 State Legislative Sessions." *Institute on Taxation and Economic Policy.*

[a] The information is incomplete given that the final tax legislation has still not been revealed as of the date.

INDEX

Note: Tables are indicated by **bold**.

adequacy approach 16; *see also* elementary and secondary education
Affordable Care Act (ACA) 21, 22, 244
Aid to Families with Dependent Children (AFDC) 37; *see also* public assistance
alcohol tax 15, 59, 60, 63, **105**, 192, 194–5, 203, **204**, 211, 269
alternative minimum tax (of corporate income tax) 79, 151
alternative to incarceration 33; *see also* tough-on-crime legislation
American federalism 154
American Recovery and Reinvestment Act of 2009 (ARRA) 21, 53, 57
American Rescue Plan Act of 2021 (ARPA) 33, 38, 39, 41, 256
American Society of Civil Engineers (ASCE) 31, 236
amnesty program 86, 100, 168, 297

balanced approach 6, 7, 55, 84, 85, 96
ballot box budgeting 74
ballot measures 6, 17, 66, 74, 208, 278; *see also* voter initiative
Brownback's tax reform package 98
budget deficit (or budget deficits) 1–4, 69, 77, 83, **84**, 85
budget fixer 185, 203, 271

budget shortfalls 7, **67**; *see also* revenue gaps
business-to-business (or B2B) 159, 164–5, 169, 178, 179

capital gain tax 81–2, 92, 130
captive REIT **143**, 144, 146
cash crisis 67
casino and racino 196, 199; "new" casino/racino states **201**; "older" casino/racino states **200**; revenue of **200**
casual users 127; *see also* marijuana tax
Centers for Medicare and Medicaid Services (CMS) 20, 240, 242, 244
Child Tax Credit (CTC) 38, 120, 128, 255–6, 262–3, 265–7, **258**
climate change 31
Colardo's Amendment 23 17
combined reporting **143**, 150–1
Commission on Fiscal Stability and Economic Growth (of Connecticut) 3, 4, 7, 89
community-based care settings (HCBS), 22, *see also* Medicaid
control state 192, **193**, **194**, *see also* alcohol tax
Coronavirus Aid, Relief, and Economic Security Act (CARES Act) 33, 39, 256

Index **323**

Coronavirus State and Local Fiscal Recovery Fund (CSLFRE) 39
corporate income tax: bases, erosion of 144–9; changes during 2008-2020 138–41; as share of state total tax revenue **137**; tax rates **140**
corrections 7, 8, 12, **13**, **32**, 33–4, **43**, 45, 46, 53, 101, 110, 273–4
COVID-19 relief funds 39; *see also* American Rescue Plan Act; *CARES ACT*

Daniel Malloy (Governor Malloy) 84–6, 89, 90
debt service 39, 41, 44, 45, 89
decoupling **143**, 145, 150
deep poverty 38
Delaware Holding Company or a passive investment company (PIC) 146
digital and service-based economy 3, 7, 58
digital products 167, 177–9; cloud computing 176–7; custom software 176; prewritten computer software 176
digital tax 177–9
discretionary spending 27, 28, 44, 45
dividends 57, 86, 115, 146, 148, 257, 272, 276

earmarking 13, 128, 247
Earned Income Tax Credit (EITC) 38, 118, 128, 256, 258, 262, 263, 265, 267; *see also* tax expenditure
E-cigarette 100, 184, 189–91
economic cycles 5, 26, 82, 88
economic nexus law (rule) 164, 171–5, 180, 256
electric vehicle 31, 228, 230, 238; *see also* fuel efficiency
elementary and secondary education 12–14, **15**, 16, 18, 20, 26, 46, **110**, 273
Enterprise Zone program 72, 144, 147, 152, 153; *see also* tax expenditure
environmental justice 33
equity approach 16; *see also* elementary and secondary education
estate tax 249–50; *see also* inheritance tax and gift tax
excise tax **187**, **193**, 207–13, 217, 219, 235

Federal Medicaid Assistance Percentage (FMAP) 18, 21, 241, 243
film incentive program (or film tax credits) **72**, 142, 152, 154; *see also* tax expenditure

financial aid 23, 25–8, 255
financial crisis 99, 101, 102, 118, 152, 163; *see also* fiscal crisis
fiscal conservative paradise 103
fiscal crisis 3, 51, 58, 63, 67–8, 70, 79, 83–5, 87, 91, 118, 121, 125, 132, 137, 138, 143, 156, 143, 156, 270
fiscal stability 1, 3–9, 46, 50, 62–3, 66, 71–4, 79–80, 83, 87–92, 111, 126, 129, 131–2, 137, 142, 150, 155–6, 159–61, 179, 185, 191, 194, 203, 204, 230, 250, 254, 261, 264–6, 269–70, 279–80
fiscal sustainability 2, 4, 72, 272
Fixing America's Surface Transportation (FAST) 31; *see also* Highway Trust Fund
flat income tax **260**, 261
flat rates 115, 257, 260–1; *see also* flat income tax
franchise tax 61, 78, 105, 109, 174
fuel efficiency 31, 238
fuel taxes 234–5; fixed rate 235; variable rate 237–9; vehicle-miles traveled (VMT) tax 237–9
full cost recovery 232–3

gambling taxes 15, 195–8, 203, 269; *see* lottery, casino and racino, and sports betting
Government Financial Officer Association (GFOA) 229, 232, 233
Governor Brownback 97, 103, 122
Governor Cuomo 77–9
Governor Eric Greitens 108
Governor Jay Nixon 108, 110, 104, 105
Governor Jodi Rell 83
Governor Kathleen Sebelius 96
Governor Mike Parson 107, 108, 265
graduate rates 5, 115, **260**; *see also* personal income tax

HB 2540 106
healthcare provider tax (provider tax) 8, 18, 50, 86, 221, 239–48, 269
higher education 1, 8, 12, 23, **24**, **25**, 26, 34, 43, 46, 54, 101, 109, 110, 224, 225, 229, 273, **274**, 276
Higher Education Emergency Relief Fund 26
Highway Trust Fund (HTF) 29, 31
HIV-positive 35
hybrid cars 29, 31; *see also* fuel efficiency

illicit market 213; see also marijuana tax
income concentration 121, 126; and state fiscal stability 129–30
Infrastructure Investment and Jobs Act (IIJA) 31
insurance tax 248–9
interest group politics 128, 166, 170
Internet-based economy 169
interstate competition 125, 137, 147, 154, 155, 166, 196, 269
investment income 57, 86, 130
IOU 67; see also cash crisis
itemized deductions **56**, 80, 99

Key, V. O. Jr. 2

last-dollar scholarship program 23
legacy cost 83, 87–92
legislative analyst's office (LAO) (of California) 67, 71
license state 192; see also alcohol tax
long-term fiscal problem 2, 218, 219
long-term obligation 4, 44
lottery 12, 54, 56, 196, 198, 199, 202, 204

maintenance of effort (MOE) 21, 37, 38, 44; see also public assistance
mandatory spending 44; see also restricted (state) expenditures
March to zero 98, 103, 104; see also Brownback's tax reform package
marijuana tax 15, 185, 207–9, 211–19, 269, 271, 272
marketplace facilitator laws 170–1, 173, 175, 180
Master Settlement Agreement 100–1, 186, 191
Medicaid 2, 8, 12, **13**, 18–23, 26, 41–6, 51, 53, 57, 77–8, 101, 108, 161, 163, 185, 228, 239–48, 250, 273, 274, 276; see also Healthcare provider tax
Medicaid Voluntary Contribution and Provider-specific Tax Amendment (MVCPSTA) 239; broad-based 240; "hold-harmless" 240, 242
medical marijuana 105, 207, 213
millionaire tax 74, 78, 82, 88, 92, 120–1, 125, 127, 304, 305
Moody's 101
motor fuel tax 228, 231, 234, 245
municipal aid 91

negative externalities 208, 209, 211, 218
net operating losses (NOL) 68, 139–40, 282, 293
new hiring credit 72; see also tax expenditure

Occupy Wall Street movement 78
online sales 7, 57–8, 164, 170–1, 173; see also economic nexus law
Oregon's Measure 5 17
Other Post-employment benefit (OPEB) 44, 89
other state funds 14, **15**, 16, 18, 23, 29, 39, **42**, 45
outmigration 82, 86, 27–128

pass-through business 99, 103–6, 109, 145, 150; entity tax 155; increase of 147–8
peer-to-peer transaction 169; see also sharing economy
pension 2, 4, 39, 43–5, 75, 83–7, **89**, 90–1, 101, 128, 262
personal income tax: as share of state tax revenue **116**; and state fiscal stability 126
personal income tax: changes during 2008–2020, cuts 121–2; changes during 2008–2020, rate increases 120–1; as a share of state tax revenue **116**; and state fiscal stability 126; tie to the federal system 116
phasing in 121–4, 257, 260, 131
poaching issue 203; see also gambling taxes
positive externalities 232
prison population 34, 35, 45; see also correction
pro-cyclical measures 7, 58
Professional and Amateur Sport Protection Act 197; see also sports betting
progressive tax 78, 82, 149; see also progressivity
progressivity 74, 81–2, 126, 129–30
promise program 23
property tax 91, 99, 116, 122, 123, 128, 160, 161, 248, 257–8, 263
Proposition 13 66, 73
Proposition 2 (California) 74
Proposition 26 (California) 74, 232
Proposition 30 61, 68–71, 73, 161

Proposition 98 (California) 74
public anti-taxation attitudes 2
public assistance 12, **13**, 35, **36**, 37–8, 46, **274**
public transit 33, 233

quarterly income tax payments 86
Quill Corp. vs. North Dakota 170; *see also* economic nexus law

rainy day funds 37, **54**, 55, **56**, 57–8, 71, 83, 86, **100**, **124**, 130, 132, 255, 271, 273–7
Reclaim California's Future 71; *see also* Proposition 30
recreational marijuana 207, **208**, 213, 215, 219, 272
red state model 99
regressive tax 160; *see also* regressivity
regressivity 81, 166, 184
regulation license 222
revenue adequacy 2, 4–7, 266, 277
revenue cap (ct) 3, 86–7, 133, 273, 279
revenue diversification 6, 7, 272
revenue gaps 51, 75, 77, 83, 96, 230; *see also* budget shortage; revenue shortage
revenue license 222
revenue shortage(s) 1, 26, 50–1, **52**, 53, 61, 83, 84, 61, 97, 100, 104, 118, 121, 125, 129, 132, 161, 186, 241, 245; *see also* revenue gaps
revenue stability 3, 124, 126, 130, 131, 149; *see also* fiscal stability
revenue trigger (tax trigger) 104–6, 108–9, 121–4, 126, 127, 131–2; *see also* SB 509 of Missouri, and state fiscal stability
revenue volatility 3, 5, 74, 129–30, 209, 267, 273, 275–6, 279; and exemption of retirement income 267; and millionaire tax 82
Road Use Charges (RUC) 230, 231

sales tax: breadth 165; destination-based sourcing 178; exemption 166–7, 178–80; origin-based sourcing 178; reliance on 159; rates **164**, **165**
sales tax holidays 162, 166, 264
SB 884 106, 207
S-CHIP 21, 39, 41
school enrollment 2, 17

School Tax Relief (STAR) program 79
S-corporation 80, 147–8; reforming 154–5, 263; *see also* passthrough business
S. Dakota vs. Wayfair 171–5; fiscal implication 173–5
Senate Bill 30 of Kansas 102; *see also* Brownback's tax reform package
Senate Bill 509 of Missouri 105
separate-entity taxation 145, 150
Serrano vs. Priest 16
severance taxes 249; sovereign wealth fund 249
sharing economy 165, 169–70; *see also* Internet-based economy
Sheldon Silver 76
sin taxes 8, 12, 50, 184–5, 191, 197, 203, **204**, 208, 218–19, 271–2; *see also* alcohol taxes; gambling taxes; marijuana taxes; tobacco taxes
single-sales factor 69, 107, 147
sports betting 196–7, 199, 202–3, 269–71
spring borrowing 74
Standard and Poor's 101
standard deduction 78, 98, 115, 116, 118, 120, 257
state Fiscal Stabilization Fund (SFSF) 57
Streamlined Sales and Use Tax Agreement (SSUTA) 176, 178
structural deficit 1–4, 6, 8, 9; sources of 3
supermajority votes 69
Supplemental Security Income (SSI) 35; *see also* public assistance
surtax 118, 120, 121, 126

Tax and Expenditure Limitations (TEL) 44, 223
tax avoidance 78, 103, 146, 190
tax base 3, 5–8, 72, 79, 80, 104, 117–20, 126, 129–30, 132–3, 138, **139**, 184, 203, 208–9, 212–13, 238, 248–9, 257, 264, 267, 269–72; broadening (expanding) 55, 56, 58, 63, 77, 83, 87–9, 92, 111, 150–1, 154–6, 179–80, 272; corporate income 141–5, 148; and erosion of sales [tax base] 73, 75, 165, 167–70, 177–9; narrowing/narrow 72, 81, 223; and sales tax break 128
tax expenditures 7, 58, 63, 71, **72**, 79, 81, 87–8, 104, 111, 133, 145–7, 151–2, 271, 278; *see also* tax incentive
tax incentive 72, 81, 137, 144–7, 152–5, 263, 271, 278–9

tax progressivity 74, 81, 126, 129–30
tax pyramiding 164–5, 168–80
tax rebate 256, **258**, 261–5
tax regressivity (regressive) 166
tax revolt 66, 223
tax volatility 5, 279
Temporary Assistance for Needy Families (TANF) 35, 37–8, 44, 127; *see also* public assistance
Temporary Taxes to Fund Education 69; *see also* Proposition 30
temporary tax increase 61, 68, 75, 77
tetrahydrocannabinol (THC) 211, 213
three factor apportionment 147; *see also* three factors (traditional equally weighted)
three factors (traditional equally weighted) 107, 136, 255
"three strikes" laws 34
timely filing discount (vendor discount) 111
tobacco tax 59–61, 63, 86, 87, **105**, 185–6, 188–92, 203–4, 213, 269
tollways 29, 221, 230, 229, 235
tough-on-crime legislation 34; *see also* "three strikes law"

trickle-down effects 104
2009 Budget Act (of California) 68
2014 CIT reform (of New York) 78–9

unemployment compensation 39, 225
user charges 221–4, 230, 232, 234, 272
user fees 220–4, 229, 230, 232, 234, 238, 269, 270

very low nicotine 190
volatility adjustment (CT) 86, 99
voter initiative 66, 73, 92, 207; *see also* Proposition 13; Proposition 26; Proposition 30; Proposition 98

Wayfair (S Dakota vs. Wayfair) 61, 62, 163–4, 170–1, 173–5, 180, 256, 271; *see also* economic nexus law
Whisky Rebellion 184
Work Opportunity Reconciliation Act (PRWORA) 37; *see also* public assistance
worldview combined reporting (complete reporting) 151

For Product Safety Concerns and Information please contact our EU representative GPSR@taylorandfrancis.com Taylor & Francis Verlag GmbH, Kaufingerstraße 24, 80331 München, Germany